Iranian/Persianate Subalterns
in the Safavid Period:
Their Role and Depiction

Middle Eastern & Islamic Studies at Gerlach Press

Robert Lacey and Jonathan Benthall (eds.)
Gulf Charities and Islamic Philanthropy in the
"Age of Terror" and Beyond
ISBN 9783940924322, 2014

Sara Bazoobandi (ed.)
The Politics of Food Security:
Asian and Middle Eastern Strategies
ISBN 9783940924308, 2014

Carool Kersten (ed.)
The Caliphate and Islamic Statehood:
Formation, Fragmentation and Modern
Interpretations (3 vols set)
ISBN 9783940924520, 2015

Esther Peskes (ed.)
Wahhabism – Doctrine and Development
(2 vols set)
(Critical Surveys in Islamic Denominations)
ISBN 9783940924506, 2016

David B. Des Roches and Dania Thafer (eds.)
The Arms Trade, Military Services and the
Security Market in the Gulf States:
Trends and Implication
ISBN 9783959940160, 2016

Helen Lackner and Daniel Martin Varisco (eds.)
Yemen and the Gulf States: The Making of a Crisis
ISBN 9783959940306, 2017

Tim Niblock with Talmiz Ahmad
and Degang Sun (eds.)
Conflict Resolution and Creation of a Security
Community in the Gulf Region
ISBN 9783959940368, 2017

Marc Owen Jones, Ross Porter
and Marc Valeri (eds.)
Gulfization of the Arab World
ISBN 9783959940320, 2018

Nikolay Kozhanov
Iran's Strategic Thinking:
The Evolution of Iran's Foreign Policy, 1979-2018
ISBN 9783959940382, 2018

David Heard
Oil Men, Territorial Ambitions and Political Agents.
From Pearls to Oil in the Trucial States of the Gulf
(2 volumes)
ISBN 9783959940641, 2019

J. B. Kelly, edited by S. B. Kelly
Desert Dispute: The Diplomacy of Boundary-Making
in South-Eastern Arabia (3 vols set)
ISBN 9783959940788, 2019

Abdulrahman Alebrahim
Kuwait's Politics Before Independence:
The Role of the Balancing Powers
(Exeter Critical Gulf Series)
ISBN 9783959940726, 2019

Noel Brehony and Clive Jones (eds.)
Britain's Departure from Aden and South Arabia
Without Glory but Without Disaster
ISBN 9783959940825, 2020

David Heard (ed.)
The Trucial Coast Diaries (1948-1957). On the Way
from Pearls to Oil in the Trucial States of the Gulf
ISBN 783959940801, 2020

Degang Sun with Dandan Zhang
Diplomacy of Quasi-Alliances in the Middle East
Translated from the Chinese by Jinan Wang
With a Foreword by Tim Niblock
ISBN 9783959940740, 2020

N. Janardhan (ed.)
The Gulf's Pivot to Asia:
From Transactional to Strategic Partnerships
ISBN 9783959941327, 2020

www.gerlachpress.com

Iranian/Persianate Subalterns in the Safavid Period: Their Role and Depiction

Recovering 'Lost Voices'

Edited by Andrew J. Newman

First published 2022
by Gerlach Press
Berlin, Germany
www.gerlachpress.com

Cover Design: Frauke Schön, Hamburg
Set by Anne Jeschke, Gerlach Press
Printed and bound in Germany
Cover image:
A Captive Central Asian Warrior, mid-17th century Deccan provenance
© David Collection, Copenhagen (21-1979) Photo credit: Pernille Klemp

© Gerlach Press and the authors 2022
All rights reserved. No part of this publication may be reprinted or reproduced, or utilised in any form or by any electronic, mechanical, or other means, now known or hereafter invented, including photocopying and recording, or in any other information storage or retrieval system, without permission in writing from the publisher.

British Library Cataloguing in Publication Data.
A catalogue record for this book is available from the British Library.

Bibliographic data available from Deutsche Nationalbibliothek
https://d-nb.info/1253739714

ISBN: 978-3-95994-152-5 (hardcover)
ISBN: 978-3-95994-153-2 (eBook)

Contents

Preface   vii

1 Liberating the "Turkoman Prisoner": An Assessment of Bound Captives in Sixteenth and Seventeenth-Century Persianate Works on Paper   1
Jaimee K. Comstock-Skipp

2 Agency and Fatalism in the Judeo-Persian *Kitab-i sar guzasht-i Kashan*   65
Alberto Tiburcio

3 The Qizilbash in Anatolia after the 1630s: Sidelined and Estranged   83
Selim Güngörürler

4 The Safavid Foundation Myth in the Subaltern Imagination   99
Barry Wood

5 The Muharram Subaltern in the Safavid Period: "Thin Description" and the Limits of European Travel Accounts   117
Babak Rahimi

6 The 'Visible Voice' or 'Vocal Visibility' of the Subalterns in Persianate Painting: The Safavid and Mughal Cases   149
Valérie Gonzalez

7 A Subaltern Hero: The 1573 Execution of Sheikh Hamza Bali as Part of the 'Sunnitisation' of the Ottoman Empire   193
Ines Asceric-Todd

8 Voices of the Caucasians at the Safavid Court: Life and Activities of Parsadan Gorgijanidze   211
Hirotake Maeda

About the Contributors   241

Preface

'Subaltern studies' refers to the importance of 'subordinate' groups in the making of history. The latter are usually defined as encompassing the urban and rural lower/under-classes, the majority in any society although, generally, the term is said to refer to all non-elites, including women. Most often the discourse concentrates on instances of social protest or at other times when the 'subalterns' make their 'voices' heard in response to, or even independent of, manipulations/interventions by elites.

The conventional understanding of the origins of this discourse looks to the work of the Italian Marxist Antonio Gramsci (d. 1937) but notes that the concept of 'history from below', of which subaltern studies is said to be a spin-off, has been extant since at least the 1960s, with the appearance of the 1963 *The Making of the English Working Class*, authored by Edward P. Thompson (d. 1993).[1] In this same tradition are the works of such others as the British historian Christopher Hill (d. 2003), whose contributions commenced in the 1940s, Eric Hobsbawm (d. 2012) and those of the American historian Gary B. Nash (d. 2021), from the 1960s.[2]

'Subaltern studies' as a distinct, named field, is usually understood to have risen to prominence in the late 1970s among historians of the Subcontinent. Beginning in 1982, under the editorship of Ranajit Guha, Oxford University Press, New Delhi, began to publish volumes in the series 'Subaltern Studies: Writings on South Asian History and Society'. By 2001, some eleven volumes, comprising more than 47 essays, had appeared. In 1988, Guha co-edited, with Gayatri Chakravorty-Spivak, a single volume entitled *Selected Subaltern Studies* with a foreword by Edward Said (d. 2003). In 1997 Guha edited *A Subaltern Studies Reader*. In 2001 David Ludden, a South Asian studies specialist, edited *Reading Subaltern Studies* with an appendix listing the contents of the series' first ten volumes. Interest in the subaltern spread: in the 1990s a Latin American subaltern studies group was established.[3]

As to the field of Islamic and Middle Eastern Studies, in the years preceding the 1978-79 Iranian Revolution it was not otherwise free from the influence of outside discourses.

The influence of 'modernisation theory' in Middle Eastern Studies long predated the 1970s. The overall, and distinctively Cold War, agenda of this discourse is perhaps no more clearly exemplified than in the title of that work which offered the economic prescription underlying modernisation theory, the 1960 *The Stages of Economic*

Growth: A Non-Communist Manifesto, by Walt Rostow (d. 2003). Early manifestations of this discourse in the field included, especially, Daniel Lerner's 1958 *The Passing of Traditional Society: Modernizing the Middle East* and Manfred Halpern's 1963 *The Politics of Social Change in the Middle East and North Africa*. As therein applied to the Middle East, 'modernisation' studies presumed that Islam was in the process of 'withering away' and that, spearheaded by a new, technocratic, and quite secular middle class, the region was fast becoming secularised and 'western'.

In these same pre-Revolution years appeared a number of other influential volumes, also from outwith the field. These included the 1972-73 English translation of Fernand Braudel's (d. 1985) 1949 *La Méditerranée et le monde méditerranéen à l'époque de Philippe II*, which opened the eyes of some to the contributions and analyses of the *Annales School*. 'World market theory' was introduced in the 1974 *The Modern World System* of Immanuel Wallerstein, a sociologist and a specialist in African Studies. Translations of the French works of the Egyptian economist Samir Amin also appeared in these years, encouraging interaction with 'dependency/underdevelopment theory', whose origins also lay outside the field.[4] Discussions, and critiques, of the latter two discourses likewise originated from outside the field.[5]

As modernisation theory and the other constructs cited above, Edward Said's 1978 publication *Orientalism* had its origins outside Islamic and Middle Eastern Studies. Said, a Palestinian, was then a member of Columbia University's Department of English and Comparative Literature.[6]

To be sure, the same decade did feature some examples of auto-critiques from within the field that challenged the conventional wisdoms then dominating the field. These critiques were given expression in some prominent, but mostly short-lived, journals.[7] One publication from those years still survives - *Middle East Report and Information Project (MERIP)*, now called *Middle East Report*, dating from 1971. In a 1975 article therein, Peter Johnson and Judith Tucker authored a history of the field in the US. Entitled 'Middle East Studies Network in the United States', the article was particularly notable for its critique of 'area studies' generally and of 'Middle East Studies' ties, and service, to 'national security institutes' and 'US global interests' following World War II. The article cast light on the rise and importance of US government funding to the field. It included a list of 'foundations' whose support was key to the 'build up [of] the Middle East studies establishment' and discussed the field's connections with other key US government and other bodies, domestic and foreign.[8]

Prior to 1979, Iranian studies, whether explicitly or implicitly, can only be said to have shared the modernisation agenda. In the literature on Iran in these years, there are no references to the faith in Iran as having any long-term 'traction' on the ground - let alone to what came to be called 'political Islam'. This material included such surveys of modern Iran as former CIA agent Richard Cottam's 1964 *Nationalism in Iran*, Peter

Avery's 1965 *Modern Iran*, and James Bill's 1972 *The Politics of Iran, Groups, Classes and Modernization*. Although it was in Iraq in early 1970s that the Ayatollah Khomeini (d. 1989) delivered the lectures that would become his famous *Islamic Government*, such scholars accorded Khomeini, let alone Shiism in Iraq, or anywhere else, little if any mention.[9] On the left, even on the eve of the Revolution itself, Fred Halliday (d. 2010), in his 1979 *Iran: Dictatorship and Development*, characterised the clergy as unable to 'sustain or channel' then-current popular feeling.[10]

The 1978-79 Iranian Revolution would seem to have demonstrated the vacuity of the modernisation paradigm and to have vindicated aspects of the 1970s' auto-critique of the field generally and Iranian Studies in particular. In fact, however, such responses as were offered in the aftermath of the field's failure to acknowledge both the faith's pre-1979 deep 'traction' across the region and the subsequent 'rise' of 'political Islam' seem to have adopted/adapted and repromulgated variants of the very Orientalist paradigms of analysis that had been questioned in the 1970s. The subsequent 'collapse of communism' in 1989 and the first Gulf War in 1991 only further encouraged the resurgence of such paradigms, with the occasional nod to contemporary events and trends.[11] The revival of pre-1979 paradigms can also be seen in such fields of research as Safavid and also Shi'i studies both of which, as with many subfields of Islamic and Middle Eastern Studies, became sufficiently populated to achieve status as distinct discourses only in the aftermath of the events of 1979.[12]

This said, if, prior to 1979, Islamic and Middle Eastern studies was largely beholden to 'modernization theory', and aware of the Annales School and underdevelopment theory, the field was not overly influenced by 'history from below', directly or not.[13]

In the longer run, as Subaltern Studies itself grew, interest therein did come to take root in Middle Eastern Studies. As in the case of the study of the Subcontinent so in Middle Eastern studies, however, both before and after the turn of the millennium, the 'modern' period preoccupied those exploring 'the below', even if not always, and explicitly, 'the subaltern'.[14] Toward the end of the first decade of the new millennium, Stephanie Cronin's 2008 edited volume *Subalterns and Social Protest* did explicitly reference this discourse. Of the twelve articles therein, only two addressed pre-nineteenth century trends and events. Of the volume's three papers on Iran, none considered its pre-nineteenth century history.[15] To that time other examples of recourse to the 'history from below' approach in Middle Eastern studies also focussed on 'the modern'.[16] In the case of Iranian studies' contributions to both 'history from below' and 'subalterns' explicitly, the predisposition to 'the modern' also obtained.[17]

In the pre-modern period, access to the voices of subaltern elements - who, being largely illiterate, left few of their own records - is usually indirect. In the years after 1979, as relates to Safavid Iran there appeared many works which, although they did not always explicitly reference either 'history from below' and/or 'subalterns', both recovered and cast valuable light on the lives of classes/groups in Safavid society which were largely unconsidered in their own right in the pre-1979 scholarship.[18] These included discussions on the veneration of Abu Muslim and Sufi doctrines and practices over the Safavid period, especially in the 17th century, by looking at clerical polemics against this veneration, Sufi-style, messianic risings across the period as pointing to their continued strength,[19] popular opposition to court-appointed clerical elites as witnessed by the resignation of these from their posts,[20] and the power of guilds as attested by firmans granting them tax concessions recorded in mosques in Esfahan, Kashan, and Yazd.[21] Other post-1979 studies included other works on Sufis[22] as well as studies on women[23], merchants[24], the *ghulam*[25], and other non-elites[26], including religious minorities.[27]

The present collection of essays derives from papers delivered at the University of Edinburgh in May 2017 as part of the larger 'Recovering "Lost Voices": The Role and Depiction of Iranian/ Persianate Subalterns from the 13th Century to the Modern Period' project. This undertaking was first conceived of in 2014. This project was generously funded later the same year by the British Institute for Persian Studies.

As noted on the project's main website, 'The aim of this project is to involve scholars from a wide range of disciplines in the commencement of an organised effort to utilise an extensive range of sources to recover evidence of the "voices" of "subalterns" across the pre-modern and modern terrains of both rural and urban society across the Persianate world. The wide-ranging sources to be explored for direct and indirect access to these voices could include elite Persian diplomatic and political-economic (court-level) materials but also those drawn from such a broad range of "cultural" spheres as, for example, art and architecture (including cinema, for the modern period), prose, poetry and other media and religious materials (Sunni, Shi`i and Sufi) of all genres in all relevant languages. The project seeks also to explore attitudes toward the subaltern by the authors of these sources. Finally, the project aims also to identify problems in accessing/using the sources and questions/avenues for further research across Persianate history and, in the process, to establish an on-going network to chart pathways for further associated research projects and support for these.'[28]

The papers delivered at the first workshop, held in Edinburgh in 2015, considered the pre-Safavid Persianate world. The 2017 gathering, the second of the workshops, called for contributions on subalterns across the Persianate world in the Safavid and Afsharid periods (1501-1747).[29]

The coverage of the eight papers from the second workshop included in this volume underlines the diversity both of the voices of subalterns located across the Persianate world of these centuries that can be recovered but also of the sources that can be utilised in that recovery.

Jaimee K. Comstock-Skipp, looking predominantly at painted works on paper spanning the sixteenth and early seventeenth centuries, brings together single-page folios of kneeling warriors constrained in a wooden yoke. These have been collectively labelled 'Turkoman Prisoners,' but this label and other ethnolinguistic typologies are not suited to the original era of the works' production. Originally assembled into albums, the author argues that the depicted bound captives render troops of the Abulkhairid-Shibanid Uzbeks. These captives are depicted elsewhere in Safavid painting traditions that accompany historical chronicles, epic poetry, and murals on palace walls. As embodiments of the attitudes and antipathies of their creators, the essay analyses the dual artistic and political function of this 'subject' as a painted representation and as a person owing obedience. Comstock-Skipp uncovers how members of Safavid society fashioned their own sense of identity vis-à-vis their subalterns in Transoxiana and synthesizes period textual and visual sources.

Alberto Tiburcio analyses the ways in which a Judeo-Persian epic from the eighteenth century portrays the situation of the Jewish community of Kashan during the Hotaki takeover of the Safavid Empire. The contribution argues that, while recognizing the reality of forced conversions, the epic also reveals the strategies through which the community was able to negotiate its status. The essay analyses the use of tropes that connect the historical events with the sacred history of Judaism in Islam. Tiburcio contends that through the counterpoint between the mythical and historical dimensions, the epic points both towards the historical agency of the Jewish community as an actor in historical time, while also portraying its fate as divinely dictated, thus suggesting that history itself was considered contingent to divine will.

Selim Güngörürler recalls that the Anatolian Qizilbaş, including those who were Ottoman subjects, were the main force of the Safavid movement that conquered Iran and set up a kingdom there. The historiography has covered their role in Ottoman-Safavid wars, in pro-Safavid uprisings within the Ottoman Empire, and in a Safavid network of allegiance from 1500 until 1640. The same goes for the later persecution of the Qizilbaş believers in an Iran undergoing Shiitization, which unfolded at the same time as the ongoing Safavid support to the Qizilbaş that had remained in Anatolia. Güngörürler investigates the twofold estrangement of the Anatolian Qizilbaş after the Peace of Zuhab (1639). This long-lasting peace in Ottoman-Safavid dealings brought about the Ottoman-Sunni establishment's stepwise acknowledgement, at least by the state if not by the clergy, of the Safavids' conversion from Qizilbaşism to Shiism. As the two states grew politically near, the Ottomans' persecution of the Anatolian Qizilbash came to a halt. This strengthens the reading that the Empire's policies against the Qizilbash had been stemming from political, not sheerly sectarian, motives. Once the imperial court came to deem it impossible for a new war with the Safavids to break out, the measures inside, which had been linked to a sense of threat, stopped. Therefore, the word *Qizilbaş* almost disappeared from Ottoman official writs, because the target community, then politically insignificant, was no longer a state matter. This ironically boosted the political estrangement of the Anatolian Qizilbaş.

Having thus lost their instrumentality for the Safavids and hence their potential to make up a fifth column against the Ottomans, they were taken off the stage of state-referenced politics on both sides. Whereas this shift might have lessened the sense of alarm and increased the sense of security felt by the community in question, it also made this population ideologically hopeless, and the state(s) now turned a blind eye to the identity that bound this community together.

The origins of the word *Qizilbash*'s shifting from a self-designation of pride to a name of slight uttered by the hardliner Sunnis, and more essentially, the figurative going-underground of the Qizilbaş as a political and religious community in Anatolia are sought not in the fighting but in the rapprochement between the Ottoman and the Safavid states.

Barry Wood notes that the so-called 'Anonymous Histories of Shah Isma'il' (published as *Alamara-yi Shah Isma'il* and *Alamara-yi Safavi*) purport to be a detailed history of the Safavid movement from the beginnings of the Safavid Order to the death of Shah Isma'il in 1524. These stories present grave problems as a record of true events, but their very distance from the rarefied sphere of official historiography makes them a valuable window into the imagination of those outside the sphere of the powerful. For these tales bear the clear stamp of coffeehouse storytellers (*naqqalan*), whose anonymous creativity moved in a dialectical relationship with the tastes of the crowds they sought to entertain and impress. The story details that survived that process are a gold mine for students of the Persian lower strata and their *mentalité*. Such details include ethnic and religious stereotypes, the attitude of the common people toward their rulers, and metaphysical expectations regarding divine support of the Safavid cause. Accordingly, the 'Anonymous Histories' afford the historian a closer understanding of the mental landscape of a segment of the Iranian population rarely heard from in historical documents.

Babak Rahimi critically examines methodologies that rely on early modern European accounts to study the Shi`i Islamic Muharram rituals, performed during first ten-days of the Islamic lunar calendar (hence the name Muharram) in commemoration of the martyrdom of Prophet's grandson, Husayn, in Karbala, 680. While focusing on the subaltern participation in Safavid-era Muharram rituals, Rahimi argues that reliance on the European travel accounts limits understanding primarily because of the discursive regimes of knowledge that the reports produced in the early modern colonial contexts. He argues instead that an alternative approach should not focus on Persian elite sources, which hardly provide any account of the rituals, but textual and visual material texts sources as historical traces with glimpses into the inner life of the ritual participants. Though fraught with danger, an interpretative approach based on the material sources, in particular Husayn Va'iz Kashifi's *Rawat al-shuhada*, could facilitate an intertextual possibility of understanding aspects of what the subaltern participants in Safavid Muharram rituals experienced. Beyond a historical realist approach, the study offers an emotive methodology based on materiality of past religious experiences.

Valerie Gonzalez suggests that in its own aesthetic way, painting attests to the role and description of subalternity in Persianate societies from the thirteenth century to the modern period. At no time in the history of Persianate painting did the subalterns ever lose their voice. They were always conspicuously visible in the images' iconography and constituted the primary site of pictorial experiment with human representation. However, to understand this phenomenon and discern through it the philosophy of subalternity within the Persianate social-political order, it is necessary to examine the pictorial approach to the duality subalterns versus royalty. Royal physiognomic portraiture emerges in the early modern era of the Safavids, Mughals and Ottomans. Yet, unlike its neighbours, it is only at the end of Shah 'Abbas I's reign that the Safavids began to depict the physical appearances of the king. Until then, they applied the concept of natural imitation only to subaltern imagery, although they used other modalities of royal portraiture. These divergences in royal portraiture signal an age-old Persian economy of human representation premised upon a semantically charged divide between subalternity and royalty. Gonzalez aims to unravel this economy and the conception of subalternity it conveys.

Ines Asceric-Todd notes that in 1573, the Istanbul hippodrome was the scene of the dramatic death of Sheikh Hamza Bali, the Bosnian-born leader of the Melami-Bayrami Sufi order: his throat was slit on the way out to the arena where he was to be executed, which was followed by one of the Janissaries leading him out cutting his own throat as a sacrifice for 'his master'. In the years preceding his execution, this seemingly minor subaltern religious leader quickly gained supporters in Bosnia, the neighbouring countries, and Istanbul itself, as well as the attention of the Ottoman authorities and the ulema. Asceric-Todd considers the persecution of Sheikh Hamza Bali and his followers in the light of the Ottoman-Safavid hostilities at the time and the Ottoman fears of a Shia-inspired insurgency. The essay examines three previously unanalysed anti-Hamzevi treatises to evaluate what they can tell us about the level of influence of the Hamzevis and other subaltern Shia-oriented movements in Ottoman society at that time, and, by extension, their role in the process of the establishment of Sunni ideological hegemony in the Ottoman Empire which was taking place for most of the 16th century.

Hirotake Maeda examines the subaltern nature of Safavid royal servants who were forcibly migrated from the Caucasus region. The first part of the essay highlights the various historical phases the Caucasus peoples experienced with the Safavid imperial authority. The second part focuses on the political-cultural activities of Parsadan Gorgijanidze, a high-ranking 'Georgian' bureaucrat with mixed background. He was raised at the court of King Rostom, a Muslim 'returned king', ruler of Kartli kingdom in eastern Georgia. Afterwards Gorgijanidze spent some forty years in

Isfahan as an imperial official. There are mixed signals in terms of the religion-national identification in Gorgijanidze's writings as being a faithful servant of the converted king in the periphery, successfully attaining a high political career inside the sovereign empire and using his 'Georgian' resources as a political leverage. His Georgian text allows us to extract the mixed subaltern moment experienced by the Caucasian peoples living in Safavid society. Maeda argues that Safavid power embraced the social tensions inside the Caucasus' local politics. They became captives of the imperial politics but not necessarily 'enslaved', rather charging themselves as the royal agents even as their peripheral identity remained intact. Georgian and other Caucasian elements living in Safavid imperial space represent various social tensions that contradicted each other and, as such, can also be examined within the framework of subaltern studies.

These gatherings and these papers were generated against the background of continued growth in the interest in 'history from below' or 'subalterns' in the Safavid period even if, as earlier such studies, these discussions did not usually refer to such terms. Works in this latter genre included studies of peasants,[30] Sufis and Sufism[31], such tribal elements as the Qizilbash,[32] religious minorities[33] and urban life more generally.[34]

To be sure, in these same years certain conventional discourses generally and in the field in particular also have continued apace.[35] The same obtains with respect to Safavid studies.[36]

Indeed, to tell the story of the Safavid period the field has long privileged what, in reality, are the voices of the Safavid minority - urban, literate elites, both those of the region and those from abroad who resided in/travelled through it. Access to works in which these voices can be heard has not proved unduly problematic. Indeed, since 1979 the availability of such material has expanded markedly.[37]

However, following on from Willem Floor's suggestion of some years ago that across the 17th century 85-90% of Iran's population, never higher than nine million in total, was rural,[38] an inversion of the Safavid social pyramid by population might be posited. As the Gall-Peters Projection corrects for the 1569 Mercator world map's distortion of the relative land masses which 'pumps up the sizes of Europe and North America,'[39] such an inversion – such that the majority Safavid 'below' becomes the Safavid 'above'[40] – underscores the reality that rather little is in fact known about that majority.[41]

At this, the works in this volume, together with the many contributions in the tradition of 'history from below' or 'subaltern studies', of which but a small number have been cited herein, suggest there are ways to recover voices of different elements of the majority of the period's population.[42]

**

Special thanks are due to the British Institute for Persian Studies for funding this project, to the contributors to this volume for their patience, and to Gerlach Press.

Bibliography

Abisaab, Rula J., 'Peasant Uprisings in Astarabad: the *Siyāh Pūshān* (wearers of black), the Sayyids, and the Safavid State', *Iranian Studies*, 49 (2016), 471-492.

Abrahamian, Ervand, 'The Crowd in Iranian Politics, 1905-1953', *Past and Present*, 41 (1968), 184-210.

Alavi, Seema, *Islam and Healing: Loss and Recovery of an Indo-Muslim Medical Tradition, 1600-1900*, New York: Palgrave Macmillan, 2008.

Amin, Samir, *Accumulation on a world scale; a critique of the theory of underdevelopment*, transl., Brian Pearce. New York: Monthly Review Press, 1974.

Amin, Samir, *Imperialism and unequal development*, New York: Monthly Review Press, 1977.

Anooshahr, Ali, 'The Rise of the Safavids According to their Old Veterans: Amini Haravi's *Futuhat-e Shahi*', *Iranian Studies* 48 (2015), 249-267.

Anzali, Ata, 'The Emergence of the Ẕahabiyya in Safavid Iran', *Journal of Sufi Studies*, 2 (2013), 149–175.

Atabaki, Touraj, ed., special issue of *International Review of Social History*, 'Special Theme – Twentieth Century Iran: History From Below', 48 (2003).

Atabaki, Touraj, ed., *The State and the Subaltern: Authoritarian Modernisation in Turkey and Iran*, London: I. B. Tauris, 2007.

Aubin, Jean, 'Revolution Chiite et Conservatisme, Les soufis de Lahejan, 1500–1514' (Études Safavides. II.)', *Moyen Orient et Océan Indien*, 1 (1984), 1–40.

Avery, Peter, *Modern Iran*, London: Benn, 1965.

Babaie, Susan, Kathryn Babayan, Ina Baghdiantz-McCabe, Massumeh Farhad, *Slaves of the Shah, New Elites of Safavid Iran*, London: I. B. Tauris, 2004.

Babayan, Kathryn, 'The "Aqaid al-Nisa": A Glimpse at Safavid Women in Local Isfahani Culture', in *Women in the Medieval Islamic World, Power, Patronage and Piety*, ed. Gavin Hambly, New York: St. Martin's Press, 1998, 349–381.

Babayan, Kathryn, *The City as Anthology, Eroticism and Urbanity in Early Modern Isfahan*, Stanford: Stanford University Press, 2021.

Babayan, Kathryn, 'In Spirit We Ate Each Other's Sorrow: Female Companionship in Seventeenth-Century Safavid Iran', in *Islamicate Sexualities: Translations across Temporal Geographies of Desire*, eds. Kathryn Babayan and Afsaneh Najmabadi, Cambridge, Mass.: Center for Middle Eastern Studies of Harvard University, 2008, 239-274.

Babayan, Kathryn, 'The Waning of the Qizilbash: The Spiritual and the Temporal in Seventeenth Century Iran', unpublished Ph.D. dissertation, Princeton University, June 1993.

Baghdiantz McCabe, Ina, *The Shah's Silk for Europe's Silver: The Eurasian Trade of the Julfa Armenians in Safavid Iran and India (1530–1750)*, Atlanta: Scholars Press, 1999.

Baltacıoğlu-Brammer, Ayşe, 'Formation of Kızılbaş Communities in Anatolia and Ottoman Responses, 1450s-1630s', *International Journal of Turkish Studies*, 20 (2014), 21-48.

Baltacıoğlu-Brammer, Ayşe, 'Those Heretics Gathering Secretly …": Qizilbash Rituals and Practices in the Ottoman Empire according to Early Modern Sources', *Journal of the Ottoman and Turkish Studies Association*, 6 (2019), 39-60.

Bayat, Asef, *Workers and Revolution in Iran, A Third World Experience of Workers' Control*, London: Zed Books, 1987.

Beinin, Joel, *Workers and Peasants in the Modern Middle East*, Cambridge: Cambridge University Press, 2001.

Bill, James, *The Politics of Iran, Groups, Classes and Modernization*, Columbus, Ohio: Charles E. Merrill, 1972.

Blake, Steve, 'Contributors to the Urban Landscape: Women Builders in Safavid Isfahan and Mughal Shahjahanabad', in *Women in the Medieval Islamic World, Power, Patronage and Piety*, ed. Gavin Hambly, New York: St. Martin's Press, 1998, 407–428.

Bosworth, C. E., *The Medieval Islamic Underworld*, Leiden: Brill, 1976.

Braudel, Fernand, *The Mediterranean and the mediterranean world in the age of Philip II*, transl., Siân Reynolds. 2 vols., New York: Harper and Row, 1972-73.

Brenner, Robert, 'The Origins of Capitalist Development: A Critique of Neo-Smithian Marxism', *New Left Review*, 104 (1977), 25-92.

Calmard, Jean, 'Popular Literature Under the Safavids', in *Society and culture in the early modern Middle East: studies on Iran in the Safavid period*, ed. Andrew J. Newman, Leiden: Brill, 2003, 315–339.

Calmard, Jean 'Shi`i Rituals and Power II. The Consolidation of Safavid Shi`ism: Folklore and Popular Religion', in *Safavid Persia: the history and politics of an Islamic society*, ed., Charles Melville, London: I. B. Tauris, 1996, 139–190.

Chalcraft, John, 'Revolutionary weakness in Gramscian perspective: the Arab Middle East and North Africa since 2021', Middle East Critique, 30 (2021), 87-104.

Cottam, Richard, *Nationalism in Iran*, Pittsburgh: University of Pittsburgh Press, 1964, 1979.

Cronin, Stephanie, *Social Histories of Iran Modernism and Marginality in the Middle East*, Cambridge: Cambridge University Press, 2021.

Cronin, Stephanie, *Soldiers, Shahs and Subalterns in Iran: Opposition, Protest and Revolt, 1921-1941*, New York: Palgrave Macmillan, 2010.

Cronin, Stephanie, ed., *Subalterns and Social Protest: History from Below in the Middle East and North Africa*, London: Routledge, 2008.

Csirkés, Ferenc, 'Popular Religiosity and Vernacular Turkic: A Qezelbash Catechism from Safavid Iran' in *Safavid Persia in the Age of Empires, The Idea of Iran* Vol. 10, ed. Charles Melville, London: I. B. Tauris, 2021, 211-239.

Cumings, Bruce, 'Boundary displacement: Area studies and international studies during and after the cold war', *Bulletin of Concerned Asian Scholars*, 29 (1997) 1, 6-26.

Deacon, E. Lucy, 'Ta'ziyeh-khani in Iranian Communities: Muharram AH 1439 (AD 2017)', *Medieval English Theatre* 42 (2020), 142-180.

Emami, Farshid, 'Coffeehouses, Urban Spaces, and the Formation of a Public Sphere in Safavid Isfahan', *Muqarnas*, 33 (2016), 177-220.

Floor, Willem, *The Economy of Safavid Persia*, Wiesbaden: Reichert, 2000.

Floor, Willem and Hasan Javadi, 'The Role of Azerbaijani Turkish in Safavid Iran', *Iranian Studies*, 46 (2013), 569-581.

Frank, André Gunder, *Capitalism and Underdevelopment in Latin America: Historical Studies of Chile and Brazil*, New York: Monthly Review Press, 1967.

Ghereghlou, Kioumars, 'On the margins of minority life: Zoroastrians and the state in Safavid Iran', *Bulletin of the School of Oriental and African Studies*, 80 (2017), 45-71.

Gholsorkhi, Shohreh, 'Pari Khan Khanum: A Masterful Safavid Princess', *Iranian Studies*, 28 (1995), 143–56.

Ghougassian, Vazken, *The Emergence of the Armenian Diocese of New Julfa in the Seventeenth Century*, Atlanta: Scholars Press, 1998

Gordon, Colin, ed. and transl., *Power/Knowledge: Selected Interviews and Other Writings, 1972-1977*, Brighton: Harvester Press, 1980.

Gran, Peter, *The Islamic Roots of Capitalism*, Austin: University of Texas Press, 1979.

Gran, Peter, *The Persistence of Orientalism: Anglo-American Historians and Modern Egypt*, Syracuse: Syracuse University Press, 2020.

Guha, Ranajit, Gayatri Chakravorty-Spivak, eds., *Selected Subaltern Studies*, New York/Oxford: Oxford University Press, 1988.

Guha, Ranajit, ed. *Subaltern Studies Reader*, Minneapolis/London: University of Minnesota Press, 1997.

Halliday, Fred, *Iran: Dictatorship and Development*, Harmondsworth: Penguin, 1979.

Halpern, Manfred, *The Politics of Social Change in the Middle East and North Africa*, Princeton: Princeton University Press, 1963.

Hashim, Ahmad, 'Military Orientalism: Middle East ways of war', *Middle East Policy*, 26 (2019), 31-47.

Holliday, Shabnam, 'The legacy of subalternity and Gramsci's national-popular: populist discourse in the case of the Islamic Republic of Iran', *Third World Quarterly* 37 (2016), 917-933.

Huat, Chua Beng, et al., 'Area Studies and the crisis of legitimacy: a view from South East Asia', *South East Asia Research*, 27 (2019), 31-48.

Johnson, Peter and Judith Tucker, 'Middle East Studies Network in the United States', *MERIP Reports*, 38 (1975), 3-20+26.

Karakaya-Stump, Ayfer, *The Kizilbash-Alevis in Ottoman Anatolia: Sufism, Politics and Community*, Edinburgh: Edinburgh University Press, 2019.

Keyvani, Mehdi, *Artisans and Guild Life in the later Safavid Period*, Berlin: Klaus Schwarz, 1992.

Khomeini, Ruhollah, *Islam and Revolution / writings and declarations, Imam Khomeini*, transl. Hamid Algar, Pennsauken: BookBaby, 2015.

Khosrowjah, Hossein, 'A brief history of area studies and international studies', *Arab Studies Quarterly* 33 (2011), 131-142.

King, Victor T., 'The problem with areas, Asia and Area studies', *Bijdragen tot de Taal-, Land- en Volkenkunde*, 168 (2012), 314-324.

Landau, Amy, 'Armenian Merchant Patronage of New Julfa's Sacred Spaces', co-authored with Theo Maarten van Lint, in *Sacred Precincts: Non-Muslim Sites in Islamic Territories*, ed. Mohammad Gharipour, Leiden: Brill, 2015, 308-333.

Lerner, Daniel, *The Passing of Traditional Society: Modernizing the Middle East*, New York: Free Press, 1958.

Lockman, Zachary *Contending Visions of the Middle East: The History and Politics of Orientalism*, Cambridge: Cambridge University Press, 2004.

Ludden, David, ed., *Reading Subaltern Studies: Critical History, Contested Meaning, and the Globalization of South Asia*, Delhi: Permanent Black, 2001.

Maeda, Hirotake, 'On the Ethno-Social Backgrounds of the Four *ghulam* Families from Georgia in Safavid Iran', *Studia Iranica*, 32 (2003), 243–278.

Matthee, Rudi, 'Prostitutes, Courtesans, and Dancing Girls: Women Entertainers in Safavid Iran', in *Iran and Beyond, Essays in Middle Eastern History in Honor of Nikki R. Keddie*, eds., Rudi Matthee and Beth Baron, Costa Mesa, CA: Mazda, 2000, 121–150.

Mignolo, Walter, 'Delinking: The rhetoric of modernity, the logic of coloniality and the grammar of de-Coloniality', *Cultural Studies*, 21 (2007), 449–451.

Mignolo, Walter, *The Politics of Decolonial Investigations*, Durham: Duke University Press, 2021.

Moreen, Vera B., 'The Problems of Conversion Among Iranian Jews in the Seventeenth and Eighteenth Centuries', *Iranian Studies*, 19 (1986), 215–228.

Moreen, Vera B., 'The Status of Religious Minorities in Safavid Iran 1617-61, The Status of Religious Minorities in Safavid Iran 1617-61', *Journal of Near Eastern Studies*, 40 (1981), 119-134.

Nash, Gary B., *The Unknown American Revolution*, New York: Viking, 2005.

Newman, Andrew J., 'Clerical Perceptions of Sufi Practices in Late Seventeenth-Century Persia: Arguments Over the Permissibility of Singing (*Ghina*)', in *The Heritage of Sufism, Vol. III: Late Classical Persianate Sufism: the Safavid and Mughal Period (1501-1750)*, eds. Leonard Lewisohn and David Morgan, Oxford: Oneworld, 1999, 135-164.

Newman, Andrew J., 'Fayd al-Kashani and the Rejection of the Clergy/State Alliance: Friday Prayer as Politics in the Safavid Period', in *The Most*

Learned of the Shi'a, ed. Linda Walbridge, New York: Oxford University Press, 2001, 34-52.

Newman, Andrew J., *The Formative Period of Period of Twelver Shī'ism: Hadīth as Discourse Between Qum and Baghdad*, Richmond, Surrey: Curzon, 2000.

Newman, Andrew J., 'The Idea of Baqer al-Majlesi as "The Idea of Iran: The Safavid Era"' in *Safavid Persia in the Age of Empires, The Idea of Iran, Volume X*, ed. Charles Melville, London: I.B. Tauris, 2021, 157-183.

Newman, Andrew, 'Safavids and "Subalterns": The Reclaiming of Voices', in *Fortresses of Intellect: Ismaili and Other Islamic Studies in Honour of Farhad Daftary*, ed. Omar Ali-de-Unzaga, London: I. B. Tauris, 2011, 477-494.

Newman, Andrew J., *Safavid Iran: Rebirth of a Persian Empire*. London; New York: I.B. Tauris, 2006.

Newman, Andrew J., 'Sufism and Anti-Sufism in Safavid Iran: The Authorship of the "Hadiqat al-Shi'a" Revisited ', *IRAN*, 37 (1999), 95-108.

Newman, Andrew J., *Twelver Shiism: Unity and Diversity in the Life of Islam, 632 to 1722*, Edinburgh: Edinburgh University Press, 2013.

Perry, John, 'Toward a Theory of Iranian Urban Moieties: The Haydariyyah and Ni'matiyyah Revisited', *Iranian Studies*, 32 (1999), 51–70.

Quinn, Sholeh, 'Rewriting Nimatallahi History in Safavid Chronicles', in *The Heritage of Sufism, Volume III: Late Classical Persianate Sufism (1501–1750)*, eds Leonard Lewisogn and David Morgan, Oxford: Oneworld, 1999, 201–222.

Rabinow, Paul, ed., *The Foucault Reader*, New York: Pantheon, 1984.

Ridgeon, Lloyd, 'Short Back and Sides, Were the Qalandars of Late Safavid Iran Domesticated?' *Journal of Sufi Studies*, 6 (2017) 82–115.

Rostow, Walt, *The Stages of Economic Growth: A Non-Communist Manifesto*, Cambridge: Cambridge University Press, 1960.

Routley, Nick, 'The problem with our maps', 6.6.17, https://www.businessinsider.com/the-mercator-projection-distorts-countries-2017-6?r=US&IR=T, acc. 19.2.22.

Rudé, George, *The Crowd in History, 1730-1848*, New York: Wiley, 1964.

Said, Edward, *Orientalism*, London: Penguin, 1978.

Sadowski, Yahya, 'The New Orientalism and the Democracy Debate', *Middle East Report*, 83 (1993), 14-21+40, repr. in *Political Islam: Essays from Middle East Report*, eds. Joel Beinin and Joe Stork eds., Berkeley: University of California Press, 1997, 33-50.

Savory, Roger, *Iran Under the Safavids*, Cambridge: Cambridge University Press, 1980.

Shosan, Boaz, *Popular Culture in Medieval Cairo*, Cambridge: Cambridge University Press, 1993.

Szuppe, Maria, 'Status, Knowledge and Politics: Women in Sixteenth-Century Safavid Iran', in *Women in Iran from the Rise of Islam to 1800*, eds., Guity Nashat and Lois Beck, Urbana: University of Illinois Press, 2003, 141–169.

Thompson, Edward P., *The Making of the English Working Class*, London: Victor Gollancz Ltd., 1963.

Wallerstein, Immanuel, *The Modern World System vol. I: Capitalist Agriculture and the Origins of the European World-Economy in the Sixteenth Century*, New York/London: Academic Press, 1974.

Yıldırım, Riza, 'The Safavid-Qizilbash Ecumene and the Formation of the Qizilbash-Alevi Community in the Ottoman Empire, c. 1500–c. 1700', *Iranian Studies*, 52 (2019), 449-483.

Zarinebaf-Shahr, Fariba, 'Economic Activities of Safavid Women in the Shrine-City of Ardabil', *Iranian Studies*, 31 (1998), 247–261.

Zonis, Marvin, *The Political Elite of Iran*, Princeton: Princeton University Press, 1971.

Notes

1 See the editor's introduction in Stephanie Cronin, ed., *Subalterns and Social Protest: History from Below in the Middle East and North Africa* (London: Routledge, 2008), 1f.
2 Nash paid tribute to Hill in his *The Unknown American Revolution* (New York: Viking, 2005), xxvii-xxviii.
3 Latin American Subaltern Studies Group, 'Founding Statement', *Boundary 2*, 20 (1993), 110-12.
4 When, in 1976, the Braudel Center for Study of Economies, Historical Systems, and Civilization was established at SUNY-Binghamton, Wallerstein was its first director. Samir Amin's works included the translation of his 1970 *Accumulation on a World Scale: A Critique of the Theory of Underdevelopment* (transl.) Brian Pearce, (New York: Monthly Review Press, 1974) and the translation of his 1973 *Imperialism and Unequal Development* (New York: Monthly Review Press, 1977). 'Dependency'/'underdevelopment' theory was first made popular by André Gunder Frank (d. 2005), whose *Capitalism and Underdevelopment in Latin America: Historical Studies of Chile and Brazil* (New York: Monthly Review Press, 1967) reveals his interests as also lying outside the field.
5 See, for example, Robert Brenner, 'The Origins of Capitalist Development: A Critique of Neo-Smithian Marxism', *New Left Review*, 104 (1977), 25-92.
6 Said was himself influenced by another 'outsider', the post-structuralist French philosopher, historian, and sociologist Michel Foucault (d. 1984), many of whose key books were available in English translation by the late 1970s. A number of the latter were in print well before the appearance of such works as Colin Gordon, ed. and transl. *Power/Knowledge: Selected Interviews and Other Writings, 1972-1977* (Brighton: Harvester Press, 1980) and Paul Rabinow, ed., *The Foucault Reader* (New York: Pantheon, 1984).
This and the discussion below are reprised from our 'Safavids and "Subalterns": The Reclaiming of Voices', in *Fortresses of Intellect: Ismaili and Other Islamic Studies in Honour of Farhad Daftary*, ed. Omar Ali-de-Unzaga (London: I. B . Tauris, 2011), 477-94.
7 No longer extant journals included *Khamsin* (1975-1986), *Review of Middle East Studies* (six issues, published from 1975-1993) and *Review of Iranian Political Economy and History* (RIPEH) (1976-1981). AMES, appearing in the latter years of the decade within the Middle East Studies Association of North America (MESA), with the 'A' in AMES standing for 'Alternatives', was similarly short-lived.
8 Peter Johnson and Judith Tucker, 'Middle East Studies Network in the United States', *MERIP Reports*, 38 (1975), 5, 8f.

9   In the original work, Cottam (see the 1979 edition, 308; Cottam's 1979 postscript begins on 320) mentions Khomeini as 'an unknown figure in Nationalist circles' leading the June, 1963 riots. In his 1971 *The Political Elite of Iran*, Marvin Zonis did mention Khomeini as well as Grand Ayatollah Burujirdi (d. 1961), but ranked 'principal religious leaders' as 20th on a list of the 30 categories of the political elite (346-8). Avery's reference to Burujirdi (505) is almost dismissive. In Bill's work (22), Khomeini is unmentioned. In the 9 photos on the cover of Bill's *The Politics of Iran*, only one was a religious figure: Sayyid Hasan Imam, identified as the Imam Jo'me.
10 Fred Halliday, *Iran: Dictatorship and Development* (Harmondsworth: Penguin, 1979), 299.
11 See Yahya Sadowski, 'The New Orientalism and the Democracy Debate', *Middle East Report*, 83 (1993), 14-21+ 40, repr. in *Political Islam: Essays From Middle East Report*, eds. Joel Beinin and Joe Stork (Berkeley: University of California Press, 1997), 33-50.
12 On the Safavids, see our *Safavid Iran: Rebirth of a Persian Empire*. London; New York: I.B. Tauris, 2006, 1-12. On Shi'i studies, see our *The Formative Period of Period of Twelver Shī'ism: Hadīth as Discourse Between Qum and Baghdad* (Richmond, Surrey: Curzon, 2000), xiii-xxvii; idem, *Twelver Shiism: Unity and Diversity in the Life of Islam, 632 to 1722* (Edinburgh: Edinburgh University Press, 2013), 1-15.
13 Exceptions include C. E Bosworth, *The Medieval Islamic Underworld* (Leiden: Brill, 1976) and Peter Gran, *The Islamic Roots of Capitalism* (Austin: University of Texas Press, 1979). In Iranian studies, see Ervand Abrahamian's 'The Crowd in Iranian Politics, 1905-1953', *Past and Present*, 41 (1968), 184-210. The latter took as its starting point George Rudé's (d. 1993) *The Crowd in History, 1730-1848* (New York: Wiley, 1964), a work well within the 'history from below' genre. The journal *Past and Present* itself was founded in 1952 by, among others, the same Edward P. Thompson.
14 In the case of the Subcontinent itself, an exception is Seema Alavi, *Islam and Healing: Loss and Recovery of an Indo-Muslim Medical Tradition, 1600-1900* (New York: Palgrave Macmillan, 2008). See also the reference to Beinin in n16.
15 The two pre-modern articles addressed street violence in Damascus and the Roma in Ottoman society. The three essays on Iran were authored by Asef Bayat, Cronin herself and Vanessa Martin. Bayat, for example, had been publishing on such elements since 1987. See his *Workers and Revolution in Iran, A Third World Experience of Workers' Control* (London: Zed Books, 1987).
16 See the works by Judith Tucker, Joel Beinin, Zachary Lockman, Ellis Goldberg, all on Egypt, as cited in Cronin's introduction, especially nn.10-12, 24 and, on peasants, again mainly focusing on Egypt, n26. See also the works cited in nn29, 30, 32, 34. Cronin (n12) noted the 'comprehensive bibliography on "history from below"' in Beinin's *Workers and Peasants in the Modern Middle East* (Cambridge: Cambridge University Press, 2001) but noted that the items therein mainly addressed 'the Ottoman Empire/Turkey, Egypt and *Bilad al-Sham*' and not 'Iran and North Africa'. It is not immediately clear that these earlier works explicitly referenced either 'history from below' or Subaltern Studies. Too, these items both were mainly published after 1979 and addressed the 'modern' period. To be sure, in n17, Cronin refers to Boaz Shosan's *Popular Culture in Medieval Cairo* (Cambridge: Cambridge University Press, 1993).
17 See, for example, such works by Touraj Atabaki as his edited special issue of *International Review of Social History*, 'Special Theme – Twentieth Century Iran: History From Below', 48 (2003), and his edited collection *The State and the Subaltern: Authoritarian Modernisation in Turkey and Iran* (London: I. B. Tauris, 2007).
    One-off conferences/seminars included the 25-26 May, 2001 'Twentieth Century Iran: History from Below', held at International Institute of Social History (IISH), Amsterdam, and the 23 January 2004 workshop 'Iran and History from Below', organised by the London Middle East Institute and the Iran Heritage Foundation. Both events covered the Qajar, Pahlavi and, to a lesser extent, the IRI periods and concentrated mainly on the political and the economic.
18 Appearing in the immediate aftermath of the Revolution but clearly produced on the cusp thereof, and, therefore, 'the last word' on the period before 1979, see Roger Savory, *Iran Under*

the Safavids (Cambridge: Cambridge University Press, 1980). On Safavid studies more generally both before and after, see the sources in n12.

19 The pioneering work on these polemics was Kathryn Babayan's 'The Waning of the Qizilbash: The Spiritual and the Temporal in Seventeenth Century Iran', unpublished Ph.D. dissertation, Princeton University, June, 1993. The present author discussed the anti-Sufi polemic and the indirect evidence it offers as to actual beliefs and practices in such works as 'Sufism and Anti-Sufism in Safavid Iran: The Authorship of the "Hadiqat al-Shi'a" Revisited', *IRAN* 37 (1999), 95-108 and 'Clerical Perceptions of Sufi Practices in Late Seventeenth-Century Persia: Arguments Over the Permissibility of Singing (Ghina)', in *The Heritage of Sufism, Vol. III: Late Classical Persianate Sufism: the Safavid and Mughal Period (1501-1750)*, eds., Leonard Lewisohn and David Morgan (Oxford: Oneworld, 1999), 135-64.

20 See our 'Fayd al-Kashani and the Rejection of the Clergy/State Alliance: Friday Prayer as Politics in the Safavid Period', *The Most Learned of the Shi'a*, ed. Linda Walbridge, (New York: Oxford University Press, 2001), 34-52.

21 On such firmans, in Isfahan, Kashan and Yazd (where the weavers were a very strong guild), see our *Safavid Iran*, 63. Floor estimates some 30% of Safavid Iran's urban population was involved in textile and leather crafts. See Willem Floor, *The Economy of Safavid Persia* (Wiesbaden: Reichert, 2000), 325; n41 below.

22 On Sufis and Sufism see, for example, Jean Aubin, 'Revolution Chiite et Conservatisme, Les soufis de Lahejan, 1500–1514' (Études Safavides. II.)', *Moyen Orient et Océan Indien*, I (1984), 1–40; Sholeh Quinn, 'Rewriting Nimatallahi History in Safavid Chronicles', in *The Heritage of Sufism, Volume III: Late Classical Persianate Sufism (1501–1750)*, eds. Leonard Lewisohn and David Morgan (Oxford: Oneworld), 1999, 201–22; Ata Anzali, 'The Emergence of the Zahabiyya in Safavid Iran', *Journal of Sufi Studies*, 2 (2013), 149–175.

23 See, for example, Shohreh Gholsorkhi, 'Pari Khan Khanum: A Masterful Safavid Princess', *Iranian Studies*, 28 (1995), 143–56; Fariba Zarinebaf-Shahr, 'Economic Activities of Safavid Women in the Shrine-City of Ardabil', *Iranian Studies*, 31 (1998), 247–61; Kathryn Babayan, 'The "Aqaid al-Nisa": A Glimpse at Safavid Women in Local Isfahani Culture', in *Women in the Medieval Islamic World, Power, Patronage and Piety*, ed. Gavin Hambly (New York: St. Martin's Press, 1998), 349–81; idem, 'In Spirit We Ate Each Other's Sorrow: Female Companionship in Seventeenth-Century Safavid Iran', in, *Islamicate Sexualities: Translations across Temporal Geographies of Desire*, eds. Kathryn Babayan and Afsaneh Najmabadi (Cambridge, Mass.: Center for Middle Eastern Studies of Harvard University, 2008), 239-274; Steve Blake, 'Contributors to the Urban Landscape: Women Builders in Safavid Isfahan and Mughal Shahjahanabad', in *Women in the Medieval Islamic World, Power, Patronage and Piety*, ed. Gavin Hambly (New York: St. Martin's Press, 1998), 407–28; Rudi Matthee, 'Prostitutes, Courtesans, and Dancing Girls: Women Entertainers in Safavid Iran', in *Iran and Beyond, Essays in Middle Eastern History in Honor of Nikki R. Keddie*, eds., Rudi Matthee and Beth Baron, (Costa Mesa, CA: Mazda, 2000), 121–50. See also such works by Maria Szuppe as 'Status, Knowledge and Politics: Women in Sixteenth-Century Safavid Iran', in *Women in Iran from the Rise of Islam to 1800*, eds., Guity Nashat and Lois Beck, (Urbana: University of Illinois Press, 2003), 141–69.

24 Mehdi Keyvani, *Artisans and Guild Life in the later Safavid Period* (Berlin: Klaus Schwarz, 1982); Riza Yildirim, 'Shi'itisation of the Futuwwa Tradition in the Fifteenth Century', *British Journal of Middle Eastern Studies*, 40 (2013), 53-70.

25 Hirotake Maeda, 'On the Ethno-Social Backgrounds of the Four *ghulam* Families from Georgia in Safavid Iran', *Studia Iranica*, 32 (2003), 243–78; Sussan Babaie, Kathryn Babayan, Ina Baghdiantz-McCabe, Massumeh Farhad, *Slaves of the Shah, New Elites of Safavid Iran* (London: I. B. Tauris, 2004).

26 Jean Calmard, 'Shi`i Rituals and Power II. The Consolidation of Safavid Shi`ism: Folklore and Popular Religion', in *Safavid Persia: the history and politics of an Islamic society*, ed. Charles Melville, (London: I. B. Tauris, 1996), 139–90; idem, 'Popular Literature Under the Safavids', in *Society and*

culture in the early modern Middle East: studies on Iran in the Safavid period, ed. Andrew J. Newman (Leiden: Brill, 2003), 315–39; John Perry, 'Toward a Theory of Iranian Urban Moieties: The Haydariyyah and Ni'matiyyah Revisited', *Iranian Studies*, 32 (1999), 51–70.

27 Vera B. Moreen, 'The Status of Religious Minorities in Safavid Iran 1617-61', *Journal of Near Eastern Studies*, 40 (1981), 119-134; idem, 'The Problems of Conversion Among Iranian Jews in the Seventeenth and Eighteenth Centuries', *Iranian Studies*, 19 (1986), 215–28; Vazken Ghougassian, *The Emergence of the Armenian Diocese of New Julfa in the Seventeenth Century* (Atlanta: Scholars Press, 1998); Ina Baghdiantz McCabe, *The Shah's Silk for Europe's Silver: The Eurasian Trade of the Julfa Armenians in Safavid Iran and India (1530–1750)* (Atlanta: Scholars Press, 1999).

28 See http://www.shii-news.imes.ed.ac.uk/projects/the-subalterns-project/ (accessed 27.1.22).

29 Videos of all the presentations at both workshops can be accessed at the above website. As these workshops involve in-person presentations by colleagues based at institutions around the world, COVID has greatly delayed further the progress of the project.

30 Rula J. Abisaab, 'Peasant Uprisings in Astarabad: the *Siyāh Pūshān* (wearers of black), the Sayyids, and the Safavid State', *Iranian Studies*, 49 (2016), 471-92.

31 Lloyd Ridgeon, 'Short Back and Sides, Were the Qalandars of Late Safavid Iran Domesticated?', *Journal of Sufi Studies* 6 (2017) 82–115.

32 Ayşe Baltacıoğlu-Brammer, 'Formation of Kızılbaş Communities in Anatolia and Ottoman Responses, 1450s-1630s', *International Journal of Turkish Studies*, 20 (2014), 21-48; idem, '"Those Heretics Gathering Secretly …": Qizilbash Rituals and Practices in the Ottoman Empire according to Early Modern Sources', *Journal of the Ottoman and Turkish Studies Association*, 6 (2019), 39-60; Ayfer Karakaya-Stump, *The Kizilbash-Alevis in Ottoman Anatolia: Sufism, Politics and Community* (Edinburgh: Edinburgh University Press, 2019); Rıza Yıldırım, 'The Safavid-Qizilbash Ecumene and the Formation of the Qizilbash-Alevi Community in the Ottoman Empire, c. 1500–c. 1700', *Iranian Studies*, 52 (2019), 449-483; Ferenc Csirkés, 'Popular Religiosity and Vernacular Turkic: A Qezelbash Catechism from Safavid Iran' in *Safavid Persia in the Age of Empires, The Idea of Iran* Vol. 10, ed. Charles Melville, (London: I. B. Tauris, 2021), 211-23. See also Ali Anooshahr, 'The Rise of the Safavids According to their Old Veterans: Amini Haravi's *Futuhat-e Shahi*', *Iranian Studies*, 48 (2015), 249-267.

33 Amy Landau, 'Armenian Merchant Patronage of New Julfa's Sacred Spaces', co-authored with Theo Maarten Van Lint, in *Sacred Precincts: Non-Muslim Sites in Islamic Territories*, ed. Mohammad Gharipour (Leiden: Brill, 2015), 308-33; Kioumars Ghereghlou, 'On the margins of minority life: Zoroastrians and the state in Safavid Iran', *Bulletin of the School of Oriental and African Studies*, 80 (2017), 45-71.

34 Farshid Emami, 'Coffeehouses, Urban Spaces, and the Formation of a Public Sphere in Safavid Isfahan', *Muqarnas*, 33 (2016), 177-220; Kathryn Babayan, *The City as Anthology, Eroticism and Urbanity in Early Modern Isfahan* (Stanford: Stanford University Press, 2021).

35 As to the first, on 'area studies', outwith the field, see Bruce Cumings, 'Boundary displacement: Area studies and international studies during and after the cold war', *Bulletin of Concerned Asian Scholars*, 29 (1997), 6-26, who calls special attention to the rise of corporate influence. More recently, see Victor T. King's review essay 'The problem with areas, Asia and Area studies', *Bijdragen tot de Taal-, Land- en Volkenkunde*, 168 (2012), 314-324; and, Chua Beng Huat, et al., 'Area Studies and the crisis of legitimacy: a view from South East Asia', *South East Asia Research*, 27 (2019), 31-48. The latter conclude (44) that 'Area Studies (sic) will struggle on.' From inside the field, see Hossein Khosrowjah, 'A brief history of area studies and international studies', *Arab Studies Quarterly* 33 (2011), 131-142, who also reviews the state of the discussion to that date. On newer/further manifestations of Orientalism, see Ahmad Hashim, 'Military Orientalism, Middle East ways of war', *Middle East Policy*, 26 (2019), 31-47; and, on the historiography of modern Egypt, Gran, Peter, *The Persistence of Orientalism: Anglo-American Historians and Modern Egypt* (Syracuse: Syracuse University Press, 2020). See also Zachary Lockman,

Contending Visions of the Middle East: The History and Politics of Orientalism (Cambridge: Cambridge University Press, 2004).

36 See our 'The Idea of Baqer al-Majlesi as "The Idea of Iran: The Safavid Era"' in *Safavid Persia in the Age of Empires, The Idea of Iran, Volume X*, ed. Charles Melville (London: I. B. Tauris, 2021), 157-183.

37 On these materials, see our *Safavid Iran*, 4f.

38 Willem Floor, *The Economy of Safavid Persia*, 2-9, 12f.

39 Nick Routley, 'The problem with our maps', 6.6.17, https://www.businessinsider.com/the-mercator-projection-distorts-countries-2017-6?r=US&IR=T, acc. 19.2.22.

40 Here the more recent attention to 'decolonialisation' might be referenced. Decoloniality was the theme of the 2020 British Society for Middle Eastern Studies (BRISMES) conference, re-scheduled for 2021: https://www.brismes.ac.uk/conference/past-conferences (acc. 31.1.22). In Latin American studies, to which this discourse owes its origins, see, for example, such works of Walter Mignolo as 'Delinking: The rhetoric of modernity, the logic of coloniality and the grammar of de-Coloniality', *Cultural Studies* 21 (2007), 449-514, for which references thanks to Mary Newman. His *The Politics of Decolonial Investigations* (Durham: Duke University Press, 2021), particularly the chapter on 'Islamophobia/Hispanophobia' (99-126), repays attention.

41 This was to say nothing of the Safavid population's myriad linguistic, ethnic, and religious differences. The first two together suggest that Persian was not as widely used across the Iranian plateau as might be thought. See the references to Floor in n38 and, also, Willem Floor and Hasan Javadi, 'The Role of Azerbaijani Turkish in Safavid Iran', *Iranian Studies* 46 (2013), 569-581; Csirkés, 'Popular Religiosity and Vernacular Turkic'. In a personal communication (15.2.22) Lucy Deacon has called my attention to some lines spoken in Turkish by Umm Kulsum to her father Imam Ali in a *taʿziyeh* text dated 1724. Deacon discusses the text in her 'Taʿziyeh-khani in Iranian Communities: Muharram AH 1439 (AD 2017)', *Medieval English Theatre* 42 (2020), 147.

Elsewhere (*The Economy of Safavid Persia*, 301), Floor suggests that 'agriculture, and its ancillary activities, was the most important sector of the economy in Safavid Persia employing about 80% of the population.' See also n21.

42 The study of just such elements in recent Iranian history continues apace. See, for example, Cronin's *Soldiers, Shahs and Subalterns in Iran: Opposition, Protest and Revolt, 1921-1941* (New York: Palgrave Macmillan, 2010); idem, *Social Histories of Iran, Modernism and Marginality in the Middle East* (Cambridge: Cambridge University Press, 2021), a chapter of which references Hobsbawm. See also Shabnam Holliday, 'The legacy of subalternity and Gramsci's national-popular: populist discourse in the case of the Islamic Republic of Iran', *Third World Quarterly* 37 (2016), 917-933.

In Middle Eastern Studies more generally, see John Chalcraft's several works utilising Gramscian perspectives, e.g., his 'Revolutionary weakness in Gramscian perspective: the Arab Middle East and North Africa since 2021', *Middle East Critique*, 30 (2021), 87-104. Note, also, the 'Gramsci in the Middle East and North Africa' Conference, planned for May, 2022, on which see https://www.lse.ac.uk/middle-east-centre/news/gramsci-in-middle-east-conference (acc. 1.2.22).

1

Liberating the "Turkoman Prisoner": An Assessment of Bound Captives in Sixteenth and Seventeenth-Century Persianate Works on Paper[1]

Jaimee K. Comstock-Skipp

Early Scholarship on the Bound Captives

This paper provides a critical examination of the "Turkoman Prisoner": a collective descriptor given to a number of single subjects found primarily in albums. Except for an insightful Hermitage Museum catalogue entry by Adel Adamova and an article by Linda Komaroff treating one such version in the Los Angeles County Museum of Art (LACMA), the oft-cited albeit cursorily-treated "Turkoman Prisoner" has not been examined as a larger group beyond three specimens following an iconographical formula.[2] An elegant warrior with wispy beard and square jaw is in a kneeling posture, rendered in submission with one arm bent in an "L" shape. He is fettered by a *palahang:* a contraption of containment to prevent the man from reaching for his bow and shooting an arrow.[3] The other arm rests on his knee. The dearth of research on this image type is remarkable for it is a repeated subject contained in albums of Persianate art assembled in the sixteenth and seventeenth centuries (Table 1: Attributions of Bound Captive Folios). I have collated thirty-five specimens in this study that are located in the collections of private individuals, museums, and libraries in Austria, Denmark, England, France, India, Iran, Russia, Turkey, and the United States. Some were discovered by tracking specific references in catalogues, and a few emerged by chance while looking through auctions, museum holdings, and hearing conference papers.[4] There are surely others waiting to be discovered.

This paper's aim is to uncover the historical context of the rendered subject, here termed the Bound Captive, to temper the emphasis on ethnicity implied by the "Turkoman" term. It becomes apparent that it is not a Turkoman depicted, but is instead a member of the Uzbek troops who attacked the eastern flank of the Safavid empire across the sixteenth and early seventeenth centuries. The Abulkhairid (Shibanid) and Tuqay-Timurid (Ashtarkhanid) dynasties carried out these military campaigns to secure the Khurasan region. My argument relies largely on period texts and visual materials painted by Safavid and Safavid-aligned artists. The majority of the artworks have a Safavid provenance, but my usage of the term "Safavid-aligned" acknowledges the few Prisoner copies that are attributed to Ottoman, Mughal, and Deccan realms. There have been a few other scholars before me to suggest an Uzbek attribution, but they do not substantiate their designation beyond a brief description based on the perceived physiognomic and ethnic traits of the depicted subject.[5] In representing the Bound Captives as inhabitants of Transoxiana, the artists give form to what they perceive as their "other": one who the artist is not. The depictions say just as much, if not more, about the renderer than the rendered.

The direction of his gaze and the position of his hands depend upon the placement of the Bound Captive in an album, and he usually faces the seam of the page break which makes him appear interiorised and withdrawn.[6] Sometimes he wears a turban but it is more common for the visor of the prisoner's *kalpak* headwear to be pulled down in front but with earflaps up.[7] His outer robe is either buttoned down the front or crossed over in the Mongol fashion, and the color of the tighter sleeves contrasts fashionably with the tunic, while a pointy-toed, high-heeled boot emerges from folds of fabric. A wispy scarf around his waist, usually striped or checked, rides on his hips and attracts attention to his armaments, sometimes just a straight dagger and riding whip. But more commonly he is equipped with arrows in a quiver, a bow, battle flail, and a sword.[8] Some iterations of this subject have been given short references in collection catalogues and surveys over the last century. These entries have perpetuated the subject's Central Asian characteristics without questioning who is represented, why the theme is repeated, and how the depictions provide insight into the historical period and social context of their producers.

Early scholars – such as Ivan Stchoukine, F.R. Martin, Armenag bey Sakisian, Laurence Binyon, and B.W. Robinson writing in the first half of the twentieth century – have been surprisingly confident in bestowing provenances. They have titled the figural subjects using a host of linguistic, ethnic, regional, cultural, and tribal designations such as Turkoman, Uzbek, Tatar, Akkoyunlu, Karakal, Mongol, Turkic, Central Asian, Gurkani, Oirat, and Qalmaq. These labels reinforce the prisoner's exoticism and exteriority as a "non-Iranian" with little to justify his Turko-Mongol designation beyond physiognomy and accessories. Scholars have traced the works to Timurid, Safavid, or Uzbek workshops. These ascriptions have at times confused both the subject matter (assumed to be an individual from a Turko-Mongol tribe and/or from Transoxiana) and the styles used to render him (interpreted as heralding from eastern schools in Herat and Bukhara, or from western workshops in Qazvin).

Moreover, this existing scholarship has affixed titles convenient for museum catalogue entries, creating categories that have reinforced a linguistic (Turkic) designation to stand for a non-Iranian subject. We must ask ourselves, however, whether the Safavid-aligned makers in fact deployed the same identity markers to distinguish the rendered subjects. The answer seems to be negative. It is worth remembering that the Safavid Qizilbash troops were, or at least were thought of, as "Turks" by the settled members of the Safavid population,[9] and the first Safavid Shah Ismail himself wrote almost exclusively in a Turkic Azerbaijani dialect when he conducted personal correspondence and composed poetry.[10] So when dealing with the early modern period, language is not an adequate means to distinguish Safavid from non-Safavid. What was actually employed to erect this division at the time is not overt within the prisoner pages but must be gleaned through visual analysis and from the historical record.

Adapting arguments pertaining to Orientalism in the arts to fit the materials, my holistic approach synthesises textual and visual sources from the period to uncover the identity of the Bound Captive when he is presented in historical chronicles, poetry manuscripts, large-scale wall paintings, and single-page album folios. Historical written evidence is taken from the following Safavid historiographies: Khwandamir's *Habib al-siyar* (a history on the early Safavid dynasty, written ca. 1523);[11] Qasimi's *Shahnama-yi Ismail* (a chronicle of Shah Ismail's conquests commissioned by Ismail himself ca. 1533);[12] Iskandar Beg Munshi's *Tarikh-i alam-ara-yi shah abbasi* (a history of Shah Abbas, ca. 1628–29);[13] Bizhan Gurji's *Tarikh-i jahangushai-yi khaqan-i sahib qiran* (ca. late seventeenth century);[14] and various *Tarikh-i alam-ara-yi shah Ismail* (histories of Shah Ismail, ca. 1680s, that are pastiches of folktales and legends preserved elsewhere in copies called *The Anonymous Histories of Shah Ismail*).[15] The Bound Captive folios and these chronicles do not count as ethnography. Rather, they are products of times and places that articulate the makers' own anxieties or adulation of the depicted individual confined within the page margins.

The first scholars to write about the folios suggested that the earliest drawings were depictions of a particular hostage or prisoner of war from the nascent Safavid period, but this specificity later evolved into a general subject for artists to repeat. F.R. Martin writing in 1912 suggested the Bibliothèque Nationale version (inscribed Mahu Khan, Table 1, entry 8) painted on silk was the original copy, and represented Murad: the last prince of the Aq Quyunlu confederation who was defeated by Shah Ismail. To Martin, it seemed "quite natural that so important a [Turkoman] prisoner should be portrayed."[16] Martin then claimed the pictorial cognates of various prisoners were a result of Shah Ismail sending copies in every direction to show that his opponent had been taken prisoner at the Battle of Shurur in 1502. Edgard Blochet corrected this historical context asserting that the Murad in question was never made prisoner by Shah Ismail, for he succeeded in escaping after a Safavid campaign in Hamadan.[17]

Whatever the fate of the alleged model, around this time the great Timurid artist Bihzad was thought to have been taken by Ismail and was appointed head librarian at the court workshop (*kitabkhana*) in Tabriz. Martin attributes Bihzad as the producer of the Mahu Khan portrait; indeed, the figure's face is very much akin to a portly foreman overseeing the building of the Great Mosque at Samarqand in the Timurid *Zafarnama* held in the library at Johns Hopkins University that was transcribed in 1467 and illustrated by Bihzad in the late-fifteenth century.[18]

However, the "Turkoman" moniker seems to have been affixed by scholars writing in the 1920s and 30s due to a dating error that unquestioningly attributed most of the Bound Captives to Bihzad who was thought to be serving his new Safavid patrons. Continuing to label these captives as Turkoman prisoners of the Safavids is not only unsubstantiated by the historical record, but it also perpetuates a scholarly bias that erects a division between Safavid and Timurid dynasties on one hand, and Turkoman and Uzbek groups on the other. Distancing the Safavids from Aq Quyunlu Turkomans is misguided since Shah Ismail evidently thought of himself as a successor more to the Turkoman state than the Timurid, and went about systematically obliterating Aq Quyunlu royal lineage so as to supplant it.[19] The initial administrative structures and the selection of the first Safavid capital in Tabriz suggest the early Safavids actually viewed themselves as a continuation of their Aq Quyunlu predecessors.[20]

The scholarly move to "Persianise" Timurids and Safavids, and "Turkicise" Turkomans and Uzbeks ignores the historical fact that after being defeated by Shah Ismail, Turkomans of various tribes rallied together and became fiercely loyal members of the Safavid Qizilbash military through most of the sixteenth century. They wore a distinctive, red-tipped baton atop a turban even into Shah Abbas's era at the end of the century, and this *taj-i haidari* headwear never appears atop the pates of the Bound Captives. In addition, a Bound Captive held in the Pierpont Morgan Library (Table 1, entry 5) was originally part of an album begun by Husain Khan Shamlu (of a Turkoman tribe) who was the governor of Herat (r. 1598–1618). The collection of calligraphic and painted materials included in the album might have been continued by his son and successor Hasan Shamlu (d. 1646). The Pierpont Captive is rendered in a style associated with Qazvin workshops that was popular between 1565–1585, and many of the captives are carried out in a similar fashion.[21] So, if at the time of their creation a majority of the Bound Captives were executed by artists trained in the Safavid capital, yet do not wear contemporary (or passé) Turkoman garb on their heads, and were even collected by Turkoman nobles working under Safavid rule, the Bound Captives must not be Turkoman prisoners.

Rethinking the Bound Captives in Terms of Chronology and Content

Beginning in the mid-1950s, the art historian Ivan Stchoukine realised the mistake of the Turkoman label and corrected the provenances to several Bound Captives. He suggested they were carried out after Bihzad's death and were done in the middle of or later in the sixteenth century, arguing that they reflected not Turkomans, but Uzbeks.[22] This better accounts for historical dynamism and acknowledges the tendency for artists to insert the preoccupations of their own age into the works. As mentioned above, at the time the Bound Captives were painted, Turkomans were no longer a separate or threatening presence but had become assimilated into the Safavid state. Instead, the Abulkhairid branch of sixteenth-century Shibanid Uzbeks and their dynastic replacements the Tuqay-Timurids of the seventeenth century *were* the Safavids' enemies in the east. These Chinggisid groups based in Central Asia conducted periodic raids and assaults on the border in Khurasan. This later production date for the Captives corresponds to a time when manuscript commissions declined in Qazvin, and artists left the courtly workshops to cater to the masses and produced less expensive, loose pages to sell. As Komaroff points out, all the known examples of the yoked prisoner are singular works mounted in albums not associated with any particular text. "[P]erhaps their meaning," she has suggested, "extends beyond any association with a specific historical figure."[23] There are scholars, however, who have refuted both Bihzad as the originator of the variations, and Murad of the Aq Quyunlu as the original subject. Nevertheless, we may surmise that some versions of the popular theme did indeed derive from an artist's actual encounter with an individual deemed to be an Uzbek subject.

Recent scholars accepting an Uzbek classification have rethought the origins of the Bound Captive artistic group, attributing Safavid artists active in the capital Qazvin with the drawings. Some even credit the genre to a singular artist – Shaikh Muhammad – who served both the Mughal emperor Humayun, and the Safavid governor of Mashhad Ibrahim Mirza.[24] Scholars suggest a few Bound Captives are rooted in Shaikh Muhammad's actual encounters with his subjects and so have interpreted the works as portraits. Abolala Soudavar reproduces the Musée Guimet drawing in his article (Table 1, entry 4), looking not unlike Sean Connery, and identifies this sitter inscribed with the name Bairam Ughlan as "the Uzbek ruler of Gharjistan who surrendered in the year 1551 to the Safavid governor of Herat."[25] It is known that both Uzbek prisoners and princes (refugee khans) passed between Mashhad and Qazvin in 1557 as they traveled to the Safavid court, which could have motivated a parallel genre of princely subjects and portraits that relate to the Bound Captives (Table 2: Attributions of Seated Prince Folios). S.C. Welch comments on the "suspicious, cautious eyes" of a drawing in the Boston Museum of Fine Arts (Table 2, entry 3) rendering an Uzbek prince seated under a tree. Welch attributes this portrait to Shaikh Muhammad who might have sketched it while in the retinue of Ibrahim Mirza.[26] Bearing striking similarities to the Captives in terms of pose, accoutrements, clothing, and headwear, this prince holds a wine cup. However, Welch alludes to the *palahang* in the "ominous symbolism of the powerful, forked trunk of the blossoming tree in the background, which a few quick hacks of a blade could have made…the traditional restraint for prisoners."[27] The ambiguity of the Bound Captive imagery is this: the Prisoners are at once pitiful and elicit pathos, yet at the same time have unmistakable expressions of pride and resoluteness that complicate reading them as simply humiliated prisoners of war.

The Seated Prince

Another way to interpret the folios of prisoners is by looking at their visual coexistence with another repeated subject in the canon of single-page paintings: the Seated Prince variously titled as amir, sultan, and khan often with an aigrette tucked into his cap or turban folds (figs. 6-8).[28] He sits with one arm bent and usually holds a wine cup or another object, be it a falcon, arrow, dagger, or kerchief (*dastarcha*). A pair of Seated Princes – the "Portrait of an Amir" reproduced by Martin (present whereabouts unknown; Table 2, entry 11),[29] and "Turkoman or Mongol Chief" in the Victoria and Albert Museum's Large Clive Album (Fig. 7) – are nearly identical mirror images of the Bound Captive in the Bodleian Library (Table 1, entry 3). All wear a turban and have a mace draped over the thigh. Perhaps pounces were used to transfer the outlines; all that is missing to identify these amirs as Bound Captives is the *palahang*. Their commonality is further emphasised through purposeful juxtaposition and placement facing each other in a double-page album spread. Staring at each other on the same eye level, the Large Clive Album pairs a thin prisoner, inscribed with the name Ibrahim Beg (Fig. 3), seated to the right of his liberated counterpart: the above-mentioned chief dressed in yellow and green (Fig. 7) who is perched on the left side of the album.[30]

Like the Bound Captive genre, the origins of the Seated Prince are uncertain, but the sideways kneeling posture and the subject's face rendered in a three-quarter view could stem from a portrait of the Timurid ruler Sultan Husain Mirza Baiqara (Table 2, entry 7).[31] In the 1931 International Exhibition of Persian Art at Burlington House in London, the portraits of Husain Mirza, whom Binyon described as "looking curiously like Henry VIII of England,"[32] and first leader of the Abulkhairid dynasty Muhammad Shibani Khan (Table 2, entry 18)[33] were placed on opposite walls. Both have been attributed to Bihzad, and both subjects adopt the two poses of the Seated Princes: kneeling sideways or cross-legged. Gulru Necipoglu has examined imperial portraiture in Turco-Persianate iconography, and has found that figures taking poses with knees bent to the side were a means of showing vassalage and humility, or a ruler's modesty when he was rendered this way.³⁴ It is understandable that the Captives would all be rendered in this stance to reinforce their submission. In contrast, a cross-legged pose with knees splayed open was reserved for monarchs and those claiming full Chinggisid blood. By rendering the Abulkhairid founder in this manner, "Bihzad certainly wanted to flatter the artistic pretensions of his new master, the last of the great warriors of the descendants of Genghis."³⁵

Historical Context of the Abulkhairid Shibanids (Uzbeks)

The portrait of Shibani Khan, the Seated Princes, and the Bound Captives accord with Safavid textual records that contain perceptions of Uzbeks. Examining the rhetoric used in these Safavid historiographies evinces conflicting tones of both admiration, trepidation, and disdain for the plundering Uzbek armies, which accounts for the captives' regality and nobility despite their shackled state. The Safavids' ambivalence towards Uzbeks is also found in historical chronicles of the period. Khwandamir's *Habib al-siyar* (ca. 1523) notes that the first Abulkhairid leader Shibani Khan was "distinguished ...for his high status and might"³⁶ with his court "adorned by great sultans and amirs."³⁷ Less flattering is the official chronicler of Shah Abbas I, Iskandar Bek Munshi, who chides Shibani for his "arrogance and ambition" and who "held any other powerful prince in low esteem."³⁸ These verbal descriptions of Shibani Khan also apply to the Prince and Prisoner copies in that most have a haughtiness about them. In various portraits of amirs, the seated figure has nothing constraining him, but he raises his hand in the same position as though he had. In the Bound Captive versions, when one arm is bent and bound in the restraining *palahang*, the subject is rendered without agency and of course the subject is subdued, but he is also defiant.

When the Safavid producers or collectors chose to distinguish the depicted prisoners, they did not resort to the typologies of tribal categories and regional names that present-day scholars have chosen. Sometimes there are passages in Persian which appear in the margins or near the Captive's feet and state the subject's or the artist's names, but exactly when the text was written or whether the writing is even contemporary to the painting is never certain. The identity of the artist is more often provided through the signature than is the identity of the sitter. In the few designations of the depicted subject where there are captions, the figures are labeled *kausaj/kusa Murad* (Table 1, entries 1 and 24 – translated as Murad of the thin-beard, seemingly a jab at his masculinity), *Amir Timur Gurkani* (Table 1, entry 3 – a spurious reference to the leader Timur from the fourteenth/fifteenth century), *Mahu Khan* (Table 1, entry 8), *Turs Giray* (Table 1, entry 33 – perhaps a Crimean Tatar dynast), and *Khwaja Beg Kuhur* (Table 1, entry 11). It is unknown what the producers of the prisoner drawings thought of each captive, or if they envisioned the products as a collective painted subject. If the captions are contemporary to the artworks, it is significant that they avoid the very classifications based on language, geography, and ethnic markers (to a certain extent) that have been selected by scholars in the twentieth century.

It is not my goal to be corrective and attribute a date, location, or ethnicity to the Captives. Yet I do posit that the majority of the prisoner artworks extant today were created by Safavid-aligned artists across the sixteenth and early seventeenth centuries. The Prisoners are windows into the Safavid psyche and show how the Safavids perceived their enemies and strengthened their own identity vis-à-vis another group. I seek to nuance a statement given by Martin, who remarked that "they are all Persian work."[39] Martin seems to take a linguistic bent and equates Safavid Iran with Persian speakers. But the term "Persian" itself is full of ambiguities. Does it imply the (presumed Safavid) producers? The language spoken by the artists? The patrons (or buyers) of the loose pages and/or albums? The sellers of the folios? The collectors and compilers of albums in which the folios were inserted? Some Captives are attributed to Mughal and Deccan workshops (such as Fig. 1), but rulers in the Indian subcontinent and the Safavids were more often allies than adversaries, so the Mughal and Deccan artists of Bound Captive materials might be considered "Safavid-aligned" depending on the era.[40] With regard to the original collectors of the materials, in addition to Safavid compilations, many of the Captives were placed in Mughal and Ottoman albums during periods in which tensions with the Safavids were at a lull.[41] Let us turn now to the function of the Captive as a non-Safavid subject, with "subject" here having a dual artistic and political function as a painted representation and as "a person owing obedience."

Interpreting the Bound Captives as Uzbeks (Abulkhairid and Tuqay-Timurid) best explains their status as political enemies of the Safavid dynasty throughout the sixteenth and into the early seventeenth century. Clashes in this period between the Safavids and Uzbeks were codified in religious and dynastic terms more than they were ethnic or linguistic. The sixteenth century marked a period of Islamic empires forging, hardening, and positioning political and religious identities in relation to other players. The Bound Captives reflect non-Safavids since they are connected to a political and regional entity sparring with the Safavid state but are rendered as captured and subdued subjects. To perceive them as non-Iranian is to resort to modern national labels that do not accord with the time period in which the artworks were produced.

Although the terms Uzbek and Turkmen are presently linked to national identities that are anachronistic in the context of Transoxiana in the sixteenth century, the term Uzbek was in fact en vogue at this time and was deployed pejoratively in Safavid sources.[42] The term referred to the Turko-Mongol tribal confederation of the Dasht-i Qipchaq that established itself in Central Asia under Abu al-Khair Khan. His grandson Muhammad Shibani Khan (1451–1510) helped situate the Abulkhairid branch of Shibanid power in Transoxiana between 1500–98.[43] Shibani Khan consolidated power and was the first to officially lead the Abulkhairid dynasty that traced its descent through Chinggis Khan's son Juchi and adhered to Hanafi Sunni Islam. The cities of Bukhara and Samarqand were the main bases of their military and political power after Muhammad Shibani Khan vanquished the Timurids in Transoxiana and Khurasan in 1507. His descendants had an uneasy alliance with the Ottomans, and repeatedly struggled with the Safavids and Mughals for territorial control. Shibani Khan met his end by the sword of the Safavid Shah Ismail, who beheaded him in the Battle of Merv in December 1510 and had his skull gilded to use as a drinking cup.[44] Less than a century later the Safavid Shah Abbas I paralleled Ismail when he wrote in November 1597 that he would go after the Abulkhairid ruler Abdallah II's head, following this his land after which he would drink sherbets from the khan's skull.[45] Perhaps much to Abbas's chagrin, Abdallah's unexpected death in 1598 would bring Abulkhairid power to an end. The Safavid ruler was thus denied a gilded cranial chalice that his predecessor Ismail had so enjoyed.

The frequency of Uzbek incursions throughout the sixteenth and seventeenth centuries appears to coincide with the frequency of their artistic depictions. The sixteenth century is peppered with these Uzbek campaigns into Safavid domains beginning with Muhammad Shibani Khan's 1507–1510 occupation of Herat. Skirmishes continued during Shah Tahmasp's reign between 1524–1576, when the Uzbeks launched five attacks on Safavid-controlled Khurasan just between 1524 and 1540. During the fourth onslaught, lasting from 1531 to 1534, the Uzbeks advanced as far as Rayy, south of present-day Tehran.[46] Later, foreign enemies took advantage of internal struggles within Iran that followed Tahmasp's death. An Uzbek attack, launched in 1578, was repulsed by the Turkoman governor of Mashhad. Uzbek tribesmen penetrated hundreds of miles into Safavid territory reaching Yazd in 1596-97.[47] Finally, there was a long span of time when the Abulkhairid Uzbeks controlled all of Khurasan between 1587–1599 where they succeeded in ravaging the holy shrine in Mashhad.[48]

By 1600, a new dynasty – the Tuqay-Timurids – replaced the Abulkhairid line.[49] During 1605–1611 there was a period of reconciliation and warm exchange between the deposed Uzbek ruler Vali Muhammad Khan and Shah Abbas as the new Tuqay-Timurid regime underwent internal struggles and brothers and nephews vied for power. However, with the accession of Imam Quli Khan (r. 1611–1642) in Transoxiana, raids on Khurasan began anew. There was a temporary truce in 1620 when an embassy including Nadhr Muhammad Khan (Imam Quli's brother, ruler of Balkh) traveled to the Safavid court to negotiate peace.[50] But several large-scale campaigns were again launched after Abbas's death in 1629, commanded by Nadhr Muhammad's son Abd al-Aziz. In the words of a period Safavid chronicler, "Abd al-Aziz Khan would go on raid against Khurasan more often than he would go to the bath."[51] But by the mid-seventeenth century, the Uzbek threat was no more and Khurasan was securely under the control of the Safavids.

In light of all the Uzbek attacks spanning the sixteenth through early seventeenth centuries, these events must have caused enormous anxiety in the Safavid heartland. It is significant that most of the prisoner drawings can be attributed to periods in which Abulkhairids and Tuqay-Timurids attempted the territorial annexation of Khurasan. The Bound Captives could have functioned as a visual device to calm the masses in Safavid Iran by rendering the fierce Uzbek troops as shackled and pacified prisoners.

Attributes of "Uzbekness"

Whereas mid sixteenth-century versions of the Captives present them as a serious menace and "armed to the teeth" as fierce warriors,[52] the pictorial tradition in the seventeenth century seems to decline and the number of extant copies diminishes corresponding to the decreased military threat of the Uzbeks. In the Bound Captive imagery of this century, such as the Metropolitan Museum of Art's version (Table 1, entry 32) and the copy from Murad III's album in Vienna (Table 1, entry 33), prisoners are stripped of their armor. They have become mere dandies with extended pinkies and pursed lips rendered in a mannered style emulating the dancing ink of Riza Abbasi. This emasculation accords with wall paintings from the Chihil Sutun palace in Isfahan, the new Safavid capital between 1590 and 1722.[53] In them, large-scale, upright Safavid shahs appear seated before Uzbek royals and nobles who are rendered as slouched, passive supplicants beholding the grandeur of their illustrious hosts.[54]

Other sources of derision can be found within small sections on the Bound Captive pages themselves, details that correspond to the rhetorical bravado of Safavid historiographical texts. My attention has been directed to animal imagery in both visual and textual forms. Bow cases featured in the Captives from the Yale University Art Gallery (Table 1, entry 11) and in LACMA (Table 1, entry 13) carry small figures of a fox (figs. 2 and 7). Safavid historiographies of the period reference this animal during battles with the Uzbeks. When chronicling a retreat of the Uzbek leader at the hands of Shah Ismail decades prior, Iskandar Beg Munshi writes in his *Tarikh-i alam ara-yi abbasi* from 1628-29, "Shahi Beg Khan [Shibani Khan]…had crept into his hole like a fox fleeing from a lion."[55]

Several other tableaus on bow cases and caps (figs. 2, 4, 5) carry birds victimising rabbits, deer, tigers, and even a dragon.[56] Birds of prey might symbolise the Safavid armies, which again is substantiated by Safavid court panegyrists. Referring to an early battle between the Safavids and Uzbeks in the vicinity of Badghis outside Herat, Khwandamir writes in the 1520s:

> The eagle of the arrow opened its beak to swallow lives, and the dragon of the spear stretched out its tongue to prick young and old alike. …Companies of

lions from the forest of pugnacity, made manifest the day of resurrection in that battle of vengeance, …with blows from crocodile-like swords and death-dealing arrows.[57]

Further evidence that the birds denote Safavid troops is found in derisive visual material from the Ottoman side that is antagonistic to the Safavids. Rather than rendering eagles opening up their beaks to swallow lives, as the Safavid artists do in the animal details adorning the Bound Captive depictions, Ottoman artists illustrating works by Ottoman eulogisers render these same birds with their necks crushed by tree branches. This detail adorns the fabric of a baldachin above Sultan Selim II's accession to the Ottoman throne in an illustration to Feridun Pasha's *Nuzhat al-akhbar dar safar-i Szigetvar* from 1568-69.[58]

Details evincing Safavid machismo in the Bound Captive pages themselves and in Safavid textiles from the first quarter of the seventeenth century reference Shah Abbas' victories against the Uzbeks in 1598. There are dispersed fragments of fabric depicting a Safavid captor on horseback with the name Abdallah written on his bowcase; he leads a prisoner sprouting a wispy beard and sporting a pointed cap with upturned visor who follows behind on foot.[59] Minute details on the very bow case of the Bound Captive from the LACMA collection (Fig. 4, detail 2) self-referentially allude to the subject's own capture at the hands of a Safavid Qizilbash. In the right corner Iranian soldiers in high-topped turbans triumphantly march forward, while in the left corner troops wearing conical caps flee.

Furthering our conversation on the important role of headgear to identify groups and sides and to provide further evidence that the Bound Captives represent Uzbek soldiers, I employ sections from Barry Wood's and Barbara Schmitz's dissertations.[60] After this headwear discussion, I will address period textual and visual sources that support my interpretation that most of the Bound Captives are Uzbek subjects depicted by Safavid artists. I will do so by looking at illustrations to Safavid historiographies and the representations of Uzbeks within them. According to Schmitz, the sixteenth century marked increasing individuation. It was the era of new costume and headwear details marking identity and affiliation, such as the Qizilbash adoption of the *taj-i haidari* turban to pronounce their connection to the founder of the Safavid dynasty Shah Ismail. This headgear later took on a Shiite religious dimension and was a way to proclaim the particularities of this branch of Islam.[61]

Bound Captives wear two types of headgear, with and without aigrettes. These head coverings are also found in illustrations to Safavid historical chronicles and epic poetry to denote group affiliation and visually label the "bad guys" antagonistic to the Safavid cause. The first head covering is associated with the turban style of the Abulkhairids. Low, squat wrappings were in vogue in Transoxiana between the 1540s and 70s, which correspond to the dates of the metropolitan Qazvin style and can further support the claim that several Bound Captives derive from this period.[62] Schmitz characterises sixteenth-century Uzbek turbans as containing a support (*kulah*) with a distinctive blunt-ended conical form. Later there was "a new type of turban during Uzbek rule in Harat from 1586–1598: a tapered kula with a truncated point. The turban cloth wound tightly and closely to the head thus differ[ed] markedly from the loosely tied Safavid turban of the 1590s."[63] Uzbek turbans – or turbanned Uzbeks – appear on Shibani Khan's followers in two folios painted by the royal Safavid artist Muin Musavvir in the seventeenth century. One illustration is in Bizhan Gurji's historiography of Shah Ismail,[64] and another is in one of the *Anonymous Histories of Shah Ismail* located in the Reza Abbasi Museum in Tehran.[65] This same scene presenting the victory of Shah Ismail over the Uzbeks even adorns the audience hall of the Chihil Sutun.[66] It is in this wall painting that we find our most definitive evidence that it is an Uzbek prisoner represented in a *palahang*, whether it is on paper or on plaster. In all of these versions, garbing the Uzbeks in their turbans emphasises a sectarian component: their adherence to Sunni Islam as opposed to the distinctive Safavid Qizilbash turban wrappings signifying Twelver Shiism.[67]

The second, and more common, head covering worn by the Bound Captives is a pointed cap (usually white) with the side flaps up, having a darker (usually black) brim pulled down. Barry Wood in his "Excursus on Haberdashery" calls it the "Turanian hat" which functions to heighten the wearer's difference to the Safavids and to reinforce his militancy and tribal affinity to Chinggis Khan. Wood explains that it is the "age-old token of the Turkic peoples of Central Asia and particularly of the Uzbeks. The headgear came to be associated with the enemies of Firdausi's Iranians in Persianate iconography, the Turkic Turanians, and is a reliable marker of that group in many *Shahnama* manuscripts."[68] Wood refers to it "as 'Turanian' to highlight the associative nature of the attribution," overlaying history with legend. This cap is found on the heads of the legendary Turanian armies in Shah Tahmasp's famous *Shahnama* of Firdausi from the 1520s to the 1530s, and in a folio depicting Ismail storming the troops of Muhammad Shibani Khan near Merv illustrated in 1579-80 by Sadiqi from the *Habib al-siyar*.[69] Within the latter illustration, one of the fleeing Uzbek soldiers in the lower left corner witnesses the gruesome death of his commander at the hands of Shah Ismail, and his cap directly resembles the Bound Captive inscribed Bairam Ughlan, whom we have met earlier (Table 1, entry 4). In an illustration from the British Library's *Shahnama-yi Ismail* (a chronicle of Shah Ismail's conquests by Qasimi Gunabadi illustrated in 1541), we see Shah Ismail victorious over a trio of Uzbek captives.[70] These Uzbeks' black and white caps most closely resemble the one worn by Mahu Khan. Taken altogether, the Uzbek troops that are featured and named in the historical chronicles help to identify the Bound Captives as these very Abulkhairid soldiers by the nature of their headwear. But the headwear also points to another popular marker of identification circulating amongst the public in the form of *Shahnama* lore, be it written by Firdausi or Qasimi. It is this association that best gets at the sentiment of the Safavid age and uncovers the social context of the Bound Captive productions.

Reading Period Sentiment in Safavid Historiographies

The Bound Captives would have triggered something in their original intended audience just by looking at them. From our vantage in the present, we must eke this out through consulting historical written sources. Historians of Persianate painting note the decline in manuscript production after Shah Tahmasp's renunciation of the arts and heightened religiosity in 1555-56 when he promulgated his so-called Edict of Sincere Repentance. As a result, artists left the courtly workshops to cater to the masses, producing loose pages to sell to a new class made wealthy from trade. To Langer, the medium of single pages necessitated "new themes that could manage without textual sources," hence the sixteenth-century interest in repeated subjects such as the Bound Captives.[71] Album paintings heralded "a general turning away from epic, romantic, and historic themes…in favor of a more focused imagery either taken out of a larger context or derived from some other literary and poetic sources."[72] The Bound Captives are examples of such imagery, and Wood reminds us that the material and mental combine together in illustrations to make meaning for their contemporaries.[73] The Captives are part of a program rooted in popular society (including the lowest levels in it) as well as the state (implying top-down power structures) to mythicise Shah Ismail and to scorn the enemies threatening Safavid borders.

Wood has published articles on a series of manuscripts which preserve the cultural memory of a key period in Iranian history.[74] These documents are a means to glean social insights into a bygone Safavid era and to ascertain "the imaginal horizons of that culture."[75] Referred to as the *Anonymous Histories of Shah Ismail* (collections of popular tales about the first Safavid ruler written down by an unknown individual)[76] or the *Shahnama-yi Ismail* (Qasimi's official panegyric), the stories within liken the exploits of Shah Ismail to legendary feats from the *Shahnama* as composed by Firdausi half a millennium earlier. The tales in the *Ismail* manuscripts initially circulated throughout early sixteenth-century Safavid society as an oral form but grew and spread so as to emerge in the corpus of book arts in the mid-century. They would become part of official Safavid historiographies by the late seventeenth century. Within the stories, Wood explains how the Uzbeks are "the enemy du jour" (ca. 1540), having recently been defeated in one of many duels to seize Khurasan. The Ismail mythologies employ Firdausian phrasing to reference Uzbeks, invoking "an awareness of Iran as a historical and 'proto-national' entity, especially as it exists in opposition to its rival-region of Turan." Moreover, Wood notes that "in the final section of the poem

Safavids are explicitly referred to as *Iranian* and their Uzbek foes as *Khanan-i Turan-zamin.*[77] Thus, many villains in the manuscripts are "depicted wearing Turanian headgear. The painter(s), it would seem, had assimilated the cultural awareness of contemporary events in the form of epic tropes and re-expressed them in appropriate visual imagery."[78] The significance of Shibani Khan as Shah Ismail's ultimate enemy is apparent in the illustrative program. Out of six illustrated manuscripts of Qasimi's *Shahnama-yi Ismail*, five copies feature this early battle of the Safavids against the Uzbeks, making it one of the two most popular and commonly illustrated scenes.[79]

It is telling that there are no surviving courtly copies of Qasimi's *Shahnama-yi Ismail* produced in the sixteenth century, which might point to its plebeian origins.[80] Instead, we see "provincial" copies in which the Uzbek enemies wear the same headgear as our Bound Captives.[81] The Italian emissary Michele Membré who visited Iran between 1539–1542 mentions the popularity of oral retellings of Shah Ismail's exploits, and "public readers explained pictures for a little money…with books in their hands, reading the battles of Ali and the fightings of the old kings and *chaich* [sic] Ismail."[82] Wood suggests these very books could have been versions of Qasimi's *Shahnama-yi Ismail*, since the work was available at the time and place of Membré's visit and its vocabulary was more accessible to the public, as opposed to the official Safavid historiographer Khwandamir whose style was too learned and verbose.[83] In this period, mountebanks entertained the masses by pointing to "long cards with figures,"[84] and elsewhere in the Ottoman realm later in the mid seventeenth century there were fortune-tellers who used large-scale pictures on paper depicting "prophets, sultans, heroes, sea and land battles, as well as love stories" to perform "a type of picture recitation" for paying customers.[85]

In light of this backdrop of repeated tales about the Uzbek defeat at the hands of Ismail taking place in sixteenth- through mid seventeenth-century Safavid society, along with single-page illustrations of such Uzbeks being depicted as prisoners, a logical supposition would be that the Bound Captives were part of the practice of using pictures in conjunction with a narrator to relate stories. We can assume that the cheering on of Safavid commanders and the jeering of Uzbek enemies had popular appeal to the masses whether through oral story-telling, illustrations in books, or in single-page folios of Bound Captives. The curses of these people are preserved in the *Anonymous Histories* with terms of abuse including the epithets bastard, unmanly, hairless, impure, uncouth, demon-faced, devil, and dog. One in particular carries pointed confessional specificity: "that bastard of a Sunni."[86] Denigrations at the courtly level instead equate Uzbek with Mongol, a pairing that evokes generational onslaughts coming from the steppes. It links sixteenth-century Uzbek perpetrators with their Chinggisid descendants in the Safavid mind, which ironically would have made the Abulkhairids quite thrilled as they sought to reinforce this very identity for themselves.[87]

The Bound Captive in Other Painted and Poetic Traditions

Returning to the walls of Chihil Sutun, we see the coexistence of Bound Captive imagery with Shah Ismail mythology.[88] On the wall of the audience hall bearing the painting "The Battle of Shah Ismail and the Uzbeks" the Safavid ruler cleaves Shibani Khan from head to waist "like a ripe cucumber" which we know is a frequently-depicted scene in the *Anonymous Histories* and official Safavid historiographies.[89] In other sections the Safavid armies dismember, lasso, tie up, and carry off Abulkhairid troops, but there is one significant detail in the lower right section of the painted plane: a portly Uzbek is constrained in a *palahang* exiting the battlefield on horseback as a prisoner-of-war. The blue of his robes, trimmed beard, red-topped turban, and comportment call to mind Bihzad's portrait of Shibani Khan. This is a rare Bound Captive depiction that does not exist as a single-subject album folio, and it is the most concrete proof that the artists of the folios and the Isfahan wall paintings come from the same Safavid political persuasion.

This is further strengthened through comparisons to depicted prisoners in restraints produced outside Safavid painting traditions which use a different iconography. The *palahang* device appears in Tuqay-Timurid works on paper, and in lithographs from late-seventeenth to early eighteenth-century European travelogues. *Shahnama* manuscripts in general rarely include the device, but it curiously appears in a few scenes from various copies that are not of a Safavid provenance. *Palahang* constraints are featured in illustrations of Bizhan confined in the pit, Zahhak captured by Faraidun, Siyavush tied up before Afrasiab, or Aulad bound in front of Rustam.[90] Elsewhere, the device is called a *giriban-i dushakha* (forked collar) and is featured in an illustration of a man in fur-lined robes done by the French jeweler Jean Chardin during his travels to Persia in the 1670s.[91] In these non-Safavid versions, the restraining stem that attaches to the hand seems longer than those I posit to be the work of Safavid artists, and the constraint seems more a product of a woodworking shop than hastily-assembled tree branches nailed together on a battlefield.

Continuing our examination of Captives depicted by other (non-Safavid) parties, it comes as no surprise that there is little, if any, comparable single-page material coming out of Transoxiana, which again bolsters the argument that the Bound Captives are Uzbek subjects produced by Safavid supporters. The only material from Bukhara or Samarqand that comes close are details found in the decorated margins attributed to Muhammad Murad Samarqandi ca. 1615–1620. In the right half of a reassembled double-page composition, a girl dressed in red struggles in a forked tree with her wrist caught between the "Y" of two branches.[92] The tree trunk and two boughs directly allude to the pose of the Bound Captives. In the left half is a male counterpart in green and brown robes also resting his bent arm against a narrow trunk.[93] There are several similar compositions in which the limbs of figures are placed in those of trees, but the meanings of these visual references are now lost to history.[94]

It is this imagery that seems more suited to Linda Komaroff's visual and verbal reading of the Bound Captives in her article on one of the LACMA prisoners (Table 1, entry 13; Fig. 5). Komaroff has read the lozenges of text surrounding the central subject and has theorised that the Bound Captive genre is to be viewed not as "an instrument of state propaganda" but as an allusion to "the type of unrequited love celebrated by Persian poets."[95] Lines of the poem read: "without your lips every moment blood flows from my pearl-raining eyes. …Happy is the prisoner [*asir*] who has someone to come to his aid."[96] In the folio she has examined, she theorises that "perhaps the depiction of the Turkman prisoner, whatever its earlier associations, might have been transformed into a visual metaphor for the prisoner of love. …The combination of word and image resulted in just the type of clever witticism that seems to have delighted a sixteenth-century Persian audience."[97]

Komaroff's broad approach looking beyond the visual component of the folios and taking in the totality of the lines of poetry around the edges of the prisoners is enlightening. However, although her "Prisoner of Love" theory may fit the particular specimen of her focus, her interpretation cannot be applied to the series as a whole. The text boxes have been cut and pasted onto the LACMA folio and might not have been part of the original artistic program when the central Prisoner image was created. Also, when exactly the completed product took its final form is unknown as is the original motivation of the assembler; analysis of text and image in *muraqqa* collections is still in its infancy.[98] An example of the challenges posed by textual inclusions is the Captive illustration that is arguably the most reproduced, which is in the Pierpont Morgan Library (Table 1, entry 5). It carries text around its central image, but the "words" contain no meaning: the pastings are calligraphic specimens and single or multiple-letter writing exercises. Where poetry has been (physically and conceptually) connected to the Bound Captive pages, it can be examined in relation to Safavid rhetoric regarding Uzbeks and other foes of Shah Ismail. Regarding poetry as a medium of expression, intentional ambiguities are present within the lines. Our understanding of this topic would be enhanced by textual and visual readings of each prisoner page, but here I will offer preliminary findings on just two of them.

Writing over a century ago, Marteau and Vever acknowledged the presence of text around the Mahu Khan depiction in the Bibliothèque Nationale (Table 1, entry 8), but spuriously cited it as coming from Nizami's *Khamsa*.[99] Komaroff acknowledges the presence of poetry here but incorrectly dismisses it as "hemistiches…in random order, without regard to rhyme."[100] Most of its *misra* do indeed rhyme depending on where one starts reading, but the poem's origins are unknown. Although the inclusion of text on album pages is not always contemporaneous to the drawing, their placement together by someone implies a certain significance. It is the relationship between the text and image on this folio that is worth exploring.

The poem surrounding Mahu Khan deals with the exchange of slaves and the value of their beauty. Lines read: "Because of the batting eyes of the ravishing one the bazaar has lots of customers. / From the locks of the beloveds' hair from Chinese Khallukh [Khalaj?] come the charming air now smelling of musk."[101] Near the end of the poem we read, "The commodity of life is cheap in this market."[102] The flirtatious text combining imagery of coquetry with commerce seems to be at odds with the militaristic image of the fettered but heavily armed Mahu Khan equipped with mace, riding whip, sword, bow, and arrows. But another line seems to directly address him and perhaps his sweethearts with the musky tresses, referring to them all as *bandagan* (slaves) who have taken vows and exchanged rings.

The inherent ambiguity of poetry applies to the ambiguity of the Bound Captive depictions themselves. They are at once pitiful and elicit pathos, but also educe disparagement. Among other cartouches surrounding Mahu Khan are those that read "His palaces are concealed under rivers," which might allude to the Oxus River separating Safavid Iran from Uzbek-controlled Transoxiana. The poem continues by mentioning his residence that is "a paradise full of Tatar houris."[103] This could be construed positively or it might be a charge leveled at the debauched courtly life from which he comes.

Another Bound Captive carries a barbed couplet taking aim at his romantic exploits couched in terms of military accomplishments. The Yale University Art Gallery prisoner inscribed with the name *Khwaja Beg Kuhur* (Table 1, entry 11; Fig. 2) is unique for his markedly disproportionate facial features that are far too small for the surface available to be filled. Not quite looking the part, a *bait* reads, "The organiser [commander] of this wondrous army is conquering [advancing through] country after country."[104] Metaphorically, what could be implied is that our Casanova is winning the hearts of many lovers.[105] The text is from a Safavid romance *Nazir u manzur* by Vahshi Bafqi which has been cut from another source and pasted onto the folio. It applies to the rendered subject by invoking a military subject, however it reads as sarcastic adulation. It praises the commander for his conquests, yet this officer appears immobilised and defeated on the page. David Roxburgh has analysed albums from the Timurid and Safavid periods and has suggested certain juxtapositions of word and image within them may have had humorous intent. Their arrangement might have been structured as jokes for the album recipient.[106] So it is not unfathomable that the Bound Captives could have had some satirical purpose when inserted into an album for a Safavid-aligned patron.

Conclusion

Having reached the end of our present discussion, I cannot state which Captive was the "*ur*-image" that instigated the rest of the group, nor can I attribute a particular artist with creating the series, and I cannot definitively name some of them as historical personages. These were the aims and approaches of previous scholars but are not mine. I instead argue that the textual and visual evidence suggests the Bound Captives were deployed by artists trained in Safavid workshops as a means to separate themselves and their potential buyers from rival powers in Transoxiana in the sixteenth century and beyond. The artists thus render a subaltern category, designating their subjects as politically and geographically outside Safavid hegemony.

Bound Captive versions may have surged in the second half of the sixteenth century due to the Safavids' political need to denigrate their Uzbek enemies; there was no Turkoman enemy to be found as the Safavids had already assimilated them. This demand to make political rivals recognisable had been previously fulfilled by *Shahnama* manuscripts of Firdausi (for the elite) and retellings of myths (for the public) in which Turanian armies were recast as Uzbek troops. After manuscript production declined, single folios proliferated and oral traditions continued to circulate recounting the heroics of the Safavid founder Ismail and other legendary figures. Album illustrations in general make us question the following: where is the narrativity of these single-page, single subjects? Does it inhere in each figure or in the historical context? Is it located in the poetry on the edges? Or in the mind of the person flipping through the complete album? From our vantage point in time and space today we will never fully arrive at answers and all we can do is piece together the fragments of visual and textual history, much like the pastiche of an album page. The Bound Captives sit, resigned to their fate while they await further judgment and scholarly critique.

It is fitting that Bihzad's portrait of Ismail's nemesis Shibani Khan was originally mounted in the album for the Safavid prince Bahram Mirza, in essence imprisoning the Abulkhairid leader between its covers. So, too, can the Bound Captives be read as perpetually confined to the sheet. Perhaps the conflated armies of Shibani Khan and those of Afrasiab from the *Shahnama* were lifted from manuscript pages and from oral traditions and were transferred to these loose pages, forever contained in the margins so as to bar their escape.

Bibliography

Adamova, Adel, *Persian Manuscripts, Paintings and Drawings from the 15th to the early 20th Century in the Hermitage Collection,* London: Azimuth, 2012.

Arberry, A.J., et al., *The Chester Beatty Library: a catalogue of the Persian manuscripts and miniatures* Dublin: Hodges Figgis, 1962.

Babaie, Sussan, "Frontiers of visual taboo: painted ‹indecencies› in Isfahan," in *Eros and Sexuality in Islamic Art,* eds. Francesca Leoni and Mika Natif, New York: Routledge, 2013, 131-56.

Babaie, Sussan, "Shah Abbas II, the Conquest of Qandahar, the Chihil Sutun, and Its Wall Paintings," *Muqarnas* 11 (1994), 125-42.

Babaie, Sussan, *Slaves of the Shah: New Elites of Safavid Iran,* London: I. B. Tauris, 2004.

Bashir, Shahzad, "Shah Ismail and the Qizilbash: Cannibalism in the Religious History of Early Safavid Iran," *History of Religions* 45, no. 3 (February 2006), 234-56.

Bernardini, M., "Hatifi's *Timurnameh* and Qasimi's *Shahnameh-yi Ismail*: Considerations for a double Critical Edition," in *Society and Culture in the Early Modern Middle East: Studies on Iran in the Safavid Period,* ed. A.J Newman, Leiden: Brill, 2003, 3-18.

Binyon, Laurence, et al., *Persian Miniature Painting: Including a critical and descriptive catalogue of the miniatures exhibited at Burlington House January-March, 1931,* London: Oxford University Press, 1933.

Blake, Stephen P., "Shah Abbas and the Transfer of the Safavid Capital From Qazvin to Isfahan," in *Society and Culture in the Early Modern Middle East: Studies on Iran in the Safavid Period,* ed. A.J Newman, Leiden: Brill, 2003, 154-64.

Blochet, E., *Musulman Painting: XIIth - XVIIth Century,* London: Methuen & Co, 1929.

Botchkareva, Anastassiia, *Representational Realism in Cross-Cultural Perspective: Changing Visual Cultures in Mughal India and Safavid Iran 1580-1750,* PhD diss., Harvard University, 2014.

Bregel, Yuri, "ABU'L-KHAYRIDS," *Encyclopædia Iranica,* online edition, 2012, available at http://www.iranicaonline.org/articles/abul-khayrids-dynasty.

Burton, Audrey, "Who were the First Ashtarkhānid Rulers of Bukhara?" *Bulletin of the School of Oriental and African Studies,* 51, no. 3 (1988), 482-88.

Feher, Geza, *Türkische Miniaturen: aus den Chroniken der ungarischen Feldzüge,* Wiesbaden: E. Vollmer Verlag, 1978.

Ferrier, R. W., ed., *A Journey to Persia: Jean Chardin's Portrait of a Seventeenth-Century Empire,* London and New York: I. B. Tauris, 1996.

Foltz, Richard C., *Mughal India and Central Asia,* Oxford: Oxford University Press, 1998.

Fragner, Bert, "The Safavid Empire and the Sixteenth- and Seventeenth-Century Political and Strategic Balance of Power within the World System," in *Iran and the World in the Safavid Age,* eds. Willem Floor and Edmund Herzig, London, 2012: I. B. Tauris, 17-29.

Hillenbrand, Robert, *Imperial Images in Persian Painting,* Edinburgh: Scottish Arts Council, 1977.

Khwandamir, Ghiyas ad-Din Muhammad, "Habib al-siyar," *A Century of Princes: Sources on Timurid History and Art,* trans. W.M. Thackston, Cambridge, Massachusetts: The Aga Khan Program for Islamic Architecture, 1989.

Komaroff, Linda, "A Turkman Prisoner or Prisoner of Love?" in *No Tapping around Philology: a Festschrift in Honor of Wheeler McIntosh Thackston Jr.'s 70th Birthday*, eds. Alireza Korangy and Daniel J. Sheffield, Wiesbaden: Harrassowitz, 2014, 369-80.

Langer, Axel, *The Fascination of Persia: The Persian-European Dialogue in Seventeenth-century Art & Contemporary Art from Tehran*, Zürich: Scheidegger & Spiess, 2013.

Lowry, Glenn, et al., *An Annotated and Illustrated Checklist of the Vever Collection*, Washington D.C.: Smithsonian, 1988.

Mahir, Banu, "A Group of seventeenth century Paintings Used for Picture Recitation," *Art Turc/Turkish Art: Proceedings of the 10th Annual Congress of Turkish Art*, Geneva: Fondation Max Van Berchem, 1999.

Marteau, Georges and Henri Vever, *Miniatures persanes: exposées au Musée des Arts Décoratifs juin-octobre 1912*, Paris: Bibl. d'art & d'archéol, 1913.

Martin, F.R., *The Miniature Painting and Painters of Persia, India and Turkey, from the 8th to the 18th Century*, London: Bernard Quaritch, 1912.

Matthee, Rudi Matthee, "Facing a Rude and Barbarous Neighbor," in *Iran Facing Others: Identity Boundaries in a Historical Perspective*, eds., Abbas Amanat and Farzin Vejdani, New York: Palgrave, 2012, 105-25.

Matthee, Rudi, "Relations Between the Center and the Periphery in Safavid Iran: The Western Borderlands v. the Eastern Frontier Zone," *Historian* (2015): 431-63.

McChesney, R. D. "The Conquest of Herat 995-96/1587-88: Sources for the Study of Safavid/Qizilbash – Shibanid/Uzbak Relations," in Jean Calmard (ed.), *Etudes Safavides*, Tehran: Institut français de recherche en Iran, 1993, 69-107.

McChesney, R. D., "Islamic culture and the Chinggisid restoration: Central Asia in the sixteenth and seventeenth centuries," in David O. Morgan and Anthony Reid (eds.), *The New Cambridge History of Islam. Vol. 3: The Eastern Islamic World Eleventh to Eighteenth Centuries*, Cambridge: Cambridge University Press, 2011, 239-65.

McChesney, R.D., "Reforms of Baqi Muhammad Khan," *Central Asiatic Journal* 24, no. 1/2 (1980), 69-84.

McWilliams, Mary, "Prisoner Imagery in Safavid Textiles," *The Textile Museum Journal* (1987), 5-23

Minorsky, V., "The Poetry of Shah Ismail I," *Bulletin of the School of Oriental and African Studies*, (1942), 1006-53.

Munshi, Iskandar Beg Munshi, *The History of Shah Abbas the Great* (Tarikh-i alamara-yi abbasi), trans. R.M. Savory, Boulder: Westview, 1978.

Necipoglu, Gulru, "Word and Image: Ottoman Sultans in Comparative Perspective," in *The Sultan's Portrait: Picturing the House of Osman*, ed. Selmin Kangal, Istanbul: Isbank, 2000.

Newman, A.J., *Safavid Iran, Rebirth of a Persian Empire*, London: I. B. Tauris, 2006.

Quinn, Sholeh, "Notes on Timurid Legitimacy in Three Safavid Chronicles," *Iranian Studies* 31, no. 2 (1998), 149-58.

Robinson, B.W., *Persian Paintings in the John Rylands Library: a Descriptive Catalogue*, London: Sotheby Parke Bernet, 1980.

Roxburgh, David, "Disorderly Conduct?: F.R. Martin and the Bahram Mirza Album," *Muqarnas* 15 (1998), 32-57.

Sakisian, Armenag bey, *La miniature persane du XIIe au XVIIe siècle*, Paris: Van Oest, 1929.

Schmitz, Barbara, *Islamic and Indian manuscripts and paintings in the Pierpont Morgan Library*, New York: Pierpoint Morgan Library, 1997.

Schmitz, Barbara, *Miniature Painting in Harat, 1570-1640*, Ph.D. diss., New York University, 1981.

Schulz, Walter P., *Die Persisch-Islamische Miniaturmalerei: Ein Beitrag Zur Kunstgeschichte Irans*, Leipzig: K.W. Hiersemann, 1914.

Soudavar, Abolala, "Between the Safavids and the Mughals, Art and Artists in Transition," *Iran* 37 (1999), 49-66.

Stanfield-Johnson, Rosemary, "Yuzbashi-yi Kurd Bacheh and 'Abd al-Mu'min Khan the Uzbek: A Tale of Revenge in the Dastan of Husayn-i Kurd," in *Muraqqa'e Sharqi, studies in honor of Peter Chelkowski*, eds. Soussie Kerman-Rastegar and Anna Vanzan, Dogana: AIEP Ed., 2007, 165-79.

Stchoukine, Ivan, *Les Peintures des Manuscrits Timurides*, Paris: P. Geuthner, 1954.

Lale Uluc, "Zülkadirli Şiraz valilerinin son döneminden resimli bir *Yusuf ve Züleyha* nüshası," in *Nurhan Atasoy'a Armagan*, ed. Baha Tanman, Istanbul: Turk Tarih Kurumu Basımevi, 2014, 387-422

Welch, S.C., *Wonders of the Age: Masterpieces of Early Safavid Painting, 1501-1576*, Cambridge, Mass.: Fogg Art Museum, 1979.

Welsford, Thomas, *Four Types of Loyalty in Early Modern Central Asia: the Tuqay-Timurid Takeover of Greater Ma Wara al-Nahr, 1598-1605* Leiden: Brill, 2013.

Wiet, Gaston, *Miniatures Persanes, Turques, Et Indiennes: Collection De Son Excellence Chérif Sabry Pacha* Cairo: Institut francais d'archeologie orientale, 1943.

Wood, Barry Wood, "The 'Shahnama-i Ismail': Art and Cultural Memory in Sixteenth-century Iran", PhD diss., Harvard University, 2002.

Wood, Barry, ed. and transl. *The Adventures of Shah Esma'il: A Seventeenth-Century Persian Popular Romance*. Leiden: Brill, 2019.

Wood, Barry, "The *Tarikh-i Jahanara* in the Chester Beatty Library, An Illustrated Manuscript of the 'Anonymous Histories of Shah Isma'il," *Iranian Studies* 37, no. 1 (2004), 89-107.

Notes

1. *Author's note:* This chapter is the result of a few versions. It began as a seminar paper for Sussan Babaie while I was her student at The Courtauld Institute of Art in 2015. I thank her for her feedback and encouragement to publish it. Its second life was as a conference paper presented at Andrew J. Newman's workshop on "Recovering 'Lost Voices': The Role and Depictions of Iranian/Persianate Subalterns from 1501-1747" (convened 19-21 May 2017 at the University of Edinburgh). I am grateful to Professor Newman and the other workshop attendants, especially Barry Wood, for their discerning insights that have helped me make this publication a reality. Lastly, I would like to offer *sipas* to my beloved Khurasani: Mohsen Qassemi H. He kindly assisted in deciphering Persian scrawls and continues to put up with my Uzbek infatuation.

2. Adel Adamova, *Persian Manuscripts, Paintings and Drawings from the 15th to the early 20th Century in the Hermitage Collection,* London: Azimuth, 2012, 212-13; Linda Komaroff, "A Turkman Prisoner or Prisoner of Love?" in *No Tapping around Philology: a Festschrift in Honor of Wheeler McIntosh Thackston Jr.'s 70th Birthday,* eds. Alireza Korangy and Daniel J. Sheffield, Wiesbaden: Harrassowitz, 2014, 369-80.

3. This device and its role is described in Gaston Wiet, *Miniatures Persanes, Turques, Et Indiennes: Collection De Son Excellence Chérif Sabry Pacha* Cairo: Institut francais d'archeologie orientale, 1943, 97-100.

4. The scholars presenting papers on this subject include Massumeh Farhad, "Artists, Paintings and their Publics: Safavid Albums in the Seventeenth Century," Yarshater Lectures in Persian Art, SOAS University of London, May 2019; and Filiz Çakır Phillip, "Battle Flail – A Differentiating Feature of the Turks," 16 International Congress of Turkish Art (ICTA), Hacettepe University, Ankara, October 2019.

5. Laurence Binyon, et al. write: "it is possible that an Uzbek, rather than a Turkman, is the subject." *Persian Miniature Painting: Including a critical and descriptive catalogue of the miniatures exhibited at Burlington House January-March, 1931,* London: Oxford University Press, 1933, 90. Barbara Schmitz also suggests an Uzbek subject in her analysis of the Pierpont Morgan prisoner – Table 1, entry 5. *Islamic and Indian manuscripts and paintings in the Pierpont Morgan Library,* New York: Pierpoint Morgan Library, 1997, 123.

6. Adamova, *Hermitage Collection,* 213.

7. *Kalpak* today refers to Kyrgyz, Uzbek, and Bashkir national headwear. It resembles black and white caps worn by figures in manuscript paintings that are engaged in outdoor pursuits such as hunting and battling.

8. This flail, the *amud al-rumi* (أَمُد الرومي), or flexible mace suspended on a chain, has been analysed by Phillip in her conference paper, "Battle Flail," at ICTA 2019.

9. R.D. McChesney, "The Conquest of Herat 995-96/1587-88: Sources for the Study of Safavid/ Qizilbash – Shibanid/Uzbak Relations," in *Etudes Safavides,* ed. Jean Calmard, Tehran: Institut français de recherche en Iran, 1993, 75.

10. V. Minorsky, "The Poetry of Shah Ismail I," *Bulletin of the School of Oriental and African Studies,* University of London (1942): 1007a.

11. According to Sholeh Quinn, this text was the most popular imitative model to Safavid historians. Begun in 1521, it includes historical events up to 1528-1529. "Notes on Timurid Legitimacy in Three Safavid Chronicles," *Iranian Studies* 31, no. 2 (1998): 149-58.

12. M. Bernardini, "Hatifi's *Timurnameh* and Qasimi's *Shahnameh-yi Ismail*: Considerations for a double Critical Edition," in *Society and Culture in the Early Modern Middle East: Studies on Iran in the Safavid Period,* ed. A.J Newman, Leiden: Brill, 2003, 3-18.

13. Mentioned in Barry Wood, "The Battle of Chalderan: Official History and Popular Memory," *Iranian Studies* 50, no. 1 (2017): 79-105.

14. Bizhan wrote this work for the penultimate Safavid monarch Shah Sulaiman (Safi II r. 1666-1694).

15 Barry Wood, "The *Tarikh-i Jahanara* in the Chester Beatty Library: An Illustrated Manuscript of the 'Anonymous Histories of Shah Isma'il," *Iranian Studies* 37, no. 1 (2004): 89-107.
16 F.R. Martin, *The Miniature Painting and Painters of Persia, India and Turkey, from the 8th to the 18th Century*, London: Bernard Quaritch, 1912, 47.
17 E. Blochet, *Musulman Painting: XIIth - XVIIth Century*, London: Methuen & Co, 1929, pl. cxix.
18 Garrett Library Manuscripts 3, f.359b.
19 This fact is pointed out by Shahzad Bashir, "Shah Ismail and the Qizilbash: Cannibalism in the Religious History of Early Safavid Iran," *History of Religions* 45, no. 3 (February 2006), 246.
20 Barry Wood, "The 'Shahnama-i Ismail': Art and Cultural Memory in Sixteenth-century Iran", PhD diss., Harvard University, 2002, 111.
21 This "Metropolitan Qazvin style" and its transmission to other centers such as Khurasan is described by A.J. Arberry, et al., *The Chester Beatty Library: a catalogue of the Persian manuscripts and miniatures* Dublin: Hodges Figgis, 1962, 73.
22 Ivan Stchoukine in *Les Peintures des Manuscrits Timurides*, Paris: P. Geuthner, 1954, corrected the work of the early scholars Sakisian, Binyon, Wilkinson, and Gray writing in the 1920s and 30s who erroneously attributed a late fifteenth-century provenance to all prisoner works.
23 Komaroff, "Prisoner of Love," 372.
24 S.C. Welch, *Wonders of the Age: Masterpieces of Early Safavid Painting, 1501-1576*, Cambridge, Mass.: Fogg Art Museum, 1979, 204-205.
25 Abolala Soudavar, "Between the Safavids and the Mughals: Art and Artists in Transition," *Iran* 37 (1999), 55 and 64, ftn. 90.
26 Boston Museum of Fine Arts 14.592. Georges Marteau and Henri Vever's attribution to Muhammadi is erroneous in *Miniatures persanes: exposées au Musée des Arts Décoratifs juin-octobre 1912*, Paris: Bibl. d'art & d'archéol, 1913.
27 S.C. Welch, *Wonders of the Age: Masterpieces of Early Safavid Painting, 1501-1576*, Cambridge, Mass.: Fogg Art Museum, 1979, 198.
28 The term *amir* refers to the head of political, military and judicial powers; military strength is however the main attribute it designates. Whether the term conveys royal or noble status is unclear, as there is no definitive law of succession. The term *sultan* is a princely title.
29 Reproduced in Martin, *Miniature Painting and Painters*, pl. 90.
30 I am grateful to Marika Sardar and Tim Stanley for providing me with images of the Large Clive Album's layout to support my argument. Several albums in the Topkapi also pair prisoners who look at each other from opposite pages. Massumeh Farhad notes an example of this is present in H.2142 (ff. 11b-12a – Table 1, entries 20, 21) in which a 17th-century Istanbul drawing faces an earlier, late 16th-century Safavid copy; according to Farhad they intentionally "play off each other" (private correspondence). Other Topkapi albums have prisoners grouped sequentially, as in H.2135, (ff. 24b, 25a, 25b – Table 1, entries 22-24). In another layout type, several prisoners are not consecutive but are scattered throughout an album (such as H.2165 and H.2133).
31 Harvard University of Art Museum 1958.59.
32 Binyon, et al., *Persian Miniature Painting*, 89.
33 Metropolitan Museum of Art 57.51.29.
34 Gulru Necipoglu, "Word and Image: Ottoman Sultans in Comparative Perspective," in *The Sultan's Portrait: Picturing the House of Osman*, ed. Selmin Kangal, Istanbul: Isbank, 2000, 25.
35 Armenag bey Sakisian, *La miniature persane du XIIe au XVIIe siècle*, Paris: Van Oest, 1929, 68.
36 Ghiyas al-Din Muhammad Khwandamir, "Habib al-siyar," *A Century of Princes: Sources on Timurid History and Art*, trans. W.M. Thackston, Cambridge, Mass.: The Aga Khan Program for Islamic Architecture, 1989, 221.
37 Ibid., 232. Not lost on Khwandamir is the irony of Shibani's epithets. Immediately after recounting the pillaging and horrors of a raid, Khwandamir then writes, "As Muhammad Khan [Shibani] ordered, his titles were announced as Imam of the Age and Viceroy of the Merciful" (233).

38 Iskandar Beg Munshi, *The History of Shah Abbas the Great* (*Tarikh-i alamara-yi abbasi*), trans. R.M. Savory Boulder: Westview Press, 1978, 59. The firsthand account of Shibani most often repeated is by Babur, the founder of the Mughal dynasty in India, who complained Shibani personally corrected the matchless calligraphy of Mir Ali Mashhadi and the marvelous artwork of Bihzad.

39 Martin provides an exception, distinguishing the copy in the Louvre (Table 1, entry 4) as a Mughal work by Akbar's court painter Farrukh the Qalmaq (*The Miniature Painting and Painters*, 47).

40 The sultanates in the Deccan were Shiite coreligionists of the Safavids, which may in part explain the Deccan attribution of the Bound Captive in the David Collection. Compared to the delicacy and humility of the others, this subject appears particularly oafish and garishly garbed, with the artist perhaps sharing the same Safavid derisive spirit.

41 With regard to non-Safavid markets for album productions, Anastassiia Botchkareva asserts that the smaller Deccani and Uzbek courts would not have had "enough resources to support artistic production" of albums compared to their dominant Safavid and Mughal neighbors. *Representational Realism in Cross-Cultural Perspective: Changing Visual Cultures in Mughal India and Safavid Iran 1580-1750*, PhD diss., Harvard University, 2014, 16.

42 Not used by the Abulkhairids themselves (who in fact preferred the term *Mughul*, or "Mongol"), "Uzbek" was wielded in period Safavid chronicles as a group designation that later became a term of abuse akin to the pejorative labels "Turk" or "Qizilbash," and was applied to "an unlettered person, a bumpkin or a rustic." Information found in R.D. McChesney, "Islamic culture and the Chinggisid restoration: Central Asia in the sixteenth and seventeenth centuries," in *The New Cambridge History of Islam. Vol. 3: The Eastern Islamic World Eleventh to Eighteenth Centuries*, eds. David O. Morgan and Anthony Reid, Cambridge: Cambridge University Press, 2011, 241.

43 Yuri Bregel spells out what is erroneous about the "Shibanid" designation to refer to the Abulkhairids and I defer to him and use the accurate latter term. "ABU'L-KHAYRIDS," *Encyclopædia Iranica*, online edition, 2012, available at http://www.iranicaonline.org/articles/abul-khayrids-dynasty.

44 Ismail was not being figurative when he "boldly said that the enemies' blood would be the wine and their skulls would be the bowls." Bert Fragner, "The Safavid Empire and the Sixteenth- and Seventeenth-Century Political and Strategic Balance of Power within the World System," in *Iran and the World in the Safavid Age*, eds. Willem Floor and Edmund Herzig, London: I. B. Tauris, 2012, 60. There are other references to cannibalism among the Qizilbash troops to prove their loyalty to their military and spiritual leader in Bashir, "Shah Ismail and the Qizilbash."

45 McChesney, "The Conquest of Herat," 93.

46 Relayed by Andrew J. Newman, *Safavid Iran: Rebirth of a Persian Empire*, London: I. B. Tauris, 2006, 27.

47 Rudi Matthee, "Relations Between the Center and the Periphery in Safavid Iran: The Western Borderlands v. the Eastern Frontier Zone," *Historian* (2015): 440.

48 To learn about what atrocities the Uzbeks may or may not have carried out while in the region, see Bregel, "BUKHARA iv. Khanate of Bukhara and Khorasan."

49 Like the Abulkhairids, the Tuqay-Timurids too descended from the Chinggisid Juchi branch but the split came in the third generation traced from the Great Khan, between his grandsons Shiban and Tuqay-Timur. Information on the dynastic shift can be found in Audrey Burton, "Who were the First Ashtarkhānid Rulers of Bukhara?" *Bulletin of the School of Oriental and African Studies*, 51, no. 3 (1988): 482-88. The broader historical context is given in-depth treatment by Thomas Welsford, *Four Types of Loyalty in Early Modern Central Asia: the Tuqay-Timurid Takeover of Greater Ma Wara al-Nahr, 1598-1605* Leiden: Brill, 2013.

50 Nadhr Muhammad Khan figures prominently in R.D. McChesney, "Reforms of Baqi Muhammad Khan," *Central Asiatic Journal* 24, no. 1/2 (1980): 70; and Richard C. Foltz, *Mughal India and Central Asia* Oxford: Oxford University Press, 1998, passim.

51 Yuri Bregel quotes Muhammad-Yusuf in "BUKHARA iv. Khanate of Bukhara and Khorasan," *Encyclopædia Iranica*, Vol. IV, Fasc. 5 (2000): 521-524. Online edition available at https://iranicaonline.org/articles/bukhara-iv (accessed on 14 March 2015).

52 Robert Hillenbrand, *Imperial Images in Persian Painting*, Edinburgh: Scottish Arts Council, 1977, 68.

53 Stephen P. Blake posits a date of 1590 for the cessation of Safavid administration in Qazvin; previous scholarship used 1598 as the year in which the Safavid capital shifted to Isfahan under Abbas I. "Shah Abbas and the Transfer of the Safavid Capital From Qazvin to Isfahan," in *Society and Culture in the Early Modern Middle East: Studies on Iran in the Safavid Period*, ed. A. J. Newman, Leiden: Brill, 2003, 154-64.

54 Sussan Babaie has examined these wall paintings depicting Safavid shahs offering refuge to Mughal and Uzbek rulers who were "suffering a reversal of fortune." In one, Tahmasp sits with the deposed Mughal emperor Humayun. In another Abbas I welcomes the Uzbek Wali-Muhammad Khan, and the likely visual source for this scene is a work on paper held in the Los Angeles County Museum of Art (M.73.5.469). The third wall painting shows Abbas II hosting Nadir (Nadhr) Muhammad-Khan, Wali-Muhammad Khan's nephew and usurper. "Shah Abbas II, the Conquest of Qandahar, the Chihil Sutun, and Its Wall Paintings," *Muqarnas* 11 (1994), 125-42. Welsford discusses the rival rulers Wali Muhammad and Imam Quli's attempts to secure Samarqand in *Four Types of Loyalty in Early Modern Central Asia*, 262-80.

55 Munshi, *History of Shah Abbas the Great*, 61. The animal allusions might also carry confessional undertones, as the important Shiite figure Ali was commonly symbolised as a lion in Safavid Iran. Mentioned in Wood, dissertation, 221.

56 Bow cases depicting *simurgh* birds preying on mammals are found in the following Prisoner copies: Pierpont Morgan Library (Table 1, entry 5), Reza Abbasi Museum (Table 1, entry 9), and an auctioned Christie's folio (26 October 2017, lot 38; Table 1, entry 7). Bibliothèque Nationale (Table 1, entry 8) and Topkapi H.2135, f.25b (Table 1, entry 24) have victimised dragons. The cap of the LACMA prisoner (85.237.28) features a *simurgh* attacking a feline (Fig. 4, detail 1).

57 Khwandamir, "Habib al-siyar," 229.

58 Topkapi Palace Library H.1339, f.110b. Reproduced in Geza Feher, *Türkische Miniaturen: aus den Chroniken der ungarischen Feldzüge*, Wiesbaden: E. Vollmer Verlag, 1978.

59 Safavid satin with metal thread specimens are extant in the Textile Museum of George Washington University (acc. no. 3.225) and Yale University Art Gallery (1951.51.86). Mary McWilliams' article on textile fragments containing Georgian captives taken prisoner by Safavid soldiers or courtiers is particularly illuminating. She substantiates her argument citing Safavid historical chronicles that extol Tahmasp's campaigns and victories against Georgians during the 1540s and 1550s. The Georgian prisoners on "textiles communicate Tahmasp's victories over a particular enemy, and his pride needed these victories. In his fifty-two year reign, …[he] had few military victories to celebrate." There are fewer fragments in comparison that seem to represent Uzbek prisoners. "Prisoner Imagery in Safavid Textiles," *The Textile Museum Journal* (1987): 19.

60 Wood, dissertation, 142-65; Barbara Schmitz, *Miniature Painting in Harat, 1570-1640*, Ph.D. diss., New York University, 1981, passim.

61 Sussan Babaie, et al., *Slaves of the Shah: New Elites of Safavid Iran*, London: I. B. Tauris, 2004, 126.

62 See ftn. 20.

63 Schmitz, dissertation, 126-27.

64 "Shah Esmail Kills Abul Khayr Khan [sic-Shibani Khan is depicted] in Battle" from *Tarikh-i alam-ara-yi shah Ismail* by Bizhan Gurji, National Museum of Asian Art (formerly the Freer Gallery of Art), Washington D.C., F2000.3.

65 Shah Ismail defeating Shibani Khan appears in another illustrated work of the *Anonymous Histories of Shah Ismail* (incorrectly labelled *[Tarikh-i] alamara-yi safavi* by the museum) in the Reza Abbasi Museum, Tehran, no.77.1.7, f.273v. Thanks to Barry Wood for this clarification.

66 Sussan Babaie, "Frontiers of visual taboo: painted 'indecencies' in Isfahan," in *Eros and Sexuality in Islamic Art*, eds. Francesca Leoni and Mika Natif, New York: Routledge, 2013, 140.
67 The sixteenth century was an era of increasing individuation in the social significance and outward declarative capacities of head coverings, with costume and headwear details used to solidify and broadcast political and religious identity and affiliation. Information also found in Babaie, et al., *Slaves of the Shah*, 126. The Abulkhairids similarly wore their own distinctively wrapped turbans throughout the late sixteenth century. Rendering the prisoners in *kalpaks* elides their religiosity and reads as an artistic move to heighten their difference from the Safavids.
68 Wood, dissertation, 156.
69 Manuscript produced in Qazvin, 1579-80, f.335a. Present whereabouts unknown. Reproduced as entry 209 in Glenn Lowry, et al., *An Annotated and Illustrated Checklist of the Vever Collection*, Washington D.C.: Smithsonian, 1988.
70 British Library Ms. Add. 7784, f.162, ca. 1541, Qazvin. Although not explicit in its comparisons, period works created parallels connecting Timur with Ismail I such as in Qasimi's *Shahnama-yi Ismail*. The deeds of Timur against Toqtamish Khan were likened to Shah Ismail's campaigns against the Uzbek leader Muhammad Shibani, as though this chapter on a single king was meant to be added to Firdausi's ancient masterpiece. Bernardini, "Hatifi's Timurnameh and Qasimi's *Shahnameh-yi Ismail*," 4.
71 Axel Langer, *The Fascination of Persia: The Persian-European Dialogue in Seventeenth-century Art & Contemporary Art from Tehran*, Zürich: Scheidegger & Spiess, 2013, 171.
72 Langer, *The Fascination of Persia*, 171.
73 Wood, dissertation, 194.
74 I can add to this Rosemary Stanfield-Johnson's work on nineteenth-century Iranian manuscripts that evidence components of older, oral life in the Safavid period. They contain the themes of revenge and humiliation of the Abulkhairid leader Abd al-Mumin at the hands of the Iranian hero Yuzbashi-yi Kurd Bacheh. "Yuzbashi-yi Kurd Bacheh and 'Abd al-Mu'min Khan the Uzbek: A Tale of Revenge in the Dastan of Husayn-i Kurd," in *Muraqqa'e Sharqi, studies in honor of Peter Chelkowski*, eds., Soussie Kerman-Rastegar and Anna Vanzan, Dogana: AIEP Ed., 2007, 165-79.
75 Wood, dissertation, 94.
76 See Wood's table of surviving copies spanning the seventeenth-nineteenth centuries in "The Battle of Chalderan," 83.
77 Wood, dissertation, 79-80.
78 Ibid., 227.
79 The other most popularly depicted subject is the wedding of Ismail, demonstrating the equal weight of the two components of *bazm u razm* (banqueting and battling) literature. Ibid., 137.
80 Bernardini and Wood have examined the surviving manuscripts and come to this conclusion that not one copy was made for a Safavid royal patron.
81 Stchoukine used the term "provincial" in *Les peintures des manuscrits safavis*. B.W. Robinson later critiqued the vapid phrase "provincial Persian" a "catch-all classification" in *Persian Paintings in the John Rylands Library: a Descriptive Catalogue*, London: Sotheby Parke Bernet, 1980, 115. Wood has since corrected the "provincial" attribution to Qasimi's *Shahnama* in the British Library (ms. Add. 7784), which bears the date 1541. The patron is unknown, but he may have been a wealthy resident of Tabriz, since the book's quality is quite good and the paintings display elements from the workshops located in Tabriz.
82 Quoted by Bernardini, "Hatifi's *Timurnameh* and Qasimi's *Shahnameh-yi Ismail*," 9.
83 Wood, dissertation, 59.
84 Wood, "Chalderan," 81; Wood, dissertation, 59; Bernardini, "Hatifi's *Timurnameh* and Qasimi's *Shahnameh-yi Ismail*," 9.
85 Banu Mahir, "A Group of seventeenth century Paintings Used for Picture Recitation," *Art Turc/Turkish Art: Proceedings of the 10th Annual Congress of Turkish Art*, Geneva: Fondation Max Van Berchem 1999, 447-48.

86 These insults found in period Safavid historical chronicles are cited by Wood, "Chalderan," 86, and in Wood's translation of *The Adventures of Shah Esmail: A Seventeenth-Century Persian Popular Romance* (Leiden: Brill, 2019). Writing in the late seventeenth century while visiting the Safavid court in Iran, the French observer Jean Chardin claimed that the Iranians looked down upon the Russians and the Uzbeks in the same way, as "filthy, uncultured, and obtuse." Reported by Rudi Matthee, "Facing a Rude and Barbarous Neighbor," in *Iran Facing Others: Identity Boundaries in a Historical Perspective*, eds., Abbas Amanat and Farzin Vejdani (eds.), New York: Palgrave, 2012: 103.

87 Khwandamir writes in *Habib al-siyar*: "Muhammad Khan Shibani…subjugated the capital of Khurasan. …From the personal possessions of the amirs and ministers of that dynasty much cash and goods were taken. …The Uzbek soldiery tormented and tortured …until they got…what they could get. The cries of many people of quality and station, reduced to misery and degradation, rose to the celestial spheres. The delicate beauties of the inner sanctum of inviolability were taken captive and tormented by the merciless Uzbeks, and Venuses of the chambers of chastity were left by ravaging Mughuls [Mongols] to wander destitute in the lanes and bazaars" (232-33).

88 Wall painting reproduced in Babaie, "the Conquest of Qandahar," 128 (Fig. 4).

89 Thanks to Barry Wood for bringing this vivid detail to my attention. References to the act are common in *The Adventures of Shah Esmail: A Seventeenth-Century Persian Popular Romance*.

90 Rare instances of the *palahang* in *Shahnama* illustrations are in a folio "Afrasiyab condemns Siyavush to Death" in the Boston Museum of Fine Arts (19.772) with an uncertain provenance posited to the late 15th century. A *Shahnama* illustrated by the artist Muhammad Murad Samarqandi who worked in Transoxiana in the first two decades of the seventeenth century depicts Aulad bound in front of Rustam. The copy is located in Tashkent's Beruni Institute (ms. 1811, f.70v) and the painting was added to the manuscript during the Tuqay-Timurid dynasty between 1604–1616. A *Shahnama* in Oxford's All Souls College, Codrington Library ms. 288, f.19v, depicts Faraidun bringing a constrained Zahhak to Mount Damavand and is thought to be a product of Ottoman-controlled Baghdad. Folios rendering the shackled Bizhan in a pit are located in the National Museum of World Cultures in the Netherlands (RV-2103-1) attributed to Iran ca. 1600, and in an Aq Quyunlu/Turkoman manuscript from 1497-1504 reproduced in Walter P. Schulz, *Die Persisch-Islamische Miniaturmalerei: Ein Beitrag Zur Kunstgeschichte Irans*, Leipzig: K.W. Hiersemann, 1914, pl. 63. Looking at other literary works, a folio from a Khamsa of Nizami (ca. 1654-1656, Bukhara) has prisoners in the constraint before Khusrau. This illustration is reproduced in Yves Porter, "Le *kitab-khana* de Abd al-Aziz Khan (1645-1680) et le mécénat de la peinture à Boukhara," *Cahiers d'Asie centrale* 7 (1999). Porter states it was taken from a Christie's auction but does not give the date or lot number. A folio of prisoners in jail in a copy of Jami's *Yusuf u Zulaikha* (Topkapi H.1084, f.149b) with illustrations from 1590s Shiraz also are rendered in the *palahang*. Image reproduced in Lale Uluc, "Zülkadirli Şiraz valilerinin son döneminden resimli bir *Yusuf ve Züleyha* nüshası," in Baha Tanman (ed.), *Nurhan Atasoy'a Armagan*, Istanbul, 2014, 387-422.

91 Illustration found in R.W. Ferrier, ed., *A Journey to Persia: Jean Chardin's Portrait of a Seventeenth-Century Empire*, London and New York: I. B. Tauris, 1996. The Persian description of this pillory is given by A.H. Morton in his review of the book within the issue of *Iranian Studies* 31, no. 1 (1998): 119-22. The caption on the illustration names the subject "Guirywânn doù Chékéh," which might refer to the Crimean dynasty "Girai," relating it to the Vienna National Library prisoner within the Murad III Album (Table 1, entry 33).

92 National Museum of Asian Art (formerly the Freer Gallery of Art), Washington D.C., 1986, 304.

93 Louvre Museum OA 7109.

94 See various examples attributed to Persianate painting workshops: the margins to a folio from a Sadi *Bustan* from Bukhara, 1649 (Chester Beatty Library, Dublin, Pers. 274, f.142b); an album page of a female nude resting her arm in the crook of a flowering tree ca. 1640-48 (Topkapi

Palace Library H.2168, f.30); an album page of a young falconer attributed to the Ottoman artist Vali Jan ca. 1580 in the Aga Khan collection (AKM97); a drawing attributed to Muhammadi in the India Office Library ca. 1575 (J.27.15); an illustration of Bebek Çelebi in the *Shaqaiq al-numaniyya* of Tashkopruzade ca. 1617-22 (Topkapi Palace Library H.1263, f. 167v).

95 Komaroff, "Prisoner of Love," 377.
96 Ibid., 373.
97 Ibid., 374.
98 A dissertation on this subject by Naciem Nikkhah (titled "Cut, Paste, Patch: A Study of Text-Image Relationships in Safavid Single-Page Compositions") is forthcoming from Cambridge University, in which she explores the relation of calligraphy attached around the borders of album paintings.
99 Marteau and Vever confuse Mahu Khan with Murad Kausaj in *Miniatures persanes: exposées au Musée des Arts Décoratifs juin-octobre 1912*.
100 Komaroff, "Prisoner of Love," 374.
101 The original lines read: *Ba jan an jins ra dilha kharidar / Zi ghamza dilbaranra tiz bazar / Zi zulf-i dilbaran-i Khallukh [Khalaj]-i Chin / Havayi janfazaish bud mushkin*. I am grateful to Mohsen Qassemi H. and Fatemeh Shams for their translation assistance and discussions concerning the poem's content. Given that *nastaliq* calligraphy is infamously imprecise in its dot demarcation, a wordplay might be going on. The likeliest locale mentioned is Khallukh: a large city in East Turkistan/Cathay, remarkable for the comeliness of its inhabitants and fragrances. But it also could refer to Khalach/Khalaj: a tribal grouping located in the region of Afghanistan today.
102 *Ba bazarash mata-i aish arzan*.
103 *Qusurash ra nahan dar taht-i anhar / bihishti kard pur huran-i tatar*.
104 *Saf arayanda-yi in turfa lashkar / chunin lashkar kashad kishvar ba kishvar*.
105 Translation and analysis provided by Mohsen Qassemi H.
106 David Roxburgh, "Disorderly Conduct?: F.R. Martin and the Bahram Mirza Album," *Muqarnas* 15 (1998), 40.

Table 1: Attributions of Bound Captive Folios[*]

Collection Attribution (as listed in catalogues)	Binyon / Wilkinson / Gray	Marteau / Vever	Martin	Robinson
1: Paris Bibliothèque Nationale Inscribed *Kausaj Murad*.			"Murad with the thin beard." 1520.	
2: Worcester Art Museum 1935.9				
3: Bodleian Library, Ms. Ouseley Add. 173 f.1 (Two copies exist, another with a gold background in a pink stenciled frame. Current location unknown.) Inscribed *Amir Timur Gurkani*.	"A Turkman Prince." Late 15th cent.	"Prince prisonnier ou blessé." Persia or Herat, end of 15th cent. or early 16th cent.	"Murad Akkuyunli taken prisoner by Shah Ismail." Herat school, attrib. to Bihzad 1502 (gold version).	"Turkman Prisoner." Qazwin, attrib. to Muhammad
4: Louvre Museum, AO 36191. Formerly Musée Guimet, Paris, no. 3619, I, a Inscribed *Bayram ughlan, signed Farrukh Beg*.			"Portrait of Murad Akkuyunli" copy attrib. to Farrukh the Qalmaq (Muhammadi's pupil), after Bihzad, 1580.	1575, Qazvin style.
5: Pierpont Morgan Library, Ms. 386-2				

[*]   Conceptual format derived from Stchoukine who listed single page folios of various subjects, historical figures, and types erroneously attributed to Bihzad in the fifteenth century by early scholars. My titling the prisoners using museum and collection accession numbers is intended to counter subjective ethnic labels in the titles. It is also a means of directing the reader to consult the good quality reproductions readily available in online catalogue collections. Other bound captive folios with uncertain provenances have been mentioned by Wiet (p. 100): Coll.

1. The Liberating the "Turkoman Prisoner"

Sakisian	Schmitz	Soudavar	Stchoukine	Welch	Miscellaneous
			Qazvin style, ca. 1575.		Reproduced in Blochet: "Portrait of a Turkoman warrior Kusej Murad." Early 16th cent.
					Reproduced in Ettinghausen & Yarshater, fig. 169. Grube: "A Prisoner." Bukhara, mid-16th cent.
"risonnier ongol." erat school, e 15th cent.	"Uzbek Prisoner." Bukharan school, Herat, 1600.	"Yoked Ozbak Prisoner." Attrib. to Shaikh Muhammad.	"Mongol prisoner." 17th cent.	Version with gold background attrib. to Shaikh Muhammad.	Reproduced in Robinson (1958), 143.
	"Nobleman Prisoner" attrib. to Farrukh Beg	"Portrait of Bayram Oghlan" attrib. to Farrukh Beg, after Shaikh Muhammad, late 16th cent.			Reproduced in Makariou & Wise, 445. Formerly in Koechlin Coll.
	"An Uzbek Prisoner." Herat, ca. 1600.	"Yoked prisoner." attrib. to Shaikh Muhammad, 1550s		"Uzbek Nobleman."	Reproduced in Grube: "A prisoner." Bukhara, mid-16th cent. Reproduced in Swietochowski & Babaie: "A Prisoner," Uzbek period, first half 16th cent.

J.M. (Catalogue de vente, Paris 1922, pl. XVI); Coll. Paravicini; Coll. Sevadjian (Catalogue de vente, Paris 1927, no. 246). Jennifer Scarce references a "seated Mongolian, ca 1590-1610" in the Nationalmuseum of Stockholm (NMH 470/1926) in "Continuity and Modernity in the Costume of the Muslims of Central Asia," *Cultural Change and Continuity in Central Asia*, ed. Shirin Akiner (USA, 1991), 256, ftn. 15. A prisoner mounted on a dappled horse is in the Pierre Jourdan-Barry collection.

6: Sotheby's auction Lot 154 15-16 April 1985 Inscribed *raqam-i Khan Muhammad 1015* (1606-07).				
7: Christie's auction Lot 38 26 October 2017				
8: Paris Bibliothèque Nationale Inscribed *Mahu Khan*.	"Turkman Prisoner (possibly Uzbek)," attrib. to Behzad. Late 15th cent.	"Prince prisonnier ou blessé." Herat or Transoxiana, early 16th cent.	"Portrait of a Mongol Prince as Prisoner." Herat school, attrib. to Behzad, end of 15th cent.	"Turkman Prisoner," 16 cent. attrib. Muhammad 16th cent.
9: Reza Abbasi Museum: Access. no. 2522.				
10: Hermitage Museum, St. Petersburg: VP 740 III Inscribed *Padshah-i Turkman*.				
11: Yale University Art Gallery: 1983.94.9 Inscribed *Khwaja Beg Kuhur*.				
12: Private Collection, Jaipur. Inscribed *Aqa Riza, amal-i murid bi-ikhlas* and another indecipherable line.				
13: Los Angeles County Museum of Art 2000.135				
14: David Collection: 21-1979				
15: Victoria & Albert Museum: Large Clive Album: IS.133-1964, f. 50a Attributed to Qara Yusuf. Inscribed *Ibrahim Beg*.				

1. The Liberating the "Turkoman Prisoner"

						"Portrait of a Tartar prisoner," attrib. to Persia.
						"Turkoman prisoner", Safavid Iran, second-half 16th cent.
risonnier ongol." erat school, [th] cent.	"Uzbek Prisoner." 16th cent.			"Mongol prisoner." Late 16th cent.		Formerly in Doucet collection. Reproduced in Blochet: "Mahu Khan," Herat, 1480.
						Reproduced in Aghdashloo. "Portrait of a prisoner." Khurasan school, early 16th cent.
						Reproduced in Adamova, et al., entry 34. "Steppe Prisoner." Qazvin, late-16th cent.
						"An Uzbek Prisoner." 19th cent.
						Reproduced in Das, 9. "Turkoman Prisoner. Copy of an old Persian picture." Ca. 1595-1600.
						Reproduced in Komaroff: "Turkman Prisoner." Iran, last quarter 16th cent.
						"A Captive Central Asian Warrior." India, Deccan, mid-17th cent.
						Attrib. to Qara Yusuf, late 16th cent.

16: Los Angeles County Museum of Art 85.237.28 "Turkoman Prisoner." Isfahan, first half-17th cent. Inscription might read: *bahr-i Ali Quli*.				
17: Boston Museum of Fine Arts 14.579		"Prince prisonnier ou blessé" attrib. to Ustad Muhammadi Bukhara or Samarkand. Safavid/Timurid. Early 16th cent.	"Portrait of Murad Akkuyunli" Copy by Sultan Muhammad after Bihzad. 1520	
18: Topkapi Palace Library H. 2142, f. 4a				
19: Topkapi Palace Library H. 2142, f.3b Inscribed *Bihzad*.				
20: Topkapi Palace Library H.2142, f. 11b Late-16th cent., Safavid				
21: Topkapi Palace Library H.2142, f. 12a 17th-cent., Ottoman (Istanbul).				
22: Topkapi Palace Library H.2135, f. 24b Inscribed *Sadiqi*.				
23: Topkapi Palace Library H.2135, f. 25a				
24: Topkapi Palace Library H.2135, f. 25b Inscribed *kusa Murad*, attrib. to Bihzad.				
25: Topkapi Palace Library H. 2156, f. 45a Inscribed *amal-i Shaikh Muhammad* on bow tip.				

						Denny: "Portrait of an Uzbek Prisoner in a Yoke."
	"A Tartar Prisoner in a Pala-hang." Herat, ca. 1585.	"Yoked prisoner" attrib. to Shaikh Muhammad, late-16th cent.			Attrib. to Shaikh Muhammad, 1595	Reproduced in Martin, vol. 2, pl. 84a. "A Captured Prince/ Album folio with a captured warrior." Persian, third quarter 16th cent. Copy of Topkapi Palace Library H. 2142, f. 4a and H.2133 -3
						Copy of Boston Museum of Fine Arts 14.579, Topkapi Palace Library H.2133 -3
						Reproduced in Kundak: "Tatar prisoner," Safavid Isfahan, early 17th cent.
	Khurasan school.				Attrib. to Shaikh Muhammad, 1580.	Reproduced in Komaroff: "Turkman Prisoner." Iran, third quarter 16th cent. (margins dated between 1572-1575). Çağman & Tanındı: Khurasani style, compiled in Herat, after 1580-81.

26: Topkapi Palace Library H.2133 -1				
27: Topkapi Palace Library H.2133 -2				
28: Topkapi Palace Library H.2133 -3				
29: Topkapi Palace Library H.2133 -4				
30: Topkapi Palace Library H.2165, f. 6b				
31: Topkapi Palace Library H.2165, f.45b Inscribed *raqam-i Bihzad.*				
32: Metropolitan Museum of Art 67.266.2				
33: Vienna National Library-Murad III Album: Mixt.313, f.38a Inscribed *Turs Girai.*				
34: Formerly Smith-Lesouëf collection. Current location unknown. Inscribed *Chini Bahadur.*				
35: Formerly Smith-Lesouëf collection. Current location unknown. Inscribed *Bahman.*				

1. The Liberating the "Turkoman Prisoner"

						Copy of Topkapi Palace Library H.2165, f.6b
						Copy of Topkapi Palace Library H.2165, f. 45b
						Copy of Boston Museum of Fine Arts 14.579, Topkapi Palace Library H. 2142, f. 4a
						Copy of Reza Abbasi Museum: Access. no. 2522
						Copy of Topkapi Palace Library H.2133-1
						Reproduced in Fetvaci. Copy of Topkapi Palace Library H.2133-2
						Reproduced in Swietochowski & Babaie: "Turkomen Prisoner," Isfahan, early 17th cent.
						Froom: "Depiction of a Captive with Mongol Features." Isfahan, 17th cent. "Turs Girai" is the name of a Crimean Tatar dynasty. Grube: Isfahan, first quarter 17th cent. Reproduced in Holter, pl. 23, attrib. to Aqa Riza (Riza Abbasi).
						Reproduced in Blochet.
						Reproduced in Wiet.

Table 2: Attributions of Seated Prince Folios

Collection Attribution (as listed in catalogues)	Marteau / Vever	Martin
1: Christie's auction Lot 207, 5 October 2010 "A Heavily Armed Uzbek."		
2: Formerly Kevorkian Collection. Current location unknown. "Mongol Warrior." India, 1620.		
3: Boston Museum of Fine Arts 14.592 "An Amir Seated Beneath a Tree." Mashhad, attrib. to Shaikh Muhammad, ca. 1557.	"Portrait de prince ou de chef d'armée." Herat, attrib. to Ustad Muhammadi (sic), early 16th cent.	"Portrait of an Amir." Attrib. to Sultan Muhammad, ca. 153
4: David Collection 86-2006 "Portrait of a Noble." Khurasan/ Herat, 1500-25.		
5: Christie's auction Lot 52 23 April 2015. "A Kneeling Prince." Bukhara late 16th cent., Mughal India early 17th cent.		
6: Shahid Mutahhari University Library, Tehran. Album folio ca. end of 16th/beginning of 17th cent.; Bukhara.		
7: Harvard University of Art Museum 1958.59. Portrait of Sultan Husain Mirza Baiqara by Bihzad. Inscribed *Sultan Husain Mirza ba-amal-i Hazrat Ustad Bihzad* [portrait of Sultan Husayn Mirza by his excellency Master Bihzad].		
8: Los Angeles County Museum of Art: M.85.237.43 "Portrait of a Kneeling Warrior, His Right Hand on the Hilt of a Dagger." Turkey, ca. 1620-30.		
9: The Keir Collection of Islamic Art on loan to the Dallas Museum of Art: K.1.2014.143 (formerly III.291) "A Turkman Prince," ca. 1575.		
10: Topkapi Palace Library: H. 2132, f.20a Seated (Qipchaq?) warrior.		

Sakisian	Schmitz	Welch	Miscellaneous
			Formerly in Kevorkian collection. Reproduced in Schulz, plate O. "Porträt eines Emir, farbig getönt." East Persian school, end of 15th c.
		Reproduced in A. Welch & Zoka. "Mongol Warrior." India, 1620.	Reproduced in Falk, pl. 142.
ortrait d'un émir." erat school, d of 15th cent.	"An Uzbek Khan's Portrait." Attrib. to Shaikh Muhammad, 1557.	"The Officer's Portrait." Attrib. to Shaikh Muhammad, ca. 1557 (S.C. Welch 1979).	Grube: "Prince Seated under a Tree," Bukhara, mid 16th cent.
			Contains Mughal seal belonging to Wazir al-Mamalik Asaf al-Daula Asaf Jah Yahya Khan Bahadur Hizabr Jang, Nawab Vazir of Oudh from 1775-97.
			Courtesy of Francis Richard.
			Resemblance to a figure drawn by Sadiqi in Khwandamir's Ḥabib al-Siyar, f. 227b, ca. 1579-80, Qazvin.

11: Portrait of an Amir. Current location unknown.		Reproduced in Martin pl. 90. "Unfinished Portrait of an Amir." Painted on silk. Herat school, end of 15th cen.
12: Victoria & Albert Museum: Large Clive Album: IS.133-1964, f. 49b Attributed to aqa Riza Jahangiri Shahi, ca. 1605. "A Turkoman or Mongol Chief holding an Arrow."		
13: "A Puzzling Amir of Bukhara" attrib. to Muhammad Murad Samarqandi, ca. 1615. Current location unknown.		
14: Boston Museum of Fine Arts 14.636 Seated Man. Safavid period, Isfahan, ca. 1595. Signed *Sadiqi Beg*.		
15: Cross-legged prince holding a wine cup. Current location unknown.		Reproduced in Martin pl. 108. "Portrait of a Amir." Attrib. to Sul Muhammad, 1530.
16: Topkapi Palace Library: H. 2134, f.24b Cross-legged prince holding a wine cup. Signed *Vali*.		
17: British Museum: 1948,1009,0.56 "Cross-legged Turkoman ruler," ca. 1550, Bukhara. Inscribed *Tatar Khan Padshah-i dasht-i Qipchaq*.		
18: Metropolitan Museum of Art 57.51.29 Portrait of Shibani Khan by Bihzad. Inscribed *surat-i Shaybek Khan, al-abd Bihzad* [portrait of Shaybek Khan by the slave Bihzad].		
19: Bonham's auction Lot 40, 18 November 2020 "A Heavily Armed Uzbek." Cup inscribed *jahan*… [indecipherable].		

				Reproduced in Witherspoon, pl. 45. "Portrait of a squatting officer with a gray beard." Safavid, late 16th c.
	Painted on cotton cloth.			Formerly in the Earl Powis collection. Mughal provenance. Reproduced in Schmitz, 123.
			The "turban exudes the energy of a Neapolitan wedding cake. The organic wriggle of the sleeves is almost intestinal." Welch, et al. (1979), 205. Misattributed to Shaikh Muhammad, 1564.	
Reproduced in Sakisian, 174. "Personnage à turban." Safavid, first half 16th cent.				
				Reproduced in İnal, fig. 11. Signed by Vali Jan.
				Reproduced in Abuseitova & Dodkhudoeva, cat. 29, p. 214; cover artwork to Lee, *Qazaqliq*.
				Extensively reproduced.
				Formerly in Kevork Essayan collection.

Print reproductions found in the following (where they are not available in online collection catalogues):

Abuseitova, M. Kh., and L. N. Dodkhudoeva. *Qazaqstan tarikhy shyghys miniatiuralarynda = Istoriia Kazakhstana v vostochnykh miniatiurakh = History of Kazakhstan in Eastern miniatures.* Almaty: Daĭk-Press, 2010.

Adamova, A. T., et al. *Persian Manuscripts Paintings and Drawings: From the 15th to the Early 20th Century in the Hermitage Collection.* London: Azimuth Editions, 2012.

Aghdashloo, Aydin, trans. Claude Karbassi. *A Collection of Iranian Miniatures and Calligraphy from the 14th to the 18th century A.D.* Tehran: Reza Abbasi Museum, 1977.

Binyon, Laurence, J. V. S. Wilkinson, and Basil Gray. *Persian Miniature Painting.* London: Oxford University Press, 1933.

Blochet, Edgard. *Les enluminures des manuscrits orientaux: turcs, arabes, persans de la bibliotheque nationale.* Paris: Editions de la Gazette des beaux-arts, 1926.

Cagman, Filiz, and Zeren Tanindi. *Topkapi Palace Museum Islamic Miniature Painting.* Istanbul: Ali Riza Baskan Guzel Sanatlar Matbaasi, 1979.

Das, Asok Kumar. *Mughal Masters. Further Studies.* Mumbai: Marg Publications, 1998.

Ettinghausen, Richard and Ehsan Yarshater, eds. *Highlights of Persian Art.* New York: Westview Press, 1979.

Falk, Toby, et al. *Treasures of Islam.* Secaucus: Wellfleet Press, 1985.

Fetvaci, Emine. "Persian Aesthetics in Ottoman Albums." Institute for Advanced Study: https://www.ias.edu/ideas/2018/fetvaci-persian-aesthetics. Accessed 20 June 2018.

Froom, Aimée Elisabeth. "A Muraqqa' for the Ottoman Sultan Murad III (r. 1574-1595): Oesterreichische Nationalbibliothek 'codex Mixtus' 313." PhD dissertation, New York University, 2001.

Grube, Ernst. *The Classical Style in Islamic Painting: The early school of Herat and its impact on Islamic painting of the later 15th, the 16th and 17th centuries.* Venice: Edizioni Oriens, 1968.

Holter, Kurt. *Persische Miniaturen.* Wien: Kunstverlag Wolfrum, 1955.

Inal, Güner. "Influence of the Kazvin Style on Ottoman Miniature Painting." In *Fifth International Congress of Turkish Art.* Edited by G. Fehér, pp. 457-476. Budapest, 1978.

Komaroff, Linda. "A Turkman Prisoner or Prisoner of Love?" *No Tapping around Philology: a Festschrift in Honor of Wheeler McIntosh Thackston Jr.'s 70th Birthday*, eds. Alireza Korangy and Daniel J. Sheffield (Wiesbaden, 2014): 369-380.

Kundak, Ali Nihat. "An Ottoman Album of Drawings including European Engravings (TSMK, H.2135)." *Thirteenth International Congress of Turkish Art: Proceedings: 3-7 September 2007, Budapest Hungary.* Eds. Géza Dávid and Ibolya Gerelyes. Budapest: Hungarian National Museum, 2009, pp. 423-37.

Lee, Joo-Yup. *Qazaqliq, or Ambitious Brigandage, and the Formation of the Qazaqs: State and Identity in Post-Mongol Central Eurasia.* Leiden: Brill Publishers, 2016.

Makariou, Sophie, and Susan Wise. *Islamic Art at the Musée Du Louvre.* Paris: Hazan, 2012.

Marteau, G. and H. Vever. *Miniatures persanes.* Paris: Bibliotheque d'art et d'archeologie, 1913.

Martin, F.R. *The Miniature Painting and Painters of Persia India and Turkey from the 8th to the 18th Century,* vols. 1-2. London: Bernard Quaritch, 1912.

Robinson, B.W. *A Descriptive Catalogue of the Persian Paintings in the Bodleian Library.* Oxford: Clarendon Press, 1958.

———. "Muhammadi and the Khurasan Style." Iran 30 (1992): 17-30.

Sakisian, A. B. *La miniature persane du XIIe au XVIIe siècle.* Paris and Brussels: Les Éditions G. van Oest, 1929.

Schmitz, Barbara. *Islamic and Indian Manuscripts and Paintings in The Pierpont Morgan Library.* New York: The Pierpont Morgan Library, 1997.

Schulz, Walter P. *Die Persisch-Islamische Miniaturmalerei. Ein Beitrag Zur Kunstgeschichte Irans [with a Volume of Plates and a Bibliography].* 2 vols. Leipzig, 1914.

Soudavar, Abolala. "Between the Safavids and the Mughals: Art and Artists in Transition." *Iran* vol. 37 (1999): 49-66.

Stchoukine, Ivan. *Les Peintures des Manuscrits Safavis de 1502 à 1587.* Paris: Librairie Orientaliste Paul Geuthner, 1959.

Swietochowski, Marie L., and Sussan Babaie. *Persian Drawings in the Metropolitan Museum of Art.* New York: Metropolitan Museum of Art, 1989.

Welch, Stuart C., and Yahya Zoka. *Persian & Mughal Miniatures: The Life and Times of Muhammad-Zaman.* Farhang-Sara (Yassavoli) Publishers, 1994.

Welch, Stuart C., Sheila R. Canby, and Nova Titley. *Wonders of the Age: Masterpieces of Early Safavid, 1501-1576.* London: Fogg Art Museum, 1979.

Welch, Anthony. "Painting and Patronage Under Shah Abbas I." *Iranian Studies,* Autumn 1974, Vol. 7 (3/4).

———. *Shah 'Abbas & the Arts of Isfahan.* New York: The Asia Society, 1973.

Wiet, Gaston. *Miniatures Persanes, Turques Et Indiennes: Collection De Son Excellence Chérif Sabry Pacha.* Cairo: Institut d'Egypte, 1943.

Witherspoon, Thomas C. *Islamic Art from the Collection of Edwin Binney 3rd. Circulated by the Smithsonian Institution Traveling Exhibition Service, 1966-1968.* Washington, D.C.: Smithsonian Institute, 1966.

Figures

Fig. 1 (corresponds to Table 1, entry 14):
A Captive Central Asian Warrior, mid-17th century
Deccan provenance
The David Collection, Copenhagen (21-1979)
Photo credit: Pernille Klemp

1. The Liberating the "Turkoman Prisoner"

45

Fig. 2 (corresponds to Table 1, entry 11):
An Uzbek Prisoner, 19th century [sic?]
Inscribed Khwaja Beg Kuhur
Yale University Art Gallery, New Haven, Connecticut 06520 (1983.94.9)
Gift of Mary Burns Foss

1. The Liberating the "Turkoman Prisoner"

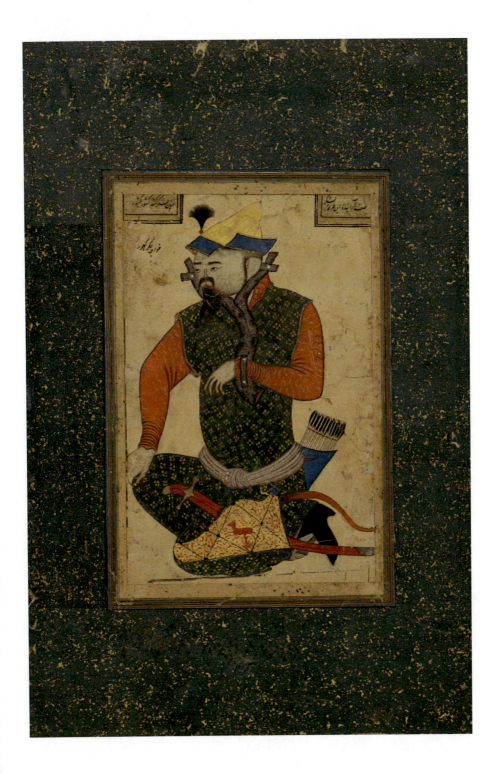

47

Fig. 3 (corresponds to Table 1, entry 15):
Turkoman Prisoner, late-16th century
Inscribed *Ibrahim Beg*
Victoria & Albert Museum
Large Clive Album: IS.133-1964, f. 50a Accepted by HM Government in lieu of inheritance tax and allo-cated to the V&A, 1964
© Victoria and Albert Museum, London

1. The Liberating the "Turkoman Prisoner"

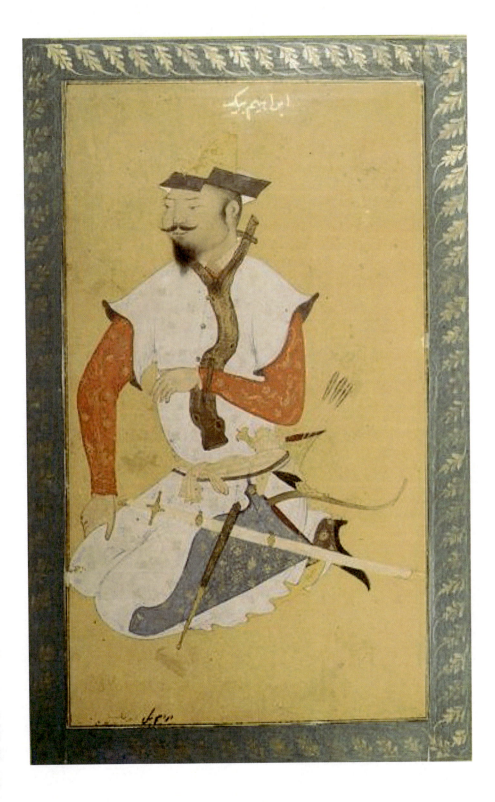

49

Fig. 4 (corresponds to Table 1, entry 16):
Turkoman Prisoner, first half of 17th century
Iran, probably Isfahan
Los Angeles County Museum of Art, The Edwin Binney, 3rd, Collection of Turkish Art at the Los Ange-les County Museum of Art (M.85.237.28)
© Museum Associates/ LACMA

1. The Liberating the "Turkoman Prisoner"

Fig. 4, detail 1: cap

1. The Liberating the "Turkoman Prisoner"

53

Fig. 4, detail 2: bow case (image enhanced)

1. The Liberating the "Turkoman Prisoner"

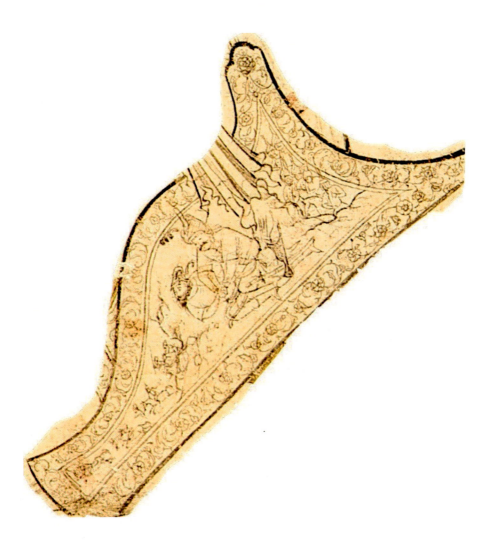

Fig. 5 (corresponds to Table 1, entry 11):
Turkoman Prisoner, second half of 16th century
Iran
Los Angeles County Museum of Art, Gift of the Ancient Art Council, Iran Trip 2000 (M.2000.135)
Photo © Museum Associates/ LACMA

1. The Liberating the "Turkoman Prisoner"

Fig. 6 (corresponds to Table 2, entry 4): The David Collection, Copenhagen (86-2006) *Portrait of a Noble*, Herat or Khurasan, ca. 1500-1525
Photo credit: Pernille Klemp

1. The Liberating the "Turkoman Prisoner"

Fig. 7 (corresponds to Table 2, entry 12):
A Turkoman or Mongol Chief holding an Arrow, 1605
Inscribed *Riza Jahangir Shahi*
Victoria & Albert Museum
Large Clive Album: IS.133-1964, f. 49b Accepted by HM Government in lieu of inheritance tax and allo-cated to the V&A, 1964
© Victoria and Albert Museum, London

1. The Liberating the "Turkoman Prisoner"

61

Fig. 8 (corresponds to Table 2, entry 8):
Portrait of a Kneeling Warrior, His Right Hand on the Hilt of a Dagger
Turkey, circa 1620-1630 or later
Los Angeles County Museum of Art, The Edwin Binney, 3rd, Collection of Turkish Art at the Los Ange-les County Museum of Art (M.85.237.43)
Photo © Museum Associates/ LACMA

1. The Liberating the "Turkoman Prisoner"

63

2

Agency and Fatalism in the Judeo-Persian *Kitab-i sar guzasht-i Kashan*

Alberto Tiburcio

Non-Shiʿis and non-Muslims are among the most marginally and poorly documented sectors of society in the Iranian historiography of the Safavid (907-1135/1501-1722) and Afsharid (1148–1210/1736-1796) periods. Not only are these groups scarcely represented in the sources, but in the rare cases where they do appear, the nature of their representation and of the sources themselves barely suffices to draw a nuanced picture of their status. Persian court chronicles, which are by and large concerned with the lives and military exploits of the rulers, devote few pages to the common folk in general, let alone religious minorities. Groups such as Armenian and Georgian Christians, Zoroastrians, and Jews do appear occasionally in the chronicles, but they usually do so as undifferentiated collectivities, with few (if any) proper names, and with seemingly no agency. European sources, consisting mostly of diplomatic and missionary reports and travelogues, contain more descriptions of these groups. While these sources exhibit the predictable biases of the foreign gaze and of implicit religious and political agendas, they are unsurmountable for getting at least a partial picture of the societal role of religious minorities.

Considering this documentary problems, the case of the Jewish community of Iran is of particular interest for at least two reasons. The first is a strictly historiographical one, this being precisely the existence of a small number of sources written from *within* the perspective of the community. Two major epic-style works are worth noting here. The first is the *Kitab-i Anusi* (*The Book of Forced Conversions*), written by Babai b. Lutf (d. 17th cent.). This work has been the subject of a thorough study by Vera B. Moreen based on manuscripts from the Jewish Theological Seminary of America in New York, the Bibliothèque Nationale in Paris, and the Ben Zvi Institute in Jerusalem.[1] The second is the *Kitab-i sar guzasht-i Kashan* (*The Book of the Fate of Kashan*) by Babai b. Farhad (d. 18th cent.), the grandson of the author of the *Kitab-i Anusi*. This work has also been edited and translated by Moreen, based on two manuscripts also kept at the aforementioned institutions in Paris and Jerusalem.[2] The second reason of interest for the Jewish case is linked to something towards which both Jewish and non-Jewish sources point: Jews were subjected to more hardships than Christian communities, with only Zoroastrians faring worse as convenient scape-goats at certain moments. This does not mean, however, that repression against Jews was necessarily a state policy throughout the history of the Safavid dynasty nor that there were not times in which Jews benefited from protection. On the contrary, the sources suggest that at least some influential members of their community were able to exercise a certain degree of bargaining power.

A close examination of the *Kitab-i sar guzasht-i Kashan* will allow us to consider the complexities of the question of agency and self-representation within Jewish sources, as well as to assess the complex relations between communal leaders, local rulers, and the state. These relations were of particular complexity for the period portrayed in this source, namely the post-1722 period, when the state was at its weakest, being contested between the Safavid claimants and the Afghan Hotaki "invaders". The present study will show how, by presenting the self-narrative of the Jewish community, the source in question suggests that the Jewish community was by no means a passive agent to which historical injustice was committed, but rather shows how at times it had the possibility of negotiating or even determining its societal status. Moreover, this study will explore how at a rhetorical level the story presents a worldview whereby two layers of historical volition are interconnected: on the one hand, there is a sense that fate as a divinely-dictated force functions as the ultimate cause of human history; but on the other, there is still a recognition of the role of human agency within the temporal limits of historical experience.

Jewish History in the Safavid Period

An overview of the status of Jews in Iran in the Safavid period is pertinent as a starting point. During the reign of Shah ʿAbbas I (r. 996-1038/1587-1629) and as a consequence of the application of scorched-earth policy in the war with the Ottomans, around 8,000 Jews from the Caucasus were forcefully relocated to the district of Farahabad in the province of Mazandaran.[3] The latter would eventually become a Jewish settlement much in the way that New Julfa became a center of Armenian Christians relocated from the Caucasus during the time for the same reasons.[4] As it happened also with the Armenians, the Jews of Farahabad went on to become strategic allies of the Shah for their role in the silk industry. As such, Jews in Iran fared better than those living in the Caucasus under Christian rule.[5] During this time, there is evidence that at least some selected Jewish scholars enjoyed some favors from the Shah. For instance, an illustrated Bible gifted to Shah ʿAbbas by the Polish cardinal Bernard Maciejowski

(d. 1608) contains marginal notes in Hebrew, which suggests that a rabbi might have had access to the court and either wrote the notes himself or was at least instrumental in training Muslim scholars in Hebrew.[6]

Drawing on the *Kitab-i Anusi*, both Vera Moreen and Mehrdad Amanat have identified instances in which Jewish apostates (who had allegedly converted to Islam out of choice) sought the Shah's intervention to take revenge against their former community.[7] In one case, an individual by the name of Abu'l-Hasan Lari (d. 1029-30/1620), obtained religious opinions (*fatwas*) from the *'ulama'* in favor of enforcing stricter dressing codes on the Jewish population. This was relatively easy, as it was common policy to prescribe special dressing regulations on *dhimmis*. In revenge, a community leader of the Farahabad Jews by the name of Eleazar incited a group of Jews to murder Lari.[8] Not long after this, a campaign of forced conversion ensued. Amanat has suggested that Eleazar may have taken their protection for granted, given the privileged status they had enjoyed until then. However – as he adds – the Shah may have acted harshly against them in order to appease other groups competing for power, including the Qizilbash. Further, Amanat also notes that this measure was not definite and that later under Shah Safi (r. 1038-1052/1629-1642) the community reconverted to Judaism.[9]

In 1620, another wave of persecutions against Jews took place in Isfahan. In this case a Jewish leader converted to Islam after being accused by his peers of mismanaging communal funds. He then accused the community of engaging in black magic against the Shah, who upon hearing this ordered all Jewish books dealing with magic to be seized and destroyed. Then, according to the abovementioned *Kitab-i Anusi*, the *Shaykh al-Islam* of Isfahan, Baha al-Din al-'Amili, better known as Shaykh Baha'i (d. 1030/1621), sought to dissuade the Shah from taking further actions against them and to target the Zoroastrians instead. But Shaykh Baha'i's efforts were unsuccessful and as many as seventy five Jews were then pressured into converting after others were fed to wild hounds.[10] In any case, what these examples show is that political motivations at a local level played a bigger role in these campaigns than any centralized policy, as the mechanisms of state coercion depended heavily on local administrators.

In the mid-1650s there were more cases of conversion within the Jewish community in places like Isfahan, Kashan, and Hamadan, mainly through the means of financial incentives.[11] The Grand Vizier of the time, Muhammad Beg (r. 1064-1071/1654-1661), has been credited with being at the forefront of many repressive policies, offering these communities only the options of conversion, exile to troubled regions of the country, or martyrdom.[12] Further, Ezra Spicehandler has identified another passage in which the Prime Minister (the *I'timad al-dawla*) declared his intention to expel the Jews from Isfahan and to relocate them to the Zoroastrian quarter of Gabrabad, in order to incite the Zoroastrian community against them.[13]

According to a missionary source, during the late 1650s the French Jesuit missionary Aimé Chézaud (d. 1664), who engaged in heated theological debates with the *ulama* and who praised the Iranians for their openness to discuss doctrinal matters, once debated an apostate rabbi.[14] Chézaud was also told by the *I'timad al-dawla* that some high dignitaries at the court considered subjecting Armenians to the same coercive treatment of force conversion to which the Jews had already been subjected, thus confirming the overall lower standing of the latter.[15] Yet, many among the *'ulama'* disapproved of this: both the *sadr* of the time and the famous theologian Muhsin Fayz-i Kashani (d. 1090-1/ 1680-1) opposed conversions and persecutions as being contrary to the precepts of the *shari'a*.[16]

The last decades of the seventeenth century, corresponding to the reigns of Shah Sulayman (r. 1077-1105/1666-1694) and Shah Sultan Husayn (r. 1105-1135/1694-1722), were particularly difficult for non-Muslim minorities. Past scholarship had attributed this to the influence of Muhammad Baqir Majlisi (d. 1111/1699), who was credited for promoting oppressive measures against Armenians, Banyan Hindus, Jews, and Sunni Muslims.[17] However, Matthee has demonstrated how it was rater Shah Sulayman's chief musketeer Budaq Sultan and, ironically, his Sunni Grand Vizier Shaykh 'Ali Khan Zanganih (d. 1101/ 1691) who pushed for the application of these policies.[18] Majlisi did write a relatively well-known piece against Jews, the *Risala-yi sawa'iq al-Yahud* (*Lightning Bolts against the Jews*),[19] but it is questionable whether the production of this kind of literature can be causally linked to any policies of systematic repression on the ground.

In his travelogue, the French missionary Nicolas Sanson (d. after 1695) bears witness to what most likely became a rapidly spreading legend, namely that the Jews were responsible for conjuring a spell on Shah Safi II, who had to be enthroned a second time with the name of Shah Sulayman:

> "on dit que les Juifs ayant fait des sortileges sur sa personne, qui l'avoient reduit dans une langueur qui le conduisoit a la mort, Chiek Ali Kan son Etmadaulet ou premier Ministre qui les decouvrit, luy conseilla de changer son nom, esperant par ce moyen éluder l'effet de ces sortileges. [They say that the Jews had casted a spell which had thrown him [Shah Safi] into a state of lethargy which almost brought him to his death. Shaykh 'Ali Khan, his *I'timad al-dawla* or Prime Minister, who discovered them, advised him to change his name, hoping thus to elude the effects of the spell]".[20]

That Shah Sulayman had to be enthroned twice because of inauspicious signs is common knowledge in Safavid history. The claim that the Jews were held responsible for it is not. It is likely that Sanson heard such rumors circulating among the locals, although it is of course difficult to assess how widespread they were.

With the fall of Isfahan to the Afghan Hotakis, the state became contested between the Afghan faction supporting Mahmud Hutak (d. 1137/1725) and the claimant to the Safavid throne, Shah Tahmasp II (r. 1135–1145/1722–1732). During the brief period in which the Hotakis managed to establish a certain degree of control, it is unlikely that they counted on the mechanisms to enforce any substantial social policy. According to the Polish Jesuit missionary Tadeusz Jan Krusinski (d. 1756) and the French engineer and polymath Louis-André de La Mamie de Clairac (d. 1752), a hierarchical scheme was put in place in which the Afghans occupied the first rank, followed by Armenians, the Sunni Dergesons (Lezgians?), the Multani Hindus, the Zoroastrians, the Jews, and finally the Persians (presumably meaning exclusively Shiʻis).[21] It is of course hard to assess what this really meant and the extent to which any policies could be executed which could have taken this scheme into account. However, it is telling that the Jews would be placed at the second to last rank, just above the "Persians" who were of course, in the circumstances of the invasion of the Safavid Empire, the main target of vengeance.

The Kitab-i sar guzasht-i Kashan

With this background in mind, let us consider the testimony of the *Kitab-i sar guzasht-i Kashan*. The story the poem recounts takes place between the months leading to the fall of Isfahan to the Afghans in 1722 and the early campaigns of Nadir Shah. It narrates the fate of the Jewish community of Kashan, from their forced conversion to Islam to their negotiated attempt to reconvert to Judaism. As it happens with many regional sources, the events it narrates do not appear in any other chronicle or travelogue. Because of this and because of its rather disconnected narrative flow, it is not easy to weave all the episodes into a coherent historical narrative.

The poem opens with some formulaic verses in reference to the biblical forefathers going back to Abraham.[22] The first passage devoted to contemporary events tells the story of a group of Jews feasting and playing loud music unaware that it was the night of remembrance of the killing of Husayn in Karbala. Interpreting this as an act of subversion, a group of Muslims conspires to have one of them executed. Upon hearing about the incident, Shah Sultan Husayn considers executing more of them, but one of his advisors at the Divan suggests to levy instead a heavy fine on the community. Then, on the night of the Sabbath, the royal musketeers (*qurchis*) round up a group of Christian and Zoroastrian mercenaries and order them to break into the Synagogue while the Jews are praying. The mercenaries drag the Jews into the plaza and threaten to burn the entire community unless they accept to pay the fine.[23]

The question of the historicity of this passage, as that of any other event in the poem for that matter, could be open for debate. The trope of Jews being chastised for feasting during a holly occasion of the people ruling over them is not necessarily novel. This passage shares a certain degree of resemblance with the Talmudic episode in which the Emperor Trajan (d. 117) represses the Jews for lighting their candles for Hanukkah on the day of his daughter's passing: "In the days of the wicked Trajan his son was born on the 9th of Av and [the Jews] fasted. His daughter died in Hannukah and they lit candles. His wife sent and said to him: Instead of conquering the Barbarians, come conquer the Jews who have rebelled."[24] Drawing parallels between biblical (and/or Talmudic) history and contemporary or more recent events in Jewish history was a practice to which even European chroniclers subscribed at times. For example, references to the story of the repression of the Jews under the rule of Haman the Agagite, from the Book of Esther (Esther, 3), appear in at least two European sources of the late Safavid period. Jean Chardin (d. 1713) mentions it in passing as he presents an overview of the history of Persia:

> "There is scarce any country in the world which makes greater figure in histories, sacred or profane, ancient or modern, than this of which we are speaking. In the scriptures the deliverance of the Jews by Cyrus; the protection they received from his successors; the memorable preservation of the whole people from the dark and deep laid plot of Haman, all refer to this potent empire and its monarchs."[25]

Here, the reference is used only to pave the way for a historical overview of Iran. However, another source which recounts the mission of the Jesuit Alexandre de Rhodes (d. 1660) to Iran makes reference to the same passage in order to draw parallels with the repression of the Jews in the late seventeenth century:

> "The Jews had spread themselves all over Persia in far greater numbers than might be supposed, and were leading a most peaceable existence without any suspicion of the terrible misfortune which was hanging over their heads. It came as an unexpected blow and threw them into dreadful consternation when, all of a sudden, an edict from the King was issued and published in every place in Persia commanding them, on pain of death, to abjure the Jewish religion and profess, thenceforth, that of Muhammad.
> The terror and consternation recorded in Scripture (Esther iii and iv), which the ancestors of this most unhappy nation suffered long ago, when Haman, their cruel enemy, caused the fatal decree obtained from the King against them to be proclaimed throughout this same kingdom, may be taken as a picture of the fear and anguish experienced by these, their descendants, at the first news of this edict."[26]

Thus, although a commonplace to a certain extent and regardless of questions of historical authenticity, Babai d. Farhad's narrative strategy of presenting the story of the feasting Jews, which resonates with this Talmudic reference, is effective and grounded in literary and historiographical precedents. It is of course unlikely that the Babai was aware of the two abovementioned European sources. However, the fact that the same kind of literary strategy can be found in works of such different nature and by authors of so dissimilar backgrounds and writing in different languages shows how widespread the practice of establishing these kinds of parallels was. These scriptural hints serve a double function: on the one hand they erase temporal barriers, bringing together ancient and contemporary –and by extension sacred and profane– time and space. And on the other hand, they allow the author to present contemporary events within a framework of causality which gives the story an equivocally fatalistic bent: on the one hand, the Jews were destined to feast during the remembrance of Husayn in the same way that they had inadvertently feasted during the death of the daughter of Trajan; but at the same time they did perform the act willingly. More importantly, whether by fate or free will, and despite the high price they have to pay for it, these unfortunate transgressions prevent the Jews from honoring a gentile festivity. Therefore, Jews end up abiding by their religious custom albeit unwillingly, and the sacrifice they have to pay for it becomes a necessary tradeoff whereby the Law of God is respected even at the expense of the community's safety.

Up to this point the situation portrayed in the story fits the commonly held image of the late Safavid period as one in which scapegoating of religious minorities and Jews in particular was common currency. However, throughout the following episodes the flow of the story becomes more complex, as the community becomes trapped within the conflict between the Afghan invaders and the Safavid claimants. The bulk of the narrative shifts to the story of the community leader or *nasi*, Nasi David, and of the mass conversion of the Jews of Kashan following the conquest of the Empire by Mahmud Hutak and his successor Ashraf (d. 1142/1730). Nasi David is summoned by the warring contender Tahmasp Quli Khan – who, as is well known, would later be enthroned as Nadir Shah – to communicate him about the new taxes to be levied on the Jews. At the same time, the opposing faction had just enthroned Ashraf, who made a brief stop in Kashan on his way to Mazandaran to fight the Qizilbash, the claimants to the succession of the Safavid dynasty backed by Tahmasp Quli Khan. In what seems as a strategy to impose fear and collect revenue to fund his campaign, the latter makes an incursion in Kashan. At his arrival, the servants greet him and entice him to force the Jews to convert:

"*Kih duzakh-and hamih jumi' -yi Yahudan/ hamin lahzih bayad gardan Musulman/ agar nah jumlih ra ma qatl arim/ yaki ra dar vilayat va nadarim* [All Jews are inhabitants from hell: they must become Muslims at once. If not, we will kill everyone. We will not leave one Jew alive in the province!]".²⁷

Tahmasp Quli Khan then decides to levy a heavy poll tax (*jizya*) on the Jews. In reaction, a small group of them goes in search of Ashraf, hoping that he will defeat Tahmasp Quli Khan and offer them protection. As this plan fails and as the defeat of Ashraf becomes inevitable, the narrative voice laments the outcome by blaming it on the Jews' own sins: "*zi aʿun kari-yi ma inha nah burdan/ agar nah tars-i ishan buvad chinin-i ma* [But Because of our sinfulness, these [the Afghans] did not win; otherwise we would not have feared them [Tahmasp Khan and his troops] so much]".²⁸ Since the new *jizya* imposed by Tahmasp Quli Khan is too burdensome for them, one of the Jewish local administrators (*kadkhudas*), Benyamin Shakshul, offers to convert to avoid paying the *jizya*: "*Biya zahir kunam man shahada ra/ bi-guftar-i Musa din-i Muhammad ra* [I shall reveal the *shahada* of Muhammad's religion in Moses's words!]". And Nasi David joins him, saying: "*Bi-gufta dast bidih bayʿat bi-sazim/ tamam-i ʿIbriyan ra sar farazim* [Give me your hand; let us swear allegiance [to the new faith], let us glorify all the Jews thereby]".²⁹

Having been relieved from the *jizya*, Nasi David summons the community to convince them of the benefits of adopting the religion of Muhammad. Some of them convert but many resist. Among the refusers are a man by the name of Abraham Yazdi and Mordechai, a rabbi from Kermanshah.³⁰ In refusing to convert, Abraham Yazdi argues that Muhammad had not required Jews to do so:

"*Yahudi nist rajuʿi kas ba man/ va gar jabr-ast kunam jala-yi vatan/ tu aknun mi kuni ma ra Musalman/ chih bad kard-ast tu-ra Musa-yi ʿImran/ va payghambar ham nah farmudih-hast an/ zi shakhshanih kuni kasi ra Musalman* [My Jewishness does not depend on anyone; if there is oppression, I will emigrate from the country. You are converting us to Islam now; what did Moses, son of ʿImran, ever do to you? The Prophet [Muhammad] did not command anyone to be converted from Moses' branch]".³¹

As the conversions and the division of the community persist, the narrative voice – that is, allegedly, Babai b. Farhad's– expresses the intention of writing a letter to the Safavid claimant Tahmasp II, asking him to allow the Jews to "reconvert" to their original religion:

Umid darim kih Shah Tahmas biyayad/ dar fathi bi-ru-yi ma gushayad/ Khudaya bar dilish andaz in ra/ biguyad jumlih bashad bar din-i Musa/ ravad Babai ham bar din-i khud baz/ kunad az nau digar avaz-u-parvaz [We hope that Shah Tahmasp will come and open the gates of victory for us. O God, cast this [thought] into his heart that he may say: "Let them all belong to the religion of Moses" Then, once again Babai will return to his own faith and swiftly make a new beginning for himself.]"[32]

The idea of petitioning the Shah to reconvert is one of the most historically valuable testimonies of the story. On the one hand, it implicitly suggests that the status of the community under the Safavids was not that of an unequivocally oppressed group, but rather that the Jews had enjoyed a certain degree of leverage and bargaining power that made their earlier condition more bearable than that of this later stage. Another point that is of particular interest, although difficult to investigate further, is whether such a practice had any precedents, and if so, on what terms such petition could have been expressed. According to the missionary Nicolas Sanson, during the last decades of the empire, tribunals allowed Armenians renegades to reconvert to Christianity:

"Le Sadre dans ce Tribunal permet aux Renegats de retourner au Christianisme. Ils luy remontrent dans une Requeste qu'ils ne peuvent pas accomplir la loy de Mahomet; qu'ils ne peuvent pas s'accoutumer à toutes les Purifications et les Pieres qu'elle ordonne [...] Le Sadre ayant lû leur Requeste, la leur rejette au nez, son Secratire la ramasse et écrit au bas qu'ils font Mortettes, c'est a dire Immondes, lâches, indignes de professer une Religion aussi sainte que celle de Mahomet. On les remet au Tribut, et ils retournent librement dans leurs Eglises. [The *sadr* of this tribunal allows the renegades to return to Christianity. They tell him in a petition that they are not able to comply with Muhammad's law, that they cannot get used to all the purifications and prayers it prescribes. [...] After reading their petition, the *sadr* throws it back at their noses, his secretary picks it up and writes at the bottom of it that they have become *murtads*, that is, repugnant, recreant, and unworthy of professing a religion as holy as that of Muhammad. The tribute [*jizya*] is once again levied on them and they return to their churches freely]."[33]

As this passage suggests, while these apostates were identified with the technical legal term of *murtad*, which in theory should have led to the death penalty, tribunals turned a blind eye on the matter and accepted their *jizya* as a reasonable settlement.

In the case of the petition of the Jews of Kashan, it is impossible to know whether it appealed to legal concepts of the *shari'a*. To judge from the words attributed to Abraham Yazdi and reproduced by Babai, it would seem as though the argument of the invalidity of conversions by force could have been brought forward. The words of Yazdi reveal an awareness of the Qur'anic principle of "there is no compulsion in religion [*la ikraha fi-l-din*]" [2:256]. To my knowledge, there is no documentary evidence to verify whether this letter was indeed ever drafted. In any case, this indirect allusion to a Qur'anic principle reveals a degree of awareness by the Jewish subjects – or at least a highly literate elite among them– of the scriptural principles of the people ruling over them. And once again, as with the subtle Talmudic reference earlier, this indirect hint to the Qur'an infuses the text with sacred undertones, although in this case appealing to the religious laws of the majority (and ruling) population.

After writing the letter, Babai approaches various members of the community in search of accomplices, trying to inquire how many among them had honestly converted in their hearts. He is faced with hostility and is advised to discuss the matter with Nasi David.[34] The latter reacts with anger at the idea of requesting permission to reconvert:

> "*Bi-gufta harf hast bi-kifayat/ shuma ra kardih-am bisiyar himayat/ riza-yi dil hamih amaditan / hamih jumlih shahadih guftihitan/ bi-khatar mirasiditan aknun Yahudi/ zi-kardar-i shuma ra nist sudi* [these are incompetent words I have protected you often. You have attained the wish of your hearts; you have all recited the shahada together. Now you have put it into your minds that you are Jews [again]; you will reap no benefit from God!]."[35]

After the affair is discussed, the renegades agree to greet Shah Tahmasp II, who was scheduled to pass through Kashan, with pages of the Qur'an while those who remained faithful greet him with Torah scrolls.[36] While perhaps less clear in this example, this image could also be said to resonate with what, by then, would have been considered sacred history: this brandishing of the scriptures to serve almost as an arbiter in a political (and military) affair evokes the image of the Battle of Siffin (37/657), in which the partisans of 'Ali and Mu'awiyya put Qur'an pages in their swords as a sign of accepting God as the final arbiter.[37] As for the portrayal of the campaigns of Shah Tahmasp II, it coincides with the picture given in other sources from the period: not only did Shah Tahmasp II benefit from a sizeable mercenary component during his campaign, but he also relied heavily on revenue extracted from Armenians and Jews. According to Krusinski, the campaign was "furnish'd by the Armenians of Julpha and particularly the Jews, with sums of money sufficient to enable him to recover the places dismember'd from his monarchy."[38]

After the defeat of Ashraf by the troops of Tahmasp Khan, a *kadkhuda* of Kashan by the name of Mir Abu'l Qasim embarks on a mission to Isfahan in the company of Nasi David, who had barely escaped a plot against him while he was on his way back from Fin Garden. Nasi David asks Mir Abu'l Qasim to intercede for his community before the Shah. He explains to him that most of the people in his community prefer to be Jews even if he himself remained committed to Islam.[39] The *mir* intercedes for them before the Divan, and does so in a way that portrays them as stubborn and as incapable of redemption, yet worthy of tolerance. A *qurchi* at the service of Tahmasp Quli Khan agrees to allow them to practice their faith in exchange of taxes. The *mir* then manages to negotiate a smaller amount of taxes in a plight for leniency, in consideration for the financial burden that the community had endured shortly before conversion.[40] A period of relative tolerance the follows. The tone of the poem, however, continues in a state of lamentation in which the calamities of the community are blamed on them for selling out of their faith:

> "*Digar az baskih dashtand Kashiyan ʿaunut / buvad hizar battar az ʿIbrut/ agar dilishan aba ham rast budi/ kiy in maṣibat-ha bi-ma ru namudi/ digar mi kardan ishan pusht bi-Turah/ nakard hich kafir u digar nasara* [The Kashanis had many sins; but their state was made a thousand times worse through transgressions [against God]. If their hearts have been right with one another would such calamities have befallen us? They turned their backs on the Torah in a manner not done even by infidels or Christians!]"[41]

The story then makes a time leap in which we are told that Shah Tahmasp II has been successfully enthroned, and that Abraham Yazdi has become the *nasi* of the community, a post he had already held before the appointment of Nasi David. David had replaced Abraham Yazdi because the latter, in his quest to remain firm in his religiosity and in his commitment to justice, had refused to pay the *jizya*, a defiance which had brought about hardship to the community. During his tenure, Nasi David had sought to appease the Muslim rulers by banning weddings and circumcision ceremonies. But as these measures did nothing to improve the situation of the Jews, Abraham Yazdi was restored to his position. As synagogues reopen and a period of relative stability follows, the narrative voice celebrates the newly regained freedom of worship:

> "*Ismishan Musalman bud ay Khudavand/ haman mi namudim ba khvish payvand/ nazar-i haqq bud kih ma dar din-i khud raftim/ vazar dadim va din ra baz kharidim/ Khudaya qawti dah bayishan dadahand zar ra/ bi-khushhali gushayand bal-u-par ra* [O God, we were called Muslims, but we stuck together. It was God's view that we could return to our religion. O God, grant strength to those who gave money; may they spread their wigs in joy!]".[42]

However, the period of calm does not last and the Jews experience increased harassment at the bazaar. In despair, members of the community reach out to Hadi, a respected man in the town known for taking care of the needy. Hadi requests a scribe and sets up to create a register. He assures the Jews that those who are not Muslim should not be afraid to register as Jews or even as Zoroastrians. Some, however, saw this with suspicion, which the narrative voice expresses thus:

> "*Khuda danad chih ayad bar sar-i ma/ khushand ya battar shavad in mihnat-i ma/ hich kudam nistand Goyim mutlaq/ va mi ravand pish kuli-yi kulih mihlaq/ chih payda shavad chih farqih tu-yi ma/ nisfih 'Ibri nisfih Goyim nisfih Mulla* [May God make all this end well, for Tahmasp Khan understands that we reneged the religion [of Islam]. If he comes, he will order everyone hanged without investigating whether he is Jew or Muslim]."[43]

And as suspected, the register is used as a pretext to target Jews, who are reprimanded for observing their own religious regulations on slaughter and for respecting the Sabbath:

> "*Yaki dar babat-i gusht shakhitih / giriftan bihanih kih karditan dukiya / va chira shanbih nakardihitan kar/ nami kunid dad u nah su-ui bazar* [One Jew was accused of declaring clean that which was forbidden in matters of slaughtering. Others were told: Why don't you work on Saturdays, why don't you do business or go to the bazaar?]" [...] "*nakhurdih-i panir ba gusht u kababi* [you did not eat kebab with cheese and meat]."[44]

As a result of these pressures, many Jews convert, leading to the downfall of Abraham Yazdi as *nasi* and to the restauration of Nasi David.[45]

The last passages of the story shift the narrative towards the fate of Jewish communities in other locations. Towards the end of the story, rumors about the "peaceful" conversion of these Kashani Jews (that is, through *nasi* David's acceptance of the *jizya*) find their way into Gulpaygan, where a fire had just killed thousands of people. Upon hearing this, the Jews of Gulpaygan celebrate a "minor Yom Kippur":

> "*Chih in harf ra shinidand an jama'at/ dar dast-i khwish bar dashtand bar shifa'at/ digar chand ruz bi-kardan Kipur Qatan/ buzurg u kuchik u mulla u khatan/ digar tuflan ra ham ruzih kardand/ va bivih zanan ham bisiyar giriyih kardand* [When that community [of Gulpaygan] heard these words, they raised their arms in intercession. They proclaimed a minor Yom Kippur for a few days, young and old, *mulla* as well as bridegroom. They even made the children fast while widowed women cried profusely.]"[46]

The poem closes telling the tragic fate of more *nasis* who were killed or had to pay heavy fines for refusing to convert.[47]

Historical Agency and the Jewish Community

As we can see, while the *Kitab-i sar guzasht-i Kashan* indeed portrays the circumstances of the Jewish community of Kashan (and beyond) as dire, it also adds complexity to the picture through one characteristic that almost no major Persian or European source can offer, namely, the recognition of agency of Jewish actors: first, Nasi David decides –albeit under difficult circumstances – to convert his community to save it from economic bankruptcy; second, the author of the source has the initiative to appeal to the authorities against the forced conversion; and third, Nasi David has the possibility to negotiate with the *mirs* to intercede for them at Divan. So although there is a fatalistic overtone in the narrative and although the final fate of the community is tragic, the Jewish characters of the story are not portrayed as passive (nor helpless) agents. Further, the unfortunate fate of the community is partly blamed –rhetorically at least–on Nasi David's weakness in accepting the conversion of his people, and thus the subsequent events are seen as a divine punishment. In a way, it would seem as though it is the non-Jewish actors that lack agency, becoming archetypical characters whose sole function is to execute such punishment or to fulfill the fate of the Jews. At the same time, the narrative also provides enough details on the background to the conflict to show that the *nasi* was trying to defend his people by converting them, because he knew (and would eventually be proven right) that they were not in the condition to pay a higher *jizya*. By revealing the intricacies of the relation between religious and socioeconomic matters, this source also serves as a window into the complexity of the relations between local administrators and the power dynamics involving influential members of marginal groups.

The time-period of the story also shows the role that dynastic changes played in the scapegoating of the community. Further, the passage on the petition to reconvert suggests that the application of *shariʿa* principles regarding conversions and apostasy were at times less important than were practical considerations regarding local administration and revenue extraction, thus countering any simplistic portrayals whereby the application of legal principles would have been inflexible. The Safavid archive is of course limited in this regard, given the lack of court records equivalent to its Ottoman counterpart. In this sense, perhaps the most important historiographical aspect of Babai's testimony is precisely the fact that it offers details on the inner workings of local administrations and their conflicts and negotiations with communal leaders. In so doing it recovers not only the voices, but also the sense of historical agency of a community which, although marginalized, was able to negotiate its status and adapt to the changing political landscape of the time. The conventions of the epic genre, with its evocation of biblical stories and with its fatalistic tone, however, endow the story with a certain degree of ambiguity, whereby the agency of the historical actors seems constrained by divine predestination. Yet, in the logic of the narrative, the notion of divinely guided fate applies to the realm of human history as a whole. While the historical actors of the story are portrayed more as plot devices than as complex characters, within this seemingly constrained framework of human history, they are nonetheless represented as willful, non-passive actors. Therefore, in the internal logic of the story there is no contradiction between the inevitability of fate and the supreme agency of the divine, and the possibility of historical agency within the constraints of the temporal (read: historical) human experience.

Further research on social history of this period should focus more on the local histories we have at hand, which share some characteristics with Babai's source. Only then are we likely to have a clearer picture of communal power dynamics in Safavid Iran and on the effects of the weakening of the state during the subsequent interregnum.

Bibliography

Primary Sources

Chardin, Jean. *The Travels of Sir John Chardin, by the Way of the Black Sea, through the Countries of Circassia, Mingrelia, the Country of the Abcas, Georgia, Armenia, and Media, into Persia Proper*, edited by John Pinkerton. London: Printed for Longman, Hurst, Rees, Orme, Cadell and Davies, 1808-14.

Clairac, Louis-André de La Mamie. *Histoire de Perse depuis le commencement de ce siècle.* Vol. 3. Paris: C.-A. Jombert, Librarie du Roi pour l'Artillerie & le Gènie, 1750.

Krusinski, Tadeusz Jan. *The history of the late revolutions of Persia: taken from the memoirs of Father Krusinski, Procurator of the Jesuits at Ispahan*. Vol 2. London: J. Pemberton, 1733.

Majlisi, Muhammad Baqir. "Risala-yi Ṣawaʿiq al-Yahud [The Treatise Lightning Bolts against the Jews] by Muhammad Baqir b. Muhammad Taqi al-Majlisi (D. 1699)", translated by Vera B. Moreen. *Die Welt des Islams*. New Series 32, no. 2 (1992): 177-195.

Moreen, Vera B. (ed.). *Iranian Jewry during the Afghan Invasion: the Kitab-i sar Guzasht-i Kashan of Babai b. Farhad*, Stuttgart: F. Steiner, 1990.

Sanson, Nicolas. *Voyage ou Relation de l'état présent du royaume de Perse. Avec une dissertation curieuse sur les moeurs, religion & gouvernement de cet Etat*. Paris: Chez la veuve Mabre Cramoisi, 1695.

Wilson, Sir Arnold T. (editor and translator). "History of the Mission of the Fathers of the Society of Jesus, Established in Persia by the Reverend Father Alexander of Rhodes." (Translation of "Relation de la mission des pères de la compagnie de Iesus. Etablie dans le Royaume de Perse par le R. P. Alexandre de Rhodes", complied by Jacques de Machaud). *Bulletin of the School of Oriental and African Studies* 3 (1925): 675-706.

Secondary Sources

Amanat, Mehrdad. *Jewish Identities in Iran: Resistance and Conversion to Islam and the Baha'i Faith*. New York; London: I.B. Tauris, 2011.

Herzig. Edmund. "The Deportation of the Armenians in 1604-1605 and Europe's Myth of Shah 'Abbas I." In *Pembroke Papers 1*, edited by Charles Melvile, 59-71. Cambridge: Cambridge University Press, 1990.

Lecker, M. (1997). "Ṣiffīn". *The Encyclopaedia of Islam, New Edition*, ed. by Bosworth, C. E.; van Donzel, E.; Heinrichs, W. P. & Lecomte, G., Volume IX: San–Sze. Leiden: E. J. Brill. pp. 552–556.

Matthee, Rudi. "Merchants in Safavid Iran: Participants and Perceptions." *Journal of Early Modern History* 3-4 (1999-2000): 233-68.

Matthee, Rudi, *Persia in Crisis: Safavid Decline and the Fall of Isfahan*. London; New York: I.B. Tauris, 2012.

Matthee, Rudi. "The Career of Mohammad Beg, Grand Vizier of Shah 'Abbas II (r. 1642-1666)." *Iranian Studies* 24, No. 1(1991): 17-36.

Matthee, Rudi, *The Politics of Trade in Safavid Iran: Silk for Silver, 1600-1730*. Cambridge; New York: Cambridge University Press, 1999.

Moreen, Vera. *Iran's Jewry's Hour of Peril and Heroism: A Study of Babai ibn Lutf's Chronicle, 1617-1662*. New York: American Academy of Jewish Research, 1987.

Moreen, Vera. "The Problems of Conversion among Iranian Jews in the Seventeenth and Eighteenth Centuries." *Iranian Studies* 19, no. ¾ (summer-autumn, 1986): 215-28.

Moreen, Vera. "The Status of Religious Minorities in Safavid Iran 1617-61." *Journal of Near Eastern Studies* 40, no. 2 (April, 1981): 119-34.

Newman, Andrew J. *Safavid Iran: Rebirth of a Persian Empire*. London; New York: I.B. Tauris, 2009.

Spicehandler, Ezra. "The Persecution of the Jews of Isfahan under Shah 'Abbas II (162-1666)." *Hebrew Union College Annual* 46 (1975): 331-56.

Tiburcio, Alberto. *Muslim-Christian Polemics in Safavid Iran*. Edinburgh Historical Studies of Iran and the Persian World, 2. Edinburgh: Edinburgh University Press, 2020.

Notes

1   Vera B. Moreen, *Iranian Jewry's Hour of Peril and Heroism: a Study of Babai ibn Lutf's Chronicle (1617-1662)* (New York; Jerusalem: American Academy for Jewish Research, 1987), 34-37.

2   Vera B. Moreen, *Iranian Jewry during the Afghan Invasion: the Kitab-i sar Guzasht-i Kashan of Babai b. Farhad* (Stuttgart: F. Steiner, 1990), 30.

3   Vera B. Moreen, "The Status of Religious Minorities in Safavid Iran 1617-61," *Journal of Near Eastern Studies* 40, no. 2 (April, 1981): 124.

4   Edmund Herzig, "The Deportation of the Armenians in 1604-1605 and Europe's Myth of Shah 'Abbas I," in Pembroke Papers 1, edited by Charles Melville (Cambridge: Cambridge University Press, 1990), 64.

5   Mehrdad Amanat, *Jewish Identities in Iran: Resistance and Conversion to Islam and the Baha'i Faith* (New York & London: I.B. Tauris, 2011), 39-40; Matthee, Rudi, "Merchants in Safavid Iran: Participants and Perceptions," *Journal of Early Modern History* 3-4 (1999-2000): 233-68.

6   Francis Richard, "Le Père Aimé Chézaud, controversiste et ses manuscrits persans." *Nameh-ye Baharestan: International Iranian Journal for Research into Islamic Manuscripts.* VI-VII, no. 11-12 (Spring-Winter 2005-2006): 15-17.

7   Moreen, "The Status of Religious Minorities," 124; Amanat, 40.

8   Amanat, 40.

9   Ibid., 40-2.

10   Ibid.; Moreen, *Iran's Jewry's Hour of Peril and Heroism*, 90-92.

11   Amanat, 42.

12   Vera B. Moreen, "The Problems of Conversion among Iranian Jews in the Seventeenth and Eighteenth Centuries," *Iranian Studies*, vol. 19, no. ¾ (summer-autumn, 1986): 217.

13   Ezra Spicehandler, "The Persecution of the Jews of Isfahan under Shah 'Abbas II (162-1666)," *Hebrew Union College Annual* 46 (1975): 337

14   Sir Arnold T. Wilson (editor and translator). "History of the Mission of the Fathers of the Society of Jesus, Established in Persia by the Reverend Father Alexander of Rhodes."(Translation of "Relation de la mission des pères de la compagnie de Iesus. Etablie dans le Royaume de Perse par le R. P. Alexandre de Rhodes", complied by Jacques de Machaud). *Bulletin of the School of Oriental and African Studies* 3 (1925): 690. See also Alberto Tiburcio, *Muslim-Christian Polemics in Safavid Iran* (Edinburgh: Edinburgh University Press): 47.

15   Ibid, 694-5.

16   Amanat, 43.

17   Rudi Matthee, *Persia in Crisis: Safavid Decline and the Fall of Isfahan* (London; New York: I.B. Tauris, 2012): 192-193. See also Tiburcio, 14-15.

18   Ibid.

19   Muhammad Baqir Majlisi, "Risala-yi Ṣawaʿiq al-Yahud [The Treatise Lightning Bolts against the Jews] by Muhammad Baqir b. Muhammad Taqi al-Majlisi (D. 1699)", translated by Vera B. Moreen, *Die Welt des Islams* New Series 32, no. 2 (1992): 177-195.

20   Nicolas Sanson, *Voyage ou Relation de l'état présent du royaume de Perse. Avec une dissertation curieuse sur les moeurs, religion & gouvernement de cet Etat.* (Paris: Chez la veuve Mabre Cramoisi, 1695): 7.

21   Tadeusz Jan Krusinski, *The history of the late revolutions of Persia: taken from the memoirs of Father Krusinski, Procurator of the Jesuits at Ispahan* (London: J. Pemberton, 1733), vol. 2: 197-198; Louis-André de La Mamie de Clairac, *Histoire de Perse depuis le commencement de ce siècle* (Paris: C.-A. Jombert, Librarie du Roi pour l'Artillerie & le Gènie, 1750), vol. 3: 5

22   Babai b. Farhad, *Kitab-i zar Guzasht-i Kashan*, in *Iranian Jewry during the Afghan Invasion*, 123-128 [Persian text] /19-26 [Morren's translation] [hereon, I will provide the page number of the Persian edited text first and of Moreen's translation next. Since hers is the standard and authoritative translation of this source, I will use it for the quotes].

23   Ibid, 27-29.

24   Talmud Yerushalmi, *Sukkah* 5:1, 55b (I would like to thank Prof. Tal Ilan for providing me with her translation of this passage).

25   Jean Chardin, *The Travels of Sir John Chardin, by the Way of the Black Sea, through the Countries of Circassia, Mingrelia, the Country of the Abcas, Georgia, Armenia, and Media, into Persia Proper,* edited by John Pinkerton (London: Printed for Longman, Hurst, Rees, Orme, Cadell and Davies 1808-14): 169

26   Wilson, 695

27   Baba'i b. Farhad, 134 / 34.

28 Ibid, 134/ 35
29 Ibid, 135/ 36/
30 Ibid, 137/ 39-40
31 Ibid, 137/ 39
32 Ibid, 138/ 40
33 Sanson, 200-201
34 Babai b. Farhad, 138-139/41
35 Ibid, 139/42
36 Ibid
37 For an overview of the battle, see Michael Lecker, "Ṣiffīn," *The Encyclopaedia of Islam, New Edition*, ed. by Bosworth, C. E.; van Donzel, E.; Heinrichs, W. P. & Lecomte, G., Volume IX: San–Sze. (Leiden: E. J. Brill): 552–556.
38 Krusinski, vol. 2: 210-211
39 Babai b. Farhad, 144-145/49-50
40 Ibid, 146/ 51-52
41 Ibid, 151/58
42 Ibid, 154/ 61
43 Ibid, 156/64
44 Ibid, 156/65
45 Ibid, 157-158/66-67
46 Ibid, 163/ 73-74
47 Ibid, 163-164/73-74

3

The Qizilbash in Anatolia after the 1630s: Sidelined and Estranged

Selim Güngörürler

Iran before the sixteenth century could be deemed a stronghold of Sunnism. This changed only when the Safavids championing the Qizilbash rite, which is not a version of Shiism but an independent belief, took over the country in the sixteenth century. Iran thus went through two separate conversions in the Early Modern Period.[1] This essay looks into the effects that the later Shiitization in Iran had on the Qizilbash in Ottoman Anatolia, the kinsmen of whom had conquered Iran for the Safavids and set themselves up as the military nobility of the land.

The Shiitization, which became entrenched in the Safavid establishment from the early seventeenth century onwards, paved the first stone towards the isolation of the Ottoman-subject Qizilbash, who had remained in Anatolia awaiting its conquest by their grandmaster-king, that is the Safavid shah. The Ottoman Empire, however, made its grip on Anatolia steadier and widened its borders eastwards at the expense the Safavids with almost each war fought between the two sides. Throughout the seventeenth century, the Anatolian Qizilbash and their brethren holding sway over Iran began to grow away from one another, without discerning that the split between them was becoming unbridgeable. Their unerring leader – the Safavid shah – who in Qizilbashism was a kind of embodiment of God, deemed himself no longer so, in line with Shiism, and was now punishing those who worshipped him. Those Qizilbash clans which had settled down in Iran were subjected to a stepwise Shiitization, and though keeping the name, they ended up being more of a chivalric order and co-ruling class rather than the original religious order organized into a military-political nobility. The Ottoman-subject brethren in Anatolia, on the other hand, stuck to the genuine Qizilbash belief.

Once the Safavid grandmaster-shah stripped himself of his godly attribution and started reigning as a worldly king, the Qizilbash in Anatolia, who remained true to their self-perceived messiah, were indeed left without a leader who would act as

83

their flagbearer. These Safavid followers in Anatolia, like the Ottoman authorities, must not have been aware of the transformation in Iran during the early seventeenth century, that is the Shiite crackdown on the Qizilbash belief. This unawareness likely lasted longer for the Qizilbash in Anatolia than it did for the Ottoman State. The former would not fully learn of the conversion of their godly leader and brethren in Iran to Shiism until well into the eighteenth century, as to be shown below. Aside from how far they may have been aware of this transformation at the start, upon learning of it they must have lost their outlook for the ultimate triumph of their God-chosen fellowship. The Qizilbash in Anatolia had earlier been entangled in clashes with the Ottoman State not as an ignored community but as a principal actor, as an adversary holding the central stage side by side with neighbouring kinsmen who had conquered Iran and set up their kingdom there.[2] As long as the Ottoman-Safavid political and military strife had been going on with the Safavid shah as the godly leader of genuine Qizilbashism, the Anatolian brethren were anything but marginalized. Later, however, the picture changed dramatically as their victorious fellows in Iran began to become Shiitized. The Qizilbash's former persecution by the Ottoman State on the one hand, and their abiding ideological as well as material troth to Safavid Iran on the other, had been keeping them central on the west Asian scene, whereas these later shifts led to their forsakenness and estrangement both in Anatolia and with regard to Iran.

After the peace of Zuhab in 1639, the Ottoman state came to see the Safavid establishment as Muslim, which must have been the outcome of an Ottoman acknowledgement that the Safavids were now Shiites and no longer the Qizilbash-believers of the earlier century. Beginning with the Ottoman diplomacy's in-passing references to the Muslimness of Safavid shahs in the 1640s, this phenomenon would reach its peak in the 1690s as the two sides officially uttered that they were co-religionists, brothers, praying for one another, shareholders in divine remuneration, and figurative addresses of God's verses in Quran.[3] This shift left its mark in many written genres. Firstly, the Ottomans' output of polemical treatises against the Safavids seemingly stopped. Secondly, the occasional exchange of letters between the two states' leading clergymen, the samples of which had functioned as accusatory manifestos and been included in Ottoman-Safavid diplomatic correspondence, discontinued. The archival, manuscript, and published collections of the post-1639 Ottoman-Safavid correspondence do not show any letter exchange between the Ottoman and the Safavid clergymen as part of diplomatic business. This contrasts with the Ottoman-Safavid relations before 1639 and the Iranian-Ottoman dealings after 1722.[4] Thirdly, the Sunni fatwas declaring the Safavids unbelievers on the grounds of genuine Qizilbashism were no longer issued, or, at least, the imperial court's pinpoint questions that were asked to get the answer of excommunication, came to a halt. All in all, this phenomenon cannot be explained with anything other than an Ottoman acknowledgement of the Safavids' Muslimness, that is Shiism and non-Qizilbashism. Yet this religious rapprochement was a political initiative by the Ottoman imperial court and bureaucracy; there is no token that Sunni clergymen partook in this process.

The definitive peace between the Ottoman Empire and Safavid Iran, which started with the protocol of Zuhab in 1639 and lasted with no break until the downfall of the Safavid kingdom in 1722, brought forth a favourable setting for the gap between the Qizilbash in Anatolia and their brethren in Iran to grow, and for the Ottoman authorities to unsee the Qizilbash element among its subjects. The political dimension of the Qizilbash issue was no longer a subject of the dealings between the two states. Although this disappearance from the central stage was not a goal of the long peace between the states, it was the natural outcome thereof.[5]

Seventeen years of stepwise normalization in relations followed the signing of the protocol of Zuhab. This timespan witnessed phenomena akin to those of former periods of truce: non-hostility without rapprochement, non-aggression without cooperation, coexistence without harmony. But now, for the first time in Ottoman-Safavid dealings, peace outlived the fragile post-pacification stage. It gradually became steady and even brought about a tangible rapprochement. The ensuing setting led to the two sides' having an inward caution but outward harmony with one another until the 1680s – a remarkable success with an eye to their history of strife. A diplomatic revolution then sealed this unprecedented achievement. Though the process was triggered by outside factors stemming from third parties, the Ottomans and the Safavids enjoyed almost twenty years of official brotherhood and alliance at the turn of the century. Although these achievements were partly undone in the next twenty years leading up to the Safavid' downfall in 1722,[6] they left a lasting mark on the relations between the Empire and the successive polities in Iran.

If war had restarted soon after the truce, or if relations had remained at this rudimentary level of non-aggression, the isolation of the Qizilbash in Anatolia could have likely not gathered speed and intensity. Because then the Ottomans would have kept on seeing them as a financial and paramilitary fifth column of the Safavids within the Empire, which in turn could have led to the adoption of certain measures with the outcome that the Qizilbash keep their sixteenth-century centrality to a certain extent, notwithstanding the loss of a portion of it owing to their split with Safavid Iran undergoing Shiitization. However, the estrangement and disregard of the Qizilbash, which had recently begun, found a fertile ground to take root, for the two sides went through a harmony of forty years. Owing to the consolidation of the Ottoman-Safavid peace, the twofold isolation of the Qizilbash in Anatolia overstepped the threshold of no return in the third quarter of the seventeenth century. The subsequent brotherhood and alliance of the 1690s between the Sunni Ottomans and the now-Shiite Safavids sealed the deal, insomuch that later setbacks in political relations and even new wars would not bring back the community in question to the central stage.

As an outcome of this process, the following phenomena arose in the 1640s and became established for good by the 1710s: firstly, the split between the Qizilbash in Anatolia and those in Iran deepened. Secondly, because the expectation of the Qizilbash Anatolia, that their godly grandmaster will fulfil the prophecy declared with İsmail Safavi's rise, was living on, superficial (but still covert) ties remained between the Qizilbash hearths in Ottoman Anatolia and their nominal grandmaster (Safavid kings of Iran) as well as the order's vicegeral organization headquartered in Ardabil – Azerbaijan. However, these ties were made hollow, because the old believers in Anatolia and the converted grandmaster as well as most of their brethren in Iran no longer shared the same set of beliefs. Later, as the House of Safi fell and eventually died out, these superficial ties must have further waned.

Thirdly, when the Ottoman state understood that its Qizilbash subjects no longer made up a fifth column in the Empire, because they had lost their military utility for the Safavids, persecutions came to a halt, harsh measures were seemingly called off, and the government stopped using the word *Qizilbash* to name the population in question.[7] Instead, the Ottomans conformed their use of this word to the Safavid practice in Iran, to designate the Safavid military, and not the religion that was living on in Anatolia as true to its sixteenth-century essence, or its Shiitized arm in Iran. In short, the religiously and ideologically forsaken Qizilbash in Anatolia no longer made up a political centre of gravity in the eyes of either state, and became cast aside in terms of identity. The shah no longer awaited of them an effective service against the Ottomans, and the imperial court, no longer deeming its genuine Qizilbash subjects a threat, turned a blind eye to their belief and identity.[8]

It is not unlikely that as part of the Ottoman state's *seyyidization* campaign in the seventeenth century, many Qizilbash patriarchs[9] were issued governmentally authenticated genealogies logging for them a descent from Prophet Muhammad's family.[10] The seventeenth century likewise witnessed the growth of a fondness between the Qizilbash in Anatolia and the Bektaşi order. This intimacy was internalized by the Qizilbash in Anatolia insomuch that after the Safavids died out and hence their order's headquarters disappeared in the mid-eighteenth century, their patriarchs would take up the Bektaşi headquarters at Hacıbektaş in central Anatolia and the lodge at Karbala in Iraq as uppermost authorities authenticating their family trees and jurisdiction over followers.[11] Association of the Qizilbash in Anatolia with existing and imperially sanctioned religious organizations must have paved the way for them to be stripped of their distinctive name in the eyes of the state, and to a certain degree to be neutralized, if not won over.

It is remarkable that in documents issued by the Safavid establishment to the Qizilbash in Anatolia or drafted by the Qizilbash in Anatolia themselves under a Shiitizing Safavid influence in the course of the later seventeenth century, we can see the traces of the abovesaid processes. A sample from the *commandment*[12] genre of Qizilbashism shows that by the middle of the seventeenth century, at the end of the initiation ceremony of an Ottoman-subject disciple from Anatolia, he was still to pledge troth to the House of Safi by counting the names of the whole line all the way from Sheikh Safi down to the reigning shah. Also, there in the devotional invocations to God were still words of prayer uttering the name of the reigning Safavid shah. Yet, some of these seventeenth-century *commandment*s strikingly indoctrinated the beliefs and practices of Twelver Shiism to the detriment of genuine Qizilbashism.[13] The Safavid establishment seemingly wanted to softly introduce its Ottoman-subject followers to Shiism. This indoctrination did not bear fruit, and must have estranged its addresses, contributing to the final split that was to come.

In 1658, dervish Majnun and dervish Mustafa of the [Qizilbash] order from Anatolia, who had formerly resettled from the Empire to Iran, were staying at the houses of royal privy physicians Mirza Muhammad Husayn and Mirza Muhammad Said with the agenda of "claiming [their] rights." Hearing about this, Abbas II visited the physicians' houses a few times to have fellowship with the dervishes. The shah likewise hosted the dervishes together with the outstanding cleric[14] *mavlana* Muhammad Muhsin Kaşi a few times at his own gatherings. In one of these gatherings, as the attendants were breaking fast together, Abbas II handwrote a Turkish decree addressed to Haji Manuçihr Xan, governor-general of Şirvan, and gave it dervish Mustafa. The royal handwrit commanded that the governor-general was to welcome Mustafa and his fellow with affection, and let them travel on, as they were going back to their own homeland over the Şirvan road.[15]

In 1678, a vicegerency-deed,[16] which most likely drawn up by the Safavid chief-vicegeral[17] office, promulgated by Shah Sulaiman himself, and issued to Sayyid Muhammad Tahir, the Sufi-vicegerent[18] of the Kavi community in the Akçadağ township in Ottoman eastern Anatolia, logs that the addressee had visited the Safavid court, most likely the order's headquarters in Ardabil. The grandmaster-shah indoctrinated, among other things, the five-time daily prayer, fasting in Ramadan, pilgrimage to Mecca, and abstaining from alcohol.[19] While the surviving contacts, visits, ties, and even documental appointments involving the Anatolian Qizilbash and the Safavid court might resemble the once-tight bonds between these two bodies, the indoctrination of canonical obligations and bans, in contrast with the Qizilbash belief which the Anatolian brethren abided by, shows the extent of the actual split between this arm and the one in Iran. The relationship between these two was living on in a shape empty of its former dimensions.

In 1711, an imposter claiming to be the Safavid prince Abbas (brother of Shah Sultan-Husayn) showed up in the Ottoman Empire with hopes of stirring up the imperial government to undertake an Iranian campaign. He failed to impress, however, and ended up in forced dwelling on an Aegean island. In 1715, he fled to the mainland and came back into sight in the middle Anatolian shire of Bozok to gather a following.

The claimant to the Safavid kingship in Iran and his 3,000-strong Ottoman-subject followers committed murders and started an uprising. But a loyalist militia crushed the movement before long.[20] This affair involving Ottoman subjects, who were in all likelihood Qizilbash, and an imposter Safavid prince in the 1710s is a telling example for the essential shift in the Ottoman state's policy towards overlooking the Qizilbash and not calling them by their distinctive name.

First of all, the imposter called his cause a "coming-out.[21]" As the imperial court saw it, "with regards to the majority of Bozok's dwellers raising of the banner of schism and unbelief, [namely] three-thousand accursed heretics, misbelief was obvious, however, the truth about their situation was hidden under the curtain of secrecy.[22]" Interestingly, the official chronicler even wrote down that trustworthy people from among the pro-state militia which crushed the uprising spoke of how the Imposter Abbas's "various sorcery-like tricks were observed, [and] that he led astray most of the people in that manner.[23]" Moreover, on the day of onslaught, it was told that the militia had suffered under a heavy storm of snow, rain, thunder, and lightning, while not a drop fell on the rebels. Reportedly, the rebel band of only 3,000 seemed to the pro-state militia as an endless sea of troops. Only after the rebels were crushed did their real number become known to the militia, whose suffering under the storm also came to a sudden end. This did not surprise the state chronicler, who remarked that the incident had happened owing to a conjunction of "such a malicious aberrant, and the shire of Bozok packed with unbelievers and heretics[24]."

From the information provided above, the following conclusions can be made. Firstly, the term *coming-out* straightforwardly calls forth the movement of Ismail Safavi as godly leader, and must have been chosen by the imposter prince so as to arouse those dynamics in Anatolia that had supported the Safavids against the Ottomans throughout the sixteenth century. Secondly, whereas the use of discriminatory words, such as *aberrant* and *accursed* against any non-state denomination was common practice in Early Modernity, especially the accusations of *unbelief* and *heresy* hint that the imperial government saw the rebels as genuine Qizilbash rather than as Twelver Shiite. The official chronicle remarkably refrains from naming them *Qizilbash* and logs the government's awareness that these were dissimulating their faith. Both attitudes afford a contrast with sixteenth century realities, when the Qizilbash in Anatolia had been central actors, had not dissimulated but proudly declared their belief even under state prosecution, and thereagainst, the state had simply called them *Qizilbash*. However, the later disregard by authorities cost them their distinctive name at the official level and shoved them towards dissimulation. The imposter Abbas's wonder-working deeds narrated from the battlefield must have been the repercussions of the propaganda of his superhuman grip stemming from his claimed godly essence. For those Qizilbash who had remained true to their sixteenth-century belief and still awaited the godly saviour in the person of the Safavid grandmaster-shah, such deeds, if they were believed to be real, made up sound evidence for the agent's being the awaited god-messiah (or, such a phenomenon could have been used as a justifying excuse to start a politically driven movement as well). Either way, it is remarkable that in an affair involving genuine Qizilbash beliefs, motifs, and followers, the state kept abnormally silent about the *Qizilbash*.

A look at the Ottoman use of *Qizilbash* in official and non-official chronicles in the 1640-1721 timespan also backs up the aforesaid. In 1647, the defeated insubordinates that fled from Baghdad to Iran are said to have "deserted to Qizilbash" and "gone to the country of the Shah."[25] In a report on the Uzbek dynastic war in 1648, the Safavid military involved is called the "Qizilbash troops."[26] In 1651, the Safavid military activity across the border at Azerbaijan and Iraq was remarked as the "movement of the Qizilbash."[27] Again, within the context of the 1701 Ottoman imperial campaign to Basra, the Iranian military deployed in southern Iraq is designated as the "Qizilbash troops."[28]

Ottoman internal and intra-governmental documents have the same feature as well. In the timespan after Zuhab, they utter the word *Qizilbash* almost only when referring to either the Safavid military (Qizilbash troops[29]), the Safavid political establishment (Qizilbash State[30]), Safavid-Iranian subjects (Qizilbash mates[31]), or the Safavid realm of Iran (Qizilbash domain/country[32]). In most cases, these references show up in borderland governors' expositions on Iran to the imperial centre telling of their observations and intelligence about stillness, unrest, abidance of peace, breaches thereof, mobilizations or other extraordinary activities, and news such as the coming of emissaries or border violations. Most of the wording in these reports was then reproduced in grand-vizierial summations, imperial decrees, and imperial handwrits.[33] In these genres, over the timespan in question, *Qizilbash* seemingly stopped designating the old believers in Anatolia. The Empire turned a blind eye to the eponymous identity of this community, because, it was now empty of its former political weight to the point of disregard, hence the loss of its distinctive name.

Last but not least, the wording in diplomatic writs in Ottoman-Safavid dealings after the peace of Zuhab also conforms to this shift. Diplomatic correspondence by monarchs, grand viziers, and governors for congratulations, friendship, alliance, treaty amendments, concerted actions, resolutions, threats, and warnings did not speak of the Qizilbash in Anatolia at all, neither in name nor with any other reference, betokening that this factor had been taken off the agenda of relations for good. Moreover, owing to the unbroken peace of eighty-four years, troops of the two sides did not formally engage one other. Thus, the military context for the shifted use of *Qizilbash* too did not become a subject of diplomatic letters or talks. Even in the imperial epistle to the shah sharing some information from the Imposter Abbas affair, which in this timespan was the only case where the genuine Qizilbash were openly involved, there is no religious or demographic reference, aside from noting that the perpetrators were from Turkish clans.[34]

By the mid-seventeenth century, the Qızılbash phenomenon, in its social and religious sense as applied to the Safavid-follower Ottoman-subjects in Anatolia, which had likely been the most important constant in both peacetime and wartime in relations since 1500, had, so to speak, faded away as a factor to be taken into consideration internationally. For a Safavid establishment converted from Qızılbashism to Shiism, the Ottoman-subject Anatolian brethren, who remained old believers, were no longer coreligionists indeed. The once active and intensive ties became passive, and continued only in form. As the Qızılbash in Anatolia lost their religious unity with and operational worth for the Safavid establishment in Iran, they were stripped of the attribute that had made them vital for Safavid policies and thus of central importance in the eyes of the Ottoman state. The imperial court therefore chose to ignore the Qızılbash identity. Yet the Qızılbash in Anatolia remained true to their beliefs and lived on in great numbers as a community. But they now lacked their distinctive name and a means to express their identity on a central stage. The origin of the phenomena, firstly that *Qızılbash* turned in Turkish into a word of slight as opposed to its original meaning, and secondly that the community in question came to be named *Alevi* instead, needs to be sought in this process of estrangement and disregard, which became enrooted from 1640 to 1720.

Bibliography

1. Archival and Manuscript Sources

Başbakanlık Osmanlı Arşivi
    Mühimme Defteri
        89, entries 106, 259.
        96, entries 875.
    YB.(21) 10/23 (1054).
    Name-i Hümayun Defteri 5-6.
Mecmua-i Mekatib. Staatsbibliothek zu Berlin. Orientabteilung, Ms. or. quart. 1577.
Mecmua-yı Mükatebat. Österreichische Nationalbibliothek. Orientalische Handschriften, Cod.Mixt. 371
Münşeat 1050-1140. Staatsbibliothek zu Berlin, OA, Hs. or. oct. 893.
Topkapı Sarayı Müzesi Arşivi. *Evrak*
    z.720 e.41 [d.302 g.3].
    z.4454 e.1 [d.696 g.17].
    z.4590 e.1 [d.698 g.8].
    z.6039 e.1 [d.753 g.19].
    z.7022 e.244 [d.796 g.27].

z.7022 e.249 [d.796 g.32].
z.7022 e.315 [d.796 g.97].

2. Published Primary Sources

Alışık, Gülşen Seyhan. "Fazlullah b. Hunci'nin Yaşamı ve Yavuz Sultan Selim Hana Yazdığı Türkçe Manzum Yakarış," *Modern Türklük Araştırmaları Dergisi* II – 4 (2005): 70-87

Düzdağ, M. Ertuğrul (editor). *Şeyhülislam Ebussu'ud Efendi'nin Fetvalarına Göre Kanuni Devrinde Osmanlı Hayatı. Fetava-yı Ebussu'ud Efendi*. İstanbul: Kapı Yayınları, rep. 2012.

Asnaad o Mokaatabaat-e Taarixi-ye Iraan az Timur taa Şaah İsmaail. Edited by Abdulhusayn Navaai. Bongaah-e Tarjoma vo Naşr-i Ketaab, 1341.

Asnaad o Mukaatabaat-e Siyaasi-ye Iraan az Saal-e 1038 taa 1105. Edited by Abdulhusayn Navaai. Tehran: Bonyaad-e Farhang-e Iraan, hs. 1360.

Fığlalı, Ethem Ruhi (editor). "İbn Sadru'd-din Eş-Şirvani ve İtikadi Mezhepler Hakkındaki Türkçe Risalesi" *Ankara Üniversitesi İlahiyat Fakültesi Dergisi* XXIV (1981).

Kaplan, Doğan (editor). *Yazılı Kaynaklara Göre Alevilik*. İstanbul: Türkiye Diyanet Vakfı, 2011.

Karaçelebi-zade Abdülaziz Efendi. *Ravzatü'l-Ebrar Zeyli*. Edited by Nevzat Kaya. Ankara: Türk Tarih Kurumu, 2003.

Katip Çelebi. *Fezleke [Osmanlı Tarihi (1000-10065 / 1591-1655)]*. Edited by Zeynep Aycibin. İstanbul: Çamlıca, 2016.

Mustafa Naima Efendi. *Tarih-i Na'ima*. Edited by Mehmet İpşirli. Ankara: Türk Tarih Kurumu, 2007.

Münşeat-ı Divan-ı Hümayun. Published in Nihal Metin, "Viyana Avusturya Kütüphanesi Nr. H.O. 180D'de Kayıtlı Münşeat-ı Divan-ı Hümayun (Name-i Hümayun Suretleri) (Muharrem 1099-Cemaziyelahir 1108 / Kasım 1687-Ocak 1697) (İnceleme-Metin)." MA. Thesis, Marmara Üniversitesi, 2014.

Nazmizade Hüseyin Murtaza Efendi b. Seyyid Ali el-Bağdadi, *Münşeat-ı Nazmizade* (Süleymaniye Yazma Eser Kütüphanesi, Esad Efendi no. 3322).

Qazvini, Mohammad Taahir Vahid. *Abbaas-naama yaa Şarh-e Zindagaani-ye 22-Saala-i Şaah Abbaas-e Saani*. Edited by İbraahim Dihgaan. Eraak: Ketaab-foruşi-ye Daavari-ye Eraak, hs. 1329.

Qazvini Isfahani, Mohammad Yusuf Vaalih. *Iraan dar zamaan-e Şaah Safi vo Şaah Abbaas-e Dovvom. Xold-e Barin*. Edited by Doktor Mohammad Rezaa Nasiri, Anjoman-e Aasaar o Mafaaxer-i Farhangi, hs. 1382.

Raşid Mehmed Efendi. *Tarih-i Raşid II. 1115-1134 / 1703-1722*. Edited by Abdülkadir Özcan, Baki Çakır, Yunus Uğur, and Ahmet Zeki İzgöer. İstanbul: Klasik Yayınları, 2013.

Sarı Abdullah Efendi. *Düsturü'l-İnşa.* Süleymaniye Kütüphanesi, Nur-ı Osmaniye no. 4304.

Sarı Mehmed Paşa. *Zübde-i Vekaiyat: Tahlil ve Metin (1066-1116 / 1656-1704).* Edited by Abdülkadir Özcan. Ankara: Türk Tarih Kurumu, 1995.

Savaş, Saim (compiler). *XVI. Asırda Anadolu'da Alevilik.* Ankara: Vadi Yayınları, 2002 – rep. Türk Tarih Kurumu, 2013.

Şah İsmail Hatai Külliyatı. Edited by Babek Cavanşir and Ekber N. Necef. İstanbul: Kaknüs Yayınları, 2006.

3. Secondary Sources

Abisaab, Rula Jurdi. *Converting Persia: Religion and Power in the Safavid Empire.* London and New York: I.B. Tauris, 2004.

Arjomand, Said Amir. *The Shadow of God and the Hidden Imam: Religion, Political Order, and Societal Change in Shi'ite Iran.* Chicago: University of Chicago Press, 1984.

Babayan, Kathryn. "The Waning of the Qizilbash: The Spiritual and the Temporal in Seventeenth-Century Iran." PhD. Dissertation, Princeton University, 1993.

Baltacıoğlu-Brammer, Ayşe. "One Word, Many Implications: The Term 'Kızılbaş' in the Early Modern Ottoman Context." In *Ottoman Sunnism: New Perspectives*, ed. Vefa Erginbaş (Edinburgh University Press, 2019), 47-70.

Bilge, Reha. *1514 Yavuz Selim ve Şah İsmail: Türkler, Türkmenler ve Farslar.* İstanbul: Giza Yayınları, 2010.

Jafariaan, Rasul. *Safaviya dar Arsa-e Din, Farhang o Siyaasat* (Tehran: Pejuheşgaah-e Havza vo Daaneşgaah, hs. 1391).

Canbakal, Hülya. "An Exercise in Denominational Geography in Search of Ottoman Alevis." *Turkish Studies* 6, no. 2 (2005), 253-71.

Eberhard, Elke. *Osmanische Polemik gegen die Safawiden im 16. Jahrhundert nach aranischen Handschriften.* Freiburg im Breisgau: Klaus Schwarz Verlag, 1970.

Emecen, Feridun. *Zamanın İskenderi Şarkın Fatihi Yavuz Sultan Selim.* İstanbul: Yitik Hazine Yayınları, 2010.

Fragner, Bert. "The Safavid Empire and the Sixteenth and Seventeenth-Century Political and Strategic Balance of Power within the World System." In *Iran and the World in the Safavid Age.* Edited by Willem Floor and Edmund Herzig. London and New York: I.B. Tauris, 2012, 17-30.

Güngörürler, Selim. "Diplomacy and Political Relations between the Ottoman Empire and Safavid Iran, 1639-1722." PhD. Dissertation, Georgetown University, 2016.

Güngörürler, Selim. "Islamic Discourse in Ottoman-Safavid Peacetime Diplomacy after 1049/1639" in *Historicizing Sunni Islam in the Ottoman Empire, c. 1450 – c. 1750*, ed. Tijana Krstic and Derin Terzioğlu (Leiden: Brill, 2020), 479-500.

Karakaya Stump, Ayfer. "Subjects of the Sultan, Disciples of the Shah: Formation and Transformation of the Kızılbash/Alevi Communities in Ottoman Anatolia." PhD. Dissertation, Harvard University, 2008.

Karakaya, Stump, Ayfer. The Kızılbash/Alevis in Ottoman Anatolia: Sufism, Politics and Community. Edinburgh: Edinburgh University Press, 2020.

Mordtmann, J.H. "Sunnitisch-schiitische Polemik im 17. Jahrhundert" in *Mitteilungen des Seminars für orientalische Sprachen an der Friedrich Wilhelms-Universitaet zu Berlin, Abteilung 2 westasiatische Studien* (1926).

Karakaya-Stump, Ayfer. *The Kizilbash/Alevis in Ottoman Anatolia: Sufism, Politics and Community*. Edinburgh University Press, 2020.

Ocak, Ahmet Yaşar. *Türk Sufiliğine Bakışlar*. İstanbul: İletişim, 1996.

Paarsaadust, Menuçihr. *Şaah Tahmasb-e Avval*. Tehran: Şirkat-i Sahaami-ye İntişaar, hs. 1381.

Posch, Walter. *Osmanisch-safavidische Beziehungen (1545-1550): Der Fall Alkas Mirza*. Wien: Verlag der Österreichischen Akademie der Wissenschaften, 2013.

Roemer, H. R. . "The Safavid Period." In *The Cambridge History of Iran* VI. Edited by Peter Jackson and Laurance Lockhart. Cambridge: Cambridge University Press, 1986, 189-350.

Sohrweide, Hanna. "Der Sieg der Safawiden in Persien un seine Rückwirkungen auf die Schiiten Anatoliens im 16. Jahrhudnert." In *Der Islam* 41 (1965), 95-223.

Söylemez, Faruk. "Anadolu'da Sahte Şah İsmail İsyanı." *Erciyes Üniversitesi Sosyal Bilimler Enstitüsü Dergisi* 17 (2004/2), 71-90.

Sümer, Faruk. *Safevi Devletinin Kuruluşu ve Gelişmesinde Anadolu Türklerinin Rolü*. Ankara, Türk Tarih Kurumu, 2nd ed. 1999.

Tekindağ, Şahabettin. "Şah Kulu Baba Tekeli İsyanı I-II." *Belgelerle Türk Tarihi Dergisi* III-IV 12-1 (1967-1968), 34-39, 54-59.

Tekindağ Şahabettin. "Yeni Kaynaklar ve Vesikalar Işığı Altında Yavuz Sultan Selim'in İran Seferi." İstanbul Üniversitesi Edebiyat Fakültesi T*arih Dergisi* XVII – 22 (1968), 49-78.

Terzioğlu, Derin. "How to Conceptualize Ottoman Sunnitization: A Historiographical Discussion." *Turcica* 44 (2012-2013): 301-338.

Winter, Stefan. "The Qizilbash of Syria and Ottoman Shiism." In *The Ottoman World*. Edited by Christine Woodhead. New York: Routledge, 2012, 171-83.

Yıldırım, Rıza. "Bektaşi Kime Derler? "Bektaşi" Kavramının Kapsamı ve Sınırları Üzerine Tarihsel Bir Analiz Denemesi," *Türk Kültürü ve Hacı Bektaş Veli Araştırma Dergisi* 55 (2010), 23-58.

Notes

1   From its seventh-century conquest by Muslim Arabs until the seventeenth century, Iran was a Sunni-majority land. Its identification with Shiism is the legacy of the Safavid-led conversion that took place in Early Modernity. The Qizilbash movement of the Safavids also left behind a large population of followers in Anatolia, Ottoman territory. In the sixteenth and seventeenth centuries, the Sunni clergy deemed Qizilbashism unrelated to Shiism. The Shiite clergy that later established itself in Iran likewise highlighted its own separate character from Qizilbashism, and did not fall short of its Sunni counterpart in calling the Qizilbash unbelievers. It is therefore essential to acknowledge this separateness of Qizilbashism and Shiism, and that they shall not be deemed an extreme version and a canonical version of a one sect. Qizilbashism was brought to Iran by the House of Safi and its warrior-followers, the Qizilbash military-nobility, who together conquered the realm and set up a kingdom at the outset of the sixteenth century. The Shiitization of Iran began not with the rise of the Safavids but as a standalone policy, which they started only later. This ensuing Shiism in Iran did not deem the original Safavid order, namely the Qizilbash belief, a branch of itself. The second conversion wave in Early Modern Iran, this time to Shiism, showed itself first in the person of Shah Tahmasb about a century after the Safavid order's original conversion from Sunnism to would be called Qizilbashism. This separate and equally revolutionary movement too needed almost a century to show widespread results, so it reached an effective level only in the seventeenth century. Above all under Abbas I's reign did the Shiite creed establish itself among the people. From the viewpoint of the victorious Shiism, the Qizilbash were unbelievers. Therefore, Iran's Shiitization was a campaign to convert not only the Sunni-majority population but also the Qizilbash rulers. I handled these phenomena in more detail and provided examples thereto in my paper "Die Frage der Abgrenzung zwischen offiziellen Konfessionen: das osmanische Reich und safawidisches Persien in der Frühneuzeit," presented in *Forschungskolloquium Lehrstuhl Geschichte Aserbaidschans, Humboldt-Universität zu Berlin* in February 2016, a revised version of which, under the title "Baaz-negari ba Gostara vo Marzhaa-ye Mazaaheb dar Çaarçub-e Ruyaaruyi-e Safaviyaan o Osmaaniyaan" is soon being published in an edited volume on the *Intellectual and Cultural Relations between Iran and Central Asia and the Caucasus* by the Research Center for Islamic History, Tehran. For supporting references, see Ayfer Karakaya-Stump, The Kızılbash/Alevis in Ottoman Anatolia: Sufism, Politics and Community (Edinburgh, 2020), 2, 4-5; Şahabettin Tekindağ, "Yeni Kaynaklar ve Vesikalar Işığı Altında Yavuz Sultan Selim'in İran Seferi," İstanbul Üniversitesi Edebiyat Fakültesi Tarih Dergisi XVII – 22 (1968): 54-55; Gülşen Seyhan Alışık, "Fazlullah b. Hunci'nin Yaşamı ve Yavuz Sultan Selim Hana Yazdığı Türkçe Manzum Yakarış," *Modern Türklük Araştırmaları Dergisi* II – 4 (2005): 70-87; Rasul Jafariaan, *Safaviya dar Arsa-e Din, Farhang o Siyaasat* (Tehran, hs. 1391), 73; M. Ertuğrul Düzdağ, Şeyhülislam Ebussu'ud Efendi'nin Fetvalarına Göre Kanuni Devrinde Osmanlı Hayatı. *Fetava-yı Ebussu'ud Efendi* (İstanbul, rep. 2012), 135-137; Walter Posch, *Osmanisch-safavidische Beziehungen (1545-1550): Der Fall Alkas Mirza* (Wien, 2013), 172-176, 266-267, 354-355; Elke Eberhard, *Osmanische Polemik gegen die Safawiden im 16. Jahrhundert nach arabischen Handschriften* (Freiburg im Breisgau, 1970), 71-75, 85-88, 99, 101, 117; Ethem Ruhi Fığlalı, "İbn Sadru'd-din Eş-Şirvani ve İtikadi Mezhepler Hakkındaki Türkçe Risalesi" *Ankara Üniversitesi İlahiyat Fakültesi Dergisi* XXIV (1981): 260-265; Ahmet Yaşar Ocak, *Türk Sufiliğine Bakışlar* (İstanbul, 1996), 237-238, 245-249; Feridun Emecen, *Zamanın İskenderi Şarkın Fatihi Yavuz Sultan Selim* (İstanbul: Yitik Hazine Yayınları, 2010), 90; Reha Bilge, *1514 Yavuz Selim ve Şah İsmail: Türkler, Türkmenler ve Farslar* (İstanbul, 2010), 311; Said Amir Arjomand, *The Shadow of God and the Hidden Imam: Religion, Political Order, and Societal Change in Shi'ite Iran* (Chicago: University of Chicago Press, 1984), 81, 110, 179; Şah İsmail Hatai Külliyatı, ed. Babek Cavanşir and Ekber N. Necef (İstanbul, 2006), 439-442, 482-483; H. R. Roemer, "The Safavid Period," in *The Cambridge History of Iran* VI, ed. Peter Jackson and Laurance Lockhart (Cambridge, 1986), 198; Saim Savaş, *XVI. Asırda Anadolu'da Alevilik* (Ankara, rep. 2013), 166, 213; Rula Jurdi Abisaab, *Converting*

Persia: Religion and Power in the Safavid Empire (London and New York, 2004), 8-12, 24, 57-59; Bert Fragner, "The Safavid Empire and the Sixteenth- and Seventeenth-Century Political and Strategic Balance of Power within the World System" in *Iran and the World in the Safavid Age*, ed. Willem Floor and Edmund Herzig (London and New York, 2012), 19; Menuçihr Paarsaadust, Şaah Tahmasb-e Avval (Tehran, hs. 1381), 607-613, 809-816, 850-853; Kathryn Babayan, "The Waning of the Qizilbash: The Spiritual and the Temporal in Seventeenth-Century Iran," (PhD. Dissertation, Princeton University, 1993), 7, 43; J. H. Mordtmann, "Sunnitisch-schiitische Polemik im 17. Jahrhundert" in *Mitteilungen des Seminars für orientalische Sprachen an der Friedrich Wilhelms-Universitaet zu Berlin, Abteilung 2 westasiatische Studien* (1926): 112-129.

2   For their role in Safavid service, see Hanna Sohrweide, "Der Sieg der Safawiden in Persien un seine Rückwirkungen auf die Schiiten Anatoliens im 16. Jahrhudnert," in *Der Islam* 41 (1965): 95-223; Faruk Sümer, *Safevi Devletinin Kuruluşu ve Gelişmesinde Anadolu Türklerinin Rolü* (Ankara, 2nd ed. 1999); Şahabettin Tekindağ, "Şah Kulu Baba Tekeli İsyanı I-II," *Belgelerle Türk Tarihi Dergisi* III-IV 12-1 (1967-1968): 34-39, 54-59; Bilge, *Türkler, Türkmenler ve Farslar*, Emecen, *Yavuz Sultan Selim*; Posch, *Osmanisch-safavidische Beziehungen*; Savaş, *Anadolu'da Alevilik*; Faruk Söylemez, "Anadolu'da Sahte Şah İsmail İsyanı," *Erciyes Üniversitesi Sosyal Bilimler Enstitüsü Dergisi* 17 (2004/2); Karakaya-Stump, Kızılbash/Alevis in Ottoman Anatolia, 26.

3   For more thereon, see my "Islamic Discourse in Ottoman-Safavid Peacetime Diplomacy after 1049/1639" in *Historicizing Sunni Islam in the Ottoman Empire, c. 1450 – c. 1750*, ed. Tijana Krstic and Derin Terzioğlu (Leiden: Brill, 2020), 479-500.

4   See the primary source bibliography in my "Diplomacy and Political Relations between the Ottoman Empire and Safavid Iran, 1639-1722" (PhD. Dissertation, Georgetown University, 2016) for the archival registers, manuscripts, and published compilations logging the relevant correspondence between the states.

5   Derin Terzioğlu, – in her "How to Conceptualize Ottoman Sunnitization: A Historiographical Discussion," *Turcica* 44 (2021-2013): 318 – calls attention to the "gradual marginalization of the Kızılbaş" in the Ottoman Empire after 1639 and our need to know more about how this relates to whatever ties that had remained between Ottoman-subject Qizilbash and the Safavids on the one hand, and how Ottoman authorities perceived all this on the other.

6   In my "Diplomacy and Political Relations between the Ottoman Empire and Safavid Iran, 1639-1722," I handle the period in a comprehensive manner.

7   Karakaya-Stump, Kızılbash/Alevis in Ottoman Anatolia, 261, 292-293. Though infrequently, Ottoman-subject Shiites in Syria were an exception. On extraordinary occasions and as a political construct, the Ottoman State could call them *Qizilbash* in the later seventeenth and the eighteenth centuries. See Stefan Winter, "The Qizilbash of Syria and Ottoman Shiism," in *The Ottoman World*, ed. Christine Woodhead (New York, 2012), 171-183.

8   In the time between the submission and the publication of this paper, colleagues have also published studies calling attention to this trend. Above all, Ayfer Karakaya-Stump remarks that the Qizilbash disappear from Ottoman archival logs after the early seventeenth century. She convincingly refutes the traditional claim that this happened owing to a withdrawal of the Anatolian Qizilbash to spots out of the state's sight. She argues instead that this disappearance from archival sources must be the outcome of, firstly, the Ottomans' unwillingness to set down people in writing as Qizilbash as long as their Qizilbash-ness was not the main subject, and, secondly, the Ottomans' new policy of an "informal accommodation," a kind of 'don't ask don't tell,' especially in the Qizilbash's dealings with state authorities, such as when paying taxes or using the courthouse. See her book *The Kizilbash/Alevis in Ottoman Anatolia: Sufism, Politics and Community* (Edinburgh University Press, 2020), 292-294. Ayşe Baltacıoğlu-Brammer, in her "One Word, Many Implications: The Term 'Kızılbaş' in the Early Modern Ottoman Context" in *Ottoman Sunnism: New Perspectives*, ed. Vefa Erginbaş (Edinburgh, 2019), 63, touches briefly upon this in her conclusion, though one should be aware of her mistaken equation of Qizilbashism with Shiism.

9   *dede*

10 Hülya Canbakal, "An Exercise in Denominational Geography in Search of Ottoman Alevis," *Turkish Studies* 6, no. 2 (2005): 253-271.
11 Rıza Yıldırım, "Beştaşi Kime Derler? "Bektaşi" Kavramının Kapsamı ve Sınırları Üzerine Tarihsel Bir Analiz Denemesi," *Türk Kültürü ve Hacı Bektaş Veli Araştırma Dergisi* 55 (2010): 33-34, 36-38, 51-52.
12 *buyruq*
13 Doğan Kaplan, *Yazılı Kaynaklara Göre Alevilik* (İstanbul, 2011), 109224-222 ,160-159 ,111-.
14 "allaamato'l-olamaa"
15 Mohammad Yusuf Vaalih Qazvini Isfahaani, *Iraan dar zamaan-e Şaah Safi vo Şaah Abbaas-e Dovvom. Xold-e Barin*, ed. Doktor Mohammad Rezaa Nasiri (Tehran, hs. 1382), 620-621; Mohammad Taahir Vahid Qazvini, *Abbaas-naama yaa Şarh-e Zindagaani-ye 22-Saala-e Şaah Abbaas-i Saani*, ed. İbrahim Dihgaan (Eraak, hs. 1329), 254-255.
16 *xilaafat-naama*
17 *xalifatu'l-xulafaa*
18 *xalifa*
19 Ayfer Karakaya Stump, "Subjects of the Sultan, Disciples of the Shah: Formation and Transformation of the Kızılbash/Alevi Communities in Ottoman Anatolia," (PhD. Dissertation, Harvard University, 2008), 184-188.
20 For the imposter-Safavid Abbas affair and references below, see my "Diplomacy and Political Relations between the Ottoman Empire and Safavid Iran, 1639-1722," 421-425, 450-451.
21 "*huruç (xoruj)*." Raşid Mehmed Efendi, *Tarih-i Raşid II. 1115-1134 / 1703-1722*, ed. Abdülkadir Özcan, Baki Çakır, Yunus Uğur, Ahmet Zeki İzgöer (İstanbul, 2013), 896.
22 "ekser-i sükkanında su-i i'tiqad nümayan velakin haqiqat-i halleri mestur-ı perde-i kitman olan ... ref'-i liva-yı rafz u ilhad ... üç bin qadar zındıq ... mela'in" *Tarih-i Raşid*, 896.
23 "gunagun hiyel-i sihr-asarı müşahede olunup ekser-i nası ol taqrip ile ıdlal ettiğinden." *Tarih-i Raşid*, 896.
24 "böyle bir müfsid-i daall, ve Bozok sancağı melahide vü zenadıq ile malamal olup." *Tarih-i Raşid*, 896.
25 "Qızılbash'a firar ettiler." / "Şah ülkesine gittiler." Katip Çelebi, *Fezleke [Osmanlı Tarihi (1000-10065 / 1591-1655)]*, ed. Zeynep Aycibin (İstanbul, 2016), 957.
26 "Qızılbash askeri." Karaçelebi-zade Abdülaziz Efendi, *Ravzatü'l-Ebrar Zeyli*, ed. Nevzat Kaya (Ankara, 2003), 21.
27 "Qızılbash ... hareket ettiğin." Mustafa Naima Efendi, *Tarih-i Na'ima*, ed. Mehmet İpşirli (Ankara, 2007), 1289.
28 "Qızılbash askeri." Sarı Mehmed Paşa, *Zübde-i Vekaiyat: Tahlil ve Metin (1066-1116 / 1656-1704)*, ed. Abdülkadir Özcan (Ankara, 1995), 711.
29 "Qızılbash askeri"
30 "Qızılbash devleti"
31 "Qızılbash taifesi"
32 "Qızılbash memleketi," "Qızılbash ülkesi."
33 Başbakanlık Osmanlı Arşivi, *Mühimme Defteri* 89, entry 106, 259; *YB*.(21) 10/23 (1054); MHM.d. 96, ent. 875; Topkapı Sarayı Müzesi Arşivi, *Evrak* z.7022 e.244 [d.796 g.27]; TSMA.e. z.7022 e.249 [d.796 g.32]; TSMK.e. z.7022 e.315 [d.796 g.97]; TSMA.e. z.4590 e.1 [d.698 g.8]; TSMA.e. z.4454 e.1 [d.696 g.17]; TSMA.e. z.720 e.41 [d.302 g.3]; TSMA.e. z.6039 e.1 [d.753 g.19].
34 See the copies of relevant diplomatic correspondence in BOA. NHM.d. 5; NMH.d. 6; Sarı Abdullah Efendi, *Düsturü'l-İnşa* (Süleymaniye Kütüphanesi, Nur-ı Osmaniye no. 4304); *Asnaad o Mokaatabaat-e Tarixi-yr Iraan az Timur taa Şaah İsmaail*, ed. Abdulhusayn Navaai (Tehran, 1341); *Asnaad o Mokaatabaat-e Siyaasi-ye Iraan az Saal-e 1038 taa 1105*, ed. Abdulhuseyn Navaai (Tehran, hs. 1360); *Mecmua-i Mekatib* (Staatsbibliothek zu Berlin, Orientabteilung, Ms. or. quart. 1577); *Mecmua-yı Mükatebat* (Österreichische Nationalbibliothek, Orientalische Handschriften, Cod.Mixt. 371); *Münşeat 1050-1140* (Staatsbibliothek zu Berlin, OA, Hs. or. oct. 893);

Münşeat-ı Divan-ı Hümayun, published in Metin, Nihal, "Viyana Avusturya Kütüphanesi Nr. H.O. 180D'de Kayıtlı Münşeat-ı Divan-ı Hümayun (Name-i Hümayun Suretleri) (Muharrem 1099-Cemaziyelahir 1108 / Kasım 1687-Ocak 1697) (İnceleme-Metin)," (MA thesis, Marmara Üniversitesi, 2014); Nazmizade Hüseyin Murtaza Efendi b. Seyyid Ali el-Bağdadi, *Münşeat-ı Nazmizade* (Süleymaniye Yazma Eser Kütüphanesi, Esad Efendi no. 3322).

4

The Safavid Foundation Myth in the Subaltern Imagination

Barry Wood

The founding of the Safavid dynasty in Iran (1501–1722) came as the culmination of a century of religious and political ferment, and as the result in particular of the millenarian strivings of the "red-head" (Qizilbash) adherents of the militant Safavid Order. Over several decades, in the teeth of resistance and oppression from Turkmans, Ottomans, Uzbeks, and others, they managed not only to survive and expand, but eventually to carve out a Twelver Shi'i state of lasting duration. At the center of these events was a charismatic action-hero in the person of the leader of the Safavid Order, Shah Isma'il I. He took leadership of the movement at the tender age of twelve and led his devoted followers to a series of victories over the course of some fifteen years, and although his meteoric career ended definitively at the Battle of Chaldiran in 1514, he had still made an indelible impact on the history of western and central Asia.

The story of the founding of the Safavid dynasty, in other words, was not only a signal event in Iranian history, it also makes for a cracking good yarn. The historian is therefore justified in asking: How did that story take root and develop in the cultural memory and imagination of the people who lived in the world that resulted from the events it describes? In one sense, the story is well preserved at the top of the social pyramid, namely in the official chronicles of the dynasty, from Khwandamir onward. The events and individuals described in these court histories, however, inhabit a rarefied dimension of ornate prose[1] and erudite self-referentiality[2] – excellent material for the prestigious and privileged, but likely out of reach of the common citizens. It was precisely this latter, though, whose mental landscape is so interesting in a context like this. For their view of the past was uncontrolled, as it were, by the need to match the facts too precisely; people were free to rewrite history according to their own value-standards, whether noble (e.g., the desire to see injustice punished) or ignoble (e.g., sectarian bigotry).[3] In popular storytelling about the past, we are afforded a valuable glimpse of history the way everyday people thought they understood it, and we can analyze and appreciate the lenses through which it was refracted for them.

It would thus be tremendously interesting to listen in on what everyday people in Safavid Iran told each other about the days of old. This is, in fact, possible, at least at a few steps' remove. The opportunity comes via a group of manuscripts that have hitherto received relatively little scholarly attention. These manuscripts are sometimes collectively referred to as the "Anonymous Histories of Shah Isma'il."[4]

Shah Isma'il was, from an early stage, the subject of stories about his dramatic life. Within two decades of his death, in fact, a Venetian traveler to Iran reported seeing men in public squares reading aloud from books and relating the battles of heroes of old, including Shah Isma'il.[5] We may also surmise that the survivors of the dramatic early years would have passed their memories down, at least within their families.[6] A mélange of actual fact, fervent exaggeration, and outright legend developed which was eventually taken up by the professional storytellers (*naqqalan*) of the thriving Safavid coffeehouse circuit. Probably owing to their popularity, the tales appear to have come to the attention of the royal palace sometime around the middle of the seventeenth century, where they were written down in manuscripts and even illustrated with miniatures.[7] Interest in the stories continued after the fall of the Safavid dynasty, as manuscript copies continued to be produced right into the nineteenth century. To date, I have located twelve manuscripts of these histories in libraries around the world; the examples in this essay are taken from the one published in 1971 as *Alamara-yi Shah Isma'il*,[8] which I have recently translated.[9]

Despite variations in the manuscripts, the general line of the narrative is consistent. The book begins with stories about Shah Isma'il's illustrious Sufi ancestors, who establish the Safavid Order in Ardabil. As the Order increases in power and influence, it attracts the enmity of the powers that be, and by the time Isma'il is born, things are sufficiently dangerous that the young boy and his brothers have to go into hiding. Within a few years, Isma'il is bidden by the Commander of the Faithful, the Imam Ali b. Abi Talib, to make his "emergence" (*khuruj*), and he takes his place at the head of his devoted followers, known as "red-heads" or Qizilbash after their distinctive headgear. The young leader embarks on a campaign of conquest and conversion, crowning himself Shah and carving out a Twelver Shi'ite state in the face of resistance from Turkmans, Uzbeks, Ottomans ("Anatolians"), and even Georgians and Ethiopians. As the divinely supported propagator of the True Faith, Isma'il enjoys seemingly unstoppable momentum, even in the face of daunting odds, and his victories mount without cease until his defeat at the hands of the Ottomans at Chaldiran – after which, his chastisement complete, the Shah continues to rule in glory and even waits for a rematch that never comes. In addition to this plotline, there are several side narratives describing the affairs of the Safavids' enemies. One relates the rise to power of Shahi Beg Khan in the vacuum created by the incompetence of the Timurid princes in Central Asia; another describes the conflict between the Ottoman ruler Bayezid and his evil-natured progeny Selim. Eventually, the Shah is summoned (somewhat abruptly) to the afterlife by his illustrious ancestors, at which point the throne passes to his son Tahmasp and the story ends.[10]

The numerous traces of oral performance in the text give away its debt to the coffeehouse storyteller's craft. In addition to the overall register of the Persian, which is tonally and grammatically informal to a fault, these traces include the verbal formulae used to change the scene, such as "Listen to two words about X," "But we have not mentioned that Y," and "You shall hear about Z." The narrator also occasionally uses popular idioms and proverbs, such as "setting Mubarak free when he's dead" (equivalent to "shutting the barn door after the horse has left"). Popular language is also found in the form of insults; the Safavids' enemies are derided as *sag* "dog," *namard* "coward," *napak* "filthy (lit. 'impure')," and *haramzada* "bastard." Stock phrases and imagery appear regularly, such as the repeated descriptions of this or that antagonist as being "like a gloomy demon" or the innumerable instances in which a hero, usually but not always Shah Isma'il, bifurcates his enemy from scalp to saddle with one mighty sword-blow. There are numerous insertions of poetic verse, intended to demonstrate cultural prowess, elevate the register of the narrative, and earn the respect of the audience.[11] There are also knowing asides intended for the moral improvement of the listener, such as the author's observations on how Shah Isma'il's pride was punished. Later manuscripts begin with an invocation of "the tellers of tales and the transmitters of stories and the sugar-chewing parrots of fine discourse," a common opening flourish in popular tales of the nineteenth century such as *Hoseyn-e Kord* and *Amir Arsalan*.[12]

The differences among manuscript versions of these tales, including variants in descriptive wording, lists of objects, character names,[13] and so on are also rooted in the practices of the *naqqalan* who passed them down. Professional storytellers worked from notebooks called *tumar*s, which simply preserved a given plot line in skeletal form; the storyteller would memorize the plotline or glance at it during his performance in the coffeehouse, freely embroidering it with details as he went.[14] Other storytellers might copy down the story as they heard it and turn that into their own *tumar*. The storyteller's apprentices, in turn, were expected to copy and memorize their own notebooks. In this way the stories grew and developed as they were passed down over the years, and in the process variations crept in.

These tales' gestation on the coffeehouse circuit is important for our understanding of their value as a window on Safavid culture. The *naqqal* did not merely transmit stories verbatim, generation after generation. The art of storytelling required its practitioners to continually modify and update their repertoire in a constant and dynamic reworking of narratives, a process that necessarily had to reflect popular thinking.[15] One reason for this was that the *naqqal* had to keep his audience interested; people were always free to go find another coffeehouse. Part of it was also that the *naqqal* saw it as his task to edify his listeners, as indicated above, which would have encouraged him to mold his narrative to supply moral lessons the audience would be responsive to. More abstractly, the influence of common cultural values exerted its own gravitational pull on the storytellers, tugging the changes they made to their narrative in the direction of commonly accepted norms of behavior – including, in the case of tales about a character like Shah Isma'il, nobility, heroism, piety, and the like.[16]

The stories of the "Anonymous Histories," then, while they have been described (not without justification) as "childish and credulous" and "essentially worthless as historical narrative,"[17] are more helpfully understood as exemplifying the voice of the people.[18] They preserve, in a palpably more direct fashion than the florid tomes penned by official Safavid court historians, a whole constellation of popular values, standards, and expectations that tell us a great deal about the mental landscape of the people who crafted and enjoyed them. *The Adventures of Shah Isma'il* is an engaging and refreshing take on Safavid history – precisely the "view from below" we seek to appreciate.

One angle from which to consider these tales and the information they provide on the mental landscape of their audience, is the perspective on the Other. What kind of people populate the mythical foundation story of the rise of Shah Isma'il, whether other ethnic groups, religious sects, or social classes?

The first kind of Other to be considered here may be termed "the Other around us," or the people of different cultural and ethnic groups thought to be of the same social level as the narrator. One guise in which "the Other around us" appears is ethnic, which in the context of these stories would mean non-Persian groups. These include Turks, Kurds, Lurs, Arabs, and even Ethiopians and Georgians.

Turks (a term which here includes Uzbeks) come in for considerable scorn. They are consistently derided as uncouth (*bi-adab*), and in particular as greedy. During Isma'il's struggle with the Aq Quyunlu, for example, the Qizilbash manage to capture Sultan Murad (whom the waggish Isma'il has nicknamed *Na-Murad*, or "The Failure"). He is placed under the watch of one Sulayman Aqa, a Qizilbash from Anatolia, who is described as "a greedy Turk who would torture his own mother for a dinar."[19] He is thus easily bribed and turns his wily prisoner loose in exchange for a jewel-encrusted armband. Later in the story, when the Uzbeks are reeling from their defeat by Shah Isma'il, Shahi Beg Khan's wife announces a reward for the head of a certain person, at which point the author says: "Hearing the word 'reward,' the Uzbek soldiers jumped up."[20] Here and there, the story's protagonists use the greed of the Uzbeks against them; in order to save the city of Yazd from the depredations of the Uzbeks, for example, the religious leader Shah Ni'matullah concocts a scheme in which he promises the occupiers a great amount of protection money, money whose payment he repeatedly delays in order to give the Qizilbash time to come save the day. The Uzbek commander Biyaqu Bahadur realizes that his men in Yazd are being duped, and he sends increasingly more insistent messages telling them to leave before the Qizilbash arrive, but each time the local Uzbek commanders see money, they forget themselves completely, until finally the royal banners appear on the horizon and the city is saved.[21]

On the other end of the realm, the Safavids have to fight a couple of times with the Kurds. The overall judgment on the Kurds is that they are a wild bunch. They are, in fact, some of the only people in the corpus of stories who manage to fight the Qizilbash to a standstill. The major confrontation occurs when the fearsome Sarim Khan the Yazidi Kurd leads an army toward Tabriz.[22] Sarim Khan, we are told, is "one of the calamities of the age"; he is a hundred and ten years old, with a white beard flowing down to his navel, and he wields a battle-axe weighing seven maunds. Two of his (seventy) sons are killed in battle, but Sarim Khan manages to seriously wound Shah Isma'il's brother Sultan Ibrahim Mirza. Another battle soon follows in which Shah Isma'il drives the Kurds into retreat but, significantly, although the Qizilbash plunder the Kurds' camp and drive them up a mountain, they are unable to defeat them completely, and the narrator ends the story by saying "the Qizilbash amirs returned to their camp without having attained their goal."[23]

Much like the Kurds, the Lurs are depicted as fiercely independent and hard fighters. They are, however, also staunch Shi'is, so Shah Isma'il is surprised and annoyed when they refuse to accept his rule, instead blocking off a certain valley and administering a painful defeat to the Qizilbash when they try to pass it. The Shah goes to Luristan himself and, in the pitched battle that ensues, marches straight up the mountain, his shield over his head to fend off the rocks that the Lurs are hurling down at him and his men. When Isma'il reaches the king of the Lurs, Malikshah Rustam, he lifts him up by the bootstrap and forces him to admit defeat. At this point the Lurs become faithful subjects, and at the celebratory royal feast, when the topic of conversation turns to a certain horse the Shah admires, the king of the Lurs tells him about the Musha'sha' Arabs and their "faith of divine Ali" [*din-i Ali-Allahi*]. Shah Isma'il and the Lurs join forces to stamp out this heresy (although not before taking a few days off to do some hunting). In battle, the Lurs fight so hard that the king of the Musha'sha' exclaims, "Now that he has Shaykh-oghli for a protector, Malikshah has become like Rustam himself!"[24]

The attitude evinced by the narrator of the "Anonymous Histories" toward Arabs is mixed. In fact, the matter seems to boil down to religion. The Musha'sha' Arabs are bad because, as we have seen, they are heretics. On the other hand, Shah Isma'il has an Arab religious advisor who sets the royal mind at ease when an Ottoman emissary presents him with a seemingly dire chronogram.[25] An Arab youth also plays a role in a vision beheld by a dervish when Isma'il's "emergence" is nigh.[26]

Toward the end of the story, a whole group of Arabs is depicted in quite a positive light.[27] This is the Egyptian commander Ghazali and his people. Ghazali appears in the story when the Ottomans are invading Egypt; originally a servant of the

Mamluk sultan Qansaw, Ghazali takes up arms against the Ottomans when his lord is treacherously killed. Sultan Selim is impressed with Ghazali's loyalty and manliness and makes him his lieutenant. Nominally a Sunni, Ghazali is obedient but standoffish with his new master, and when he duly leads a campaign into Safavid territory and ultimately meets the Qizilbash in battle, he finally sees Shah Isma'il in the flesh and is immediately filled with a sense of devotion. Shah Isma'il takes him prisoner but understands that this man is one of his followers at heart. Ghazali quickly converts to Shi'ism and reviles the first three caliphs. He then writes to his son Ghazali-oghli and tells him to take the Arabs and head for the Shah's royal court. Ghazali and his people, as it turns out, are descended from prisoners released at the behest of Shah Isma'il's ancestor as a favor to Timur, and they have inherited an intense devotion to the Safavid house. After a difficult and eventful journey, which is openly referred to as a pilgrimage, these Arabs reach the feet of the Shah, who first tests their beliefs and then sends them to settle in Shushtar and Huvayza.

Linked to the Arabs in the narrator's mind are the Zangis or Ethiopians, who figure in a fascinating episode in the lead-up to the Battle of Chaldiran.[28] Sultan Qansaw of Egypt is holding a feast at which one of his black slaves gets drunk and begins boasting about how he could tear up "Shaykh-oghli" (i.e., Shah Isma'il)[29] like a linen shirt. A Sufi of the Safavid order just happens to be present, and he warns the slave not to tangle with a hero like Shah Isma'il, nor even with his servants, like Khan Muhammad Khan the governor of Diyarbakr. The slave vows to bring back Khan Muhammad Khan's head, and Sultan Qansaw, glad to be rid of him, sends him along with three hundred other Zangis to get the job done. En route to Diyarbakr, the Zangis run across a group of Qizilbash who are out hunting, and in the ensuing battle most of the Zangis are killed or driven into the wilderness; twenty are captured and sent as prisoners to Diyarbakr, where the populace marvel at them. Some convert to Shi'ism and are taken into service; those who refuse are sent to Tabriz as booty, where the Shah makes a few his retainers and sends the rest back to Egypt to tell Sultan Qansaw what happened. This story clearly had appeal for the exoticism of its content, from the enormous, demon-like Zangis to the strange weapons they wield in battle. In fact, this episode is the only one in the entire "Anonymous Histories" narrative to consistently appear in every copy that has illustrations.

A final ethnic group mentioned in the "Anonymous Histories" is the Georgians. They appear twice. The first time is early in the narrative, when the Georgian king Bagrat Khan, feeling threatened by the growing prestige and influence of the Safavid order, invades Ardabil in an attempt to stamp it out.[30] Much later in the story, long after Shah Isma'il has established his realm, three Georgian kings rebel against Safavid suzerainty.[31] One of them is even described as demonic and wielding a giant mace, reminiscent of Sarim Khan the Kurd from an earlier story. The overall impression given is that Georgians are treacherous infidels guided by priests. One Georgian king, however (Manuchihr Khan), converts to Shi'ism upon being treated courteously by his Qizilbash captors and hearing of the divine qualities of the Shah.

The Other in these tales may also be categorized according to religion. Here the distinction in the mind of the author(s) is quite clear and simple: Shi'is are good, and Sunnis are bad.

The narrator's sectarian prejudice against Sunnis is apparent on virtually every page of the narrative, literally from the opening passage, which sets the scene by saying that in the old days, most places in Iran "clung to the paths of Sunnism and Christianity, and the true sect of the Twelve Imams was hidden."[32] As the narrative progresses, the author's dim view of Sunnism shows itself with regularity. In the numerous battles, for example, defeated enemies are frequently offered security at the price of conversion, and particularly of cursing the first three Caliphs as enemies of the faith. This the Sunnis in the story abhor explicitly, virtually always to the point of preferring death. Sunnis are also seen as untrustworthy, such as the village head who refuses to help the pregnant queen the night she gives birth to Tahmasp.[33] One story in which the author gives full rein to his anti-Sunni feelings is that of Qulijan. Shah Isma'il is en route to Herat, and he wants to send someone ahead to make sure the city's population gives him the royal welcome he deserves. Amir Najm II suggests his servant Qulijan. When Qulijan reports for duty, Shah Isma'il asks him whether he is friend or foe to the Sunnis; Qulijan replies, "Amir Najm knows how much I love the Sunnis," and Amir Najm clarifies that Qulijan loves them so much that "if he killed a thousand of them a day every day, he wouldn't hold back if even more showed up."[34] Qulijan is sent to Herat, where he single-handedly so terrorizes the populace that they put together a welcome for Shah Isma'il such as even Sultan Husayn Bayqara never received.

Conversely, in the narrator's eyes, Shi'is are invariably good. Since it is a running trope of the story that the Twelver sect is oppressed and dominated by their Sunni enemies throughout Iran, making it Shah Isma'il's sacred mission to propagate and elevate that faith, the story is frequently moved ahead by invoking Shi'is who have been hiding their beliefs and come out at the appropriate time to save a Qizilbash in trouble, including the Shah himself. In the aforementioned story of the Sunni village head who refused to help the pregnant queen, Her Majesty's party is looked after by another village head who happens to be a Shi'i, not to mention fabulously wealthy, as will be discussed below. Another important crypto-Shi'i in the story is Sultan Husayn Bayqara, the last Timurid prince. He tries to promulgate the Twelver faith in Herat, but is foiled by the insubordination of the populace. In the meantime, though, a Shi'i sayyid from Jabal Amil has heard of Sultan Husayn's Shi'ism and is on his way with forty thousand households. He is dismayed to hear of the situation in Herat, but he has a vision in which he is told to wait in Sabzavar for seventeen years, at which time a scion of Ali will announce the True Faith in Khurasan. The sayyid waits patiently and, sure enough, seventeen years later he learns of the rise of Shah Isma'il. He even takes his people into the fight against the Uzbeks as a show of his devotion.[35]

It is interesting, too, the lengths to which the author(s) will go to make prominent pre-Safavid historical figures palatable to a militant Shi'i audience. Even if such figures are not claimed to be crypto-Shi'is, like Sultan Husayn Bayqara, they are usually portrayed as having, in some way, benefited or benefited from Shi'ism, and in particular the Safavid Order. Timur, for example, has a fascinating series of encounters with Shah Isma'il's ancestor Sultan Ali "the Black-Clad."[36] Hasan Padishah, i.e., Uzun Hasan Aq Quyunlu, is said to have ascended the throne "with the help of the house of the saintly Shaykh Safi."[37] Babur, the future founder of the Mughal empire in India, is not explicitly said to have converted, but he does put on a Qizilbash *taj*, which he himself refers to as "the crown of fortune."[38] He also departs Iran for India when Shah Isma'il presciently suggests that he will have better luck there – at which point Babur notes that a yogi once told him that the Chaghatay would prosper in India thanks to the house of Shaykh Safi al-Din.[39]

In addition to "the Other around us," the author(s) of the "Anonymous Histories" had interesting notions about "the Other above us," meaning those in power. The appearance of specific rulers in the text affords us a valuable glimpse of the popular attitude toward the powerful in the lives and cultural memory of people in Safavid Iran.

The author's attitude toward Shah Isma'il, to take the most important example of a royal figure, is, as might be expected, adulatory and even worshipful. The Shah is referred to throughout the narrative by titles such as "the Perfect Guide," "the Most Noble Ruler," the "Ruler Who Achieves His Desires," the "Ruler Who Is the Shadow of God," and so on. The devotion of his followers is absolute. Just how absolute it was is apparent in a telling episode which occurs during the account of an Ottoman emissary's visit to Iran in the lead-up to the battle of Chaldiran.[40] Part of the message the emissary brings from Sultan Selim is how outraged the Ottomans are that Shah Isma'il, when he conquered Baghdad in 1508, dug up the bones of the Sunni jurisprudent Abu Hanifa, burned them, and buried a dog in their place. In response, Shah Isma'il takes the emissary and the Safavid religious scholars on a hunting trip. While out hunting, they spot a shrine, which the Shah is told is the shrine of the prophet Qaydar.[41] A pilgrimage is ordered. The party has just finished performing the rites when someone comes running up holding the body of one of Shah Isma'il's hunting dogs, saying it was accidentally killed by a kick from a horse. The Shah acts crestfallen; he says, "I saw great wisdom in this dog, such as human beings do not possess," and he orders that the dog's body be wrapped in silk brocade – and then that his men break open the wall of the shrine and bury the dog inside! The Ottoman emissary, already shocked at this command, is even further scandalized to see the Safavid religious scholars striving to outdo each other in obedience. He asks one of them the reason for his obedience and is told, "When the Perfect Guide gives a command, what else can we do? We recognize that reward and punishment belong to him."[42] The Shah's chief religious advisor later tells the emissary, "Can there be a better reason than this, that the Perfect Guide is now Padishah? He gave an order saying, 'Bury the dog near a prophet of God.' We all knew it was a heinous and most evil act, but for the sake of pleasing the Shah we did it, for we are the *ulama* of the Islamic nation; we dug up the ground and obeyed His Majesty so that he would be satisfied with us and we might obtain a high position near him."[43] He also invokes a parallel with the burial of the first two Caliphs.[44]

It is not all cheerleading, however. On a couple of occasions, rare as they may be, the narrator inserts moralizing comments about Shah Isma'il. In particular, the narrator gently chides the Shah for swelling with pride after his defeat of Shahi Beg Khan.[45] This pride ultimately comes back to haunt His Majesty, as before the battle with the Ottomans at Chaldiran both he and the Qizilbash take no heed of the massive enemy force being assembled; the narrator observes at this point that "The Shah was being a bit arrogant."[46] Two manuscripts even highlight Isma'il's failure to say "God willing" before going into battle against Sultan Selim.[47]

At one point, before a certain battle, Shah Isma'il overhears some Qizilbash griping that they do all the fighting while he takes all the credit – a line inserted, perhaps, only to give Isma'il a chance to show his importance by temporarily withholding his efforts, but interesting nonetheless as a brief moment of subaltern criticism of those in power.[48]

In addition to Shah Isma'il himself, his son Tahmasp is also an object of clear reverence in these stories. The author, in fact, tries to make it sound as if Tahmasp is alive and on the throne when the stories are being written, although he gives away the ruse a couple of times with, for examples, posthumous references to Shah Abbas I (who died in 1629).[49] Tahmasp, as the young son of the divinely sanctioned champion of the True Faith, naturally is shown in a devout light. At one point, when the city of Herat is under siege and in danger of falling, Tahmasp's prayer saves the city.[50] Shortly thereafter, the young prince is brought into the room where Isma'il lies ill. The mere sight of the boy cures the Shah of his fever, and he sits up with paternal joy, already on the mend.[51]

Shahi Beg Khan, who maneuvers his way to the top of the Uzbek heap and becomes Shah Isma'il's chief antagonist in the east, is depicted as arrogant and power-hungry. He rises to the throne by effectively outwitting and outfighting the feckless, squabbling heirs of Sultan Husayn Bayqara. Besides this, though, Shahi Beg Khan is also portrayed as something of an object of derision, if not a comic figure, as he keeps getting thwarted. For example, his first attempt to take Samarqand is a complete farce: As his army is preparing to assault the city, the population comes streaming out the gate, armed to a man with cudgels; they bash in the brains of two thousand of Shahi

Beg Khan's troops and rob half as many more.[52] Later on, when Shahi Beg Khan conquers Herat, he is determined to enter the city with fully as much pomp and glory as Sultan Husayn Bayqara used to, but his evil fate keeps catching up with him. As he enters the city, a child spontaneously recites an ominous quatrain (for which Shahi Beg Khan kills the boy with his own tambourine).[53] Shortly thereafter, Shahi Beg Khan orders the nobles of the city to assemble in the Friday mosque and hear the *khutba* recited in his name. The preacher begins to recite the titles and honorifics of the new ruler, as he is about to speak Shahi Beg Khan's name itself, his tongue is turned by the Unseen and he says instead, "Shah Isma'il Safavi al-Musavi al-Husayni Bahadur Khan, Shadow of God, may He prolong his rule!"[54] The enraged Shahi Beg Khan has the preacher killed; he then orders the bazaars of Herat plundered, further cementing his image in the mind of the tales' audience as a force for evil. Shahi Beg Khan's last and most important failure, of course, is his falling for Shah Isma'il's phony retreat at Marv. To round out the picture, Shahi Beg Khan is henpecked by his wife, who is clearly intimated to be more intelligent than he is, and he is also openly contradicted by his high-ranking officers. It is hard not to conclude that the molders of the "Anonymous Histories" narrative saw him as rather a contemptible figure.

Shah Isma'il's nemesis in the west, the Ottoman sultan Selim I, is also shown as arrogant, brutal, and obsessed with power. Unlike Shahi Beg Khan, however, Sultan Selim seems to be taken fairly seriously.[55] Even his beginnings are sinister. As a seven-year old boy, he is already described as bad-tempered, disrespectful, and even "like a poisonous snake,"[56] and when he is only ten years old his own father, Sultan Bayezid, brains him with a mace in the harem. The boy is secretly nursed back to health, though, and re-discovered at age eighteen, when his strapping virility finally elicits his father's respect.[57] As an adult, Selim is depicted as a barely-controllable hothead, in contrast to the prudent and phlegmatic Sultan Bayezid. When Shah Isma'il sends the straw-stuffed head of Shahi Beg Khan to the Ottoman court, for example, Selim is ready to kill the Safavid emissary just for looking at him with insufficient respect, whereas Sultan Bayezid is unruffled even by Shah Isma'il's "gift," saying that it shows the loftiness of his station that he should be sent the head of the ruler of all Turkistan.[58] Eventually Selim overthrows his father and commences his rivalry with Shah Isma'il, which culminates (but does not end) at the Battle of Chaldiran. For all his wrathful and violent nature, though, Selim is also shown as henpecked by his mother[59] and conspicuously craven in battle,[60] and his demise is as humiliating as it is just, as will be discussed shortly.

One final royal figure to consider is the future founder of the Mughal dynasty, Babur (who is consistently referred to as "Babur Padishah," despite the fact that he hasn't founded the empire yet). Babur is portrayed as haughty, wayward, and somewhat incompetent. Early in the narrative, he gets locked out of his own city (Samarqand) when the people there see that he was unable to defeat Shahi Beg

Khan.⁶¹ He keeps conquering cities, then losing them and asking Shah Isma'il for help in reconquering them; this leads Isma'il's lieutenant Amir Najm II to call him crazy (*divana*). Babur's troubled relationship with Amir Najm, in fact, is an important part of the story. The two men get off to a rocky start when Babur treats Amir Najm with contempt on their first meeting, viewing him as "nothing more than a peasant."⁶² Later, when the two lead an expedition into Central Asia to punish the Uzbeks, Babur has to deal with Amir Najm's increasingly erratic behavior, including his hanging of his own nephew in the name of discipline (regret for which only makes him more unstable), culminating in the massacre of civilians at Qarshi and the ignominious defeat of the Qizilbash army. This is, of course, blamed on Babur, and he is forced to make a humiliating pilgrimage of apology to the royal court, his sword around his neck in submission.⁶³ Eventually, Babur departs for India on the advice of Shah Isma'il, whom he never met in real life.⁶⁴

One fascinating aspect of the author's impression of the Other above him is the material dimension of their existence, particularly the exotic objects they own and wield. We hear, for example, about Shahi Beg Khan's armbands, which are "encrusted with eighteen diamonds and rubies and emeralds and engraved with the name of Changiz Khan, and each stone of which was worth the income of an entire city,"⁶⁵ and about his battle-drum, which is made of seven metals and can be heard four leagues away.⁶⁶

Shahi Beg Khan himself is described as envious of a certain tent that Sultan Husayn Bayqara once owned. The narrator states:

> It was sewn in Anatolia from European satin; the artists wove images of different sorts of trees and pictures of wild animals and birds into its interior on their looms, and a hundred and forty thousand tumans were spent on it. It came to be known by the name *Iftah* [Arabic: "conquer!"], because whenever Soltan Hosayn Mirza went on campaign with this tent, he was never defeated but always conquered.⁶⁷

The narrator really pulls out all the stops in his description of Qasim Khan, the lord of the steppe, to whom the defeated Uzbeks look for support in their quest for revenge on Shah Isma'il:

> Jani Beg Sultan looked at Qasim Khan and saw that he was like a gloomy demon. He was sitting upon the Changizid throne, which was made of gold and fashioned in a novel way, with its four corners made in the likenesses of a lion, a leopard, a tiger, and a dragon. He wore Changiz Khan's jeweled crown, which was worth nearly seventy thousand tumans, and he had bright white eyes, bushy eyebrows, and long moustaches. Several very long hairs had also grown

from his chin, including three big hairs, one of which reached down to his right breast, one to his left, and one all the way down to his navel. This was a sign of his status as a Changizid, as every descendant of Changiz Khan with such hairs was entitled to rule.[68]

Perhaps the most interesting exotic royal possession is almost a character in itself. This is Shah Isma'il's horse, which is usually referred to, for reasons that are unclear, as the "mare of Mansur." This horse is at once fleet and wise. For example, after his defeat outside Marv, Shahi Beg Khan flees and gets stuck in a bog; Shah Isma'il heedlessly tries to ride after him, but the "mare of Mansur," realizing the danger before its master does, plants its legs firmly and stands as motionless as the pole star.[69] In the aftermath of this victory, when Isma'il sends the severed hand of Shahi Beg Khan to the recalcitrant king of Mazandaran, the messenger who takes the grim package requests, and is granted, the use of the horse.[70] And when Shah Isma'il himself is later defeated at Chaldiran and falls into another bog, the first thing he does after a Qizilbash pulls him out is to arrange to have someone find his horse.[71]

A final category of Other to take into consideration when reading the "Anonymous Histories" for insight into the subaltern mentality is "the Other beyond us," or the transcendental Other. By this I mean the numerous references to the divine as a mover of events and rewarder or punisher of persons. The metaphysical expectations of the author(s) are revealing.

The imprint of divine will on the storyline is most apparent in the guidance provided to the actors in the narrative, particularly Shah Isma'il himself. He is frequently told what to do in dreams, such as when, fretting over the potential public resistance to his declaration of Shi'ism in newly conquered Tabriz, Isma'il receives detailed instructions on how to position his men in the Friday mosque so as to kill anyone who protests the recitation of the Shi'i *khutba*.[72] The Shah is occasionally alerted in a dream that certain of his followers are in trouble and need his assistance.[73] Divine guidance is also offered once while Isma'il is awake, in that he beseeches God for help in capturing a particularly strong fortress and is rewarded with a trance-like state in which one of the Imams describes the best means of attack.[74] In one episode, Shah Isma'il even submits to the Unseen a request for advice in writing: He leaves a petition atop the grave of the Imam Riza in Mashhad overnight, and in the morning, when the Shah and his men open the shrine and check, they find a note in the Imam's handwriting telling them what to do.[75] Other means of determining the right course of action include reliance on astrologers and readers of animal shoulder-bones (who, it is interesting to note, are never wrong). At one point the Qizilbash even take an augury by watching a fight between their own dogs and the enemy's; although outnumbered, the Qizilbash dogs drive the others from the field yelping, which both sides interpret as an omen in favor of the Qizilbash.[76]

Naturally, the higher powers of the universe are more than willing to help Shah Isma'il eradicate the enemies of the True Faith. On one occasion, during the Safavid conquest of Baghdad, the Qizilbash ford the Tigris river at a point where the enemy has destroyed the bridge. After they are across, Shah Isma'il orders his men to check and see if the water did not support anyone. Lo and behold, one man has drowned, and he turns out to have been a Kurd who had gotten mixed up in the ranks of the Qizilbash during the previous battle and was concealing his identity.[77] Another instance in which a villain is felled by unseen powers is the episode near the end of the narrative, when the Turkman official Amir Khan, who has been lying about his murder of a sayyid, declares that if he is guilty, then the Commander of the Faithful (i.e., Ali) shall become his enemy. No sooner has Amir Khan said this than he is struck down with unbearable pain, and he dies that very evening.[78]

The divinely occasioned demise that most stands out is probably that of Sultan Selim, the supreme villain of the whole story. During his preparations for a second invasion of Iran, Selim goes hunting. As he is pursuing a partridge up a mountain, he thinks to himself that when he conquers Ardabil, he will raze the tomb of Shaykh Safi. Immediately he has a vision of a white lion attacking him. A Janissary, noticing that the Sultan is petrified with fear, asks him what he had just been thinking, and when Selim repeats his intention aloud, he miraculously falls off the mountain and dies.[79]

It is interesting that large-scale miracles are few in this narrative. Minor miracles include tongue-turnings, such as the one mentioned above that happens to Shahi Beg Khan. A similar slip occurs in Tabriz when Sultan Selim is occupying the city in the wake of his victory at Chaldiran.[80] Such inspired mistakes on the part of Friday preachers demonstrate Shah Isma'il's rightful, divinely sanctioned claim to power. But aside from things like these and the instances of guidance and targeted execution mentioned above, there are few outright interventions in worldly affairs by divine powers.

One miracle, in fact, seems to have dropped out of the canon early on. This is Isma'il's vision of a youth riding a camel from the direction of Mashhad during a crucial battle, which appears in the Chester Beatty Library manuscript[81] but not in the version published as *Alamara-yi Shah Isma'il*. Was this early miracle edged out of the narrative in favor of less overt reliance on divine might?

It is apparent, in conclusion, that the corpus of tales known collectively as the "Anonymous Histories of Shah Isma'il" offer the attentive historian, if not a reliable body of historical fact, a great deal of insight into the mental landscape of the people passing around their memories of the early days. In these pages, we get a powerful sense of the Safavid foundation myth as it existed in the minds of the sub-royal classes in seventeenth-century Iran: A divinely supported Shah spread the True Faith in a world populated by treacherous Sunnis, various rough and tumble tribes, and world-moving individuals of good and evil character – a world in which those who opposed the Shah's rightful mission got their comeuppance, whether by his own royal blade or by being hurled off a cliff for an impious thought. Such stories must have been particularly appealing as the power of the Safavids waned[82] and was finally destroyed; hearing or reading about the good old days, when the forces of good simply couldn't lose, would have been a tonic for people living through the chaos of eighteenth-century Iran, when many of the extant manuscripts seem to have been written down. For twenty-first century historians, the appeal comes from the opportunity to consider the view of people other than those in the chancery, in the name of looking at Safavid history from the perspective of those who lived it and not just those who made it.

Bibliography

Anooshahr, Ali. "The Rise of the Safavids According to their Old Veterans: Amini Haravi's *Futuhat-e Shahi*." *Iranian Studies* 48, no. 2 (March 2015): 249–267.

Gallagher, Amelia. "The Transformation of Shah Ismail Safevi in the Turkish *Hikaye*." *Journal of Folklore Research* 46, no. 2 (May 2009): 173–95.

Hanaway, William. "*Amir Arsalan* and the Question of Genre." *Iranian Studies* 24, no. 1 (1991): 55–60.

Hanaway, William. "Iranian Identity." *Iranian Studies* 26, no. 1 (Winter–Spring 1993): 147–50.

Horst, Heribert. *Timur und Hoga Ali: Ein Beitrag zur Geschichte der Safawiden*. Abhandlungen der Geistes- und Sozialwissenschaftlichen Klasse, Jahrgang 1958, no. 2. Mainz: Akademie der Wissenschaften und der Literatur; in Kommission bei F. Steiner, Wiesbaden, 1958.

Mahdavi, Shireen. "Amusements in Qajar Iran." *Iranian Studies* 40, no. 4 (September 2007): 483–99.

Marzolph, Ulrich. "A Treasury of Formulaic Narrative: The Persian Popular Romance *Hosein-e Kord*." *Oral Tradition* 14 (1999): 279–303.

Marzolph, Ulrich. "Persian Popular Literature in the Qajar Period." *Asian Folklore Studies* 60, no. 2 (2001): 215–36.

Matthee, Rudi. *Persia in Crisis: Safavid Decline and the Fall of Isfahan*. London: I. B. Tauris, 2012.

McChesney, R. "Alamara-ye Sah Esma'il." *Encyclopædia Iranica*, I/8, pp. 796–97; an updated version is available online at http://www.iranicaonline.org/articles/alamara-ye-sah-esmail-an-anonymous-narrative-of-the-life-of-shah-esmail-r (accessed 1 November 2015).

Membré, Michele. *Mission to the Lord Sophy of Persia (1539–1542)*. Translated by A. H. Morton. Warminster: E. J. W. Gibb Memorial Trust, 1999.

Morton, A. H. "The Date and Attribution of the Ross Anonymous. Notes on a Persian History of Shah Isma'il I." In *History and Literature in Iran: Persian and Islamic*

Studies in Honour of P. W. Avery, edited by Charles Melville, 179–212. Pembroke Papers 1. New York: British Academic Press, 1998 (1990).

Morton, A. H. "The Early Years of Shah Isma'il in the *Afzal al-tavarikh* and Elsewhere." In *Safavid Persia; The History and Politics of an Islamic Society*, edited by Charles Melville, 27–51. Pembroke Papers 4. London: I. B. Tauris, 1996.

Muntazir Sahib, Asghar, ed. *Alamara-yi Shah Isma'il*. Majmu'a-yi matun-i farsi 43. Tehran: BTNK, 1349.

Page, Mary Ellen. "Naqqali and Ferdowsi: Creativity in the Iranian National Tradition." PhD diss., University of Pennsylvania, 1977.

Page, Mary Ellen. "Professional Storytelling in Iran: Transmission and Practice." *Iranian Studies* 12, no. 3/4 (Summer–Autumn 1979): 195–215. http://www.jstor.org/stable/4310320.

Quinn, Sholeh A. "Rewriting Ni'matu'llahi History in Safavid Chronicles." In *The Heritage of Sufism, vol. III: Late Classical Persianate Sufism (1501–1750); The Safavid & Mughal Period*, edited by Leonard Lewisohn and David Morgan, 201–22. Oxford: Oneworld, 1999.

Quinn, Sholeh A. *Historical Writing during the Reign of Shah 'Abbas: Ideology, Imitation, and Legitimacy in Safavid Chronicles*. Salt Lake City: University of Utah Press, 2000.

Shukri, Yad Allah, ed. *Alamara-yi Safavi*. Tehran: Bunyad-i Farhang-i iran, 1350.

Wood, Barry D. "The *Shahnama-i Isma'il*: Art and Cultural Memory in Sixteenth-Century Iran." PhD diss., Harvard University, 2002.

Wood, Barry D. "The *Tarikh-i Jahanara* in the Chester Beatty Library: An Illustrated Manuscript of the 'Anonymous Histories of Shah Isma'il.'" *Iranian Studies* 37, no. 1 (March 2004): 89–107.

Wood, Barry. "The Battle of Chalderan: Official History and Popular Memory." *Iranian Studies* 50, no. 1 (January 2017): 79–105.

Wood, Barry, ed. and transl. *The Adventures of Shah Esma'il: A Seventeenth-Century Persian Popular Romance*. Leiden: Brill, 2019.

Yamamoto, Kumiko. *The Oral Background of Persian Epics: Storytelling and Poetry*. Brill Studies in Middle Eastern Literatures 26. Leiden: Brill, 2003.

Notes

1 And some poetry; there exists a panegyric epic, commissioned by Shah Isma'il himself, describing (highly selectively!) Isma'il's career in the style of the *Shahnama*. See Barry Wood, "The *Shahnama-i Isma'il*: Art and Cultural Memory in Sixteenth-Century Iran" (PhD diss., Harvard University, 2002).

2 See Sholeh A. Quinn, *Historical Writing during the Reign of Shah 'Abbas: Ideology, Imitation, and Legitimacy in Safavid Chronicles* (Salt Lake City, 2000) for an exploration of this phenomenon.

3 See Barry Wood, "The Battle of Chalderan: Official History and Popular Memory," *Iranian Studies* 50, no. 1 (January 2017): 80–81.

4   For an introduction, see R. McChesney, "Alamara-ye Sah Esma'il," *Encyclopædia Iranica* I/8, pp. 796–97.
5   Michele Membré, *Mission to the Lord Sophy of Persia (1539–1542)*, trans. A. H. Morton (Warminster, 1999), 52. Interestingly, just over the (linguistic) border, the Shah Isma'il character took on a completely different life of its own in Turkish folklore, for which see Amelia Gallagher, "The Transformation of Shah Ismail Safevi in the Turkish *Hikaye*," *Journal of Folklore Research* 46, no. 2 (May 2009): 173–95.
6   A. H. Morton surmises as much in "The Early Years of Shah Isma'il in the *Afzal al-tavarikh* and Elsewhere," in *Safavid Persia: The History and Politics of an Islamic Society*, ed. Charles Melville (London, 1996), 27–51. See also Ali Anooshahr, "The Rise of the Safavids According to their Old Veterans: Amini Haravi's *Futuhat-e Shahi*," *Iranian Studies* 48, no. 2 (March 2015): 249–267 for an official source based in eyewitness accounts by the Qizilbash.
7   For one of the illustrated copies, see Barry D. Wood, "The *Tarikh-i Jahanara* in the Chester Beatty Library: An Illustrated Manuscript of the 'Anonymous Histories of Shah Isma'il,'" *Iranian Studies* 37, no. 1 (March 2004): 89–107. The corpus of manuscripts is dealt with briefly in Wood, "The Battle of Chalderan." For the way in which the stories were brought to bear on official historiography, see A. H. Morton, "The Date and Attribution of the Ross Anonymous. Notes on a Persian History of Shah Isma'il I," in *History and Literature in Iran: Persian and Islamic Studies in Honour of P. W. Avery*, ed. Charles Melville (New York, 1998 [1990]), 179–212.
8   Asghar Muntazir Sahib (ed.), *Alamara-yi Shah Isma'il* (Tehran, 1349/1971) (henceforth *AASI*). Another version, from a different manuscript, is Yad Allah Shukri (ed.), *Alamara-yi Safavi* (Tehran, 1350/1972).
9   Barry Wood (ed. and trans.), *The Adventures of Shah Esma'il: A Seventeenth-Century Persian Popular Romance* (Leiden, 2019) (henceforth Wood, *Adventures*).
10 The narrator does his best to make it sound as if Tahmasp is alive and on the throne, but several clues in the text give away the true date of the tales' composition. See Morton, "Date and Attribution."
11 Mary Ellen Page, "Naqqali and Ferdowsi: Creativity in the Iranian National Tradition" (PhD diss., University of Pennsylvania, 1977), 227–28.
12 Ulrich Marzolph, "A Treasury of Formulaic Narrative: The Persian Popular Romance *Hosein-e Kord*," *Oral Tradition* 14 (1999): 287.
13 The character Mansur Beg Purnak, for example, is named Zahrab Sultan in the version published by Shukri.
14 For the practices of the *naqqalan*, see Page, "Naqqali and Ferdowsi," as well as Mary Ellen Page, "Professional Storytelling in Iran: Transmission and Practice," *Iranian Studies* 12, no. 3/4 (Summer–Autumn 1979): 195–215. See also the mention in Shireen Mahdavi, "Amusements in Qajar Iran," *Iranian Studies* 40, no. 4 (September 2007): 490.
15 Page, "Professional Storytelling in Iran," 213.
16 Interestingly, the tradition seems eventually to have come full circle; one scholar notes that modern Iranian *naqqalan* believe that Shah Isma'il used storytellers to spread the Twelver Shi'i faith (Kumiko Yamamoto, *The Oral Background of Persian Epics: Storytelling and Poetry* [Leiden, 2003], 20–21).
17 Morton, "Date and Attribution," 203.
18 William Hanaway, "Iranian Identity," *Iranian Studies* 26, no. 1 (Winter–Spring 1993): 150.
19 *AASI*, 106; Wood, *Adventures*, 87.
20 *AASI*, 374; Wood, *Adventures*, 282.
21 *AASI*, 329–33; Wood, *Adventures*, 252–54.
22 This may be the memory of an early-sixteenth century rebellion by the Yazidis.
23 *AASI*, 151–60; Wood, *Adventures*, 128.
24 *AASI*, 170–88; Wood, *Adventures*, 147.
25 *AASI*, 516; Wood, *Adventures*, 385.

26 *AASI*, 41–43; Wood, *Adventures*, 39–40.
27 *AASI*, 564ff; Wood, *Adventures*, 427–440.
28 *AASI*, 234–40; Wood, *Adventures*, 183–87.
29 Shah Isma'il's enemies consistently refer to him as "Shaykh-oghli," meaning "son of a shaykh," as a contemptuous reference to his dervish heritage.
30 *AASI*, 5–6; Wood, *Adventures*, 7.
31 *AASI*, 604ff; Wood, *Adventures*, 450–55.
32 *AASI*, 1; Wood, *Adventures*, 3.
33 *AASI*, 82ff; Wood, *Adventures*, 69–70.
34 *AASI*, 397; Wood, *Adventures*, 297.
35 *AASI*, 343–46; Wood, *Adventures*, 261–63.
36 *AASI*, 14–21; Wood, *Adventures*, 16–21. See also Heribert Horst, *Timur und Hoga Ali: Ein Beitrag zur Geschichte der Safawiden* (Wiesbaden, 1958).
37 *AASI*, 87; Wood, *Adventures*, 72.
38 *AASI*, 391; Wood, *Adventures*, 294.
39 *AASI*, 499; Wood, *Adventures*, 448–50.
40 *AASI*, 515ff; Wood, *Adventures*, 384–87.
41 Son of Isma'il, son of Ibrahim; his shrine still exists in Zanjan Province.
42 *AASI*, 517; Wood, *Adventures*, 386.
43 *AASI*, 519; Wood, *Adventures*, 387.
44 Ibid. The point may be a religious one, i.e., praising the virtues of following a leader and demeaning the Sunni concept of consensus (*ijma'*) in matters of faith.
45 *AASI*, 369; Wood, *Adventures*, 278.
46 *AASI*, 520; Wood, *Adventures*, 388.
47 Chester Beatty Library MS Per. 278, folio 216b; *Alamara-yi Safavi* (ed. Shukri), 477. *AASI* leaves out this detail.
48 *AASI*, 202ff; Wood, *Adventures*, 159–60.
49 E.g. *AASI*, 377 (Wood, *Adventures*, 283).
50 *AASI*, 457; Wood, *Adventures*, 340.
51 *AASI*, 460; Wood, *Adventures*, 342.
52 *AASI*, 253; Wood, *Adventures*, 200.
53 *AASI*, 308; Wood, *Adventures*, 237.
54 *AASI*, 308; Wood, *Adventures*, 238.
55 No doubt because he was the only one to defeat Shah Isma'il.
56 *AASI*, 232; Wood, *Adventures*, 181.
57 *AASI*, 233–4; Wood, *Adventures*, 182.
58 *AASI*, 383–4; Wood, *Adventures*, 288.
59 Before the Battle of Chaldiran, she berates her son for picking a fight with Shah Isma'il, who has the Twelve Imams themselves on his side (*AASI*, 513; Wood, *Adventures*, 382).
60 At Chaldiran, he does not fight in person, preferring to watch from a hill, and when the battle is going against him, he cannot bring himself to fire his cannons, having promised earlier not to do so (*AASI*, 524; Wood, *Adventures*, 391).
61 *AASI*, 261–2; Wood, *Adventures*, 205.
62 *AASI*, 391; Wood, *Adventures*, 293. Amir Najm II is dismissed as a peasant by several people in the story; it would be interesting to track down the potential reasons.
63 *AASI*, 412ff; Wood, *Adventures*, 351–52.
64 The foundation of the Mughal Empire, as pointed out above, is thus indirectly credited to the hero of the Safavid founding.
65 *AASI*, 382; Wood, *Adventures*, 287. These are presented to the Ottoman sultan as "a modest little trifle."
66 *AASI*, 489–90; Wood, *Adventures*, 362.

67 *AASI*, 297–98; Wood, *Adventures*, 231.
68 *AASI*, 483; Wood, *Adventures*, 358.
69 *AASI*, 368; Wood, *Adventures*, 277.
70 *AASI*, 376; Wood, *Adventures*, 283.
71 *AASI*, 528; Wood, *Adventures*, 394.
72 *AASI*, 60; Wood, *Adventures*, 52–3.
73 E.g. *AASI* 64–5, 155–56 (Wood, *Adventures*, 56, 124).
74 *AASI*, 118–19; Wood, *Adventures*, 97.
75 *AASI*, 348–49; Wood, *Adventures*, 264.
76 *AASI*, 228; Wood, *Adventures*, 178.
77 *AASI*, 163; Wood, *Adventures*, 131.
78 *AASI*, 617; Wood, *Adventures*, 460.
79 *AASI*, 596–7; Wood, *Adventures*, 443.
80 *AASI*, 533; Wood, *Adventures*, 397–98. Unlike Shahi Beg Khan, Sultan Selim does not execute the preacher, on the (uncharacteristically charitable) grounds that he was acting out of habit when he spoke.
81 Chester Beatty Library, MS Per. 278, fol. 209b.
82 This late-Safavid nostalgia for early Safavid history has been remarked upon; see e.g. Rudi Matthee, *Persia in Crisis: Safavid Decline and the Fall of Isfahan* (London, 2012), xxiv and 126–28.

5

The Muharram Subaltern in the Safavid Period: "Thin Description" and the Limits of European Travel Accounts

Babak Rahimi

By and large, Subaltern Studies has been an overlooked method of inquiry in the subfield of Safavid studies. With the new set of research questions engendered by developments in early modern studies since the late twentieth century, the question of subaltern and challenges in representing its standpoint have seen scant attention in scholarly works on the Safavids. There are three reasons for this.

First, scholarly research on the Safavids has mostly relied on the elite culture of court chronicles, jurisprudence texts or literary works with an "Isfahani-centeric perspective" that tends to represent history from the perspective of literate male subjects with the privilege of self-representation through cultural capital and network ties.[1] With few exceptions, the focus on elite cultural sources has mainly contributed to bypassing the question of subalternity of displaced social groups positioned on the margins of power relations with the ruling class(es) who maintain a dominant role.[2] Second, and yet connected with the first reason, the focus on (male) elites, in particular the royal household, court officials, merchants, military figures and more importantly the clerics, has served as a normative way to expand on the contested notion of "Safavid polity," its civic and religious institutions, state bureaucracies and military organizations across the vast Iranian landmass that nominally identified the Safavid imperium. The elite-centric bias has been justified in the assumption that the advent or the breakdown of politics revolves around elite interaction, and that those in the margins with diverse social backgrounds are precisely as such: shadowy backgrounds to elite histories who are in control over the competing forces to shape or maintain political order.

The third reason is inherently tied to the production of academic knowledge. Since its inception during the inter-war period, when joint efforts between state and corporate Foundations gave rise to area studies, academic discourses of various disciplines have given rise, to use Michel Foucault's term, a "corpus of knowledge" that has presupposed a way of looking at history marked by certain organization of concepts and types of enunciations in the exclusion of subalternity.[3] This is particularly true in the case of the Middle Studies. As Sabra J. Webber has shown in her 1997 study, the study of subaltern or "small voices" has been viewed in the field of the Middle East Studies as a byproduct of South Asian studies and therefore limited for its focus on the colonial period when regions such as Subcontinent India saw the rise of anti-colonial and anti-bourgeoise movements comprised by the marginal populations.[4] What sidelined as historical discourse was a broader attempt to think of history "from below" with a keen eye on the invisible agencies of subaltern social classes and their contribution to history.

Since 1997 the Middle East Studies has seen a range of new works that apply the analysis of subalterity from anthropological, historical and sociological perspectives. Edited volume by Stephanie Cronin, *Subaltern and Social Protest: History from Below in the Middle East and North Africa* (2008), exemplify a set of new studies that seek to identify the interweaving relations between social movements, politics, gender and the unemployed in urban-rural settings.[5] The publication of Manata Hashemi's *Coming of Age in Iran: Poverty and the Struggle for Dignity* (2020) also suggests an emerging current in the field of Iranian studies where class, marginality and counter-elite cultures take on more of the scholarly spotlight. Despite challenges, especially due to limitation of sources, such new studies seek to reconceputalize agency in ways that go beyond the binary paradigms of "tradition" and "modernity" and more importantly, against the solipsistic tendencies to write the histories of preponderant groups.

The subfield of Safavid studies, which grew in prominence in 1970s, thanks largely to the British-Canadian scholar, Roger Savory, however, has yet to engage – perhaps until the present volume – in a critical and in-depth discussion on the question of subaltern in its early modern context. Such discussion, I suggest, would need to rethink historical knowledge for a more inclusive and wide-ranging historical analysis drawn from various schools of thought, including Subaltern Studies, to recover themes of agency in Safavid history. This critical inquiry should also be done in the context of global modernities and complex formations of indigenous and colonial histories since the early modern era. Such ambition should also include a critical effort to study intersections of class, gender, ethnicity, race and sexuality on the urban and rural levels. Historically speaking, the idea is an attempt to problematize assumed notions of culture, economy and politics in the era of gunpowder empires when historical changes went well beyond the military revolution from the sixteenth to seventeenth centuries.[6]

The present study aims to contribute to a nascent discussion on Safavid subalternity. The focus here is primarily on methodological challenges in examining the subaltern features of Muharram rituals, performed during first ten-days of the Islamic lunar calendar (hence the name Muharram) in commemoration of the martyrdom of Prophet's grandson, Husayn, in Karbala, 680. It was in the Safavid period (1501-1722) that the diverse and changing Shi'i ceremonies, dating back to the early years of Islamic history, developed into both state and civic events. The Isfahani phase of Safavid rule (1590-1666) marked a period when the public rituals attained considerable popularity especially in urban areas where they underwent institutional transformations in staging and collective performances in line with the construction of new architectural sites in Isfahan under Shah Abbas I (r.1588-1629).[7]

The seventeenth century is also important for the study of subaltern of Muharram as the royal regime promoted the commemorative rituals, partly, as a way to distract from crisis that ensued the ascension of Safi (1629-1642) to the throne in February 1629.[8] The combination of foreign military incursions (especially the Ottoman capture of eastern Iraq), decreasing global demand for Safavid silk, and ongoing economic challenges in the centralization of taxation as a way to empower the central government and its new military apparatus away from the Qizilbash served as fertile ground for the revival of Sufi-messianic movements, despite the suppression of Nuqtavis early Abbas's reign.[9] In this sense, Muharram and, by and large, Imami commemorative cultures offered an alternative official religious culture to the growing messianic millenarianism in Isfahan and the provinces. The growth of popular spiritual currents among artisans, craftsmen and the poor in expanding urban spaces, paradoxically, could have also signaled the incorporation of Sufi rituals in Muharram ritual culture. All in all, the growing presence of the underclass in Muharram rituals after the death of Abbas I (1692) bespeaks of major cultural and religious changes that were caused by economic and political reconfigurations in an Empire that increasingly sought to impose Imami religion on the population.

However, since the establishment of Safavid rule in 1501, the main objective for promoting Muharram was the consolidation of state power with the popularization of ritual culture as an ideological source of legitimacy. The promotion of Muharram was partly aimed at promoting Shi'i Imami Islam but also to construct a new imperial social order based on what Sussan Babaie calls "Perso-Shi'i" identity in major urban centers, in particular Isfahan where new city spaces shaped emergent social networks and urban (sub)cultures.[10] The spread of the rituals served as a form of social solidarity on an imperial scale and, hence, open to denizens of all urban neighborhoods, including the subaltern groups who also participated in social spaces with the growing Sufi-urbanite and ('Abu Muslim) messianic cultures of the bazaars, coffeehouses and taverns since the late sixteenth century.[11] While the intersection between messianic and 'Alid devotional cultures, upheld by Sufi-brotherhood guild networks, adds a complicated dimension to the study of Safavid-era Muharram culture, we can speak of the rituals as state practices inclusive to all inhabitants regardless of class status.[12]

The argument here is that while there is considerable potential to learn from the subaltern life of Safavid society in the seventeenth-century course of developments with Muharram--together with other ritual performances such as *futuwwat* Sufi-urban guild fights between Haydaris and Nimatullahis – there is a dearth of primary sources on the "inner" life of the marginal population who participated in Muharram.[13] The European travel accounts, the bulk of our primary sources on the ceremonies, represent a set of problematic sources of knowledge, and accordingly the discussion focuses on the methodological limitation of these travel reports.[14] The second, the shorter part, is more suggestive. It argues that Husayn Va'iz Kashifi's *Rawat al-shuhada* [hereafter *Rawzat*) might provide us with an indigenous source to reimagine the "inner" life of the Muharram subaltern subject in a multivocal sense of ritual practices.

Aware of the intractable nature of definitions, the notion of "subaltern" that the present study adopts is a generic one. The notion of subaltern class is made in reference to how Antonio Gramsci (1891-1937) understood the concept when he coined the term interchangeably with *"classi subordinate,"* and in close relation with the ruling class, in the first half of twentieth-century Europe.[15] Far from a monolithic identity, the subalterns are "social groups" who stand outside of the hegemonic sphere of ruling elites, and they range from workers to peasantry, from the underclass to ethnic minorities and women. The subaltern can also imply an independent collective, also known as "masses," who carry the potential for resistance even when capitalism has not taken form in particular in agrarian settings. The postcolonial question is, therefore, an extension and not an essential feature of the subaltern.

Historical and social contexts, of course, are key. What we do not evidently discern in the case of Safavid subaltern is the formation of "parties" and "civic associations," as Gramsci saw it as a promising future of this distinct social group in twentieth-century Europe. In unraveling the subaltern in the modern period, though, one cannot but problematize changing societal processes that characterize a particular "society," if such term can be generically employed here. While a discussion on subaltern forms of life can be expanded in nineteenth-century Qajar Iran, as Touraj Atabaki has shown in his study of subaltern migrant Iranian community in the Caucasus, in the case of Safavid Iran we are limited to the urban elite and visible groups that textually and visually appear in court documents, chronicles or the foreign travel reports.[16] A study of subaltern in the Safavid period would, therefore, seek to tentatively identify a spectrum of indiscernible subordinated and related social groups, ranging from the urban unemployed, the roaming peasantry, guild workers, migrant women and children, who most likely participated in Muharram as city dwellers.[17] The intractable problem, however, is the very discourse to identify groups who possess subordinate and invisible status in a society that revolved around hierarchies of class, gender, race and sexuality. How can the voice of the subaltern, whose history remains muted in the archives of knowledge, be excavated for another kind of discourse?

In what follows I discuss the shadowy contours of subaltern in the Safavid-era Muharram performances solely based on limited accounts of European textual and visual testimonies presented the literary form of travel literature. Yet what I attempt to show is that the fragmented understanding we gather from the European travel accounts on the rituals is stringently sketchy and partial to scattered remarks based on a "thin description" of the travel genre, often oriented in descriptions of outwardly ritual behaviors that mostly reflect perceptions of the (Western) European visitors than the social life of Muharram subalterns.[18] In other words, the Gayatri Spivak's classic question "Can the subaltern speak?" in reference to the Safavid society has to be complemented with questions of early modern European perceptions entrenched in claims of objective authority over depictions of Muharram.[19] The key concern here, first, is what the depictions fail to include, which ultimately evinces practices of reading or interpreting non-European cultures in an early modern context. Second, the project of subaltern in Safavid society would also attend to histories that either implicitly or explicitly focus on locating visible bodies within a polity that revolved around performances of power through which the elites appear as the principal speaking subjects in history. This objective of this study is the former concern.

Despite claims to firsthand knowledge, the study argues, the early modern European travel accounts of Muharram, which mostly span across the seventeenth century, not only lack insight but, for the most part, projected a set of discursive practices in what they reported as objects of knowledge. Expressed in combined personal and impersonal observations, the descriptions of encountered culture in the travelogues are filtered through a selective process to which, especially with the writings of Jean Chardin in the later half of the seventeenth century, reveal an encyclopedic collection for fragmented imageries of Muharram. The encyclopedic tendency in some of the accounts should be viewed as discursive regime that primarily aimed at offering an assumed objective account to which the traveler would legitimize authority to speak for a readership rather than merely reveal the inner life of the society under observation.

For the most part, a singular and pervasive authorial presence of the traveler overshadowed the presence of the observed ritual participants, in particular the marginal and the poor, excluded, for the most part, to a systematic extent. What we have is not merely the failure to give account of the subaltern, a twentieth-century term essentially absent from the travel writings, but a way to conform to the prevailing expectations of the readers at home about the depicted Orient. Most of the reports aim to inform their audiences an apparently on-the-spot observations, and in doing so participated in a broader set of knowledge-making practices of data collection that defined the early modern colonial networks that eventually gave rise to high imperialism of the nineteenth century.

Before a study of the travel accounts, albeit briefly, let us begin with the travel accounts, which are mostly the only sources we have available about Muharram from the period.[20]

European Travel Accounts of Safavid-era Muharram

The rise of Shah Ismail (1501-1524) to power in 1501 marked a significant shift in Islamic history. The emergence of Safavids, first, signaled the formation of a major Shi'i state since the Fatimids (909-1171) and, second, the rise of a gunpowder empire in the early modern global era, a period of considerable change marked by the European conquest of Americas and the expansion of contact across the world. The Safavids exemplified an early modern empire that identified an emerging age of Islamicate societies with complex multi-ethnic, tribal and urban networks.

The Safavids, originally a Sufi-brotherhood movement from Anatolia, emerged as a force to counter-balance the Sunni Ottoman power, which by fifteenth century had gained considerable territories after the conquest of Constantinople in 1453. While by the late fifteenth century the Ottomans had been cemented as a major power in the region, the Safavid came to establish the first major Shi'i Empire since the collapsed of the Fatimad caliphate in Egypt in 1171. Although facing numerous external and internal challenges, the imposition of Shi'i Imami Islam in Persia, then widely of Sunni adherence, marked a transformative moment in the expansion of the Safavid Empire. This crucial period largely included the dissemination of Shi'i dogmas and practices that aimed for the consolidation of Safavid power with the construction of a new religious imperial identity.[21]

Muharram rituals identified the most significant civic event in the Safavid imperium. The commemorative ceremonies, mostly expressed in the form of self-mortification and public mourning, have been performed by Shi'i mourners since the massacre of Karbala, subsequently forming a rich body of ceremonies that largely entailed various commemorative performances, reenacting the story of Husayn along with seventy-two of his followers and family members. Although Muharram undergone various changes since the tenth century, especially when it received patronage under the Buyids (945–1055) and became a politicized form of urban ceremonies, the early ritual performances, usually performed in the form of household-based elegies, were largely limited to the Shi'i community.[22] The lamentation rituals were performed to keep alive the collective memory of the martyrdom of Husayn, forming a community of remembrance based on the ideals of salvation through penitence and suffering.[23]

It was not until the ascent of the Safavid dynasty in the early sixteenth century when Muharram received government patronage, sanctioned by the newly established regime to legitimize state authority (*vilyayat*) through spectacles of devotion for the Imams, which the Shah Ismail associated lineage with the 'Alid household through the seventh Imam Musa al-Kazim (i.e. Husayn as the "Prince of Martyrs" became the head sovereign of the empire with the Safavids as his representative).[24] By the late sixteenth century, Muharram, in close connection with the growing popularization of 'Alid loyalty, became one of the most important official festivals. As the Safavid state underwent a major political transformation under Abbas I with a series of centralization reforms, which included the construction of a new capital in Isfahan, Muharram transformed into major public events. Under 'Abbas, as Calmard explains, "Muharram ceremonies which had until then been apparently rather limited to their devotional and folkloric aspects, became a great festival, both civil and religious."[25]

The interaction between "civil" and "religious" underlined a growing tendency to interweave the religious culture into everyday life and Muharram, along with other important calendarial rituals and festivities, emerged to play a critical role in the process of shaping collective identities. Seen in this context, Abbas' ambitious policy to expand Isfahan into a new imperial capital included the institutionalization of extraordinarily rich repertoire of spectacles and visual representations of power through architecture, urban space and royal rituals.[26] This new visual regime identified monarchical power a stable and permanent institution, and accordingly royal support for the Muharram, initiated as way of promoting an integrated imperial identity.[27] Such urbanization patterns helped dramatize 'Alid ideology in the Muharram pomp, performed in the new royal square of Isfahan, similar to the Ottoman circumcision rituals or the Palm Sunday ceremonies at the Kremlin during the reign of Ivan the Terrible (1547-1575) or the regal processions of Louis XIV (1643-1715).[28] With the spread of Muharram, even after the collapse of the dynasty in 1722, the ritual culture of devotional mourning attained far-reaching social implications for a population that had been deeply shaped by Shi'ism under the Safavids, along with pre-Islamic Persian and non-soteriological religious practices such as Central Asiatic animism and Qizilbash shamanism.[29]

But the socio-political developments that brought Muharram to the fore of historical knowledge can be credited to the Safavid economy. The key institution was the Abbas court, which played an active role in expanding foreign trade, monopolizing export and import of luxury goods, while concurrently encouraging Europeans to participate in domestic markets. Meanwhile, Safavid's reach for global commerce coincided with the transhemispheric economic expansion, leading to increase in European integration into a world economy. By the sixteenth century the rise of newly competing centralized states in Western Europe and expanding urbanization, closely tied to cultural and religious changes, partly, as a result of print technology, witnessed a new class of (male) travelers. Conquest and colonization marked by competition for new trade routes gave way to rapid advances in practical knowledge, which travel reports served as a key means in the process. It is no wonder that by the early seventeenth century the new Isfahan saw an increase of European merchants, ambassadors and missionaries that aimed to advance their commercial or political interests at the royal court amid competition between European dynastic powers vis-a-vis the Ottomans.[30] As visitors in residence at Isfahan, and at times other Safavid domains, the experience of travel not only enhanced the social status of the traveler but also provided a bid for authority over what was encountered, recorded, archived and later published for the consumption of a reading public back home.

Broadly speaking, in the post-Mongol era, the early modern European experience of travel gave through long distance commerce, and by extension exploration, gave rise to competing desires for knowledge as cultural commodities, new social curiosities about foreign lands such as Persia, imagined as a great civilization with the late Humanist taste for ancient history. On a practical level, seventeenth-century gentlemen-travelers like the Sherley brothers also sought new personal and financial opportunities with the ongoing Ottoman-Safavid conflict.[31] Knowledge about the foreign was fused with an emerging sense of adventure for collection and exploration, in what Michael Nerlich has called "ideology of adventure" operating within complex history of emergent capitalistic commerce in the early modern period.[32]

The sixteenth-century travel writings, in particular those from the northern Mediterranean, dominated by Genovese and Venetian economic interests, developed out of the impetus to gather data and archive the flow of information from diverse zones of trade and possible spheres of political influence. The first European depiction of Muharram by Michel Membré (1541) represents the only example of a travel report from a period when the Venetian commercial interests, still at its height, reached the Safavid domains. By the seventeenth century, as economic and political competition shifted towards Western Europe, in particular England and France, the travel depictions of Muharram emerged through a new order of things, a discourse field of knowledge that increasingly participated in the growing networks of commercial capitalism tied to rising territorial states.

It is important to bear in mind that this important stage in the development of travel literature also corresponded with the growth of Muharram, as its politicization began under the reign of Shah Tahmasb (1524-1576). For the most part, the Shi'i commemorative practices spread as part and parcel to the Imamization of Safavid Iran, while the shah turned to the further strengthening of Imami institutions across the new empire. It was during this crucial period of expansive religious policy of Imami imposition that Muharram became a major official event, similar to the public performance of Friday prayers in the new capital, Qazvin.[33] The Imami ritualization of everyday life such as cursing the Sunni Caliphs in major urban centers especially in the capital, Tabriz (1540), bespeaks of major social engineering projects that shaped the reign of Tahmasb and the newly Safavid imperium.[34]

Under the reign of Abbas I the depiction of the ceremonies also underwent considerable changes, as noted earlier, largely due to the increasing number of Europeans travelling to the empire with an appetite to write down what they saw. While in the mid-sixteenth century Muharram rituals had less pomp and representational features, and endorsed by a regime that lacked centralized authority, the seventeenth-century version of the performances represented an increasingly staged and symbolical elaborate, underscoring the consolidation of the Safavids as a centralized-territorial state, but equally important literary discursive changes in depicting the rituals.

The European reports combine into a total of twenty-three accounts, each providing a distinct local description of Muharram ritualization from the mid-sixteenth to the early eighteenth centuries.[35] From Membré (1541) to Krusinski (1714), the depictions include a range of discourses that shifted in textual and visual strategies from the early phase of the Safavid rule, under Shah Tahmasb's reign, when the empire was still in its formative stages, to the reign of Sultan Husayn (1694-1722), whose despotic rule paved the path toward the disintegration of the dynastic rule. The narrative descriptions became richer in description as Muharram underwent dramatic transformations as Abbas I asserted authority after defeating Uzbeks in 1598-99 and Ottomans later in 1602-03.

The development in both travel writings and Muharram coincides when Safavid political structure reasserted power in response to domestic political and religious challenges. The building of new civic spaces, in particular the Maydan Naqsh-e Jahan, was partly constructed for social integration of the empire, but also to generate a sense of awe among denizens and visitors. As an architectural feat, the Maydan served as a new public domain, one in which the English traveler, Thomas Herbert, would describe as "…without doubt as spacious, as pleasant and aromatic a market as any in the universe."[36] By 1618-19, as observed by travelers such as Pietro Della Valle and Don García de Silva Figueroa, Muharram had developed into an organized public event along with the construction of the new Maydan. The development ranged from display of dramatic spectacles of mourning performances to ceremonial pageantries and urban fights in the city square.[37] The realistic representation of key figures from the Karbala story and elaborate processions underscores the degree of public participation in the rituals as a public event.

By the mid-seventeenth century, personal accounts of Muharram became fused with more impersonal description of Safavid political and social life. While the narratives reflected the changing sociocultural life of European societies, heralding the deep-seated transformation of early modern public literacy, the demand from the European reading public and growing book markets encouraged the publication of more travel accounts. However, as print production increased along with the number of travelers visiting Safavid territories, the gender-specific identity of writers did not change. The entire ensemble of travel reports, with a range of description of Muharram, were written by men somehow linked to an institution, a polity or a noble family, as in the case of Sherley brothers. Although the contents of accounts differ according to the historical periods during which the texts were written, edited and later published, the collection of travel reports shared the common practice of referencing other reports, at times freely borrowing and at other times correcting the previous published texts, while all aiming to shape the opinion of the readers they sought to entertain back at home.[38]

The first European depiction of Muharram ceremonies appears in correlation with the way the rituals evolved from obscure rites of passage (in the sixteenth century) to full-blown political festivals in the form of extraordinary spectacles that staged state power (in the seventeenth century). Michele Membré's 1540 account of the rituals at Tabriz, the first report of the rituals, reflects the perception of a Venetian diplomat who described the ceremonies in their esoteric, relatively exclusive form. As the first European traveler who produced a short account of the ceremonies, Membré wrote his report for the Venetian Doge, the city's most powerful civic-political institution. As a diplomat-merchant traveler, his readership was limited to a Catholic political body with a desire for diplomacy and commerce with an Ottoman rival.

On 1540 in Tabriz, Michele Membré gives the following account in his *Relazione*:

> "In the month of May they perform the passion of a son of Ali (una passion per uno fio*lo de Ali)*, wherefore they call him Imam Hussain, who fought a certain race which they call Yazid, and had his head cut off…I saw young men make their bodies black and go naked on the earth. I saw another thing someone make a hole underground like a well, and put himself in it naked and leave only his head out, with all the rest of the hole, packed in with earth up to the throat; and that was to perform that passion. This I saw with my own eyes."[39]

Membré's short description is significant for two reasons, and is worth analyzing, I argue, as a way to understand the subaltern in the ceremonies. First, the narrative depicts the view of a privileged outsider, as someone who is able to document the events while visiting Safavid Persia as a Venetian ambassador to Tahmasb's court. His audience too, as earlier noted, is restricted to the Venetian political establishment back at home, which he also a member. Second, and more importantly, Membré relies on a textual staging based on the authority of sight that produces a personal narrative through face-to-face encounter based on the spot experience of visual observation. This is the first instance when Muharram is described from a personal perspectivist narrative. In this sense, the reference "This I saw with my own eyes" qualifies the author to present an account of Muharram that its focal point lies in claimed immediacy of what is observed through sight. Likewise, the authority of sight validates the short account that depicts the ceremonies to be unambiguously articulated, transparent in the brevity of its eyewitness description.

Note that Membré does not allocate any textual space to interpret the ceremony. The observation is the limit of the account. Equally important is the function and meaning of a reportage account that is intimately linked with the personal observation, an emphasis on eye-witness account as a common feature of sixteenth-century travel reports with the European discovery of Americas. The authority inherent to the report is devoid of intermediaries or secondhand accounts. The first-person verb ("I saw") lends an authoritative status, especially as the account also entails an impersonal description that is rhetorically distant and yet present at the dramatic events unfolding before Membré. Meanwhile, the first-person pronoun "I" refers back to a singular perspective that circulates back to the narrator, whose interlocutors participating in Muharram remain frozen in the visualized experience of the writer. The interplay between personal and impersonal augments Membré description as trustworthy and authentic for the readers, which would serve as the most objective of the narrative.

The perspective of a personal narrative is evident in this sixteenth-century report, which shows that Membré writes in the post-Medieval travel literary traditions: an objective strategy to collect and represent perceived data and transfer, as accurately as possible, into the written account of a report. Yet a narrative feature key of the Membré's narrative is the evocation of realistic, however peculiar, images that would allow Muharram's depicted scenes to appear visible to a curious reader at home. The rhetorical strategy revolves around the practice of seeing as a form of self-evidence ("This I saw with my own eyes"), which comes at the concluding sentence. Sight records a form of travel experience of a non-Christian religious culture that registers little but no emotional reaction from the observer as writer; rather an external observation that gives an objective form to the narrative.

Another significant feature in this narrative is the use of the Christian cultural terminology. Membré's representation of Muharram, primarily described in terms of "festivals," "celebration," "spectacles" and, in the most culturally technical terminology, "passion plays," recall the author's self-cultural understanding of similar public events in the form of Catholic festivals back at home. The use of familiar tropes serves to describe aspects of the religious or cultural life of the native Persians that his readership can understand. Anthony Pagden's concept of "principle of attachment" is useful here.[40] Travellers such as Membré give attachment to unfamiliar and new experiences to familiar cultural references and meaningful frameworks that the readers can relate. As a rhetorical technique, this would, accordingly, allow Membré's audience, mostly the literate noblemen, to better interact with the alien culture described by the writer. The experience of sight serves as means to enable the writer and his readers to apprehend, in unmediated way, Safavid religious life.

It is perhaps in this literary technique of referring troupes of familiar that Membré did not find the need to elaborate on the ritual participants. The general reference to "young men" perhaps resembles a familiar description of ritual participants in a religious festival in northern Italy, although the description does not provide an understanding of the age, class and social position of the described men. The description of self-burial in a well, naked up to the throat, a practice that is also noted by later travel accounts, is qualified with the term "passion," which has a specific meaning in the Catholic devotional tradition. Yet what is overlooked from this description is the social context around the rituals performed by men, lumping a range of male participants into the generic pronoun "they". Females are entirely absent in this short description, invisible to the observing eye of a male Venetian. In many ways, Membré exemplifies a travel report tradition that through personal encounter depicts a foreign culture in fragmented, snapshot narrative, one that provides us with a thin description of Muharram in the early Safavid period.[41]

By the early seventeenth century the narratives about Muharram undergo change, as did the political conditions of Safavid politics and global commerce. As noted earlier, while Muharram became a highly elaborate form of state ritual, the seventeenth-century European accounts also became increasingly multifaceted, with descriptions that would constantly shift positions, perspectives and rhetorical languages between personal and impersonal in correlation with the changing, emotionally-charged ritual events observed in mostly urban contexts. For the most part, all the accounts, in varied lengths and variation of perspective, combine the enmeshed personal and impersonal descriptions, the latter also evident in Membré personal account. While the entire ensemble of texts reaffirms the legitimacy of personal narrative in subordinate to impersonal description, they also heavily rely on sight as a means of representing evidential information about Safavid social life. The crafting of travelogues in terms of eye-witness accounts served as a way to stage self-presentation of the traveler over the Safavids who are excluded the power of presenting themselves.[42] The presence of narratorial self becomes a common feature in the writings of De Gouvea, (the second traveler in 1602-040 to the last travelers to provide accounts of Muharram, namely, De Brun (1704) and Krusinski (1714). In these two critical centuries, when new scientific ideas and methods spread out across colonial networks in tandem with the growing epistemic community of readers and writers, personal narrative and impersonal descriptions became indistinguishable, as the travelogues provide more detail information about host societies. Detail serves as a medium for objectivity.

The most significant development appeared with the publication of the travel book by the wealthy French Huguenot, Chardin. The description of the rituals by Chardin, who traveled three times to Isfahan (1666-67; 1669; 1673-7), is significant for three main reasons. First, Chardin's report represents one of the earliest and best examples of a writing genre that reflected the increasing mobility of European exploration and colonization of the globe. It is worth noting that Chardin operated in close association with the East India Company, which its aggressive expansionist activities throughout the seventeenth century led to an increasing number of Europeans traveling to numerous territories around the globe.[43] Second, Chardin's travel book represents the first objectivist narrative of Safavid society that marks a distinguished feature in comparison to previous travel reports.[44] Such objectivism reflected a rising worldview for comprehensive scientific knowledge acquired through experience and inductive reasoning. The classificatory system of cataloguing the natural world went hand in hand with scientific exploration and the establishment of new scientific associations, such as the Royal Society (established in 1660), which Chardin, after his travels to Iran and upon settling in England in 1681, belonged. Third, and in connection with presenting scientific knowledge, the 1711 publication of Chardin's ten-volume *Voyages de Monsieur le Chevalier Chardin* presents a major shift away from journal format style to disembodied observer of panoramic-like writing. The emphasis in this form of writing would be on the acquisition of precise knowledge by which proto-ethnographic information can be presented for study and discussion based on a realist perspective.

A study of Chardin's travel account of Safavid Persia goes beyond the present study. Here I focus on his descriptions of Muharram. In one of the most detailed account on the rituals, Chardin elaborates on the rituals which is worth quoting:

> "It must be noted first that during these ten days no trumpets or drums are sounded at the normal times. Devout people do not shave themselves, neither on the face nor on the head, take no baths, do not set off on their travels and generally speaking undertake little business. Several dress themselves in black or purple which are the colors of grief. Everyone puts on a sad demeanor and appearance and each one clothes themselves in public mourning…. One would have thought oneself in the hall of an armory. Besides, mixed with paper and crystal lanterns, were quantities of lamps and chandeliers which were lit at one o'clock at night. The common people of the district assembled and went in procession. At the same time some Sufi or other somber and devout men start to regale the people with stories of the celebrations until the preacher arrives who takes part in the proceedings with a reading from a chapter of the book *Al-Qatl*, which contains the life and death of Husein in ten chapters, for the ten days of the festival. He preaches on this subject for two hours rousing the people to lament… *I would never have believed the agony which grips the people. It is inconceivable.* They beat their chests. They wail and howl, especially the women, tearing themselves and crying in floods of tears. I have been at these sermons and admired the concentration of the audience who could only have attended out of an *intense devotion, although the preacher was extremely moving…* (my italics)."[45]

At first glance, something salubrious appears in Chardin's description of Muharram. The focus on the experience of rituals enables Chardin to convey to his readers an image of a foreign culture that self-expresses in "devotion," a religious rite with Christian resemblance, as also noted by Membré. However, by positioning himself as a close-observer of the ceremonies, Chardin is able to shift his perspective from a far-distant external observer to the nearest position of a participant observer, as someone with close proximity to the rituals and yet with an observable distance to maintain an apparent objective perspective. The staging of his observation in terms of both distance and proximity places Chardin in a rational register with a far less personalized style of narrative accounts evident in some other travel reports. The narratorial subject is present but only through a distance of impassive observation. Emotions are depicted, but to a limit. The emotive views of Chardin are partial to the implausible ("inconceivable"), hence preventing a look at the interiority of those he depicts and his own subjective views in relation to the inner life of the Safavid mourners.

A key idea here is the immediacy of an external perception, narrated and printed for (educated) readers who, along side Chardin, view the rituals through the materiality of the printed text. Appeal to immediacy through encounter is a key feature in Chardin's description, and also a common feature of numerous travel reports in late seventeenth and eighteenth centuries. But immediacy also involves the use of cultural simile in language of description. The statement, for instance, "One would have thought oneself in the hall of an armory" serves as literary technique for a more immediate experience that allows the reader to understand a foreign culture through familiar spatial imagery known at home. The traveler-writer engages in a proactive visualization that immerses his writing within the events as privileged access to the "intense" practices of the observed rituals. But the visual descriptions limit the report to a discursively privileged vantage point from a distance, a detached outward gaze which the authorial position is to document, report, with the aim of information-gathering.

One should bear in mind a subjective dimension that Chardin is eager to convey to his readers. Recalling his account, "I have been at these sermons and admired the concentration of the audience who could only have attended out of an *intense devotion, although the preacher was extremely moving...*" By describing the emotions of Muharram participants, Chardin is able to attribute a spiritual fervor, an "intense devotion" to "the common people" he observes. Equally important, he also admires the sermons for displaying intense devotion to the martyred Imam. But something diverges in the narrative. The reference to have witnessed the rituals ("I have been at these") defines Chardin's physical presence not in attempt to delve into the emotive experiences of the perceived ritual participants, but the bolstering of a position of observation that evokes an objective register based on a personalized focus. However, most of Chardin's account revolves around an impersonal narrative of listing and recording ritual behaviors, and other cultural practices of the Persians, that merit description. What is striking though is not how much Chardin reveals himself through his travel narrative but, rather, how little. His emotive expressions are primarily secondary to objective perception of the encountered society.

The question of empathy should be viewed here from a critical light. At first glance, the account gives identification to the ritual expressions articulated by Chardin. However, a critical look at an expression such as "intense devotion" reveals Chardin's projection of an assumed state of mind, in this case a devotional one based on a Christian (most likely a Protestant) understanding of ritual practice. Chardin's "the common people" hardly speak through his text about their experiences and emotional states in the course of the ceremonies, and only do so in emotive expressions of pain such as "agony," "wail" and "howl". Emotions, after all, are moving objects, and for an objective gaze to depict them inner movements would need to be frozen into depictions of external expressions.

Chardin's ostensible interpretation of the subaltern "common" displays a discursive framing with a singular perspective. What such perspective underscores is an overreliance on the external perception of the observer rather than the voice(s) of the observed. Here, I argue, the observational narrative with the prioritization of description over interpretation of Muharram emotions sets the discursive limit to Chardin's report, viewed by many of his contemporaries as the most reliable travel writer. Although like Membré he situates himself in an optically privilege position as a keen observer of Safavid society, Chardin writes as a detached documentarian, whose account aims at objectively offering a chronological gathering of information about the rituals as they unfold through the act of seeing. The implicit authority in the on-the-spot observation is the ability to see the rituals, but not necessarily understand it, as perhaps a modern reader of an unknown culture would expect.

While this should not surprise us, as Chardin is not a modern ethnographer, a contentious concept to begin with, the key feature to bear in mind is the detached prose style of the description that allows only feelings to enter in the form of implausibility, and limited admiration without explanation of what is admired, that sets the limits of the observation. Equally important are the readers, who Chardin does not expect to inquire about the rituals, but only its description framed in accessible though exotic terms. Though an assumption of expressed devotion is clearly made, ("*I would never have believed the agony which grips the people. It is inconceivable*"), Chardin's objective is less about expressing the meaning behind the mourning practices but the outward behavioral activities that enhance the foreignness of the host society. Yet a key feature to Chardin's account is his own presence in the form of an outsider's gaze representing an authorial focal point as a way of self-fashioning in the style of encyclopedic erudition of reportage and archive.

Seen in a discursive regime of categorization of mapping an external landscape, the subaltern in Muharram becomes inherently relegated in a thin descriptive account. Chardin possibly acknowledges the subaltern ("common people") but ultimately fails to speak their intentions, desires or hopes of participants in their lived contexts. The subaltern not only does not speak through Chardin's narrative, but primarily remains a mere moving body, made visible only through the printed account. Note that the reference to "devotion" is the thickest description that one could find in this thin account, and, as noted earlier, this should be suspect to projecting a Christian theological reading into the rituals.

Despite its limitations, no other European traveler provides such a unique account of Muharram as Chardin. The six reports (António De Gouvea (1602-14), Kakash (1603-04; 1618-19), Pietro Della Valle (1602-03), Figueroa (1618-9), Afanasievich Kotov (1624-5), Thomas Herbert (1628) during the reign of Shah Abbas continue with eye-witness accounts, similar to Membré, except that a (rather brief) comparative discussion of Shi'ism also accompanies some of the reports. In De Gouvea's 1602-4 report, for example, we encounter the first detailed account of combat fights between city guilds, which signals the participation of guild workers who either associate as either Haydari or Nimatullahi factions.[46] The guild fights and the participation of diverse social classes, including the travelers as audiences, introduces a new ritual development as Muharram becomes more carnivalesque with the occurrence of volley-firing of arquebus fired by a number of male participants parading in front of the empty coffins.[47]

The other notable report is of Della Valle, whose extensive 1618-19 description includes one of the most interesting references to the subaltern, though certainly with limitations. He writes:

> ...They all live in a state of dejection; they all in fact dress sadly, and many wear black, which otherwise they rarely put on; no one shaves head or beard; no one takes a bath; and they all abstain, not only from what is thought sinful, but also from every kind of enjoyment. Many poor people, too, are in the habit of burying themselves in busy streets up to the neck and even part of their heads in earthenware jars, wide all around from the feet and narrow to fit the head at the top. And these are sunk into the ground, out of sight, holding back the earth all about from the men who crouch inside, seeming as if they are really buried. And they remain like this from sunrise to nightfall, each keeping another poor wretch sitting down nearby, saying prayers and asking for alms from all the passers-by.[48]

It is with Della Valle's report that we receive one of the best descriptions of the subaltern ("many poor people") playing a visually central role in the ceremonies. The rituals of self-burial appear to be performed by the "poor," who are accompanied by another who recites prayers and asks for alms from passers-by. Also, Della Valle observes the presence of women in the ceremonies, although their economic background is not explained. The economic status of the male "poor" is also not clarified, though most likely they represent the destitute population of Isfahan who relied on charity and public institutions, similar to Muharram, for help. Meanwhile, the appearance of what Willem Floor calls "professional entertainers" as men, painted in black or red who receive money for their performances, underscores the increasing marketization of the ceremonies in this period.[49]

The introduction of camel sacrifice ceremonies and ensuing rituals fights in Muharram in Figueroa's 1618-19 account of Muharram in Isfahan is an intriguing report. First, the camel sacrifice ceremonies, as a reinvented tradition, most likely involved the poor and the underclass of Isfahani population, and perhaps those from the countryside, who sought charity and consumption of blessed food from the ceremonies.[50] Second, and more importantly, Figueroa's account offers an important insight on a major ritual development, which is also discussed in Della Valle's detailed account, but it does not examine the socio-economic or subjective experiences of the rituals. The missing account adds to a style of travel writing that in all six accounts focus on description in a distance, failing to explain the motives, meanings and agencies of participants, in particular the "poor," in the ceremonies.

In the post-Abbas period, the remaining fifteen travel reports (Olearius (1637), Philippe de La Sainte-Trinité (1630-40?), Raphaël Du Mans (1647-1696?), Gabriel De Chinon (1650-1668?), D'Armainville Poullet (1660), De Montheron (1641), Jean de Thévenot (1665), Chardin (1666-67, 1669, 1673-7), J.B. Tavernier (1667), Petrus Bedik (1670-5), John Struys (1671), Engelbert Kæmpfer (1684-5), Gemelli Careri (1694), Gauderea (1695), Krusinski (1714), become more comprehensive, as the rituals too become more popular and elaborate in their ceremonial pomp at performed in the Maydan of Isfahan and other major cities. Despite richness of detail, the reports continue to favor perceived behavior over meaningful content, marked by a thinness of description derived from a documentarian approach that attends to the cultural fixedness of indigenous people under observation.

This is most evident in the case of Chardin, as earlier discussed, but other reports also include similar discursive approach. In the case of Adam Olearius, a German diplomat sent by Frederick II Duke of Hostein to Iran in 1637, for example, Muharram is depicted in its final tenth-day, Ashura, at Ardabil. In its non-Isfahani context, Olearius writes about two different mourning ceremonies, one for the foreign dignitaries and another for denizens of Ardabil. Representatives of five quarters of the city recited eulogies for Ali and his martyred son, Husayn, while seven young poor boys, called "Tzatzaku," painted in black, knocked on small stones and their chests.[51] Based on Olearius's account, the underclass boys appear to have enacted rituals that had specific ritual performance, though the specific name ("Tzatzaku") remains unclear to the reader. Olearius' description of the seven boys, along with their depiction in the engraving in the 1647 edition of the book, as noted by Brancaforte, illustrated a sketchy account that limits the presence of the subaltern in the rituals to mere dancing entertainers, resembling "devils," for the European gaze.[52]

Although space precludes me to study each travel report, a general observation that can be made about the seventeenth-century accounts is that the textual and illustrative depictions of Muharram provide a literary resource for the European book market and readership. Here I reference Elio Brancaforte's original analysis of several reports, particularly Della Valle, Adam Olearius and Jean de Thévenot, and the use of engraving and other illustrative works, published along with the texts that rather than providing an "accurate" account of Muharram obfuscated the Safavid "Other". The published travel reports, Brancaforte argues, underwent editorial, censorship, and translational changes either by the author, artist, publisher, state or religious officials so to "fit the expectations of a reading public…," resulting in published works that would depicts something different from what the travelers witness in their travels.[53] Brancaforte echoes Sonja Brentjes' study of early modern European maps, engravings and textual sources about Safavid Iran, which, she argues, were rarely "… true or objective in the sense that they directly and reliably reflect the Iranian conditions at stake in a particular representation."[54] Representation is an enterprise fraught with quandaries of bias.

With respect to the (proto) Enlightenment literary culture of the seventeenth century, the published travel writings reflect the cultural norms and textual practices of the emerging European public sphere. For this reading public, the subaltern is made invisible as a mere crowd, the multitude that gathers to mourn the death of Husayn in ceremonies that receive mixed descriptions as exotic, demonic or farcical. The "poor," the "women," and "children" become background noise, either textually or visually, to rituals that gradually by the eighteenth century get categorized into a distinct set of social behavior.[55] The main problem with the travel accounts of Muharram subalterns is that they rarely permit the ritual participants to speak; accounts of participant expressions only occur in the course of ritual bodily enactments or chants such as *"ja Hossein…,"* which is less a "voice" than a ritual shout to dramatize the narrative.[56] At their best, the reports, including the most detailed by Bruyn and Chardin, neglected to provide any significant insight on agency of the ritual participants, including the subaltern.

Whilst most seventeenth-century travel accounts normalized eyewitness narratives as a way to gather facts through empirical inquiry, discourses on foreign societies saw a radical reorganization in knowledge. By and large, as an outcome of Spanish and Portuguese colonial conquests of the "New World," travel became a source of practical information used for entangled networks of commerce, religion and empire. Objects, plants, humans and ideas, gathered from around the globe, served as new site of nomenclature, taxonomy and rational classification for universal knowledge. As Linda Schiebinger has astutely shown in her work, *Plants and Empire*, the early modern European collection of objects, in varied hierarchy of assortments, was intimately informed by coalesced practices of scientific knowledge and commercial colonialism.[57] By the eighteenth century, exploration and informal networks of colonial expansionism worked closely with scientific fields of inquiry, as travel played an integral role in the process.

As cultural objects from the Muslim Orient, in particular the exotic Persia, depictions of Muharram found their way into the print cultural archive of the

Enlightenment in the early eighteenth century. The representation of Muharram, as "*FÊTE d'HUSSEIN*" by Bernard Picart (1673-1733) in the 7th volume of the encyclopedic book of religion, *Cérémonies et coutumes religieuses de peuples du monde* (1723-1743), references Chardin and Thévenot as source of the illustration, which should be best described as inspirational rather than referential. In the pages that both textually and visually describe Muharram, readers encounter depictions that are classified and categorized with other rituals, described as festivities, to which the cultural life of the Muslim society are revealed from an optical view. Sight intertwines with factual representation of encyclopedic imaginary.

Here the engraving of Muharram is an odd reconstruction of the two French traveler's account. The imaginary Muharram ceremony is illustrated in a panoramic frame, a wide view that surrounds the reader as observer. Most male mourners appear as nude figures, frozen in movement while dramatically performing various penitent scenes, assembled and juxtaposed in an urban texture. Similar to an object in a cabinet of curiosity, Bernard Picart's representation is intended as one object of mysterious exoticism among others. Similar to Chardin's objectivist perspective, the prompted vision is one of detachment that views the Safavid mourner, including the subaltern men who perform the begum ritual of self-burial at the center of the picture, from an exterior landscape. The Safavid religious world opens outward toward the sight of the European reader, who steadily watches the theatrics of a foreign culture from a panoramic vantage point. Knowledge of Muharram is archived in a work of encyclopedia that identifies Muharram as one among other classified public activities that are defined as religious rites.

The use of the term "knowledge" is inherently problematic since it assumes that a rendering of an "objective" historical account can be attained by observable perception for an accurate description, either in words or images. But observation, faithful and accurate to what has been observed, does not equal to "knowledge" but underscores the limits of perception according to who is doing the describing based on changing socio-cultural standpoint. The appeal to objectivity by some of the travel writings (in particular Chardin), therefore, should be critically viewed as part and parcel to a broader regime of Enlightenment discourse that solidified the systematizing world view of information gathering through which the Other, Safavid or other non-Europeans, can be categorized into objects of knowledge, archived for practical usage of traveling empires.

The above discussion should also undermine the reliability of amicable position of some of the travel narratives on the Safavids. The troublesome truth of the early modern European travel reports, as a source of knowledge, is not the extent to which they offer "accurate" or "meticulous description" of what was observed, as though we can easily separate "fact" from "truth" of discourse. Rather, the problem lies in the limit of self-reflexivity expressed in a style of writings and illustrations that methodically fail to recognize agency with the Safavids. In particular case of subalterns, in some accounts the Safavids under observation are even questioned for their intention in participating in the rituals. Yet, for the most part, the travelers' method of collecting observable events is shrouded in how Persia is imagined as an exotic land of curiosity, lumped together with an imagined "Orient". What we should reject, henceforth, is the simple assumption that a positive description of an indigenous population lends itself to a more accurate account of the subject under study. Accuracy and reverence are hardly the same.

Muharram Subaltern: A View from Inside?

In the previous section, I argued that the early modern European reports on Muharram reveal not ethnographic "evidence" but rather a set of thin descriptions as part of discursive regime of knowledge. What the reports represent are changing imageries, in textual and visual forms, of a non-European culture in crude portraits, selective in temporal focus on externalized behavior rather than internal processes of the ritual participants. The Muharram subalterns are, textually, marginal players in the travel reports precisely because the reports rarely aim to reveal the inner life of the people, especially the poor and the underclass, under observation; the everyday social life merely serves as background to representations of selected practices, assumed exotic for a literate European society who could find the rituals entertaining for cultural consumption. In fact, one could argue that the seventeenth-century travel reports reflect a growing scientific culture of a cabinet of curiosity wherein the Safavid-era Muharram became categorized as a cultural object, among many others especially from the "New World," in which institutionally positioned the European men as objective observers and reporters of a world awaiting exploration, and ultimately collection for present or future market consumptions.

I should briefly note here that while thin description entails serious methodological limitations, we must not entirely dismiss various fragments of perceptions they offer about Safavid society. They can partly help us reconstruct Safavid history through a careful critical approach so to underscore the complex connections between knowledge, material practices and power. Moreover, an interpretative account would not have inherently provided a more immediate or accurate discourse on the mental life of Muharram subalterns. Moreover, an interpretative approach maintains limitations based on the perspective of the narrators and his or her cultural capital tied to various forms of institutional settings. Authorial narrative cannot be overcome through mere interpretation of ethnographic research.

For any textual or visual representations, the following two questions remain: who represents and who is represented? More specifically, we should ask: what is the socio-institutional basis of the writers? For the most part, I argue, the presence of the European men of "literate" culture along with their reading publics would not diminish in authorial presence with a "thick description". The assumed superiority of Europeans as bearers of civilization over those observed is evident in the very act of exploration and by extension textual production that symbolically renders knowledge as hegemonic.

So, would primary sources from a Safavid perspective, then, help us with a more informed understanding of Muharram subaltern? The answer is a tentative no. The historical documents, which are very few, could be used to map out a relative understanding of the Safavid, contingent in how they are used, but not as a source of knowledge while disregarding their ideological framework in what they depict. The Persian textual sources have serious limitations as well. The only available sources by Iskandar Beg, the "Munshi," (secretary) and Munajjim Yazdi, for instance, revolve around a chronicle discursive framework and, especially in the case of Munshi, the tropes carry a biased in favor of the monarchy and little but no acknowledgment of the subaltern, as 1604 description by Munshi serve as a good example.[58] When it comes to the subaltern, the Persian sources reflect an insider view of an elite culture that equally views the subaltern as invisible aspects of an imperial landscape of royal power and state pomp.

The best sources, I suggest, that we can benefit are textual and visual materials that were most likely read or ritually used by the participants in the course of the rituals. The turn to material culture, which here I also include textual sources, could serve as a way to rethink the inner life of Muharram participants. This is ostensibly risky since it would require us to engage in an imaginary methodological mode of inquiry, which is highly suspect in numerous academic fields, which continue to adhere to the principle of observational factualization in discerning social historical truths. How could we rethink a lost historical experience through material cultural artifacts? The intractable methodological problem should, first, focus on the reliability of the source and the extent to which it can shed light on Muharram rituals. The second issue is how to think of the participants' experiences across gender, ethnic and class lines while critically engaging with one's projection of interpretative framework, especially modern categories that we impose on a historic society under study.

By way of an example, I briefly turn to Husayn Va'iz Kashifi's *Rawzat*. Perhaps the most read source in Muharram history, *Rawzat* is a profound textual elegy in the tradition of Islamic martyrology. The significance of this late Timurid-period text is that, as Kaempfer notes in his report, sections of the eulogy were recited by the *futuvvat* circles during Muharram.[59] Divided into ten sections, plus a conclusion, and composed in both Persian poetry and prose, along with some Arabic poetry, the *Rawzat* can be recognized as both a theological and a numinous historical text, a sort of salvation narrative of mystical (*'irfan*) quality, representing the Karbala tragedy and its characters by describing their emotions and responses to events leading up to, during, and after the battle. Such salvational and mystical history is devoid of an austere sequential narrative strategy since it aims to describe the martyrdom of sacred figures based upon the doctrine of intercession. By this I mean to suggest that the martyrological narrative is discursively arranged in such a way that, through the described events of the battle of Karbala, deliverance from sin on the day of resurrection is promised to the orators and the audience of the text; through their miraculous role as intercessors with God for the forgiveness of sins, the recitation of the narratives serves as a medium for the redemption of devotees. Combined with the element of mysticism, this soteriological aspect constitutes a central motif in the *Rawzat* of Kashifi, which could play a significant role in how we could understand experiences of Muharram participants across a wide range of social backgrounds.

As a poetic discourse of collective memory, *Rawzat* is multivocal, that is, interconnected of fictive voices that in multitude of expressions articulate an alternative sacred history lost to time and yet potentially relived through recitation. In what the late Russian literal theorist, Mikhail Bakhtin, called "polyphony" or many-voiced, *Rawzat* incorporates many styles of expressions from multiple perspectives that underline living conversations in a dialogical process for future responses.[60] It is no wonder that the language of *Rawzat* is interwoven with vivid though shifting prose and verses with melodic overtones of melancholic character. The language reflects a heteroglot paradigm of an imagined, mythical world of Karbala. Using a dramatic device, the narrative of Karbala merges incongruent incident of events, characters or places related to Husayn's martyrdom and in metaphoric and often deliberately esoteric ways transgress boundaries between genres. The phenomenon of dialogization of narrative facilitates various descriptions and powerful emotions, in which voices and characters confront one another in free and equal, though conflictual, dialogues. In multithemed prose, similar to the ghazal genre of lyrical love poetry, the intricate mélange of poetical and prose narratives, at times lucid and at other times obscure, transpire into a dramatic descriptive plot of aesthetic importance. By mediating between the profane and the sacred world, the text restores a dynamic of intertextuality to the reading or listening ritual participants, allowing them to freely interpret symbols and myths, and relive the disparity between this-worldly and other- worldly realities throughout the narrative.[61] The feature of free interpretation is what Bakhtin describes as "plurality of multiple consciousnesses," creating distinct worlds of experiences for each and simultaneously "as someone else's consciousness," which underlines the social sphere.[62]

Imagine witnessing, no, participating in a *Rawzat* ceremony in Ardabil, Isfahan or Shiraz sometime in the seventeenth century. Imagine how a subaltern with needs, desires, hopes and dreams of personal, familial, and social importance can participate in a living text with multithemed contents, utterances that entail open responses, metaphors that permit multiple interpretations in a narrative that is ultimately about redemption and hope for a better future. What might a rereading of *Rawzat* look like with the attempt to reimagine the world of the marginal whose voices are silenced in both European and Persian sources? Perhaps the subaltern can speak through *Rawzat*.

To write the history of Muharram subaltern, I suggest, one should begin with such textual dream world, which gives us impressionistic access to multiple experiences that would have made Muharram a public event for the subaltern. However, such beginning would require us to reframe not only our analytical approach, but also the very focus of our research for historical knowledge. We can use the European accounts, as I have done in this study, in a critical discussion and yet recognize their limitations.

What is important to bear in mind is that there are essential limits to all sources, archival or living ones, such as *Rawzat*, which continues to be used across the Persianate world. This is so because there is an inescapable risk of projecting a distinct historically contingent stylized perspective into a martyrological narrative that is inherently open to interpretation. However, the combined use of various sources, in particular material sources, can help us reconstruct subjective histories through imaging past experiences. The focus on multisensory interpretation, mindful of range of historical subjectivities and mostly invisible to archival texts produced by elites, can signal a paradigm shift in our knowledge of the subaltern not in Safavid but global histories. Moving beyond the realist approach, we can recognize that, although knowledge is impossible, history is the imaginative act of reading the past through interweaving traces, subject to erasure and multiple interpretations in which we, as observers, equally participate.

Bibliography

Abisaab, Rula Jurdi, *Converting Persia: Religion and Power in the Safavid Empire*. London: I.B. Tauris, 2004.

Andrea, Bernadette, "The Global Travels of Teresa Sampsonia Sherely's Carmelite Relic," in *Travel and Travail: Early Modern Women, English Drama, and the Wider World*, eds., Patricia Akhimie and Bernadette Andrea, Lincoln/London: University of Nebraska Press, 2019, 102-20.

Appadurai, Arjun, "Introduction: Place and Voice in Anthropological Theory," *Cultural Anthropology*, Vol. 3, 1 (1988), 16-20.

Atabaki, Touraj, "Disgruntled Guests: Iranian Subaltern on the Margins of the Tsarist Empire," *International Review of Social History*, vol. 48, 3 (2003), 401-426.

Ayoub, Mahmoud, *Redemptive Suffering in Islam: A Study of the Devotional Aspects of 'Āshūrā in Twelver Shī'ism*. The Hague: E.J. Brill, 1978.

Babaie, Sussan, *Isfahan and Its Palaces: Statecraft, Shi'ism and the Architecture of Conviviality in Early Modern Iran*. Edinburgh: Edinburgh University Press, 2008.

Babayan, Kathryn, "In Spirit We Ate Each Other's Sorrow: Female Companionship in Seventeenth-Century Safavid Iran," in eds. Kathryn Babayan and Afsaneh Najmabadi, *Islamicate Sexualities: Translations across Temporal Geographies of Desire*, Cambridge, Mass.: Center for Middle Eastern Studies of Harvard University, 2008, 239-274.

Babayan, Kathryn, *Mystics, Monarchs, and Messiahs: Cultural Landscapes of Early Modern Iran*. Cambridge: Harvard University Press, 2002.

Babayan, Kathryn, "Sufis, Dervishes, Mullas: the Controversy over Spiritual and Temporal Dominion in Seventeenth-Century Iran," in, *Safavid Persia: The History and Politics of an Islamic Society*, ed. Charles Melville, London: I.B.Tauris, 1996, 117-38.

Bakhtin. Mickail, *Problems of Dostoevsky's Poetics*. Minneapolis; London: University of Minnesota Pres, 1984.

Bembo, Ambrosio, *The Travels and Journal of Ambrosio Bembo*, translated from the Italian by Clara Bargellini, Berkeley: University of California Press, 2007, 351-354.

Bernard, Jean Frederic, *Cérémonies et coutumes religieuses de peuples du monde*, Amsterdam, 1723, Vol. 7.

Brancaforte, Elio, "Between Word and Image: Representations of Shi'ite Rituals in the Safavid Empire from Early Modern European Travel Accounts," in *Remapping Travel Narratives (1000-1700): To the East and back again*, ed. Montserrat Piera, Leeds: Arc Humanities Press, 2018, 129-155.

Brentjes, Sonja, "Immediacy, Mediation, and Media in Early Modern Catholic and Protestant Representations of Safavid Iran." *Journal of Early Modern History* 13, no. 2–3 (2009), 173-207.

Calmard, Jean, "Shi'i Rituals and Power II. The Consolidation of Safavid Shi'ism: Folklore and Popular Religion," in edited by Charles Melville, *Safavid Persia: The History and Politics of an Islamic Society*. London: I.B. Tauris, 1996, 139-90.

Çelebi (Effendi), Evliya, *Narrative of Travels in Europe, Asia, and Africa in the Seventeenth Century*. Translated by Joseph von Hammer-Purgstall. Volume II, London, 1834-50.

Cronin, Stephanie, ed., *Subalterns and Social Protest: History from Below in the Middle East and North Africa*. London; New York: Routledge, 2008.

Daneshpajohesh, Manoucher (ed), *Baresiy-i safarnamihay-i dori-yi Safavi*. Isfahan: Isfahan University Press, 2006.

De Gouvea, A. *Relation de grandes guerres et victoires obtenues par le roi de Perse Chah Abbas*, French translation. Rouen: Nicolas Loyselet, 1646.

Della Valle, Pietro. *The Pilgrim: The Travels of Pietro Della Valle*, trans., abridged, and introduced by G. Bull. London: Hutchinson, 1990.

Della Valle, Pietro. *I Viaggi . . . Lettere dalla Persia*, ed. F. Gaeta and L. Lockhart, *Il Nuovo Ramusio*, I, Rome: Istituto poligrafico dello Stato, 1972.

Ferrier, R.W. *A Journey to Persia: Jean Chardin's Portrait of a Seventeenth-Century Empire.* London; New York: I.B. Tauris, 1996.

Floor, Willem, *The History of Theater in Iran.* Washington D.C.: Mage Publishers, 2005

Foucault, Michel, *The Archaeology of Knowledge and the Discourse on Language.* Translated by A.M. Sheridan Smith. New York: Vintage Books, [1972] 2000

Geertz, Clifford, *The Interpretation of Cultures: Selected Essays.* New York: Basic Books, 1973

Gramsci, Antonio, *Selections from the Prison Notebooks of Antonio Gramsci.* Edited and translated by Quintin Hoare and Geoffrey Nowell Smith. New York: International Publisher, 1971.

Guha, Ranajit, "On Some Aspects of the Historiography of Colonial India," in *Subaltern Studies I: Writings on South Asian History and Society,* ed. Ranajit Guha, Delhi: Oxford University Press, 1982, 1-8.

Halm, Heinz, *Shi'a Islam: From Religion to Revolution.* (trans.) Allison Brown. Princeton: Markus Wiener, 1997.

Herbert, Thomas, *Travels in Persia 1627-29.* London: J.W. Parker and Son, 1928.

Hunt, Lynn, M. C. Jacob and W. Mijnhardt, *The Book that Changed Europe: Picart and Bernard's Religious Ceremonies of the World.* Cambridge, MA: The Belknap Press of Harvard University Press, 2010.

Kæmpfer, Engelbert, *Am Hofe des Persischen Grosskönigs 1684–85,* trans. W. Hinz. Leipzig: K.F. Koehler Verlag, 1940.

Lockman, Zachary, *Field Notes: The Making of Middle East Studies in the United States.* Stanford, California: Stanford University Press, 2016.

Olearius, Adam, *Offt begehrte Beschreibung der newen orientalischen Reise,* Schleswig, Germany: Bey Jacob zur Glocken, 1647.

Olearius, Adam, *The Voyages and Travels of the Ambassadors Sent by Frederick Duke of Holstein to the Great Duke of Muscovy and the King of Persia,* London: Printed for John Starkey and Thomas Basset, 1669.

Matthee. Rudi, "Prostitutes, Courtesans, and Dancing Girls: Women Entertainers in Safavid Iran," in, *Iran and Beyond, Essays in Middle Eastern History in Honor of Nikki R. Keddie,* eds. Rudi Matthee and B. Baron, Costa Mesa, CA: Mazda, 2000, 121-150.

Matthee, Rudi, "The Safavids under Western Eyes: Seventeenth-Century European Travelers to Iran," *Journal of Early Modern History,* 13, 2009, 137-71.

Membré, Michael, *Mission To The Lord Sophy of Persia (1539-1542).* Translated with introduction and notes by A.H. Morton (trans.) London: Trustees of the Gibb Memorial, 1993.

Muir, Edward, *Ritual in Early Modern Europe.* Cambridge: Cambridge University Press, 1997.

Munajjim, Jala al-Din, *Tarikh-i 'Abbasi ya ruzname-ye Mulla Jalal.* Edited by Sayfallah Vahidniya. Tehran: Intisharat-i Vahid, 1987.

Munshi, Iskander, *History of Shah 'Abbas the Great*, R M. Savory, ed and transl., Boulder: Westview Press, vol. 2, 1978.

Nerlich, Michael, *Ideology of Adventure: Studies in Modern Consciousness, 1100-1750.* Minneapolis: University of Minneapolis Press, 1987.

Newman, Andrew, "Preface to the 'Travel to Iran' Special Issue," *Journal of Early Modern History* 13 (2009), 99-103.

Newman, Andrew, "Safavids and 'Subalterns': The Reclaiming of Voices," *Isma'ili and other Shi'i Studies: Essays in Honour of Farhad Daftary,* ed. in O.Ali-de-Unzaga, London: I.B.Tauris, 2010, 473-490.

Newman, Andrew. *Safavid Iran: Rebirth of a Persian Empire.* London; New York: I.B.Tauris, 2006.

Padgen, Anthony, *European Encounters with the New World, from Renaissance to Romanticism,* New Haven and London: Yale University Press, 1993.

Quinn, Sholeh A., *Historical Writing During the Reign of Shah 'Abbas: Ideology, Imitation, and Legitimacy in Safavid Chronicles,* Salt Lake City, UT: University of Utah Press, 2000.

Rahimi, Babak, "From Assorted to Assimilated Ethnography: Transformation of Ethnographic Authority from Michel Membré to John Chardin, 1542-1677," in *Unravelling Civilization: European Travel and Travel Writing,* ed. Hagen Schulz-Forberg, Brussels, Belgium: P.I.E.-Peter Lang, 2005, 107-27.

Rahimi, Babak. *Theater State and the Formation of Early Modern Public Sphere in Iran,* Leiden; Boston: Brill, 2012.

Savory, Roger, *Iran Under the Safavids,* Cambridge; New York: Cambridge University Press, 1980.

Schiebinger, Londa. *Plants and Empire: Colonial Bioprospecting in the Atlantic World.* Cambridge, Massachusetts/London: Harvard University Press, 2004.

Spivak, Gayatri. *A Critique of Postcolonial Reason: Toward a History of the Vanishing Present,* Cambridge: Harvard University Press, 1999.

Webber, Sabra J. "Middle East Studies & Subaltern Studies." *Middle East Studies Association Bulletin,* Vol. 31, 1 (1997), 11-16.

Notes

1 See Rudi Matthee, "The Safavids under Western Eyes: Seventeenth-Century European Travelers to Iran," *Journal of Early Modern History,* 13, 2009, 151. For a critical study of Safavid court chronicles, see Sholeh A. Quinn, *Historical Writing During the Reign of Shah 'Abbas: Ideology, Imitation, and Legitimacy in Safavid Chronicles,* Salt Lake City, UT: University of Utah Press, 2000. For a critical reflection on elite-centric historical scholarship on the Middle East and North Africa, see Stephanie Cronin, 'Introduction,' Stephanie Cronin, ed. *Subalterns and Social*

Protest: History from Below in the Middle East and North Africa. London; New York: Routledge, 2008, 1-22.

2   Andrew Newman's study, particularly in the context of socio-political and economic crisis in post-'Abbas period, is the only work known to me that discusses the subaltern in the Safavid historical context. Andrew Newman, "Safavids and 'Subalterns': The Reclaiming of Voices," in *Isma'ili and other Shi'i Studies: Essays in Honour of Farhad Daftary*, ed. O.Ali-de-Unzaga, London: I.B.Tauris, 2010, 473-490. The other notable examples are the original works of and Sussan Babaie and Kathryn Babayan, whose groundbreaking studies on urban architecture and popular cultures have shed light on the everyday life of Safavid society, though the question of subaltern has a limited focus in both works. Rudi Matthee's studies of prostitutes, courtesans, and the social life of stimulants in the period are also noteworthy, although his studies are devoid of subaltern analysis. See Rudi Matthee, "Prostitutes, Courtesans, and Dancing Girls: Women Entertainers in Safavid Iran," in *Iran and Beyond, Essays in Middle Eastern History in Honor of Nikki R. Keddie*, eds. Rudi Matthee and B. Baron, Costa Mesa, CA: Mazda, 2000, 121-150.

3   Michel Foucault, *The Archaeology of Knowledge and the Discourse on Language*. Translated by A.M. Sheridan Smith. New York: Vintage Books, [1972] 2000, 33. See also Zachery Lockman, *Field Notes: The Making of Middle East Studies in the United States*. Stanford, California: Stanford University Press, 2016.

4   Sabra Webber, "Middle East Studies & Subaltern Studies." *Middle East Studies Association Bulletin*, Vol. 31, 1 (1997), 11-16; Ranajit Guha, "On Some Aspects of the Historiography of Colonial India," *Subaltern Studies I: Writings on South Asian History and Society*, ed. Ranajit Guha, Delhi: Oxford University Press,1982, 1-8.

5   Stephanie Cronin, ed., *Subalterns and Social Protest: History from Below in the Middle East and North Africa*. London; New York: Routledge, 2008.

6   In terms of gender and sexuality, I draw attention to Kathryn Babayan's "In Spirit We Ate Each Other's Sorrow: Female Companionship in Seventeenth-Century Safavid Iran," in *Islamicate Sexualities: Translations across Temporal Geographies of Desire*, eds. Kathryn Babayan and Afsaneh Najmabadi, Cambridge, Mass. : Center for Middle Eastern Studies of Harvard University, 2008, 239-274.

7   Kathryn Babayan, *Mystics, Monarchs, and Messiahs: Cultural Landscapes of Early Modern Iran*. Cambridge: Harvard University Press, 2002, 219-232; Andrew Newman, *Safavid Iran: Rebirth of a Persian Empire*. London; New York: I.B.Tauris, 2006, 58-59; Babak Rahimi, *Theater State and the Formation of Early Modern Public Sphere in Iran*, Leiden; Boston: Brill, 2012.

8   Andrew Newman, "Safavids and 'Subalterns': The Reclaiming of Voices," in *Isma'ili and other Shi'i Studies: Essays in Honour of Farhad Daftary*, ed. O.Ali-de-Unzaga, London: I.B.Tauris, 2010, 477-480.

9   Andrew Newman, *Safavid Iran: Rebirth of a Persian Empire*. New York; London: I.B.Tauris, 2006, 74-75.

10 See Sussan Babaie, *Isfahan and Its Palaces: Statecraft, Shi'ism and the Architecture of Conviviality in Early Modern Iran*. Edinburgh: Edinburgh University Press, 2008.

11 Kathryn Babayan, "Sufis, Dervishes, Mullas: the Controversy over Spiritual and Temporal Dominion in Seventeenth-Century Iran," in *Safavid Persia: The History and Politics of an Islamic Society*, ed. Charles Melville, London: I. B. Tauris, 1996, 117-38.

12 Adam Olreaius's 1637 report of Muharram includes reference to recitation of elegies, which Babayan explains, came from the guilds. Babayan, 2002, 219. For an account of Alid devotional culture in the *futuvvat*, see Kathryn Babayan, *Mystics, Monarchs, and Messiahs: Cultural Landscapes of Early Modern Iran*. Cambridge: Harvard University Press, 2002, 161-196.

13 The term "inner" refers to conceptual challenges historians face to reconstruct the meaningful experiences manifested in "voices" of a ritual community, especially the silenced subaltern, through archived literary discourses. Yet the conceptual challenge is not just about recovering lost voices, but how we, as historians, also participate in reconstructing the historical experience in

our contemporary interpretation of the text. "Our dialogue," Arjun Appadurai writes in a famous introductory article on place and voice, "is not just a dialogue "in the field," between self and other, but it is also a dialogue over time between anthropological text and their ever-changing readings." Arjun Appadurai, "Introduction: Place and Voice in Anthropological Theory," *Cultural Anthropology*, Vol. 3, 1 (1988), 17.

14 Our only non-European travel report of Safavid-era Muharram, from the Ottoman traveler, Evliya Çelebi (1611-1682), is a useful but limited account of the rituals. Çelebi's description of Muharram in Tabriz in 1647 and 1655 depicts self-violent performances and use of razors, along with varies representations of bodies from the Karbala story. However, the Ottoman description, similar to most European accounts from the period, is limited to mostly male performers and lacks a detail account of the rituals and their meaning. Çelebi's narrative should be studied as a distinct travelogue with its own reading public and within the *Seyahatmame* tradition. See Evliya Çelebi (Effendi), *Narrative of Travels in Europe, Asia, and Africa in the Seventeenth Century*, Translated by Joseph von Hammer-Purgstall. Volume II, London, 1834-50, 138.

15 Antonio Gramsci, *Selections from the Prison Notebooks of Antonio Gramsci*. Edited and translated by Quintin Hoare and Geoffrey Nowell Smith. New York: International Publisher, 1971, 52-55.

16 Touraj Atabaki, "Disgruntled Guests: Iranian Subaltern on the Margins of the Tsarist Empire," *International Review of Social History*, vol. 48, 3, 2003, 401-426.

17 The connection between rural and urban is one of migration, which most likely involved labor migration to developing urban centers under the reign of Abbas I when textile industry in the form of workshops saw a sharp increase in numbers. The relationship between guilds and retail markets in the Isfahani-phase of rule played an important role in a migration process, which remains understudied.

18 "Thin description" is derived from Clifford Geertz's famous methodological concept of "thick description". While thin description aims to uncover meaning behind actions or behaviors of a society for an external observer, thick description represents without seeking to examine the meanings for the actions.

Clifford Geertz, *The Interpretation of Cultures: Selected Essays*. New York: Basic Books, 1973, 3-30.

19 See Gayatri Spivak, *A Critique of Postcolonial Reason: Toward a History of the Vanishing Present*. Cambridge: Harvard University Press, 1999, 244-311.

20 See Babak Rahimi, *Theatre State and the Formation of Early Modern Public Sphere in Iran: Studies on Safavid Muharram Rituals, 1590-1641*. Leiden, Boston: Brill, 2012, 199-234.

21 Rula Jurdi Abisaab, *Converting Persia: Religion and Power in the Safavid Empire*. London: I.B. Tauris, 2004.

22 Heinz Halm, *Shi'a Islam: From Religion to Revolution*, Allison Brown (transl.). Princeton: Markus Wiener, 1997, 41-44.

23 Mahmoud Ayoub, *Redemptive Suffering in Islam: A Study of the Devotional Aspects of 'Āshūrā in Twelver Shī'ism*. The Hague: E.J. Brill, 1978.

24 Kathryn Babayan, "Sufis, Dervishes, Mullas: the Controversy over Spiritual and Temporal Dominion in Seventeenth-Century Iran," in *Safavid Persia: The History and Politics of an Islamic Society*. ed. Charles Melville, London: I.B.Tauris, 1996, 123.

25 Jean Calmard, "Shi'i Rituals and Power II. The Consolidation of Safavid Shi'ism: Folklore and Popular Religion," in *Safavid Persia: The History and Politics of an Islamic Society*. ed. Charles Melville, London: I.B.Tauris, 1996, 143.

26 See Sussan Babaie, *Isfahan and Its Palaces: Statecraft, Shi'ism and the Architecture of Conviviality in Early Modern Iran*. Edinburgh: Edinburgh University Press, 2008.

27 Kathryn Babayan, *Mystics, Monarchs, and Messiahs: Cultural Landscapes of Early Modern Iran*. Cambridge: Harvard University Press, 2002, 226.

28 See Edward Muir, *Ritual in Early Modern Europe*. Cambridge: Cambridge University Press, 1997.

29 See Babak Rahimi, *Theater State and the Formation of Early Modern Public Sphere in Iran*, Leiden; Boston: Brill, 2012, 199-271.

30 Roger Savory, *Iran Under the Safavids*, Cambridge; New York: Cambridge University Press, 1980, 100.
31 See Bernadette Andrea, "The Global Travels of Teresa Sampsonia Sherely's Carmelite Relic," in *Travel and Travail: Early Modern Women, English Drama, and the Wider World*, eds. Patricia Akhimie and Bernadette Andrea, Lincoln; London: University of Nebraska Press, 2019, 104-108.
32 Michael Nerlich, *Ideology of Adventure: Studies in Modern Consciousness, 1100-1750*. Minneapolis: University of Minneapolis Press, 1987.
33 Babak Rahimi, *Theater State and the Formation of Early Modern Public Sphere in Iran*, Leiden; Boston: Brill, 2012, 217-218.
34 It is not known if the ceremonies were performed in Qazvin later in 1548.
35 The names of European travelers Muharram observation are as follow: Michele Membré (1540); António de Gouvea (1602-4); Etienne (Stefan) Kakash (1603-04); Pietro Della Valle (1618-9); Garcia de Silva y Figueroa (1618-9); Fedot Afanasievich Kotov (1624-5); Thomas Herbert (1628); Adam Olearius (1637); Pére Philippe de la Sainte-Trinité (1630-1640?); De Montheron (1641); Pére Raphaël du Mans (1647-1696?) Gabriel de Chinon (1650-1668?); d'Armainville Poullet (1660?); J. Thévenot (1665); J.B.Tavernier (1667); Jean Chardin (1666-7, 1669, 1673-7); Petrus Bedik (1670-5?); Jan Jansz. Struys (1671); Engelbert Kaempfer (1684-5); Gemelli Careri (1694); Abbé Gaudereau (1695); Cornelis de Bruyn (1704); P. Judasz Tadeusz Krusinski (1714). For a detail list of publications of the travel books, see Calmard, 1996:182-4. For a detailed list of travel reports, dates and publications, see Calmard 1997. For a thorough study of illustration of Muharram in European travel reports, see Elio Brancaforte, "Between Word and Image: Representations of Shi'ite Rituals in the Safavid Empire from Early Modern European Travel Accounts," in *Remapping Travel Narratives (1000-1700): To the East and back again* ed. Montserrat Piera, Leeds: Arc Humanities Press, 2018, 129-155.
36 Thomas Herbert, *Travels in Persia 1627-29*, London: J.W. Parker and Son, 1928, p. 127.
37 Jean Calmard, "Shi'i Rituals and Power II. The Consolidation of Safavid Shi'ism: Folklore and Popular Religion," in *Safavid Persia: The History and Politics of an Islamic Society*, ed. Charles Melville, London: I.B. Tauris, 1996, 154.
38 Manoucher Daneshpajohesh, Manoucher (ed). *Baresiy-i safarnamihay-i dori-yi Safavi*. Isfahan: Isfahan University Press, 2006, 33.
39 Michael Membré. *Mission To The Lord Sophy of Persia (1539-1542)*. Translated with introduction and notes by A.H. Morton, London: Trustees of the Gibb Memorial, 1993, 43.
40 Anthony Padgen, *European Encounters with the New World, from Renaissance to Romanticism*, New Haven and London: Yale University Press, 1993, 17.
41 Babak Rahimi, "From Assorted to Assimilated Ethnography: Transformation of Ethnographic Authority from Michel Membré to John Chardin, 1542-1677," in *Unravelling Civilization: European Travel and Travel Writing*, ed. Hagen Schulz-Forberg, Brussels, Belgium: P.I.E.-Peter Lang, 2005, 107-127.
42 For a study of power of presentation in travel reports, see Debbie Lisle, *The Global Politics of Contemporary Travel Writing*, Cambridge: Cambridge University Press, 2006, especially 11-17.
43 Chardin's *Voyages* played a crucial role in the development of relativism and, by and large, Enlightenment thought such as Edward Gibbon and Voltaire. His influence, for example, on Montesquieu's *Persian Letters* can be found in letters 7, 67, 121 and 143. See Junko Thérèse Takeda, *Iran and a French Empire of Trade, 1700-1808*, Liverpool: Liverpool University Press, 28 and Nicholas Dew, Orientalism in Louis XIV's France, New York: Oxford University Press, 2009, 132.
44 This would also include Chardin's contemporary travel reports by Adam Olearius, whose account also offers one of the most sophisticated descriptions of Muharram. See Elio Brancaforte, 2018, 140-147. Also consider the work of Ambrosio Bembo, a Venetian nobleman who visited Isfahan in the late 1670s. His report offers a traditional account of Safavid native life that typifies the convention of fusing personal and impersonal description in his published

travel report. Although he does not provide a description of Muharram, Bembo employs a similar technique of associating the notion of "ceremony" with everyday cultural practices of the native society, including marriage and funeral. See Ambrosio Bembo, *The Travels and Journal of Ambrosio Bembo*, translated from the Italian by Clara Bargellini, Berkeley: University of California Press, 2007, 351-354.

45 Translation quoted from R.W. Ferrier, *A Journey to Persia: Jean Chardin's Portrait of a Seventeenth-Century Empire*. London; New York: I.B. Tauris, 1996, 107-108. Chardin, Jean. ed. Le Laglés. *Voyages...en Perse, et autres lieux de l'Orient*. Vol 9, 1811, 52-6.

46 See A. de Gouvea, *Relation de grandes guerres et victoires obtenues par le roi de Perse Chah Abbas*, French translation. Rouen, 1646, 75–77.

47 De Gouvea writes: "I could never understand whether this feast was for pleasure or for lamentation, since some people laughed, danced and sang, whereas others cried and wailed." "Feste estoit de resioüissance, ou de tristesse." A. de Gouvea, *Relation de grandes guerres et victoires obtenues par le roi de Perse Chah Abbas*, French translation, Rouen: Nicolas Loyselet, 1646, 76.

48 Pietro Della Valle, *The Pilgrim: The Travels of Pietro Della Valle*, trans., abridged, an introduced by G. Bull. London: Hutchinson, 1990, 142–44; for the original, see *I Viaggi... Lettere dalla Persia*, ed. F. Gaeta and L. Lockhart, *Il Nuovo Ramusio*, I, Rome: Istituto poligrafico dello Stato, 1972, 84–85, 115–18, 134–34.

49 See Willem Floor, *The History of Theater in Iran*. Washington D.C.: Mage Publishers, 2005, 129.

50 Babak Rahimi, *Theater State and the Formation of Early Modern Public Sphere in Iran*, Leiden; Boston: Brill, 2012, 226-229.

51 Adam Olearius, *The Voyages and Travels of the Ambassadors Sent by Frederick Duke of Holstein to the Great Duke of Muscovy and the King of Persia*, London: Printed for John Starkey and Thomas Basset, 1669, 161–76; Adam Olearius. *Offt begehrte Beschreibung der newen orientalischen Reise*, Schleswig, Germany: Bey Jacob zur Glocken, 1647, 329-330.

52 Elio Brancaforte, "Between Word and Image: Representations of Shi'ite Rituals in the Safavid Empire from Early Modern European Travel Accounts," in Montserrat Piera (ed.), *Remapping Travel Narratives (1000-1700): To the East and back again*, Leeds: Arc Humanities Press, 2018, 147.

53 Elio Brancaforte, "Between Word and Image: Representations of Shi'ite Rituals in the Safavid Empire from Early Modern European Travel Accounts," in *Remapping Travel Narratives (1000-1700): To the East and back again*, ed. Montserrat Piera, Leeds: Arc Humanities Press, 2018, 131.

54 Sonja Brentjes, "Immediacy, Mediation, and Media in Early Modern Catholic and Protestant Representations of Safavid Iran." *Journal of Early Modern History* 13, no. 2–3 (2009), 175. For a general critical account of the travel reports, see Andrew Newman, "Preface to the 'Travel to Iran' Special Issue," *Journal of Early Modern History* 13 (2009), 99-103; See also Babak Rahimi, *Theater State and the Formation of Early Modern Public Sphere in Iran*, Leiden; Boston: Brill, 2012, 24-27.

55 See Lynn Hunt, M. C. Jacob and W. Mijnhardt, *The Book that Changed Europe: Picart and Bernard's Religious Ceremonies of the World*. Cambridge, MA: The Belknap Press of Harvard University Press, 2010.

56 Adam Olearius, *Offt beghrte Beschreiburng der newen orientalischen Reise*. Schleswig, Germany: Bey Jacob zur Glocken, 1647, 327.

57 See Londa Schiebinger, *Plants and Empire: Colonial Bioprospecting in the Atlantic World*. Cambridge, Massachusetts, London, England: Harvard University Press, 2004.

58 Iskander Munshi, *History of Shah 'Abbas the Great*, R M. Savory, ed and transl., Boulder: Westview Press, vol. 2, 1978, 846 and Mulla Jala al-Din Munajjim, *Tarikh-i 'Abbasi ya ruzname-ye Mulla Jalal*. Edited by Sayfallah Vahidniya. Tehran: Intisharat-i Vahid, 1987, 360.

59 See Engelbert Kæmpfer, *Am Hofe des Persischen Grosskönigs 1684–85*, trans. W. Hinz . Leipzig: K.F. Koehler Verlag, 1940, 144.

60 Mikhail Bakhtin, *Problems of Dostoevsky's Poetics*. Minneapolis; London: University of Minnesota Pres, 1984, 5-46.

61 See Babak Rahimi, *Theater State and the Formation of Early Modern Public Sphere in Iran*, Leiden; Boston: Brill, 2012, 273-320.
62 Mikhail Bakhtin, *Problems of Dostoevsky's Poetics*. Minneapolis; London: University of Minnesota Pres, 1984, 6-7.

Figure 1: La Fête d'Hussein.

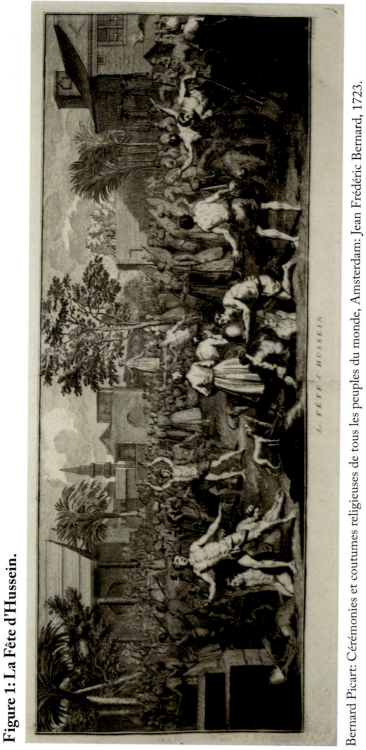

Bernard Picart: Cérémonies et coutumes religieuses de tous les peuples du monde, Amsterdam: Jean Frédéric Bernard, 1723.

6

The 'Visible Voice' or 'Vocal Visibility' of the Subalterns in Persianate Painting: The Safavid and Mughal Cases

Valérie Gonzalez

Looking at Persianate Subalternity Through the Lens of Painting

A look at painting for the purpose of recovering the lost voices of the subalterns in Persianate societies from the thirteenth-century to the Modern period will lead, not to the recovery of any loss, but to the rediscovery of the most 'visible-vocal' faces in this visual material, namely the subalterns' faces. To clarify the terminology, in the pictorial domain the term 'subalterns' stands for the represented individuals of all social ranks united except for the ruler, its relatives and the nobility that form the opposite iconographic category of 'royalty'. The latter is obviously dominated by the king's figure, while subalternity appears in the multiform of not only the royal entourage of courtiers, army officers, clerics, administrators, etc., but also of the court's servants, artists, domestics workers of all kinds, in sum the commoners.[1]

At no time in the history of Persianate painting did the subalterns ever lose their voice. Always conspicuously visible in the iconography, they served as the primary site of pictorial experiment with human representation. In the highly stylized and otherworldly framework of Persian painting, namely the common lore of the diverse Persianate pictorial schools, the subalterns actually constitute the most 'vocal' presence in the sense that they consistently present the most tangible and palpable figures, by contrast with the ethereal archetypal princely figuration. (Fig. 1) These qualities of tangibility and palpability of subaltern imagery are the product of a form of individualisation of the figures, and of an intent to vary their facial expression so as to reflect in a certain manner the natural versatility of the human body and mind.

This dichotomic plastic treatment of subaltern and royal iconography began to be challenged with the emergence of the quasi-physiognomic and full-fledged physiognomic princely portrait in the early Modern period. (Fig. 2) However, in this period, this novelty whereby the topoi of subalterny and royalty entered into a kind of aesthetic competition, only concerns Mughal and Ottoman art. It is only at the end of Shah 'Abbas I's reign that the Safavids slowly began to depict the physical appearances of the sovereign. Until then, they applied the concept of natural imitation only to subaltern imagery, thus maintaining for some time, in Modern Iran, the pre-Modern partitioned figurative order.

This complex economy of human representation in Persianate painting, aesthetically and stylistically differentiating between the two registers of subalternity and royalty, conveys a particular conception of the human order and specific socio-political values. This article aims to unravel these conception and values by examining the modalities of their aesthetic translation in the pictorial medium. However, the inquiry focuses more particularly on the evidence of this phenomenon found in early Safavid and Mughal painting until the period of Shah Abbas I's reign (1588-1629) in Iran, and of Jahangir's reign (1605-1627) in India. For these pictorial productions are particularly revelatory of the fundaments of the said economy of human representation and what it tells us about subalternity in the Persianate societies.

The Context: Portraiture in Early Modern Persianate Painting

The early Modern period of the Ottoman, Safavid and Mughal empires constitutes a milestone in the history of Persianate painting as the portrait genre became like never before a prominent iconographic trope.[2] Most remarkable in this historical-artistic development is the aforementioned emergence of the physiognomic royal portrait by which, for the first time, the ruler's figure appears recognisable through the rendition of its natural looks. This fact requires critical attention because it holds the key of the problematic of subalternity in question. But prior to engaging in this critique, it is necessary to expound what, in theory, the mimetic or physiognomic portrait and the other modalities of portraiture consist of. For owing to the lack of terminological definition and a certain casualness in the use of aesthetic concepts, the studies on Persianate painting turn out to be often confusing and misleading.[3]

About the Art of Portraiture

To define the theoretical underpinnings of the Persianate stylistic treatment of the dual iconography of subalternity and royalty, the primary sources are not more helpful than the studies. In her landmark essay on the Persian literature about human figuration, Priscilla Soucek remarks that 'when 'local tradition' describes something as a 'portrait', the goal should be to understand how that type of portraiture functioned.'[4] Precisely, the latter point cannot be figured out by referring to these sources, as they elaborate on the relationship between the image and what it represents only at an abstract philosophical level. As useful as they may be to penetrate the Persian aesthetic consciousness, these texts' theories do not account for the pictorial practice itself that, as the archaeological evidence shows, clearly differentiated between the various possibilities of picturing the human figure and deliberately made choices among these possibilities in order to fulfil specific semantic needs. Depending on the location and precise period of the Persianate world's history in which it was practiced, the portrait genre took on different forms and a fortiori induced different cognitions and experiences, hence the necessity of a proper methodology to study this genre and define its semantic workings.

Although they acknowledged this discrepancy between the Persian philosophy of visual art and the pictorial reality this philosophy is supposed to enlighten, Soucek and the Islamic art historians who have studied these texts did not provide any satisfactory answer to this fundamental question of the nature and functioning of portraiture in Persianate artistic culture.[5] The reason for this shortcoming resides in the traditional method of art history on which they rely. This method is not attuned to art and aesthetic theory, therefore it does not allow for the identification and cognisance of these constitutive nuances of the portrait as an artistic complexity with a multifaceted aesthetic and semantic operatory system. Yet, the knowledge of these nuances is particularly important in the Islamic context, characterised by a distinct metaphysical approach to figurative representation.[6]

In Islamic art studies, scholars categorise generically as portrait a greatly varied spectrum of images figuring people, individuals and archetypes of individuals. In theory, the human figure can be portrayed according to two main models: the model that I call 'the conceptual-modular signaletic portrait', and the familiar physiognomic likeness. The first model operates in the region of the symbol and the concept inasmuch as the figuration makes meaning by means of an encoded system of signs forming figurative modules that is the equivalent of a script or a grammar in the domain of visual forms. These signs and modules convey a more or less wide range of standard informative data about the subject depicted, for example a breast or a moustache signifies the figure's gender, a skin colour its ethnicity, specific paraphernalia its social function, a particular garment its cultural affiliation, etc. In a given signaletic portrait, the selection of data constructs a visual *semiosis* (a set of significations semiotically signified or signified by signs) that gives a certain idea of the figure, but that does not account for the ipseitic physical traits that this figure possesses, possessed or hypothetically would have possessed in the natural world, in a word its carnality.[7] We may say that rather than picturing its subject, the signaletic portrait institutes its identity in the image. By inference, in this type of portrait the beholder cognises, rather than *re*cognising, the subject's identity. In sum, the signaletic model is a disincarnated instance of portraiture. Traditional Persian human representation mainly follows this model.[8] (Fig. 1)

The process of pictorial incarnation is, on the other hand, the very objective of the physiognomic portrait or likeness. A familiar example of this second model is classical European portraiture that reached its peak of realism with painters like Diego Velasquez and Anthony van Dyck. Importantly, whether artists have/had an actual knowledge of the figure's real physical aspect allowing them to represent it truthfully, or in the lack of thereof have/had to imagine it, it is the impression of naturalistic rendering that makes of a portrait a physiognomic likeness. For example, Jahangiri painting is reputed for the veracity not only of the contemporary portraits of the Mughal emperor and his subjects, but also of the reinvented likenesses of Jahangir's ancestors, Timur, Babur and Humayun.[9] The latter lend the Timurid Mughal genealogical family portraits the appearance of a living reality.

As we shall see, while some portraits attest to the implementation of one of these two models in a clear-cut manner, other cases may be more ambiguous. In halfway between the carnal and the conceptual or the natural and the signaletic, these ambiguous portraits may raise issues of categorisation or misdirect their interpretation. Yet, to understand any portrait's meaning, it is mandatory to determine whether within the generic genre of portraiture this portrait fundamentally, if not exclusively, operates in the region of the sign or of the natural form. This question of definition appears in all its acuteness when it comes to discuss early Modern Persianate portraiture that gave the impulse to the mimetic likeness in Islam.

Contrasting Approach to the Subalternity-Royalty Duality in Early Modern Persianate Painting

In early Modern Persianate painting, the technics of picturing attained a peak of sophistication and opened up an unprecedented range of strategic plastic possibilities. These technics included modelling and shading, the palette's enrichment and a refined use of drawing that, by pictorial law, allow for an efficient imitative rendering of Nature's complex forms as they appear to the eye. Landscape, for example, become more three-dimensional in this period.[10] If one compares with one another images of the late Timurid and early Safavid, Mughal and Ottoman era, one may easily observe this technical evolution. (Figs. 1-5) In the perspective of our inquiry on subalternity, the following questioning arises: to which ends were these technical conquests employed in early Modern Persianate human iconography?

A close observation of the artefacts reveals that the early Modern technical achievement did not necessarily serve the same purpose in the aesthetically distinct pictorial schools of the Safavids, the Mughals and the Ottomans, although these schools converge on one notable aspect of image-making. That point of convergence significantly lies in the use of these advanced pictorial modalities to animate the multitude of modular human representations with lively naturalist figures of subalternity. In the idealistic metaphysics of the Persian pictoriality common to the Safavid and Ottoman schools of painting, these lively human depictions puncture and open up the image's space onto the reality of the phenomenal world, particularly in the scenes de genre (depictions of ordinary life activities) such as views of encampment or of building construction; these apertures let the viewer get a concrete palpable sense of the contemporary life. In Mughal painting, however unlike in its Safavid and Ottoman counterparts, these lively figures of subalternity do not tear the images' fabric but blend with it, as in this painting the Persian pictorial model has been remodelled into a mimetic imagistic space. (Figs. 4 and 5) Nonetheless the fact however remains that despite these regional differences, the *topos* of the subalterns was definitely not given a secondary importance in Persianate pictorial representation in general, especially if we compare their depiction in the sphere of images with that in the textual sources in which this microworld of the anonymous people is most of the time unspoken about. In painting, by contrast, this hyper-visible/vocal microworld constitutes an essential element of the worldly vision this medium intends to project.

Yet, this unifying feature of the Safavid, Mughal and Ottoman pictorial productions located in subaltern iconography contrasts with their divergence, mentioned earlier, in the approach to the subject of royalty in the early Modern period, thus signalling that a specific philosophy of the relationship between the two groups underpins this unanimous aesthetic assertion of the subalterns in the humanistic construct projected by the paintings. That divergence manifests itself more precisely in the difference between, on one hand, the Safavids' approach to royal imagery, and on the other hand, the Mughals and the Ottomans'. And in the light of this asymmetric state of affairs, the contrast between Safavid and Mughal portraiture is the most revelatory of all.

Contrasting Approach to the Subalternity-Royalty Duality in Early Modern Safavid and Mughal Painting

The Mughal Case

As it is well known, within the whole of Persianate painting, Mughal art distinguishes itself by its naturalistic inclination.[11] In what I describe in a previous work in terms of 'the Indian body-centric metaphysics of the picture', as opposed to 'the logocentric metaphysics of the Persian picture' (logos/language/script/text centred), the ultimate mimetic manifestation is the realism of the human face.[12] Like their European contemporaries, the Mughal artists made pictures of people based on direct observation, regardless of their social rank. In the Mughal royal register, the poignant drawing of a downcast-eyed Akbar from the British Library, and in the subaltern register, the artists' self-likenesses illustrate well this practice. (Fig. 6) We may consequently say that, in the Mughal pictorial context, the Persian duality of subalternity/royalty *stylistically* dissolves itself. This means two things.

First, the subalterns and royals have the same stylistic value in Mughal imagery as a reflection of the world's concreteness in which all human beings share the same property of carnality.

Second, in the Mughal pictorial context, the Persianate social-political partition of royalty versus subalternity, rather than being formally showed, is signified by the discourse of the picture. In other words, Mughal painting thematises this partition only *discursively* or *narratively*, not stylistically. If, from the stylistic viewpoint, the realistic rendition of the Mughal emperor's corporeity keeps him down-to-earth, so to speak, and at the same aesthetic plane as the rest of humanity (subalternity), his divinely attributed ontological superiority inspired by the Iranian ideology of sovereignty expresses itself through the organisation and semantic of forms, for example through courtly scenes hierarchically composed or the display of royal visual attributes and paraphernalia.[13]

In Jahangiri imagery, this iconographic semantic articulating the divide between the royals and the subalterns takes on a hyperbolic rhetorical turn with the symbolic semantisation or metaphorisation of the imperial portrait. This process consists in loading the picture with highly referential symbols such as the halo around the emperor's head, solar rays, the globe-pedestal, and various allegorical settings that design a world apart for the royal figure: a superior world closer to God.[14] Thus, although thanks to its unprecedented realistic quality Jahangiri portraiture metaphysically anchors the picture in the mundane more deeply than ever, this iconographic symbolisation introduces in the same picture a new dimension of idealistic order, thereby creating a dialectical polarisation between empiricism and idealism in the imperial portrait's metaphysics. Beyond the imagistic semantic, it is this metaphysical polarisation that, in Jahangiri painting, pictorialises with the most potency the Persianate social-political dichotomy between royalty and subalternity.

The Safavid Case

In the otherworldly universe of Safavid painting, there is no such a stylistic dissolution like in Mughal pictoriality. Putting narration aside, style segregates and constitutes the most powerful tool of semantic differentiation with which the Safavid picture thematises the dichotomy in question, until things changed at the end of Shah

'Abbas I' rule. This reading of the material, however, is to be argued against the studies because of their problematic interpretations of this question of style and aesthetics in Safavid portraiture. A recent article by Kishwar Rizvi published in the authoritative journal *The Art Bulletin*, 'The Suggestive Portrait of Shah 'Abbas: Prayer and Likeness in a Safavid *Shahnama*', will serve this critique.[15] (Fig. 7)

To begin, there is a need to deconstruct an assumption widely shared by the scholarship and reported by Rizvi in this statement: 'Art historians have noted that early Safavid painting is remarkable for its resistance to verisimilitude'.[16] Not only this statement is plainly wrong, but in addition, the expression '*resistance* to verisimilitude' betrays the lingering currency in this scholarship of the outdated Orientalist Eurocentric vision of art that posits *mimesis* (imitation of Nature) as the universal norm based on which both Western and non-Western artworks are to be apprehended, evaluated and interpreted.[17] Significantly, we would not find in these studies any mention of a 'resistance to abstraction', for example in the study of Mughal painting that, from its inception, re-fashioned the textual-geometric space of the Persian paradigm (abstraction) into a penetrable scene of mimetic projection (verisimilitude).[18] To state what ought to be obvious, the use of the artistic concepts of abstraction and verisimilitude in non-Western visual cultures are not be construed against a preconceived normativity that only concerns the history of Western art. In the Persianate Islamic context, the apprehension of these concepts is the product of an inner logic of creativity stemming from the culturally determined artistic development of each of the Persianate polities.

Furthermore, to recall our earlier remarks, the transhuman Safavid pictoriality does implement the imitative strategy, although selectively, in these apertures onto the phenomenal world formed by the naturalistic tableaux of the subalterns' life.[19] (Fig. 3) One may find these tableaux nested in the most surreal images, for example in some illustrations of Shah Tamasp' s *Shahnama*.[20] Some scholars did underscore this aspect of Safavid painting, but their observations have nevertheless not led the scholarship to challenge this false certitude about a 'Safavid resistance to verisimilitude'.

Thus, Rizvi analyses a folio from a 1605 *Shahnama* in which she detected various innovations reflecting the artistic evolution in the period. (Fig. 7) The folio, she argues convincingly, features a portrait of Shah 'Abbas I in place of the figure of the *Shahnama*'s warrior Gushtasp, in the canonical epic scene of the latter's confrontation with a dragon. In other words, the portrait consists of a double image conflating the mythic figure and the historic monarch. Rizvi furthers her interpretation of this folio with a narrative of breakthrough in this presupposed history of Safavid resistance to verisimilitude, as she identifies in the said portrait of the Shah an unprecedented physiognomic albeit suggestive likeness. We may designate this alleged breakthrough 'a surrender to verisimilitude', to use the same terminology of violence. The momentous artistic event, the scholar purports, took place against the background of a hiatus in portraiture between the Timurid period and the era of Shah 'Abbas I' reign because, for religious reasons, the first four Safavid sovereigns did not wish to represent themselves in painting. This art historical narrative of resistance and surrender is to be examined as understanding the evidence of this royal portrait has a direct implication in our endeavour to unravel the Persianate philosophy of the subalternity-royalty divide.

The Two Faces of Shah 'Abbas I

There exist several renditions of Shah 'Abbas I including, at the very end of his reign, a Safavid portrait from the Louvre's collection that clearly tends toward the physiognomic likeness. In this group of images, among the earliest examples are this folio discussed by Rizvi and a study in live of the shah's face and a painted version attributed to the Hindu Mughal artist Bishndas that Jahangir especially commissioned, with the graceful agreement of the Shah. (Figs. 7 and 8) This commission is well documented in the sources chronicling the diplomatic relationship between the two empires.[21] These two Mughal works are particularly important because they served as a substitute for the living model in order to elaborate a few famous Mughal political pictures representing together Jahangir and his Safavid rival. Yet, even though her topic of inquiry concerns a portrait of Shah 'Abbas I, Rizvi barely mentions these rare data *d'après modèle vivant*, stipulating in an endnote that 'the differences in the Mughal and Safavid versions cannot be explored here...'[22] The comparison, however, brings forth substantial information.

The paralleling of Bishndas' face study and the 1605 *Shahnama* folio discloses a conspicuous discrepancy between the two portraits, as if they depicted two different persons: one figure presents a rather round face, the other an elongated one; Shah 'Abbas' aquiline nose described in the period texts is not visible in the Safavid depiction but is apparent in the Mughal artefact; and while the latter endeavors to render the natural shapes and folds of the facial organs in minute details, a conventional iconographic repertoire picture these organs in the Safavid version. Given these divergences of style and the refinement that Mughal naturalism had achieved in the Jahangiri period, it is easy to determine which one of the two renditions represents the Shah's physical ipseity with the most accuracy. Overall, by comparison with the Mughal rendition, the Safavid portrait appears as an approximation of likeness much closer to the signaletic formula than to the physiognomic model, even though the image does possess a certain quality of carnal tangibility through which one may sense the intention of individualising the modular depiction. It is actually one of these ambiguous cases previously mentioned that may potentially mislead. A comparative look at the 1605 piece with the much later Safavid likeness of the shah from the Louvre supports this interpretation. (Figs.7 and 9)

The only common feature the study and the folio share is the dropping mustache and cut of facial hair that, according to Rizvi's finding, were set in fashion by Shah 'Abbas I. For her, this feature constitutes a proof of the subject's royal identity in the figure of Gushtasp, and of the nature of the portrait as naturalist representation. Rizvi then adds this proof to the other evidence constituted by the objects displayed around the warrior in prayer that she meticulously deciphers as paraphernalia of 'Abbas' Shi'ite piety and royalty.

In iconological terms, this identification is most valid. There is indeed no doubt about Shah 'Abbas' presence in this folio and about the dual nature of the portrait. The aesthetic interpretation, however, is more problematic. Despite the tension toward carnal individualisation, the mimetic characterisation of the image of the Persian king is not sustainable. Here is my alternative reading of it, based on the underlying of this characterisation's flaws.

First, although hair is an organic element of human physiology, the particular fashion that shapes it does not suffice to confirm the physiognomic nature of a portrait. Other figures may bear the same hair pattern, hence, like dress, hair fashion partakes of the wide range of signaletic items by which a human representation may declare the identity of the figure(s) represented without involving the rendition of their corporeal particulars.

Second, the main compositional element that allows the beholder to pinpoint Shah 'Abbas, instead of a Gushtasp groomed *a la mode* set by this monarch, is in fact the prominently displayed Shi'ite and royal paraphernalia that, combined with the gesture of prayer, form a powerful identifying semiotic apparatus. The latter delivers a religious-political *semiosis* by which the beholder cognizes, but does not recognizes, the kingly figure in the folio's iconography.

Third, if the mustached figure of Gushtasp alias 'Abbas does reflect the general tendency to give more prominence to human figuration in this period, however, it does not attest just yet to any aesthetic shift from resistance to surrender to verisimilitude in the Safavid construction of royal imagery. Quite on the contrary, owing to its strong signaletic discursive features and the rather conventional picturing of the subject's face, the portrait only confirms its inscription in the old Persian pictorial order that consistently presents royal subjects in archetypal or symbolic forms, by contrast with the subjection of subaltern imagery to aesthetic experiment.

Thus more accurately defined, the 1605 Safavid portrait of Shah 'Abbas is not the radical novelty that Rizvi describes. It evidences instead the artistic continuity with the Safavid precedents, for example in the *Shahnama*-i Ismail studied by Barry Wood that contains basic signaletic images of the contemporary historic ruler.[23] If these images do not present the same degree of elaboration by comparison with the

1605 folio, nonetheless they implement the same non-physiognomic convention-based representational scheme. Moreover, it ought to be noted that, like the mimetic likenesses, they do materialize the sovereign's presence in the paintings. As Rizvi's narrative does not connect the folio with these previous Safavid royal portraits she misconstrues the period between Shah 'Abbas I's rule and the Timurid era as a hiatus in the art of Persianate portraiture.

On the other hand, as it was revealed by the two portrayed faces of this ruler, an aesthetic shift indeed occurred in this period of the history of Persianate portraiture, but not in Iran, outside of it, in Mughal India, and in Ottoman Turkey. This configuration of events along the line 'inside versus outside' of Iran clearly indicates that the causes of this shift lie in the displacement of the Persian artistic culture to other geopolitical spaces, and in the heeding of new local parameters of the pictorial practice in these spaces. We cannot deal with this question here because it would drive us away from our main preoccupation concerning the conceptual underpinnings of the traditional Persian partitioned conception of human representation. Now the relevant matter to investigate is Rizvi's perception of the signaletic Shah 'Abbas/Gushtasp portrait as 'suggestive'.

A Not So Suggestive Portrait of Shah 'Abbas I

The term 'suggestive' incorrectly describes the double image by which Shah 'Abbas I appears in the 1605 *Shahnama*. If this image is indeed complex because of its double discursive and iconographic layer, however, it does not suggest. In fact, it does exactly the opposite: it asserts. Suggestion implies a lack of straightforwardness, a pattern of ambiguity or opacity, and forces the act of guessing. Rizvi refers to this process because she sees in Gushtasp a figure of concealment: Shah 'Abbas is hiding behind this figure, therefore he is not immediately visible; only a few (signaletic) elements 'suggest' his presence. Yet, the image's aesthetics and its historical context of use allow for a different hermeneutics of the artefact that rules out this idea of suggestion. Above all, the depiction contours both its forms and meaning with the utmost clarity and directness, without leaving any grey zone. It provides all the necessary informative elements for the immediate legibility and discernment of the two superimposed narratives, namely the paradigmatic presentation of the Persian sovereign as the righteous Muslim ruler before God, and the mystic-mythic encounter between the Persian warrior and the dragon. The meaning that these narratives convey as well is straightforwardly disclosed: the suprahuman hero Gushtasp is a reflection of Shah 'Abbas', the ultimate guardian of Islam and vice versa.

This construing of the structurally complex albeit semantically limpid folio as a mirroring double portrait takes on its full meaning in the light of the *Shahnama*'s function as 'the mirror of kings', in other words as a specific form of portraiture. As it is well known, the kingly users of Firdawsi's epic would identify themselves, mentally through reading and performatively through storytelling, with the text's 'good' protagonists as paradigms of kingship, heroism and righteousness.[24] The figures in the illustrated manuscripts would provide a visual support and effect a kind of materialisation of this process of virtual transference of human character, from literary protagonists to historic figures and vice-versa.[25] To be effective and performative, this materialisation would not necessarily require the actual presence of the ruler's material portrait in the illustrations. In his 2008 novel, *The Enchantress of Florence*, situated in the historical context of the Mughal emperor Akbar's reign, Salman Rushdie beautifully describes this Persianate strategy of virtual construction of portraiture not with the *Shahnama*, but with another famous epic that assumed a similar reflexive function: The *Hamzanama*.[26] Referring to a court painter, Rushdie writes:

> 'Over and over again, he painted the legendary hero Hamza on his three-eyed fairy horse overcoming improbable monsters of all types, and understood better than any other artist involved in the fourteen-year-long Hamza cycle which was the atelier's pride and joy that he was painting the emperor's dream-autobiography into being, that although his hand held the brush it was the emperor's vision that was appearing on the painted cloths. An emperor was the sum of his deeds, and Akbar's greatness, like that of his *alter ego* Hamza, was not only demonstrated by his triumphs over enormous obstacles – recalcitrant princes, real-life dragons, *devs*, and the like – it was actually created by those triumphs. The hero in Dashwanth's pictures became the emperor's mirror, ... 'Together we are painting the emperor's soul', Dashwanth told his collaborators sadly. 'And when his spirit leaves his body it will come to rest in these pictures, in which he will be immortal'.'[27]

I call 'the event portrait' this form of *performed* portraiture by mental reflexivity and mirroring with the visual aid of the painted manuscript, as opposed to 'the apparent portrait' that takes the materialisation of the virtual transference to another level by means of double images such as the figuration of Shah 'Abbas I/Gushtasp. These two types of portraiture are, however, intimately linked as the former prepared the advent of the latter, and the latter constitutes the logical outcome of the former. Rizvi could not grasp this aesthetic logic of portraiture in relation to the performative workings of the *Shahnama* and akin literature, as for her, a real portrait can only be a literal likeness. As a result, to explain the folio's meaning and the breakthrough it allegedly occasioned, she turns to the religious-political context of the Shah's reign. For want of a better argument, she inevitably concludes with a seldom enlightening historical generalisation placing the portrait in the framework of the monarch's spectacular patronage of the arts in Esfahan, subtended by his politics of religious assertion in the competitive Persianate political arena. As if those elements were not already present in the dynamics of art making during the rule of Shah 'Abbas' predecessors.

It is true though that, in admitting that the actual material, as opposed to the virtual mental superimposition of the royal image on the representation of a *Shahnama* protagonist, was a new act, one ought to investigate the motivation of this act in the context of Shah 'Abbas' artistic culture; an act that took place in the framework of this practice of the performative portrait. The intense relationship between the Mughal and Safavid kingdoms in this period, through which Mughal art exerted a considerable impact on its Iranian counterpart, is the path of inquiry to explore.[28] But again, what interests us is the information that this process of superimposition may harbor about the Persian conceptualisation of the social-political duality of royalty versus subalternity.

The Double Duality of Myth versus Reality and Royalty versus Subalternity in Persian Painting

What does the double portrait of Gushasp/Shah Abbas I philosophically and metaphysically tell us in relation to the naturalistic images of subalterns? The use of an illustrated *Shahnama* as site to picture the king situates him assertively in the region of myth. Let us recall, however, that in the Persian Muslim context, 'myth' is a region where legend and history meet, more exactly were the legendary past prolongs and expands history and time and space mingle. This historicising conception of the myth frames and legitimises the construction of a Persian ideology of the Muslim ruler as an extraordinary being bestowed with superior qualities by divine grace, 'a real myth' in a way: 'God's shadow on earth'. That is what the 'event portraits' would perform, this mythologising construction of the Persian Muslim ruler's persona. However, to signify powerfully, this construction required to be made against the oppositional construct of an ordinary humanity, precisely that of the subalterns and of the mundane reality to which they belong.

Indeed, in the pictorial medium the Persian ideology of the divinely sanctioned authority of the king articulates itself by positing in the forms the opposition between myth and reality. This opposition above all insures the Muslim humanistic linkage between the two worlds through the Persian re-writing of history embedded in the *Shahnama* and the performed spatiotemporal re-composition in which myth only expands reality. Each utterance and reading of the epic's verses, and each visualisation of its illustrations would allow for the construction of this alternative Persian world. In accordance with this vision, on the broad Persianate pictorial scene the subalterns reign as the masters of the sphere of pure concreteness. Sometimes, this aesthetic of subalternity may even express the highest humanistic values of justice and ethics, like in the striking depiction of a real event by Abd ul-Samad, a Persian artist who worked at the Mughal court: 'The Arrest of Shah Abu'l Ma'ali by the Dependable Tolaq Khan Qushi', in Bodleian Library, Oxford.[29]

Royal Myth and Subaltern Reality Confronted: 'The Arrest of Shah Abu'l Ma'ali by the Dependable Tolaq Khan Qushi', c.1556-60

Like the Safavid folio previously discussed, this image consists of a double portrait and similarly produces an evidence of the Persian partitioned philosophy of royal and subaltern representation. However, it does so in the explicit terms of an active and tense confrontation, within the one and same pictorial space, between the two naturalistic and idealistic styles literally applied to the iconographic divide of royalty and subalternity. This 'confrontation' takes place at three levels of the image.

At the first purely iconographic level, instead of two figures in one like in the *Shahnama* folio, the painting represents two distinct individuals, a court officer and a Mughal prince. Through this binary configuration, the royal register directly confronts the subaltern register. At the second aesthetic-stylistic level, this binary configuration sets up, in rhetorical antinomic terms, a confrontation between a detailed physiognomic example of subaltern naturalistic depiction and an instance of the signaletic-archetypal model of royal portraiture in the purest Persian tradition. At the third narrative level, the two represented individuals are literally involved in an act of physical confrontation, thus metaphorizing somehow violently albeit most persuasively the double opposition between royalty and subalternity, and between myth and reality.

The pictorially reported event, the arrest of an infamous courtier of Humayun whom his son and successor Akbar condemned to execution for challenging his authority, is also chronicled in the primary sources so that the artefact fits the category of historical painting. This historical inscription of the image only reinforces the thesis of the subalterns' voice in Persian painting that this essay has all along endeavoured to demonstrate. A careful reading of this fascinating image will make the point.

This series of confrontational patterns produces a threefold semantic that posits subalternity, reality, and realism as the picture's dominant forces. Indeed, the subaltern stylistically appears as both the most tangible figure of the picture and its rhetorical centrepiece. The detailed morphological characteristics expressing the personality of the mature and experienced man impose their crushing power upon the delicate conventional features of the prince thematising its royal origins. Clashing with this visually impacting realism of the subaltern, the regal figure's ethereal rendition exudes weakness and fragility, while still retaining the nobleness of its social extraction. Empowered by his authoritative corporeality, the dependable seems to subdue effortlessly the ageless and ideally beautiful yet foolish member of Mughal royalty.

Obviously, by no means this visual *semiosis* implies a challenge to the Mughal socio-political order. It is, on the contrary, an assertive expression of it. The violence of the scene built up at the three levels of the picture's aesthetic operation and the triumph of the stylistic realism it brings forth deliver nothing less than a disciplinary rhetoric of punishment and death to the service of an ideology of absolute power, namely Akbar's power.

Subalternity, realism and death form again a powerful triad in another image of a Persianate subaltern: the portrait of a beloved courtier of Jahangir, Inayat Khan, lying on his deathbed. There exist two renditions of this same portrait, a painting attributed to Balshand, c. 1618–19 at the Bodleian Library, and a drawing in the Museum of Fines Arts, Boston.[30] (Fig. 10) These artefacts are the ultimate evidence of the vocal visibility or visible voice of the subalterns in Persianate painting, as they turn the subaltern subject into a true icon, an icon of death. The evocation of this portrait will serve as a conclusion to this essay.

Dying Inayat Khan: The Persianate Subaltern Iconified

The *Jahangirnama* records in detail the story behind the two hyper-realistic images of Inayat Khan agonising on his deathbed. In Ajmer in 1618, Jahangir narrates the imminent passing of his close courtier:

> 'On this date news came of the death of Inayat Khan. He was one of my closest servants and subjects. In addition to eating opium, he also drank wine when he had the chance. Little by little he became obsessed with wine, and since he had a weak frame, he drank more than his body could tolerate, and was afflicted with diarrhea. [While so weakened he was overcome two or three times by something like epileptic fits. By my order Kakim Rukna treated him, but no matter what he did it was to no avail. In addition, Inayat Khan developed a ravenous appetite, and although the doctor insisted that he not eat more than once a day, he couldn't restrain himself and raged like a madman. Finally, he developed cachexia and dropsy and grew terribly thin and weak] Several days prior to this, he requested that he be taken ahead to Agra. I ordered him brought to me to be given leave to depart. He was put in a palanquin and brought. He looked incredibly weak and thin. 'Skin stretched over bone.' Even his bones had begun to disintegrate. Whereas painters employ great exaggeration when they depict skinny people, nothing remotely resembling him had ever been seen. Good God! How can a human being remain alive in this shape? [...] It was so strange I ordered the artist to draw his likeness.'[31]

This likeness constitutes a visual commemoration of a beloved individual, a Mughal subaltern, whose imminent death was made unforgettable for ever by means of an iconifiying pictorial representation. In that, this representation joins the global pantheon of icons of death, gruesome yet glorious homages to beloved or remarkable individuals, subalterns, kings, free beings, friends or lovers, such as *Marat* dead in his bath on July 13, 1793, by Jacques-Louis David, and *Felix, June 5th, 1994* by A.A. Bronson, picturing Felix Partz about three hours after he died from AIDS.[32] (Fig. 11) The striking visual similitude between the latter and the painting of dying Inayat Khan underscores with great might the transcendental value of these icons.

Bibliography

Adle, Chahryar, "*Recherche sur le Module et le Tracé Correcteur dans la Miniature Orientale*, I" *Le Monde Iranien et l'Islam* Vol. 3 (1975): 81-105.

Arjomand, Said Amir, *The Shadow of God and the Hidden Imam: Religion, Political Order, and Societal Change in Shi'ite Iran from the Beginning to 1890*, Chicago: University of Chicago Press, 1984.

Asher, Catherine B., "A Ray from the Sun: Mughal Ideology and the Visual Construction of the Divine", in Matthew T. Kapstein (ed.) *The Presence of Light: Divine Radiance and Religious Experience*, Chicago: University of Chicago Press, 2004, 161-194.

Beveridge, Henry (ed.) *Tuzuk-i Jahangiri* (*Memoirs of Jahangir*), Alexander Rodgers, (transl.), 2 vols., London: Royal Asiatic Society, 1968.

Crill, Rosemary and Japil Jariwala, eds., *The Indian Portrait*, London: National Gallery of Portraits, 2010.

Duran, Jane, "Naturalism and Mannerism in Indian Miniatures" *The Journal of Aesthetic Education* 35 4 (Winter 2001): 57-63.

Gonella, Julia, and Christoph Rauch (eds.), *Heroic Times, A Thousand Years of the Persian Book of Kings*, Berlin: Staatliche Museen zu Berlin, 2012.

Gonzalez, Valerie, *Aesthetic Hybridity in Mughal Painting, 1526-1658*, series "Transculturalisms", Farnham: Ashgate Publishing, 2015, 17-63.

Gonzalez, Valerie, "The Physiognomic Royal Portrait: A Centerpiece of Moghul Painting". in Miriam Malachi (ed.), *In the Maharajah's Court*, Jerusalem: The Israel Museum, Jerusalem, 2020, 97-105, 82-87.

Grabar, Oleg and Mika Natif, "Two Safavid Paintings: An Essay in Interpretation" *Muqarnas* 18 (2001): 173-202.

Hillenbrand, Hillenbrand (ed.), *Shahnama: The Visual Language of the Persian Book of Kings*, Aldershot: Ashgate, 2004.

Juneja, Monica, "Translating the Body into Image: The Body Politic and Visual Practice at the Mughal Court during the Sixteenth and Seventeenth Centuries", in *Images of the Body in India: South Asian and European Perspectives on Rituals and Perfomativity*, ed. Axel Michaels and Christoph Wulf, New Delhi: Routledge, 2011, 235-260.

Kearney, R. and B. Treanor (eds.), *Carnal Hermeneutics*, New York: Fordham University Press, 2015.

Khan, Sayyid Ahmad (ed. in Persian), *Tuzuk-i Jahangiri (Memoirs of Jahangir)*, Henry Beveridge (ed.) Alexander Rodgers, (transl.), 2 vols., Alighar, 1864.

Koch, Ebba *Mughal Art and Imperial Ideology*, New Delhi/New York: Oxford University Press, 2001.

Koch, Ebba, "The Mughal Emperor as Solomon, Majnun, and Orpheus, or the Album as a Think Tank for Allegory" *Muqarnas* 27 (2011): 277-312.

Leoni, Francesca, "The Shahnama of Shah Tahmasp", in *Heilbrunn Timeline of Art History*, New York: The Metropolitan Museum of Art, 2000.

Losty, J.P. and Malini Roy, *Mughal India, Art, Culture and Empire*, London: British Library, 2012.

Melville, Charles (ed.) *Shahnamah Studies*, Cambridge: Center for Middle Eastern and Islamic Studies, University of Cambridge University, 2006.

Melville, Charles, and Gabrielle van den Berg (eds.), *Shahnamah Studies II, The Reception of Firdausi's Shahnama*, Leiden: Brill, 2012.

Mitchell Lynette, and Charles Melville (eds.), *Every inch a king: comparative studies on kings and kingship in the ancient and medieval worlds*, Leiden: Brill, 2013.

Muzaffar, Alam, Françoise Delvoye Nalini, and Marc Gaborieau (eds.), *The Making of Indo-Persian Culture: Indian and French Studies*, New Delhi: Manohar Publishers, 2000.

Natif, Mika, "The painter's Breath and Concepts of Idol's anxiety in Islamic Art", in *Idol Anxiety*, ed. Josh Ellenbogen and Aaron Tugendhaft, Stanford: Stanford University Press, 2011, 41-55.

Necipoğlu, Gülru "The Serial Portraits of Ottoman Sultans in Comparative Perspective", in *The Sultan's Portrait: Picturing the House of Osman*, Istanbul: Isbank, 2000, 21-61.

Page, Mary Ellen, "Professional Storytelling in Iran: Transmission and Practice" *Iranian Studies* Vol. 12, 3-4 (1979): 195-215.

Palyiu, Cheryl Ann, "Dying Inayat Khan, Nature, Spirituality and Mortality in the *Jahangirnama*" *Journal of the Lucas Graduate Conference* 3 (March 2015): 66-81.

Porter, Yves, "From the "Theory of the Two Qalams" to the "Seven Principles of Painting": Theory, Terminology, and Practice in Persian Classical Painting" *Muqarnas* 17 (2000): 109-118.

Porter, Yves, "La forme et le sens. A propos du portrait dans la littérature persane classique", in *Pand-o Sokhan, Mélanges offerts à Charles-Henri de Fouchécour*, Téhéran: Institut Français de Recherche en Iran, 1995, 219-231.

Rizvi, Kishwar, "The Suggestive Portrait of Shah "Abbas: Prayer and Likeness in a Safavid *Shahnama*" *Art Bulletin* Vol. 94, 2 (June 2012): 226-250.

Roxburgh, David, *Prefacing the Image: The Writing of Art History in Sixteenth Century Iran. Muqarnas Supplements*, Leiden: Brill, 2000.

Rushdie, Salman, *The Enchantress of Florence*, London: Jonathan Cape, 2008.

Seyller, John (ed.), *Eva and Konrad Seitz Collection of Indian Miniatures: Mughal and Deccani Paintings*, Museum Reitberg. with introductions and interpretations by Konrad Seitz, Seattle: University of Washington Press, 2011.

Seyller, John and Wheeler M. Thackston, *The Adventures of Hamza: Painting and Storytelling in Mughal India* Washington DC: Arthur M. Sackler Gallery, Smithsonian Institution, 2010.

Skelton, Robert, "Imperial Symbolism in Mughal Painting", in Priscilla Soucek (ed.), *Content and Context of Visual Arts in the Islamic World*, University Park: Pennsylvania State University Press, 1988, 177-192.

Soucek, Priscilla, "Persian Artists in Mughal India: Influences and Transformations" *Muqarnas* 4 (1987): 166-81.

Soucek. Priscilla, "The Theory and Practice of Portraiture in the Persian Tradition" *Muqarnas* 17 (2000): 97-108.

Soudavar, Abolala, "Between the Safavids and the Mughals: Art and Artists in Transition" *IRAN* 37 (1999): 49-66.

Tanindi, Zeren, "Transformation of Words into Images, Portraits of Ottoman courtiers in the Diwans of Baki and Nadiri", *Res* 43 (Spring 2003): 131-145.

Topsfield, Andrew, *Visions of Mughal India: The Collection of Howard Hodgkin*, Oxford: Ashmolean Museum, 2012.

Von Folsach, Kejeld, and Joachim Meyer, *The Human Figure in Islamic Art. Holy Men, Princes, and Commoners*, Copenhagen: Strandberg Publishing, 2017.

Wood, Barry D. "The Shahnamai Isma'il: Art and Cultural Memory in Sixteenth-Century Iran', Ph.D. dissertation, Harvard University, 2002.

Wright, Elaine (ed.), *Muraqqa', Imperial Mughal Albums from the Chester Beatty Library, Dublin*, Alexandria VA: Art Services International, distributed by University Press of New England, 2008.

Yamamoto, Kumiko, *The Oral Background of Persian Epics. Storytelling and Poetry*, Leiden: Brill, 2003.

Zarzycka, Marta, and Bettina Papenburg (eds.,) *Carnal Aesthetics*, London, New York: IB Tauris, 2014.

Notes

1. For a study of the depiction of the human figure in general see Kejeld Von Folsach and Joachim Meyer, *The Human Figure in Islamic Art. Holy Men, Princes, and Commoners*, Copenhagen: Strandberg Publishing, 2017.
2. See Valerie Gonzalez, "The Physiognomic Royal Portrait: A Centerpiece of Moghul Painting". In *In the Maharajah's Court*, ed. Miriam Malachi, Jerusalem: The Israel Museum, 2020, bilingual English and Hebrew, 97-105 and 82-87; Rosemary Crill and Japil Jariwala, eds., *The Indian Portrait*, London: National Gallery of Portraits, 2010; Zeren Tanindi, "Transformation of Words into Images, Portraits of Ottoman courtiers in the Diwans of Baki and Nadiri" *Res* 43 (Spring 2003): 131-145; Gülru Necipoğlu, "The Serial Portraits of Ottoman Sultans in Comparative Perspective", in *The Sultan's Portrait: Picturing the House of Osman*, Istanbul: Isbank, 2000, 21-61; Monica Juneja, "Translating the Body into Image: The Body Politic and Visual Practice at the Mughal Court during the Sixteenth and Seventeenth Centuries", in *Images of the Body in India: South Asian and European Perspectives on Rituals and Perfomativity*, ed. Axel Michaels and Christoph Wulf, New Delhi: Routledge, 2011, 235-260.
3. See my critique of the problematic methodology used in the study of painting in Islam, in Valerie Gonzalez, *Aesthetic Hybridity in Mughal Painting, 1526-1658*, series "Transculturalisms" Farnham: Ashgate Publishing, 2015, 17-63.
4. Priscilla Soucek. "The Theory and Practice of Portraiture in the Persian Tradition" *Muqarnas* 17 (2000): 98.
5. David Roxburgh, *Prefacing the Image: The Writing of Art History in Sixteenth Century Iran. Muqarnas Supplements*, Leiden: Brill, 2000; Yves Porter, "La forme et le sens. A propos du portrait dans la littérature persane classique", in *Pand-o Sokhan, Mélanges offerts à Charles-Henri de Fouchécour*, Téhéran: Institut Français de Recherche en Iran, 1995, 219-231, and "From the "Theory of the Two Qalams" to the "Seven Principles of Painting": Theory, Terminology, and Practice in Persian Classical Painting" *Muqarnas* 17 (2000): 109-118; , Gülru Necipoğlu, "The Serial Portraits of Ottoman Sultans in Comparative Perspective", in *The Sultan's Portrait: Picturing the House of Osman*, Istanbul: Isbank, 2000, 21-61.
6. Mika Natif, "The painter's Breath and Concepts of Idol's anxiety in Islamic Art", in *Idol Anxiety*, ed. Josh Ellenbogen and Aaron Tugendhaft, Stanford: Stanford University Press, 2011, 41-55.
7. For more theoretical inputs on this trope of carnality in the arts and other humanistic domains, see, *Carnal Hermeneutics*, eds. R. Kearney and B. Treanor, New York: Fordham University Press, 2015; *Carnal Aesthetics*, eds. Marta Zarzycka and Bettina Papenburg, London, New York: IB Tauris, 2014.
8. Chahryar Adle, "*Recherche sur le Module et le Tracé Correcteur dans la Miniature Orientale*, I" *Le Monde Iranien et l'Islam* Vol. 3 (1975): 81-105.
9. Realism is a stylistic variant of naturalism that, thanks to sophisticated pictorial technics, enables images to imitate the appearances of things and beings with a high degree of faithfulness. See the rich production of illustrated catalogues of Mughal painting in which portraiture constitutes a central theme: Crill, Rosemary and Japil Jariwala, eds., *The Indian Portrait*, London: National Gallery of Portraits, 2010, Andrew Topsfield, *Visions of Mughal India: The Collection of Howard Hodgkin*, Oxford: Ashmolean Museum, 2012; John Seyller (ed.) , with introductions and interpretations by Konrad Seitz, *Eva and Konrad Seitz Collection of Indian Miniatures: Mughal and Deccani Paintings*, Museum Reitberg. Seattle: University of Washington Press, 2011; Elaine Wright (ed.), *Muraqqa', Imperial Mughal Albums from the Chester Beatty Library, Dublin*, Alexandria VA: Art Services International, distributed by University Press of New England, 2008.
10. It must be noted, however, that this stylistic feature of the nature-like texturing of these elements by no means entails that the scenes' settings in which it is used are of realistic or imitative order. Style and iconography are different constituents of the image's composition. For example, in Safavid painting the rocks' landscapes present a high degree of texturing and modeling that lends

them qualities of concreteness such as three-dimensionality; yet the movement that animates them and the variegated figurative crypto-images they foster, animal profiles, monsters, etc. inscribe them in the category of imaginary landscapes, not in that of naturalistic landscapes.

11   See Jane Duran, "Naturalism and Mannerism in Indian Miniatures" *The Journal of Aesthetic Education* 35 4 (Winter 2001): 57-63; Crill, Rosemary, Susan Stronge and Andrew Topfield (eds.), *Arts of Mughal India: Studies in Honour of Robert Skelton*, Ahmenabad and London: Mapin Publishing in Association with the Victoria and Albert Museum, 2004; J.P. Losty and Malini Roy, *Mughal India, Art, Culture and Empire*, London: British Library, 2012.

12   For a detailed explanation of these concepts of body-centrism and logocentrism in pictoral metaphysics in the Persianate context, see Valerie Gonzalez, *Aesthetic Hybridity in Mughal Painting, 1526-1658*, 149-154, 170-173, and 184-203.

13   About the Persian conception of kingship see *Every inch a king: comparative studies on kings and kingship in the ancient and medieval worlds*, eds. Lynette Mitchell and Charles Melville, Leiden: Brill, 2013; Said Amir Arjomand, *The Shadow of God and the Hidden Imam: Religion, Political Order, and Societal Change in Shi'ite Iran from the Beginning to 1890*, Chicago: University of Chicago Press, 1984.

14   See Catherine B. Asher, "A Ray from the Sun: Mughal Ideology and the Visual Construction of the Divine", in *The Presence of Light: Divine Radiance and Religious Experience*, ed. Matthew T. Kapstein, Chicago: University of Chicago Press, 2004, 161-194; Ebba Koch, *Mughal Art and Imperial Ideology*, New Delhi/New York: Oxford University Press, 2001, 5-8, and "The Mughal Emperor as Solomon, Majnun, and Orpheus, or the Album as a Think Tank for Allegory" *Muqarnas* 27 (2011): 277-312; Robert Skelton, "Imperial Symbolism in Mughal Painting", in *Content and Context of Visual Arts in the Islamic World*, ed. Priscilla Soucek, University Park: Pennsylvania State University Press, 1988, 177-192.

15   Kishwar Rizvi, "The Suggestive Portrait of Shah "Abbas: Prayer and Likeness in a Safavid *Shahnama*" *Art Bulletin* Vol. 94, 2 (June 2012): 226-250. This article provides a substantial bibliography on Persianate painting in the Modern era.

16   Ibid, 243.

17   About this serious problem of epistemology in the studies on painting in Islam, see my criticism in *Aesthetic Hybridity in Mughal Painting*, 84-87.

18   About this and other aspects of the aesthetics of Mughal painting, see ibid.

19   See, for example, the iconological analysis of Oleg Grabar and Mika Natif, "Two Safavid Paintings: An Essay in Interpretation" *Muqarnas* 18 (2001): 173-202.

20   See Francesca Leoni, "The Shahnama of Shah Tahmasp", in *Heilbrunn Timeline of Art History*, New York: The Metropolitan Museum of Art, 2000. http://www.metmuseum.org/toah/hd/shnm/hd_shnm.htm (June 2008)

21   Duly reported by Rizvi in her article, this event is narrated in detail in Henry Beveridge (ed.) *Tuzuk-i Jahangiri* (*Memoirs of Jahangir*), Alexander Rodgers, (transl.), 2 vols., London: Royal Asiatic Society, 1968, 116-17.

22   Rizvi, 'The Suggestive Portrait of Shah 'Abbas, 249 (note 84).

23   See Barry D. Wood's unpublished thesis, "The Shahnamai Isma'il: Art and Cultural Memory in Sixteenth-Century Iran', Ph.D. dissertation, Harvard University, 2002.

24   Kumiko Yamamoto, *The Oral Background of Persian Epics. Storytelling and Poetry*, Leiden: Brill, 2003; Julia Gonella and Christoph Rauch (eds.), *Heroic Times, A Thousand Years of the Persian Book of Kings*, Berlin: Staatliche Museen zu Berlin, 2012; Charles Melville (ed.) *Shahnamah Studies*, Cambridge: Center for Middle Eastern and Islamic Studies, University of Cambridge University, 2006; Charles Melville and Gabrielle van den Berg (eds.), *Shahnamah Studies II, The Reception of Firdausi's Shahnama*, Leiden: Brill, 2012; Mary Ellen Page, "Professional Storytelling in Iran: Transmission and Practice" *Iranian Studies* Vol. 12, 3-4 (1979): 195-215.

25   Robert Hillenbrand (ed.), *Shahnama: The Visual Language of the Persian Book of Kings*, Aldershot: Ashgate, 2004.

26 See John Seyller and Wheeler M. Thackston, *The Adventures of Hamza: Painting and Storytelling in Mughal India* Washington DC: Arthur M. Sackler Gallery, Smithsonian Institution, 2010.
27 Salman Rushdie, *The Enchantress of Florence*, London: Jonathan Cape, 2008, 119.
28 There is much to be done critically concerning this aspect of the cross-fertilisation between the two artistic cultures. On the other hand, the displacement of Persian artists to the Mughal court has been well studied. See Priscilla Soucek, "Persian Artists in Mughal India: Influences and Transformations" *Muqarnas* 4 (1987): 166-81; Abolala Soudavar, "Between the Safavids and the Mughals: Art and Artists in Transition" *IRAN* 37 (1999): 49-66; Alam Muzaffar, Françoise Delvoye Nalini, and Marc Gaborieau (eds.), *The Making of Indo-Persian Culture: Indian and French Studies*, New Delhi: Manohar Publishers, 2000.
29 See Andrew Topsfield, *Visions of Mughal India: The Collection of Howard Hodgkin* Oxford: Ashmolean Museum, 2012, 14.
30 See ibid, 62, and Cheryl Ann Palyiu, "Dying Inayat Khan, Nature, Spirituality and Mortalityin the *Jahangirnama*" *Journal of the Lucas Graduate Conference* 3 (March 2015): 66-81. https://openaccess.leidenuniv.nl/handle/1887/31524
31 *Tuzuk-I Jahangiri*, ed. in Persian by Sayyid Ahmad Khan, and translated by Alexander Rogers, and ed. Henry Beveridge Alighar, 1864, Vol. 2, 43-44.
32 This very large image was recently exhibited in the Whitney Museum, New York. Together with Jorje Zontal, Partz and Bronson formed a three head-group of artists named "General Idea", created in 1975.

Figures

Fig. 1: 'Conquest of Baghdad by Timur', folio from a Zafarnama (Book of Victories), June-July 1436. Ink, opaque watercolour, and gold on paper. Rogers Fund, 1955. Accession number 55.121.17. © 2000–2018 The Metropolitan Museum of Art.

6. The 'Visible Voice' or 'Vocal Visibility' of the Subalterns in Persianate Painting

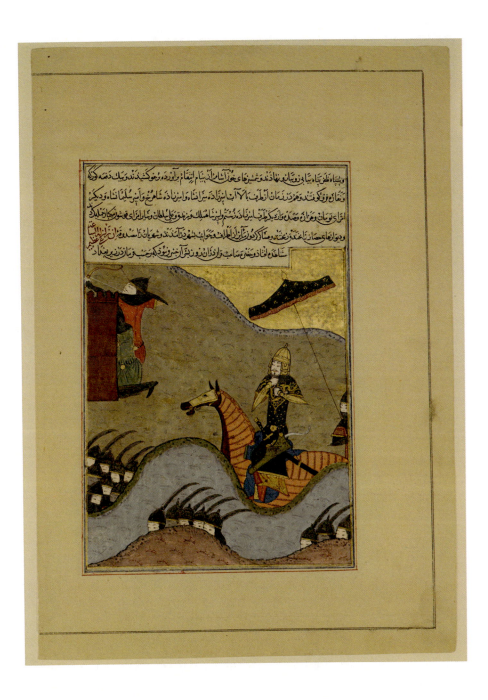

Fig. 2: 'Hamid Bhakari punished by Akbar', attributed to Manohar (active ca. 1582–1624), c. 1604. Illustrated album leaf from an Akbarnama by Abu'l Fazl (1551–1602). Mughal India. Ink, opaque watercolour, and gold on paper. Accession Number: 30.95.174.8. Theodore M. Davis Collection, Bequest of Theodore M. Davis, 1915 © 2000–2014 The Metropolitan Museum of Art.

6. *The 'Visible Voice' or 'Vocal Visibility' of the Subalterns in Persianate Painting*

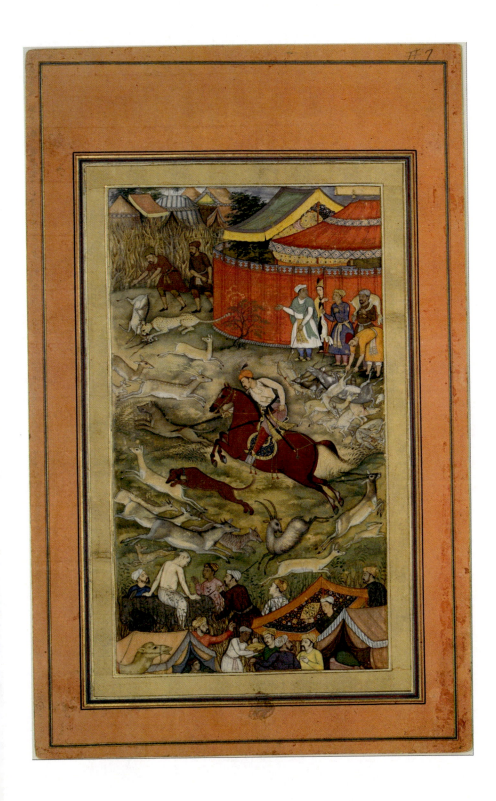

Fig. 3: Illustration of the *divan* of Hafiz, 'Allegory of drunkenness', by Sultan Muhammad, c.1531-33, Tabriz, Iran. Ink, opaque watercolour, and gold on parchment. Gift of Mr. and Ms. Stuart Carey Welsh. Accession number 1988.430. Jointly owned by the Metropolitan Museum of Art and the Arthur M. Sackler Museum, Harvard University. © 2000–2018 The Metropolitan Museum of Art.

6. *The 'Visible Voice' or 'Vocal Visibility' of the Subalterns in Persianate Painting*

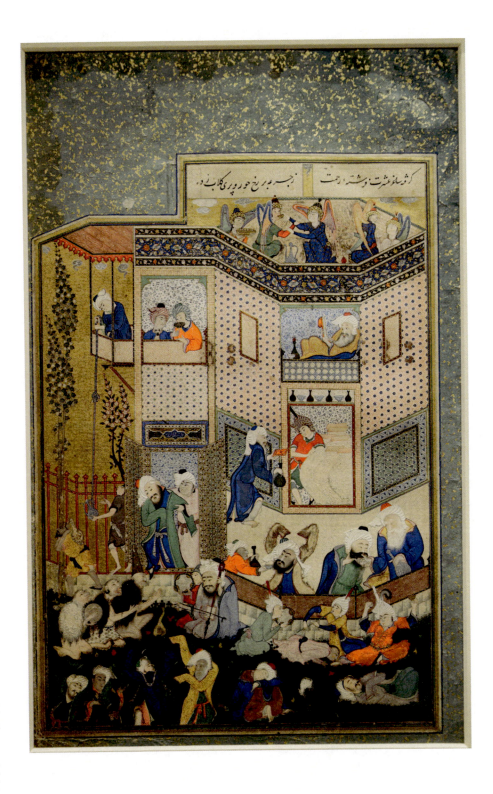

Fig. 4: 'Jahangir and Parviz', detail, attributed to Manohar, c. 1610-1615. Album leaf. Mughal India. Opaque watercolour, and gold on paper. Acquired at auction in 1925. Accession Number: IM.9-1925 ©Victoria and Albert Museum, London.

6. The 'Visible Voice' or 'Vocal Visibility' of the Subalterns in Persianate Painting

Fig. 5: 'Battle of Nicopolis' (1396), Ottoman miniature, Topkapi Palace, Istanbul. Accession number hazine 1523. Photograph in the public domain.

6. *The 'Visible Voice' or 'Vocal Visibility' of the Subalterns in Persianate Painting*

Fig. 6: 'Jahangir seating on an hourglass throne', by Bichitr, c. 1625, from the St Petersburg Album. Detail of the King James' likeness and Bichitr's self-portrait. Ink, opaque watercolour, and gold on paper. Freer Gallery of Art, Washington D.C. Photograph in the public domain.

6. The 'Visible Voice' or 'Vocal Visibility' of the Subalterns in Persianate Painting

Fig. 7: 'Gushtasp and the dragon of Mount Sakila', 1605, from a *Shahnama* by Firdawsi. Iran. Opaque watercolour, ink and gold on paper. @Staatsbibliothek zu Berlin – Preußischer Kulturbesitz (MS or. Fol. 4251, fol. 460a).

6. *The 'Visible Voice' or 'Vocal Visibility' of the Subalterns in Persianate Painting*

Fig. 8: 'Portrait of Shah 'Abbas I', attributed to Bishndas, c. 1617. Mughal India. Ink and opaque watercolour on paper Dimensions: 19.5 x 15.6 cm (7 11/16 x 6 1/8 in.) Harvard Art Museums/Arthur M. Sackler Museum, Gift of Stuart Cary Welch, Jr. Image Number: 73648 Accession Number: 1999.304. Courtesy of Imaging Department © President and Fellows of Harvard College.

6. The 'Visible Voice' or 'Vocal Visibility' of the Subalterns in Persianate Painting

185

Fig. 9: Portrait of Shah Abbas I and his page, signed by Muhammad Qassim, Esfahan, Iran, Mars 12, 1627, ink on paper. MAO 494. @musee du Louvre/Claire Tabbagh.

6. *The 'Visible Voice' or 'Vocal Visibility' of the Subalterns in Persianate Painting*

187

Fig. 10: 'The Dying Inayat Khan', by Balchand, c. 1618. MS Ouseley Add. 171, f. 4v. @Bodleian Libraries, University of Oxford.

6. *The 'Visible Voice' or 'Vocal Visibility' of the Subalterns in Persianate Painting*

Fig. 11: *Felix, June 5th 1994*, by A.A. Bronson exhibited in 2017, in the Whitney Museum, New York. Photo: courtesy of Elah Hanany.

6. *The 'Visible Voice' or 'Vocal Visibility' of the Subalterns in Persianate Painting*

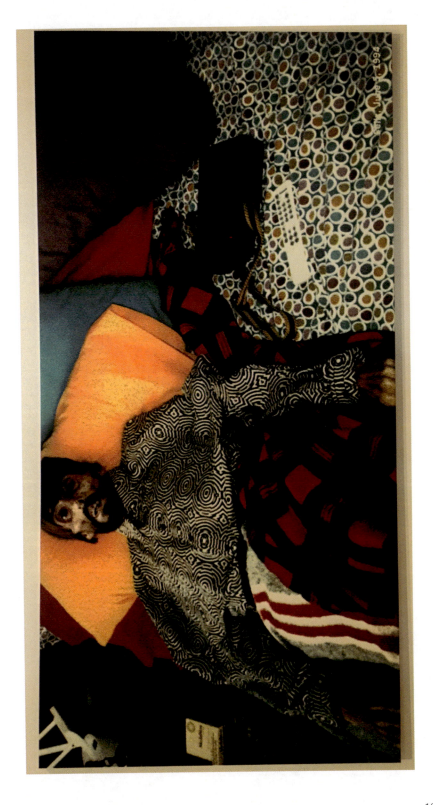

191

7

A Subaltern Hero:
The 1573 Execution of Sheikh Hamza Bali as Part of the 'Sunnitisation' of the Ottoman Empire

Ines Asceric-Todd

Introduction: the Hamzevi Phenomenon and the Sources

On the 6th of June 1573, the Istanbul Hippodrome, the Atmeydan, was supposed to witness the execution, by stoning, of Sheikh Hamza Bali, a charismatic Melami-Bayrami[1] sheikh from northern Bosnia, charged with heresy and atheism.[2] The planned execution, however, never took place, since it became apparent that large numbers of Hamza's followers had gathered at the Hippodrome, which is why the guards were ordered to slit his throat before they reached the arena. The event was made much more dramatic by one of the Janissaries who was present at Hamza's death, slitting his own throat as a sacrifice and, according to reports, 'an eternal witness to his master's innocence'.[3]

The Hamzevi[4] phenomenon first caught significant scholarly attention around the middle of the last century with the discovery of a number of documents, mostly imperial decrees (*hukum*) from the *Muhimme defterleri* ('the registers of important affairs'), relating to the persecutions of Sheikh Hamza Bali and his followers in the second half of the 16th century.[5] Starting in the 1950s, a flurry of articles was published in the following two decades, occasionally outside the former Yugoslavia, but mostly in a number of academic journals inside Bosnia. While some of those articles did contain analytical sections, the purpose of most of them was to publish and/or translate the original documents in question in order to make them available to the wider academic community.[6] In most cases, the documents themselves were not further analysed. One such article was Ibrahim Mehinagic's 1973 "Cetiri neobjavljena izvora o Hamzevijama iz sredine XVI vijeka" ('Four unpublished sources about the Hamzevis from the middle of the 16th century'), which, in addition to one short poem about the Hamzevis, first brought to light the three known extant contemporary anti-Hamzevi treatises. The article provided full translations into Bosnian of all three documents, as well as the facsimiles of the originals in Ottoman.[7] It did not, however, analyse the documents, and, apart from short mentions in a number of discussions on the subject of the Hamzevis since then, the contents of these three documents have never thus far been examined in any detail.

The first substantial synthesis of the existing knowledge on the Hamzevis was made by Dzemal Cehajic in his hitherto unsupplanted introduction to the Sufi orders in the lands of the former Yugoslavia, in the chapter entitled 'The Hamzevi order of dervishes'.[8] The most recent study of the Hamzevis and their history was provided by the present author in Part 3 of the monograph *Dervishes and Islam in Bosnia* (2015), entitled 'Political Roles of Bosnian Dervishes: the Hamzevis – A Dervish Order or a Socio-Political Movement?'.[9] There, I propose that the swift and ruthless measures taken against Hamza and his followers were essentially due to this order acquiring very strong socio-political and sectarian character, something that has always existed in the Melami-Bayrami tradition, and was in the case of the Hamzevis manifested in clear tendencies towards political independence and the disowning of the official authorities through, for instance, formation of their own local government and courts.[10] This conclusion is supported by the fact that it is not entirely clear which, if any, of the accusations of heresy levelled at Hamza were actually proven at his trial, and his execution was ordered essentially on the basis of him being the *halife* of the same order as Ismail Masuki.[11] Likewise, it is very difficult to determine what exactly Hamza's teachings were, as neither he, nor his immediate followers left any writings to that effect, and the only sources of information on the subject are the official documents on his persecution, such as the arrest warrants or edicts, or the *fatwa* justifying his execution, and the three anti-Hamzevi treatises mentioned above.[12] These latter sources – which are mentioned in the above monograph, but not examined in any detail there – have to be treated with caution with regard to making any firm conclusions on the exact nature of Hamza's teachings. However, it seems reasonable to assume that, if examined more closely, their contents and the heretical teachings or practices ascribed to Hamza and his followers in these documents, whether accurate or imputed, may provide some valuable information on the attitudes and opinions of these documents' authors, and, by extension, the attitudes of their milieu and those who may have commissioned them.

The Context: The Ottoman Suppression of the Kızılbas and Other Shia Orders and the 'Sunnitisation' of the Ottoman Empire

The Ottoman government's persecution of 'heretics' and 'heretical' movements throughout the 16th century has also been a subject of continued scholarly interest since around the 1960s. The academic debate on the subject has mainly centred on the rebellions of the Safavid-supported Kızılbas[13] leaders and communities in Anatolia, and their subsequent suppression by the Ottoman state, as well as the exact correlation between that process and the Ottoman-Safavid wars which took place in the same period.[14] Specifically, scholars have been trying to ascertain to what extent the state-sponsored suppression of the Kızılbas was motivated by security concerns due to the Safavid backing of these rebellious elements, and to what extent the religious concerns themselves played a part in this process. Given that the persecution of the 'Kızılbas' very quickly expanded to include any Sufi elements with even the slightest Shia-tinged beliefs or practices, another important question arises here, this time in relation to the 'Sunnitisation' of the Ottoman Empire – namely, the 16th-century process characterised by the Ottoman administration's and religious institution's active policy of defining themselves as representatives and defenders of orthodox Sunnism as the official religion of the empire.[15] This question can be formulated as follows: was this process the reason behind the Ottoman government's suppression of all Shia-oriented elements in the Ottoman society, or was the rise and prominence of these elements in fact one of the underlying causes of the Sunnitisation process in the first place?

In her article "Sufis in the Age of State-building and Confessionalization", Derin Terzioglu argues that classical scholarship – represented first and foremost by Mehmet Fuat Koprulu and Ahmet Yasar Ocak – tended to consider the Ottoman state as inherently Sunni orthodox and therefore in natural opposition to any 'popular' or 'folk' religious movements and Sufi orders with Shia tendencies, thus implying that the already Sunni-oriented state was the reason behind the suppression and re-organisation of Shia elements within Ottoman society. Moreover, while these elements were previously allowed to co-exist, in the shape of 'folk' Islam, side by side the official religion of the empire, it was the rise of a rival Shia dynasty, the Safavids – who attracted the loyalty of some of these popular Sufi movements – that triggered the persecution of these elements throughout the Ottoman realm.[16] She further suggests that more recent scholarship has criticised this view, principally on the basis that it unjustifiably presents a clear-cut dichotomy between 'orthodox' and 'heterodox' Islam in late medieval and early modern Ottoman Empire.[17]

This criticism does not seem entirely justified since the classical scholars certainly admitted to the Ottoman state's and ruling elite's ambivalence regarding their own religious orthodoxy, and were aware that the dividing line between the 'official' state religion and the 'folk' religion of the popular Sufi orders, many of whom had Shia character, was often quite blurred, especially in the early periods during the formative centuries of the Ottoman Empire. After all, Koprulu himself, for instance, was among the first to subscribe to the view that the medieval Anatolian brotherhoods of the Akhis, who were closely linked to popular dervish orders, played a crucial role in the formation of the Ottoman Empire.[18] This could not have been done without the involvement of those who were or were later to become the Ottoman ruling class. Even Halil Inalcık, who certainly comes under the heading of classical Ottomanists, and who did indeed champion the view that there was a dichotomy between the 'high' culture of Ottoman cities and the court, and the 'low' culture of the countryside, dominated by ghazis and popular heterodox dervish orders, had to admit to the sometimes close relationship between the Ottoman ruling elite and these subaltern dervish movements and their leaders, as in the case of Murad II (r. 1421–44 and 1446–51) and the founding figure of the Bayrami order of dervishes, Haci Bayram Veli (d. 1430).[19] He further also suggested that it was in fact the struggle with the Kızılbas that served to strengthen the position of the 'narrow' Sunni Islam within the Ottoman state,[20] in other words, it aided the Sunnitisation process, which means that the formal orthodox identity of the Ottoman state was far from completely crystalized by that stage. Finally, even if the classical scholars' views did suffer from such shortcomings to the extent proposed above, it is very difficult to fit within these views the 'anomaly' of the Janissaries, one of the pillars of the Ottoman state and ruling elite, being so closely linked to Bektashism, one of the most heterodox Sufi orders within the Ottoman realm.[21]

While there is no need to completely disagree with the 'classical' scholarship on this issue, Terzioglu's observations that the picture of reality on the ground in the late 15th and 16th centuries would have shown very fluid religious boundaries, and that this period saw many transformations in religious affiliations, both towards orthodoxy, in the shape of the Sunnitisation process of the Ottoman ruling elite, and towards heterodoxy, in the form of 'Shiitisation' of different parts of Ottoman population, certainly seem valid.[22]

Ayse Baltacıoglu-Brammer goes somewhat further in her criticism of the existing scholarship and suggests that the classical scholars wrongly considered Ottoman persecutions of the Kızılbas communities predominantly as a security concern, while 'revisionist' scholars either still maintain the view of a religious dichotomy between the 'high' and 'low' Islam, or have a very one-dimensional stance regarding the relationship between the Ottoman authorities and their Kızılbas subjects, one which sees this relationship purely in terms of confrontation and persecution.[23] While a more nuanced approach to the Ottomans' relationship with their Shia subjects is certainly welcome, here too, the criticism of the existing scholarship seems somewhat exaggerated: as already mentioned, the classical scholars were aware of the lack of clear division between the official orthodox Islam and heterodox movements in the early Ottoman periods, and Baltacıoglu-Brammer herself in fact shows that the Kızılbas/Shia persecutions were very much linked to security concerns and that the largest waves of persecutions coincided with the main periods of Ottoman-Safavid conflicts.[24]

It seems clear from everything said so far about this subject that the only conclusion that can be made about the 16th –century Sunnitisation of the Ottoman Empire is that this was a complex and continued process, caused by a number of religious and political factors, including both the rise and threat of the Kızılbas and their followers, and the Ottoman-Safavid conflict, the two being in turn mutually linked. Without the need to reject the classical scholarship and their findings, the present paper will take the above-cited observation about there occurring in the Ottoman society in this period religious transformations in both directions, as the vantage point from which to consider the appearance and spread of the Hamzevi 'heresy' in the mid-16th century. It will examine the contents of the existing anti-Hamzevi treatises in order to see how this phenomenon fits in with both the Sunnitisation and Shiitisation processes which these transformations comprised.

The Hamzevi Persecutions as Part of the Ottoman Sunnitisation Process

After the death of his spiritual mentor (*mursid*) and head of the Melami-Bayrami order, sheikh Husameddin Ankaravi (d. 1557), Hamza Bali, in spite of becoming sheikh Ankaravi's successor (*halife*), left Istanbul and returned to his homeland of Bosnia, where he started his proselytizing activities, initially as a minor subaltern religious leader. In the years leading up to his execution, however, he had gained many supporters, whose numbers apparently went into several thousands, not only in Bosnia, but also in the neighbouring regions and back in Istanbul itself.[25] Hamza was arrested on the basis of an imperial arrest warrant (*hukum*) dated 22 April 1573, and, not long after, executed on 6 June 1573, on the basis of a *fatwa* issued by the Seyhulislam Ebu Suud Efendi.[26]

The dramatic events of Hamza's arrest and the subsequent trial and execution thus coincide with the second large phase of the Kızılbaş persecutions, which started in the latter half of the 16th century, peaking in the 1570s.[27] This already indicates a connection between the two issues. Moreover, the processes followed were also very similar, even down to the language used in the official correspondence sent by the central government to the local *kadi*s entrusted with dealing with these problems. Thus, for instance, an imperial order for an investigation and arrest of all suspected Hamza sympathisers in the province (*sancak*) of Herzegovina, dated 25 August of 1573, requests the local *kadi*s, not just to identify the suspected '*melahide*' (atheists), but to carry out an investigation, and then arrest all the suspects if they find the charges against them justified.[28] At the same time, an imperial order dealing with the Kızılbas in the rural communities in eastern Anatolia, issued to the *kadi*s of Diyarbekir and Ruha, in September 1574, likewise requests the *kadi*s there to investigate the allegations of atheism (*ilhad*) themselves before arresting the suspects, in this case two individuals accused of both heresy and having connections with Iran.[29] The language and the tone of the two orders bear remarkable similarities, leaving the impression that as far as the central government was concerned they hardly saw any difference between a Kızılbas Safavid sympathiser in Anatolia, and a member of a Melami-Bayrami order of dervishes hundreds of miles away in southern Europe.

Hamza Bali's rise to prominence occurred several decades after the biggest Kızılbas revolts at the start of the 16th century – Sah Kulu's rebellion in 1511, Sah Veli uprising in 1520, and the Kalender revolt in 1527 – and the persecutions and suppression of the Kızılbas which came in the wake of those, as well as several decades after the execution in 1529 of the Melami-Bayrami *kutup* Ismail Masuki and his twelve followers, which seemingly put a halt to the more extreme tendencies of this order.[30] This would seem to suggest that neither the Kızılbas persecutions nor the suppression of the Melami-Bayrami order in the first half of the 16th century had the desired effect. In Anatolia, the Kızılbas were still a problem, and, judging by some of the documents from the second half of the 16th century, the Safavid propaganda among them was as strong as ever.[31] Deep inside the European part of the Ottoman Empire, in northern Bosnia, the Melami-Bayrami order with Shiism-tinged heterodox tendencies, and based on non-conformist, sectarian form of organisation, flourished and attracted thousands of followers. Both of these occurrences, but especially the reinvigoration of the Melami-Bayrami order, in the shape of the Hamzevis, indicate that the Sunnitisation process, which may have started decades before, did not come very far by that stage. The anti-Hamzevi treatises dating from that period seem to confirm this conclusion.

Two of these documents are short instructional treatises (*risale*) on the correct Sufi doctrine and method,[32] written in the style of advice to a young Hamzevi follower, according to one of them, called Veled,[33] with the aim of returning him to the straight path. The two treatises appear together in an undated manuscript, but because of their references to the Hamzevis, their composition can easily be situated in the second half of the 16th century, and specifically before June 1573, since both mention Hamza as still alive and active. The first was written by a certain Mehmed Amiki and the second by Yigit-bası Ahmed Efendi, and although we don't know anything about them, it seems safe to conclude that they were both certainly Mevlevis, and, in the case of the second author, possibly the head of the local branch of the order:[34] firstly, both treatises were written with the aim of providing instruction on the correct way of joining the Sufi path and the correct method of the progression along this path; secondly, the authority repeatedly invoked in both of the documents, on both matters of doctrine and practice, is that of Jalal al-Din Rumi (d. 1273);[35] and thirdly, both texts are interspersed with Mesnevi or Mesnevi-inspired verses in Persian.

The very existence of these treatises is in itself evidence of obvious popularity of the Hamzevi order and the evident need of the establishment, and representatives of the officially-sanctioned forms of Sufism, to take active steps towards curbing this popularity. Whether they were commissioned by the *ulema*, or written at the initiative of the Mevlevis themselves, they are certainly part of the Sunnitisation process that was taking place across the Ottoman Empire at the time, and thus provide an insight into the role that the *ulema*-approved Sufi orders played in this process.

The first treatise, written by Mehmed Amiki, as already mentioned, starts by an introductory section, explaining the motives behind its composition.[36] According to this introduction, the author himself had met the young *sipahi* and a Hamzevi follower called Veled, which inspired him to write this treatise about both the proper way of entering the Sufi path, and the errors of the Hamzevis, and in particular of Hamza himself, whom the *sipahi* in question had obviously accepted as his *mursid*: throughout the treatise, Hamza is referred to as 'your sheikh and master'. The introduction further suggests that the Hamzevi 'heretics' use the ignorance of the masses and the uneducated in order to recruit them into their ranks, which is why there is a need for a clear and accessible guide against the Hamzevis and their teachings to be written.

The first chapter accuses Hamza Bali of preaching against the need for the prescribed forms of worship ('*amel ve mucahede*'), which, according to the author Amiki, is contrary to the proper Sunni teachings and is caused by the misinterpretation of the Qur'anic verses regarding this subject.[37]

The next one, albeit somewhat indirectly, accuses the Hamzevis of false modesty – namely, of displaying outward signs of piety and poverty, but secretly coveting money and this-worldly riches – and of drinking alcohol. The author puts this in a roundabout way, suggesting that 'many dervish lodges and monasteries (*zivaya ve savami*) are populated by *pirs* and *murids* of 'Qarmatian' leanings' who wear dervish robes to attract followers but have corrupt souls.[38] Since the deliberate adoption of poverty does belong to the Melami tradition, and Hamza Bali himself was said to have followed this to an extreme degree of dressing in rags and starving or eating food thrown to street cats and dogs,[39] this is something that his disciples may well have embraced themselves. The other two accusations, however, namely, the disregard for the prescribed prayers and other forms of worship, and approval of unlawful or non-Sunni practices, such as wine drinking, were common elements of 'heresy tests' employed by jurists at heresy trials. The test would be carried out by assessing the accused's views on licit and forbidden acts under the Sharia law. If the suspect was found to consider the obligatory acts (such as prayer or fasting) as voluntary, and approved of illicit acts (such as wine drinking), their heresy was proven and they could be convicted.[40]

Such accusations are therefore often symbolic and appeared as a matter of form in relation to all groups considered heterodox in some way. Moreover, they are much more readily associated with Shia sects like Bekatshism, and Bektashi-like orders such as the Kızılbas. Given that in both instances, neither Hamza himself nor Hamzevis are mentioned by name in relation to these accusations, this seems like a case of deliberate ambiguity and attempt at ascribing guilt 'by implication', as it were. This would seem to apply especially to the wine-drinking allegations, since contemporary sources have described one of Hamza's recruitment techniques as consisting of visits to taverns and preaching against wine drinking, suggesting substituting 'the wine of God's love' for the wine of the Satan.[41] In any case, whatever the amount of truth in these accusations may be, for our purposes, they certainly seem to point to the fear, on the part of their author and his milieu, of the more extreme Shia practices such as those adopted by the Kızılbas and their followers.

The next chapter in the treatise is somewhat longer and is devoted to the issue of the interpretation of dreams. The author starts with the statement that he 'has heard' that the young man's sheikh, in other words, Hamza Bali, denied the existence of meanings to dreams and rejected the science of dream interpretation.[42] The fact that this is based on what Amiki 'has heard' suggests that this may well have been a conjuncture on his part, or on the part of whoever passed this information, but one which the author nevertheless found important and necessary to address. The treatise thus spends a considerable proportion of the text demonstrating importance and usefulness of dreams, especially in the context of a right Sufi path, and providing evidence from the Qur'an and the Mesnevi.[43] According to Amiki, denying dream interpretation is unlawful and against the Sunna, but also detrimental to one's spiritual progression on the Sufi path. Thus he says: 'Oh Veled! Know that the true essence of the Sufi path ('*hakikat-i suluk*') is not some sort of formal determination or physical struggle, but it is a mystical path and spiritual training. Therefore, the science of dream interpretation is the foundation of the Sufi path.'[44]

In the final chapter, the text criticises Hamza's spiritual methods on the example of him wrongly revealing to his disciples 'the eighteen thousand hidden worlds'. The chapter explains the traditions relating to these worlds, their exact number and their character, though it does not elaborate any further on the meaning of the alleged 'revelation' by Hamza Bali and its wrongfulness.[45]

The second, shorter, treatise from the same manuscript, by Yigit-basi Ahmed Efendi, is written in the same style, addressing the young disciple called Veled and instructing him in the appropriate way of following the Sufi path. The first issue with which the treatise is concerned is miracle performing and different kinds of magic. In this context, Hamza Bali, referred to as 'Hamza Sultan', is accused of ostentatiousness and gratuitous performance of miracles, which is something that, according to Ahmed Efendi, true servants of God, i.e. saints, would not do, except in the case of some very grave need. Because of that, Hamza's miracles should be classified as belonging to 'lesser' magic and not true '*keramat*'.[46] The fact that Hamza is called by his honorific Sufi title of 'Sultan' and that he is acknowledged as being able to perform miracles, seems rather at odds with proclaiming him a heretic – which is definitely the aim of the first work in the collection – and denouncing him as a false spiritual leader. In fact, this treatise does not unequivocally do either on any occasion throughout the text, which makes Ahmed Efendi's objections to Hamza Bali seem not as strong as those of Amiki, and one can't help but wonder about his conviction in his own words against Hamza, and the actual motives for writing this *risale*.

The second part of the treatise is concerned with refuting the doctrine of '*wahdat al-wujud*', the name given to the set of teachings developed by the great Sufi scholar and mystic Ibn Arabi (d. 1240) and traditionally a matter of contention between the *ulema* and Sufi orders generally. The author here interprets it as a unity of nature between 'the creator and the created', which is an 'impossibility' and thus constitutes a 'heresy' (*zandaka*).[47] As already mentioned,[48] this doctrine is known to have been adopted by the Melami-Bayramis and other non-conformist orders like them, and it is, therefore, perfectly plausible to assume that it would have formed part of Hamza Bali's teachings. Here, however, neither Hamza himself nor the Hamzevis generally are explicitly mentioned as either espousing or propagating this doctrine. Given this, and the point mentioned above about the certain lack of conviction in Ahmed Efendi's attacks on Hamza, it seems plausible to conclude that he was perhaps tasked with writing something matching the first treatise, and denouncing the heretical Hamzevis, but that he either did not know much about them, or was not actually convinced of what he had been told about them, their leader, and their teachings.

The third document is much more overt about its anti-Hamzevi sentiments and reveals much stronger fears of their sectarian character and possible political agenda. This 16th century fragment from a religious treatise, by an unknown author, and apparently found in Bosnia,[49] mentions the Hamzevis several times and in the same breath as the Hurufis.[50] In the first instance, it is stated that Hurufis, Hamzevis and other heretics (*zindik*) and atheists (*mulhid*) have appeared in the world and are quickly spreading.[51] They are described as being very successful at spreading their teachings, and that if there were not for the *ulema* they would draw the whole world into their heretical schools of thought (*mezhepler*) within a few days: 'Their schools of thought are whim (*heva*) and not the noble Sharia, which is why the *ulema* have issued a *fatwa* for them to be killed'.[52] Thus, although anonymous and undated, it is safe to assume that this treatise was written at the height of the Hamzevi persecutions, either just before or perhaps even just after Hamza Bali's execution in 1573, since this mention of the *fatwa* must be in reference to the one issued by Seyhulislam Ebu Suud Efendi justifying Hamza'a execution. Both the Hurufis and the Hamzevis are further accused of deceiving the ordinary people into joining their ranks: 'The ignorant masses do not know the Hurufis and the Hamzevis. They think that they are from among us, from among the Sunnis'.[53] The text carries on by accusing the Hurufis and Hamzevis of spreading anti-*ulema* propaganda, by saying that the latter were not acting in accordance with their knowledge and should not be listened to. Finally, the text warns that if more is not done to educate these ignorant Muslim masses, they will stop listening to the *ulema* altogether and will gradually accept Hurufi teachings: 'The Hurufis will then use the opportunity and find a suitable way to publicly announce their sectarian school of thought (*mezhep*) and their missionary books the '*Cavidan-i kabir*' and '*Cavidan-i saghir*'.'[54] As for the Hamzevis, they will 'at the same time, or perhaps earlier, when there are about a hundred thousand of them, rise up [in rebellion?], and will carry out a massacre (*katl-i am*) of all those who refuse to enter their order, and will rob their possessions, and burn down their property.'[55] In another part of this fragment, an unnamed source is reported to have been in the company of some Hamzevis and has learnt that they approved of drinking wine, prostitution and homosexuality.[56] While the above fears of the Hamzevi teachings spreading and the possibility of a Hamzevi-led rebellion do not seem that far-fetched, the last section sounds much more like formulaic anti-Hamzevi propaganda, based, once again, on the standard components of the heresy tests, namely, approval of illicit acts, wine-drinking, prostitution and homosexuality being the most extreme and therefore highly symbolic examples of such acts. The latter should thus be treated with much more caution.

Conclusion

What all three documents examined above have in common is that they are evidently representative of the developments within the 16th-century process of the Sunnitisation of the Ottoman Empire, initiated and carried out by the Ottoman establishment in part as a response to the Safavid-supported Kızılbas insurrections. The documents reveal real fears of the Shia leanings of the Hamzevi order and of its sectarian tendencies, both of which are also the primary characteristics of the Kızılbas, who had by then been collaborating with the Safavids and revolting against the Ottoman authority for decades. Even though the Kızılbas suffered a major wave of persecutions and suppression by Sultan Selim I (r. 1512-1520) after their biggest revolt of 1511, the Kızılbas threat did not dissipate that easily: in 1520 there was another rebellion in Anatolia, and more waves of persecutions also followed, many aimed at preventing the Kızılbas support during campaigns against the Safavids, such as, for instance, the persecutions carried out in the wake of Suleyman I's (r. 1520-1566) campaigns in 1534-35, or those just before the start of the 1578 Ottoman-Safavid war. The appearance of the Hamzevi order in the second part of the 16th century was clearly not arbitrary, as it and the immediate attempts at its suppression came hand-in-hand with the further Kızılbas uprisings in Anatolia and the second large phase of the Kızılbas persecutions in the 1570s.[57] Judging by the manner in which they dealt with them, even the language with which they described them, the Ottoman authorities themselves evidently thought of and treated the two phenomena as connected. Both of these phenomena, namely, the continuous rebellions of the Kızılbas, and the rise and proliferation of the Hamzevi and other Shia or Shia-oriented Sufi orders, could thus be characterised as belonging to the Shiitisation part of the religious transformations that were taking place in the Ottoman Empire since the late 15th century, mentioned here earlier. While not a completely clear-cut case of cause and effect, and while the opposite may at times have been the case, the Sunnitisation process was obviously in large part prompted by the Shiitisation one.

A further similarity between the Hamzevis and the Kızılbas is that the Hamzevis too had a military dimension, since they clearly had support from among different sections of the Ottoman army: according to the above treatise by Mehmed Amiki, the Hamzevi that needed returning to the right path was a *sipahi*; and the Hamzevi following among the Janissaries – who, through their links with Bektashism, were already a Shia-oriented organisation – was a serious problem for the Ottomans and brought the issue into the heart of the capital and the empire. Bearing this in mind, it is not difficult to understand how at that stage even a hint of Shia tendencies could be seen as potential Safavid loyalties and had to be treated as harshly as possible: for just like Shiism was an essential part of Safavid identity and the basis of their legitimacy, so was Sunnism rapidly becoming a corner-stone of Ottoman power-base, carved out in part precisely as a counter-measure to the Safavids and many Safavids-sympathetic movements inside the Ottoman territory.

The above documents also reveal the role the mainstream orthodox Sufi orders played in the Ottoman Sunnitisation process: in the case of the first two treatises, the senior Mevlevi figures were recruited to compose them presumably because of their standing in society generally, and their influence among the Sufi orders more specifically.[58] Yigit-basi Ahmed Efendi, the author of the second treatise, apart from being a senior Mevlevi was also very likely a senior guild official, probably a saddler, thus a member of one of the strongest guilds in Bosnia at the time. The choice of Yigit-basi Ahmed Efendi for this role may not have been arbitrary: given that the Hamzevis themselves – in line with the Melami tradition – exerted considerable influence over certain crafts and guilds in northern Bosnia,[59] this may have been a deliberate attempt at curbing the Hamzevis' influence and its further spread within this particular social context. To this, one other observation can be added: the present author has shown on several occasions that the tradition of *futuwwa* – the code of noble and chivalric conduct based on Sufi tradition and adopted by *futuwwa* fraternities such as the Anatolian Akhis – was strongly preserved by Ottoman guilds in this period, and particularly those in Bosnia.[60] This tradition, which had Shia overtones from the outset, according to some scholars, experienced even further Shiitisation in late 15th and early 16th century,[61] which fits in very well with what has already been said about the religious transformations taking place within the Ottoman Empire at this time.

In terms of the contents of the treatises, only the unknown author of the third anonymous document seems to display a strong conviction in their denouncement of the Hamzevis; even there though, the treatise seems to be concerned more with the Hurufis and the Hamzevis are criticised and denounced by association, rather than directly. As for the other two, the Mevlevi-authored treatises, the accusations levelled at the Hamzevis are either not very specific or not direct, and in the case of Amiki's treatise, for instance, the accusations regarding false modesty and drinking alcohol seem to be imputed and based either on formulaic heresy 'traits' or on what is known about other heterodox orders or movements, rather than anything specific to the Hamzevis. Moreover, the seemingly most important contentious doctrinal issues discussed in the treatise, namely, the importance of the interpretation of dreams, is addressed on the basis of what, in the words of the author himself, he 'has heard'. This perhaps indicates that Amiki was indeed commissioned to write this treatise, and, more importantly, that he was reluctant to accuse the Hamzevis of any doctrinal wrongdoings he did not know about himself and with certainty, hence the need to include this caveat. The lack of conviction in Yigit-bası Ahmed Efendi's denouncement of the Hamzevis has already been pointed out: nowhere in this treatise is Hamza directly accused of being a heretic or a false spiritual leader, he is acknowledged as being able to perform miracles, and is throughout referred to as 'Hamza Sultan', a title of respect one would expect to be used by his followers rather than the author of an anti-Hamzevi exposition.

Hamza's execution in 1573 did not have the desired effect: Hamza became a patron-saint of the Melami-Bayrami order, and the order formally adopted the name 'Hamzevis' in his honour. He seemed to have carried on acquiring supporters even after his death and another wave of Hamzevi persecutions and executions was carried out in 1582.[62] This, together with the above indicators, seems to point to only one conclusion: while the Ottoman establishment carried out its Sunnitisation process, as far as the ordinary people in the Ottoman Empire were concerned this may just as easily have turned into a Shiitisation one, and things may have taken a very different course were there not for the determination and ruthlessness of the Ottoman authorities in suppressing any such sensibilities.

Bibliography

Primary Sources

Mehmed Amiki's anti-Hamzevi treatise from the 16th century
Yigit-bası Ahmed Efendi's anti-Hamzevi treatise from the 16th century
16th –century fragment from a religious treatise mentioning Hamzevis

All three published with a translation into Bosnian in: Mehinagic, I. "Cetiri neobjavljena izvora o Hamzevijama iz sredine XVI vijeka" [Four unpublished sources about the Hamzevis from the middle of the 16th century]. *Prilozi za Orijentalnu Filologiju* XVIII-XIX/1968-69 (Sarajevo 1973), 217-266.

Secondary Sources

Abisaab, Rula, *Converting Persia: Religion and Power in the Safavid Empire*. London and New York: I. B. Tauris, 2015.
Allouche, Adel, *The Origins and Development of the Ottoman-Safavid Conflict (906-962 / 1500-1555)*. Berlin: Schwarz, 1983.
Asceric-Todd, Ines, "The Noble Traders: The Islamic Tradition of "Spiritual Chivalry" (*futuwwa*) in Bosnian Trade-guilds (16th-19th centuries)", *The Muslim World* 97/2 (2007), 159-173.
Asceric-Todd, Ines, *Dervishes and Islam in Bosnia: Sufi Dimensions to the Formation of Bosnian Muslim Society*. Leiden and Boston: Brill, 2015.
Asceric-Todd, Ines, "Fotovvat in Bosnia". In *Javanmardi: The Ethics and Practice of Persianate Perfection*, edited by Lloyd Ridgeon, London: The Gingko Library, 2018, 163-181.
Azamat, Nihat, "Hamza Bali", *IA*: 503-505.
Babinger, Frantz, and Fuat Koprulu, *Anadolu'da Islamiyet*, translated by Ragıp Hulusi. Istanbul: İnsan Yayınları, 1996.
Baltacıoglu-Brammer, Ayse, "The Formation of Kızılbas Communities in Anatolia and Ottoman Responses, 1450s-1630s". *International Journal of Turkish Studies* 20/1-2 (2014), 21-47.
Baltacıoglu-Brammer, Ayse, "'Those Heretics Gathering Secretly …": Qizilbash Rituals and Practices in the Ottoman Empire According to Early Modern Sources'. *Journal of the Ottoman and Turkish Studies Association* 6, no. 1 (2019), 39-60.
Bayramoglu, Fuat, and Nihat Azamat, "Bayramiyye". *IA*: 269-273.
Birge, John Kingsley, *The Bektashi Order of Dervishes*. London: Luzac, 1937.

Cehajic, Dzemal, *Derviski redovi u Jugoslovenskim zemljama, sa posebnim osvrtom na Bosnu i Hercegovinu* [Dervish orders in Yugoslav lands with special reference to Bosnia-Herzegovina]. Sarajevo: Orijentalni Institut u Sarajevu, 1986.

De Jong, Frederick, Hamid Algar, and Colin Imber. "Malamatiyya". *EI2*: 223-228.

Hadzijahic, Muhamed, "Tekija kraj Zvornika – postojbina Bosanskih Hamzevija?" [The lodge near Zvornik – the original homeland of Bosnian Hamzevis?]. *Prilozi za Orijentalnu Filologiju* X-XI/1960-61 (Sarajevo 1961), 193-203.

Handzic, Adem, "Jedan savremeni documenat o sejhu Hamzi iz Orlovica" [One contemporary document about sheikh Hamza from Orlovici]. *Prilozi za Orijentalnu Filologiju* XVIII-XIX/1968-69 (Sarajevo 1973), 205-215.

Handzic, Adem, "O progonu Hamzevija u sjeveroistocnoj Bosni 1582. Godine" [On the persecution of the Hamzevis in North-East Bosnia in 1582]. *Muzej Istocne Bosne u Tuzli: clanci i gradja za kulturnu istoriju istocne Bosne*, knj. XI (Tuzla, 1975), 33-38.

Handzic, Adem, and Muhamed Hadzijahic. "O progonu Hamzevija u Bosni 1573. godine" [On the persecution of the the Hamzevis in Bosnia in 1573]. *Prilozi za Orijentalnu Filologiju* XX-XXI/1970-71 (Sarajevo 1974), 51-69.

Imber, Colin, *Ebu's-su'ud: The Islamic Legal Tradition*, Edinburgh: Edinburgh University Press, 1997

Inalcık, Halil, *The Ottoman Empire: The Classical Age, 1300-1600*. London: Phoenix Press, 2000.

Karamustafa, Ahmet T., *God's Unruly Friends: Dervish Groups in the Islamic Later Middle Period, 1200-1550*. Oxford: Oneworld, 2006.

Koprulu, Mehmet Fuat, *Les origins de l'empire ottoman*. Paris: E. De Boccard, 1935.

Le Gall, Dina. *A Culture of Sufism: Naqshbandīs in the Ottoman World, 1450-1700*. Albany: State University of New York Press, 2005.

Mehinagic, I., "Cetiri neobjavljena izvora o Hamzevijama iz sredine XVI vijeka" [Four unpublished sources about the Hamzevis from the middle of the 16th century]. *Prilozi za Orijentalnu Filologiju* XVIII-XIX/1968-69 (Sarajevo 1973), 217-266.

Mir-Kasimov, Orkhan. "Hurufiyya", *EI3*, Brill Online.

Morgan, David, *Medieval Persia 1040-1797*. London and New York: Routledge, 2nd ed., 2016.

Ocak, Ahmet Yasar, *Babailer Isyanı*. Istanbul: Dergah Yayınları, 1980.

Ocak, Ahmet Yasar, *Osmanlı Toplumunda Zındıklar ve Mulhidler: 15. ve 17. Yuzyıllar*. Istanbul: Turkiye Ekonomik ve Toplumsal Tarih Vakfi, 1998.

Repp, Richard C., *The Mufti of Istanbul: a Study in the Development of the Ottoman Learned Hierarchy*. London: Ithaca Press, 1986.

Terzioglu, Derin, "How to Conceptualize Ottoman Sunnitization: A Historiographical Discussion". *Turcica* 44 (2012-13), 301-338.

Terzioglu, Derin, "Sufis in the Age of State-building and Confessionalization", in *The Ottoman World*, edited by Christine Woodhead, 86-99. London and New York: Routledge, 2013.

Wittek, Paul, *The Rise of the Ottoman Empire*. London: Royal Asiatic Society/Luzac, 1958.

Yildirim, Riza, "Shi'itisation of the *futuwwa* tradition in the fifteenth century". *British Journal of Middle Eastern Studies* 40/1 (2013), 53–70.

Zarinebaf-Shahr, Fariba, "Qizilbash 'Heresy' and Rebellion in Ottoman Anatolia during the Sixteenth Century", *Anatolia Moderna* 7 (1997), 1-15.

Notes

1 '*Melami*' is the term applied to all Sufi groups which adhere to the tradition of '*melamet*' – concealment of one's piety and spiritual station, which can lead to being perceived as reproachable (Ar. '*malama*' = blame, reproach). An extreme example of adherence to this tradition is provided by antinomian Sufi groups or individual Sufis who purposely sought to attract reproach through unconventional behaviour, such as, for instance Qalandars, Haydaris or Abdals. For more on these popular Sufi groups, see a number of works by Ahmet T. Karamustafa, but especially: *God's Unruly Friends: Dervish Groups in the Islamic Later Middle Period, 1200-1550*, Oxford: Oneworld, 2006. For more on '*melamet*', see Frederick De Jong, Hamid Algar and Colin Imber, "Malamatiyya", *EI2*, 223-228. The Melami-Bayrami order represents a second phase in the history of the Bayrami order which, following the death of its founder Hajji Bayram Veli in 1430, adopted the tradition of '*melamet*'; see Fuat Bayramoglu and Nihat Azamat, "Bayramiyye", *IA*: 269-273.

2 The technical terms used for these particular accusations were '*zandaqa*' and '*ilhad*' respectively and were formulated in the *fatwa*s issued by prominent members of the Ottoman *ulema*, such as Mufti Hamza, Seyhulislam Ebu Suud Efendi and Kemalpasazade, during a number of anti-Shia purges which took place throughout the Ottoman Empire during the 16th century. See Fariba Zarinebaf-Shahr, "Qizilbash 'Heresy' and Rebellion in Ottoman Anatolia during the Sixteenth Century", *Anatolia Moderna* 7 (1997), 5.

3 Ines Asceric-Todd, *Dervishes and Islam in Bosnia: Sufi Dimensions to the Formation of Bosnian Muslim Society*, Leiden and Boston: Brill, 2015, 164.

4 Already during Hamza Bali's time, the term Hamzevi appears in relation to his followers, and, by extension, to members of the Melami-Bayrami order at that time generally. Initially seemingly coined as a pejorative term by the Ottoman authorities, after Hamza Bali's execution the term was readily adopted by the Melami-Bayramis themselves.

5 Although some brief mentions of the subject can be found even as early as the start of the 20th century.

6 Examples of the former are: Muhamed Hadzijahic, "Tekija kraj Zvornika – postojbina Bosanskih Hamzevija?" [The lodge near Zvornik – the original homeland of the Bosnian Hamzevis?], *Prilozi za Orijentalnu Filologiju* X-XI/1960-61 (Sarajevo 1961), 193-203; and Adem Handzic and Muhamed Hadzijahic, "O progonu Hamzevija u Bosni 1573. godine" [On the persecution of the Hamzevis in Bosnia in 1573], *Prilozi za Orijentalnu Filologiju* XX-XXI/1970-71 (Sarajevo 1974), 51-69. Examples of the latter are more numerous and, among others, include: Adem Handzic, "Jedan savremeni documenat o sejhu Hamzi iz Orlovica" [One contemporary document about sheikh Hamza from Orlovici], *Prilozi za Orijentalnu Filologiju* XVIII-XIX/1968-69 (Sarajevo 1973), 205-215; Adem Handzic, "O progonu Hamzevija u sjeveroistocnoj Bosni 1582. Godine"

[On the persecution of the Hamzevis in North-East Bosnia in 1582], *Muzej Istocne Bosne u Tuzli: clanci i gradja za kulturnu istoriju istocne Bosne*, knj. XI (Tuzla 1975), 33-38.

7   Ibrahim Mehinagic's, "Cetiri neobjavljena izvora o Hamzevijama iz sredine XVI vijeka" [Four unpublished sources about the Hamzevis from the middle of the 16th century], *Prilozi za Orijentalnu Filologiju* XVIII-XIX/1968-69 (Sarajevo 1973), 217-266.

8   Dzemal Cehajic, *Derviski redovi u Jugoslovenskim zemljama, sa posebnim osvrtom na Bosnu i Hercegovinu* [Dervish orders in Yugoslav lands with special reference to Bosnia-Herzegovina], Sarajevo: Orijentalni Institut u Sarajevu, 1986, 185-208.

9   Asceric-Todd, *Dervishes and Islam*, 161-179.

10 Asceric-Todd, *Dervishes and Islam*, 171-173.

11 Also known as Oglan Seyh, this was a Melami-Bayrami sheikh accused and convicted of heresy, and executed in 1529; see R C Repp, *The Mufti of Istanbul: a Study in the Development of the Ottoman Learned Hierarchy*, London: Ithaca Press, 1986, 236-238. See also Ahmet Yasar Ocak, *Osmanlı Toplumunda Zındıklar ve Mulhidler: 15. ve 17. Yuzyıllar*, Istanbul: Turkiye Ekonomik ve Toplumsal Tarih Vakfı, 1998, 274-290.

12 Although we do know about some of the common Melami-Bayrami spiritual traditions which, together with the practice of '*melamet*', served to categorise them as heterodox and Shiism-oriented, such as the keen nourishment of Ibn Arabi's '*wahdat al-wujud*' ('unity of being') doctrine, the 'polishing of the heart' theory and practice, and the strong emphasis on the personality of the *kutup*, the spiritual pole of the order. For more on these teachings see Cehajic, *Derviski redovi*, 188-190.

13 'Kızılbas' = literally 'red head' in Turkish, refers to the turban traditionally worn by the followers of the Safavi Sufi order, and goes back to one of its 15th-century leaders, Sheikh Haydar (r. 1460-1488), who is said to have invented the red twelve-gored cap around which the cloth of the turban is wound. This particular shape of the cap was later interpreted as symbolising the twelve Shia imams. David Morgan, *Medieval Persia 1040-1797*, London and New York: Routledge, 2nd ed. 2016, 108; Rula Abisaab, *Converting Persia: Religion and Power in the Safavid Empire*, London and New York: I. B. Tauris, 2015, 8.

14 The main periods of war between the Ottoman and the Safavid Empires were 1532-1555, 1578-1590, and 1623-1639 (Ayse Baltacıoglu-Brammer, "The Formation of Kızılbas Communities in Anatolia and Ottoman Responses, 1450s-1630s", *International Journal of Turkish Studies* 20/1-2 (2014), 23, n. 6).

15 This process is also sometimes referred to as 'confessionalization'; see, for instance, Derin Terzioglu, "Sufis in the Age of State-building and Confessionalization", in *The Ottoman World*, ed. Christine Woodhead (London and New York, 2013), 86-99. For more on this process see also: Derin Terzioglu "How to Conceptualize Ottoman Sunnitization: A Historiographical Discussion", *Turcica* 44 (2012-13), 301-338.

16 Terzioglu, "Sufis", 87. Examples of such classical scholarship include: Franz Babinger and Fuat Koprulu, *Anadolu'da Islamiyet*, trans. Ragıp Hulusi, Istanbul: İnsan Yayınları, 1996; Ahmet Yasar Ocak, *Babailer Isyanı*, Istanbul: Dergah Yayınları, 1980 and *Osmanlı Toplumunda Zındıklar ve Mulhidler* (see note 10 above). See also Adel Allouche, *The Origins and Development of the Ottoman-Safavid Conflict (906-962 / 1500-1555)*, Berlin: Schwarz, 1983.

17 Terzioglu, "Sufis", 87. She gives Karamustafa's *God's Unruly Friends* and Dina Le Gall's *A Culture of Sufism: Naqshbandis in the Ottoman World, 145-1700*, Albany: State University of New York Press, 2005, as examples of this scholarship.

18 See Mehmet Fuat Koprulu, *Les origins de l'empire ottoman*, Paris: E. De Boccard, 1935. One may also add here Paul Wittek and his Ghazi theory, which is based entirely on the suggestion that the early Ottoman polity and the ruling elite were inextricably linked to the popular traditions of the Anatolian 'dervish knights', the Ghazis; see Paul Wittek, *The Rise of the Ottoman Empire*, London: Royal Asiatic Society/Luzac, 1958.

19 Halil Inalcık, *The Ottoman Empire: The Classical Age, 1300-1600*, London: Phoenix Press, 2000, 192.

20 Inalcık, *The Ottoman Empire*, 197.
21 John Kingsley Birge, *The Bektashi Order of Dervishes*, London: Luzac, 1937, 74. See also Asceric-Todd, *Dervishes and Islam*, 48-49.
22 Terzioglu, "Sufis", 87.
23 See Baltacıoglu-Brammer, "The Formation of Kızılbas Communities".
24 Baltacıoglu-Brammer, "The Formation of Kızılbas Communities", 23-24.
25 Nihat Azamat, "Hamza Bali", *IA*: 503.
26 Asceric-Todd, *Dervishes and Islam*, 162-163.
27 Zarinebaf-Shahr, "Qizilbash 'Heresy'", 9.
28 Handzic and Hadzijahic, "O progonu Hamzevija u Bosni 1573. godine", 54, 57.
29 Zarinebaf-Shahr, "Qizilbash 'Heresy'", 10.
30 See note 11 above.
31 Zarinebaf-Shahr, "Qizilbash 'Heresy'", 10-11. On the Safavid propaganda more generally see also Ayse Baltacıoglu-Brammer. "'Those Heretics Gathering Secretly …'": Qizilbash Rituals and Practices in the Ottoman Empire According to Early Modern Sources.' *Journal of the Ottoman and Turkish Studies Association* 6, no. 1 (2019), 39-60.
32 The manuscript of the two documents is housed in the Croatian (formerly Yugoslav) Academy of Science and Art (HAZU) Archive in Zagreb, Oriental Collection, under the MS. No. 1285. As already mentioned, both were published, with translations into Bosnian, in Mehinagic "Cetiri neobjavljena izvora o Hamzevijama". Here, the Bosnian translation of the documents is used in conjunction with the original text in Ottoman.
33 In its introduction, the first manuscript suggests that a son of a *sipahi* (a member of Ottoman landed cavalry) called Veled ('*Veled-nam bir sipahi-zade*') had joined the ranks of the Hamzevi followers, and hence the reason for composing the treatise was to return him, and others like him, to the right path. Throughout the treatise, the separate chapters/sections are indicated by a vocative '*Eyyuha el-Veled*!' The use of this invocation is replicated in the second treatise, which does not have an introduction, but its general style, including this particular stylistic device, and the contents suggest that the two are connected, and written either at the same time with the same aim, or one is an imitation of the other.
34 In Sarajevo, for instance, the Mevlevi order was linked to the saddlers' guild, and there is evidence which suggests that the Mevlevi elders, including, at times, the heads of the order, were also senior members of the guild administration, such as the *yigitbası*, the assistant and deputy to the head of the guild. In fact, according to Sarajevo's saddlers' register (*defter*) from 1745, the *yigitbası* at that time was 'Dervish Ahmed Mevlevi' (see Asceric-Todd, *Dervishes and Islam*, 123), whose name is thus identical to that of the author of our treatise. If these treatises were written in Bosnia, which seems highly likely, it is equally likely that our Yigit-bası Ahmed Efendi was a senior member of the Mevlevi order there (as well as obviously a member of a guild, presumably the saddlers').
35 The great 13th century Sufi mystic and poet, and patron-saint of the Mevlevi order of dervishes.
36 See note 33 above.
37 Mehinagic "Cetiri neobjavljena izvora", 233-234, 241-242.
38 Mehinagic "Cetiri neobjavljena izvora", 234, 242.
39 Asceric-Todd, *Dervishes and Islam*, 162.
40 Colin Imber, *Ebu's-su'ud: The Islamic Legal Tradition*, Edinburgh: Edinburgh University Press, 1997, 92.
41 From verses attributed to Hamza Bali by Ataaullah Nevizade Atayi (1583-1634), quoted in Cehajic, *Derviski redovi*, 192.
42 Mehinagic "Cetiri neobjavljena izvora", 235, 243.
43 Mehinagic "Cetiri neobjavljena izvora", 235-237, 243-245.
44 Mehinagic "Cetiri neobjavljena izvora", 236-237, 244.
45 Mehinagic "Cetiri neobjavljena izvora", 238-240, 246-248.

46 Mehinagic "Cetiri neobjavljena izvora", 251, 261.
47 Mehinagic "Cetiri neobjavljena izvora", 251-252, 261.
48 See note 12 above.
49 The manuscript is 8 pages long, is incomplete both at the start and the end, and has some pages missing in the middle. According to Mehinagic, who published and translated it, it was found somewhere in Bosnia by a private manuscript collector who then gave it to Muhamed Hadzijahic, one of the scholars who worked on the Hamzevis at the time. What has become of the manuscript since then is unknown. Mehinagic "Cetiri neobjavljena izvora", 217.
50 The Hurufis were a mystical messianic movement whose founding figure was Fadlallah Astarabadi (d. 1394), and whose teachings combined Shia and Sufi elements, and were inspired by the 'science of letters' (*'ilm al-huruf*), hence their name. They are known to have had political agenda at times, and there is evidence of their activities within the Ottoman Empire towards the end of the 15th and in the first half of the 16th century. After that, however, their teachings were mainly preserved by the Baktashis. For more see Orkhan Mir-Kasimov, "Hurufiyya", *EI3*, Brill Online.
51 Mehinagic "Cetiri neobjavljena izvora", 223, 229.
52 Mehinagic "Cetiri neobjavljena izvora", 223, 226.
53 Mehinagic "Cetiri neobjavljena izvora", 223, 226.
54 Mehinagic "Cetiri neobjavljena izvora", 224, 226.
55 Mehinagic "Cetiri neobjavljena izvora", 224, 226.
56 Mehinagic "Cetiri neobjavljena izvora", 224, 231.
57 See note 27 above.
58 This also provides a good example of 16th – century Sufi politics evident in both the Persian and Ottoman contexts. At the time when the official Safavid and Ottoman state policies were being crystallised around either Shia or Sunni identity, the Sufi *tariqas* themselves were also evolving and trying to find their place in the new order of things. In the Safavid territory, mainstream Sufi orders would have struggled to redefine themselves in the face of the rise of the Safavids and the proliferation of their brand of Shia-inspired militant Sufism, or even their later adoption of Twelver Shiism as their official religion. Within the Ottoman realm, however, the mainstream *tariqas* such as the Mevlevis clearly found themselves a role within this new order, that of the *ulema*-approved champions of the Sunnitisation process. Whether this was based on genuine conviction or simply part of 'Sufi politics' as means of self-preservation, is, of course, another issue – see the rest of the Conclusion here.
59 Asceric-Todd, *Dervishes and Islam*, 169.
60 See: Ines Asceric-Todd, "The Noble Traders: The Islamic Tradition of "Spiritual Chivalry" (*futuwwa*) in Bosnian Trade-guilds (16th-19th centuries)", *The Muslim World* 97/2 (2007), 159-173; Asceric-Todd, *Dervishes and Islam*, several sections, but especially Ch. 5, 93-112; Ines Asceric-Todd, "Fotovvat in Bosnia", in *Javanmardi: The Ethics and Practice of Persianate Perfection*, ed. by Lloyd Ridgeon, London: The Gingko Library, 2018, 163-181.
61 Riza Yildirim, "Shi'itisation of the *futuwwa* tradition in the fifteenth century", *British Journal of Middle Eastern Studies* 40/1 (2013), 53–70.
62 Asceric-Todd, *Dervishes and Islam*, 169-173.

8

Voices of the Caucasians at the Safavid Court: Life and Activities of Parsadan Gorgijanidze[1]

Hirotake Maeda

Iran and the Caucasus

The peoples of the Caucasus maintained close cultural, economic, and political relations with the Iranian commonwealth from ancient times. The linguistic influence of the Iranian languages also spread across the North and South Caucasus. A clear manifestation thereof is the existence of two Elbrus(es), one in the Caucasus and the other along the Caspian coast. According to the *Georgian Chronicle* (*Kartlis Tskhovreba*) Parnavaz (fourth to third Century BC), the legendary first king of Georgia, was a nephew of viceroy of the Persian empire and his mother was from Isfahan[2]. He killed the regent of Alexander the Great (III of Macedon) and established the first unified Georgian kingdom. Georgian kings were under strong Iranian influence but from medieval times the Bagratid princes stressed the ancient Judaic roots to transcend the Muslim as well as Byzantine hegemony[3]. Iranian cultural markers, however, were still important in the south Caucasus throughout the medieval and early modern period. The heyday of medieval Caucasian literature corresponded with the Iranian cultural resurgence. Nizami Ganjavi (1141-1209) and Mosis Khorenatsi (1130-1213), two literary men of prominence, one writing in Persian and the other in Armenian, were both from Ganja. In nearly the same period the twenlveth century Georgian poet Shota Rustaveli authored the national epic poem *Vepkhistqaosani* (*The Knight in the panther's skin*) supposedly at the court of Queen Tamar (r. 1184-c. 1213) in Georgia[4].

While the Iranian plateau was under Seljuk and Mongol rule, a new political system of dual structure, a hybrid polity of Turk-Tajik, was established. Nomadic tribesmen constituted the military elites while the sedentary population provided financial and administrative resources. The new geo-political settings and the technical innovation in the sixteenth and seventeenth centuries enhanced by massive flow of peoples and goods resulted in drastic change in the political structures in the region.

The early modern world conditioned the emergence of the new imperial entities. There was an urgent need for the army equipped with firearms and peoples as well as estates to sustain the enlarged royal domain. The Safavids undertook the massive transportation of "the Caucasian society" into the Iranian highlands and integrated the peoples of the Caucasus within the imperial household institutions. The long-standing Iran-Caucasus relations entered a new phase[5].

Beyond Islamic Discourse

V. Minorsky examined the role of Caucasian elements in the remodeled Safavid state structures and called them the "third force". R. Savory confirmed that their presence was already visible in the court of Shah Tahmasp. Babayan et al. researched the phenomena and placed the Caucasus' royal *gholam*s and Armenian merchants as the two pillars of the Safavid empire after the reformation of Shah 'Abbas I (d. 1629)[6]. According to them, the two elements symbolized the imperial transfiguration from the Shah-disciple to the Shah-slave doctrine. This insight connects the discussion on the Caucasian elements in the Safavid empire with broader Islamic slave institutions. The characterization, however, could not escape the traditional understanding of the slaves of the Islamic world, as faceless servants to the absolute monarch often with the Islamized, Asianized connotations. The "Islamic slave paradigm and/or the military slavery in the Muslim polity" also suffered the nationalist interpretations whether they stressed the casualty towards nation building or lamented own weakness[7].

This study intends to bridge the "divided" history of trans-bordering peoples, examining the boundaries they crossed. The current attempt also aims to incorporate the discussion on Safavid "slave" soldiers with the ongoing reconsideration on "slave studies" in the early modern period[8]. Recent studies, expanding its boundaries, depend on the connectedness, inter-dependency, and impact on the representation and collectiveness or collective identities[9].

Traditionally the central argument regarding Ottoman slaves was based on the institutional model, with the influence of Byzantine or Islamic heritage being the main concern of discussion. More nuanced accounts on "Ottoman society with slaves" have recently appeared. These deliberately (re)examined the history of the political elite society including eunuchs (those who transcended gender boundaries), the trans-bordering imperial subjects, and those who crossed the religious boundary, i.e. the "renegades" with their polemical writings, especially in the Mediterranean Sea[10]. For example, Dikici analyzed the careers of Ottoman eunuchs in detail. Her discussion on the eunuchs' origins (outsider or homegrown etc.), and the (re)producing process are worth mentioning. Differences between white and black eunuchs and the former's upholding of male gender role in society as brothers and uncles are similar to Safavid cases. In the reigns of Shah 'Abbas I through 'Abbas II (d. 1666) we confirm the active political role of the royal *gholams* (non-castrated, military elite) who were male relatives of influential eunuchs and their female family members[11]. Various forms of dependency and their mobilizing aspects of early modern Mediterranean bondage are also scrutinized[12]. These works profoundly changed the attitudes of scholars in the relevant fields to the history of trans-bordering peoples and trans-imperial subjects. Senses of the belongings, their strategic choices, conscious or not, and the larger and minor scale identity politics are part of this debate.

Turning to the Safavid political society, royal slaves from the Caucasus played a crucial role in the restructured Safavid state, that of a "household empire", after the reformations of Shah 'Abbas I. They were physically brought into the imperial spaces by forced invitation. They were not simply an oppressed minority, but a symbolic social component of what "royal" meant in the early modern imperial society in Iran. They were directly subordinated to the shah, i.e. they became *khassa* (private) members of the royal household. As royal represented primarily a state in premodern society, their servitude meant they were serving the sovereign and state organizations.

The royal *gholam* corps consisted of one of the two military-elites (the other was *qorchis* corps). They were capable warriors and bureaucratic elites of the empire. This partly confirms the claim of Georgian scholars of twentieth century who described the Georgian *gholams* as the new aristocracy[13]. They, in fact, formed a semi-dynastic elite element of the empire. The elite *gholams* were often from the aristocratic families from Georgia[14]. In this sense they were not representing subaltern elements in the Safavid society or at home in the Caucasus.

When they moved to Iran, however, we witness their refugee status, being separated from the local society they were coming from[15]. Whatever perceived and often associated with the place of their origins, the Caucasian elements in the Safavid society built migrated societies under the imperial jurisdiction. Naturally or paradoxically, in exile they often strengthened their sense of "national" or at least clan identification that they sometimes projected into their land of origin.

We must pay attention to the fact that the Safavid policy was not always consistent over the two centuries. Shah 'Abbas I was eager to transport the local society of the Caucasus and tried to modify the local ruling institutions to his own benefit[16]. Targeted societies suffered the forced migration policies. Nevertheless, Shah Tahmasp I (d. 1576) and Shah 'Abbas I were the only shahs who directly intervened in the local political regime. The two shahs ordered the distribution of land of Georgian nobles sometimes directly. This could be a threat to the power of the Bagratid dynasty. These acts were attested by Persian-Georgian documents but the effect was always limited even in their own time and other shahs seemingly only acknowledged the precedence (thus local landed nobility sometimes utilized the shah's past orders)[17]. At the same time the indigenous principalities and the landed nobilities kept fighting for their autonomy.

The dynamism that those trans-bordering peoples experienced challenges the rejected simple interpretation that they were uprooted absolute slaves for the shah. Rather we pay much attention to the effect in what was meant to be placed in the Safavid subjugation.

Caucasians Experiencing "Mixed" Subaltern Moment

To investigate the historical realities of these "Caucasian captives" in Safavid society, a socio-economic approach is difficult to apply given the lack of static data and source materials[18]. Herein we pay more attention to their spontaneous adaptation to local society as is symbolized by churches in New Julfa, endorsing local customs with multi-cultural influences. Considering this subaltern moment as experienced by these Caucasian migrants to the Safavid imperial society, several narratives of the "Caucasus slaves" by European travelers are scrutinized to explore the meaning of the subordinate.

In 1617 Davud Beg, head of hundred *gholam* soldiers (*yuzbashi*), welcomed the Italian traveler Pietro Della Valle to the suburb of Isfahan. Della Valle was astonished at the dazzling clothes he wore. Davud deliberately told him that even a humble servant had such clothes[19]. Davud was a son of Allahverdi Khan, the governor-general of Fars, the most prominent *amir* of the whole empire and the most successful "shah's slave"[20]. They became state elite in the Safavid "household empire" portrayed themselves as humble servants of the shah. In his statement and attitude, logic, reality and perceptions (of one's own and those from societies) overlapped.

The Spanish ambassador García de Silva Figueroa was in Iran around the same period and met a young Georgian boy who was in a dance company[21]. He might have been an actual victim of the Safavid expedition into Georgia. No longer paying much respect to religious items, the boy handed an icon of Holy Mother to de Silva Figueroa, the latter praised the act of devotion[22]. These two men of Georgian origin, one from the highest stratum of society and the other from its lowest, were both immigrants (or their direct descendants) to Iran. We remember that Allahverdi's ancestry is not easily traced and Allahverdi could had only a modest origin in Georgian aristocratic society (possibly the Undiladze clan). Emamqoli, Allahverdi's son and successor, strengthened his Georgian connections by the shah's will and this contributed to the total downfall of his family early in Safi's reign. This family experienced mixed social tensions, i.e. a minor Georgian noble became the richest provincial ruler, cultivating "national" ties, and inviting calamity in the end[23]. We recognize the various range of social connotation behind the realities.

Della Valle's description includes extensive information on the peoples from the Caucasus living in the Safavid realm. He visited Iran during the 1610s when Shah 'Abbas undertook a policy of forced migration on a monumental scale in the Caucasus. In eastern Georgia hundreds of thousands were registered to be sent to

Iranian highlands. He witnessed the immigrant society in Mazandaran and elsewhere. One of those "forced hostages" became his second wife. He married a Georgian girl Mariuccia after his return to Rome. She was then adopted by his first wife Maani in Isfahan. According to Della Valle Mariuccia's original name was Tinatin Ziba[24], perhaps a combination of the names of the Georgian "Tinatin" and the Persian "Ziba" (meaning beautiful). She was a refugee, possibly escaping the Safavid invasion, but part of the great paradox was the fact that she moved to the Safavid realm where her relative was serving the shah. The latter then became afraid of forced conversion and entrusted her to Maani. This story contains many entangled social moments full of complexity that includes serious decisions taken in a series of crucial situations[25]. Their actions symbolized the various phases of Safavid subaltern moments the Caucasian immigrant experienced.

We could further observe the overlapping nexus. Della Valle reported that Abedik, an Armenian merchant, liberated forty thousand Christian captives by paying their ransoms. Abedik borrowed the sum from Khusraw Khan, an influential *gholam* and the governor-general of Shirvan, offering silk and his property in security. Khusraw was an Armenian by origin and his house was situated in New Julfa[26]. As a darugha of the city, Khusraw was in charge of 200 tomans' annual tribute to the shah paid by Julfa Armenians. He shared this responsibility with Safraz, a kalantar of New Julfa who was a son of the first kalantar of the district Khoja Safar. In the spring of 1637, Shah Safi visited Khusraw's house with the Mughal ambassador on the day of Christian religious ceremony[27]. Thus the converted elite courtiers acted partly as "representatives" of his former co-believers[28]. His son Allaverdi became one of the most influential courtiers at the time of 'Abbas II. As a governor-general of Shirvan, located near the North Caucasus, Khusraw was sending young boys and girls to the central court for the New Year tribute. Instead of simple terminology of "migration", and originally voluntary or not, we observe an intriguing nexus of Christians and the former Christians emerged in Safavid society as they were liberated, reunited, financed, presented, converted, donated, etc[29]. Della Valle also left us a unique observation. Each youth sent by Khusraw Khan wore their local dress, meaning they had not lost their sense of where they were even as they preserved and showed their "original identities"[30]

Question of Servitude

The traditional understanding of "Islamic slave soldiers" is that the forcibly removed people became rootless slaves in the host polity. Their existence was invisible and absent in the modern historiographies of nationalized homeland influenced by strong nationalist discourse as well as the "host society" and its successor "nation" state. Both the societies where they originated and to which they immigrated seemingly accepted a unilateral view on the "Caucasian elements" in the Safavid imperial society. A countless number of people left their homeland not of their own free will. The Caucasus was known for slave trading from ancient times[31]. Their history, at the same time, is witness to a large number of trans-imperial military elites[32]. This seemingly paradoxical phenomenon was a part of geo-political features of the Caucasus region as a periphery, loosely connected with neighboring imperial polities and civilizations.

The Safavid *gholam* phenomenon had a specific feature. The resurgence of Safavid power in the region during the reign of Shah 'Abbas saw the rise of Caucasian elements inside the imperial administration. The region was under Ottoman rule during the first two decades of 'Abbas's reign and the Safavid army included many Caucasian elements at the reconquest of the region during the 1603-07 war. Naturally the Caucasian elements in the royal court exercised a certain leverage because the shah's recovery operation led to the reorganization of the political order in the north-west frontier of the Safavid empire and its relationship with the indigenous societies. At the same time, this often happened on the broader political stage of international politics. Ottoman military pressure was constant throughout 'Abbas's reign. Competition and resistance among the local powers influenced the certain political behavior of the imperial elites and thus produced its own dynamics inside the court. The "slave" elites of the Safavid dynasty represented both the central and peripheral dynamics bearing the label of imperial elites.

As a matter of fact, the erasing of the previous identity, as had been stressed in the previous studies on the Middle Eastern military slavery, does not apply in the Safavid case. In reality the identity of their places of origin could matter[33]. Adding different strata could be a key matter of concern. The reality of servitude and (inter-)dependency of the trans-bordering imperial elites of the Safavid dynasty should be investigated.

The problem is further complicated in the Safavid case when "slave elements" from the Caucasus represented the royal. The peripheral-central dynamics and their "duality" echoed the making of a household empire that came about through the new elements which had been private but "official" in the newly transformed Safavid state after the reign of Shah 'Abbas. This was partly slave elites representing imperial agency even while maintaining their local and peripheral identity. The Safavid empire embraced Caucasian society through 'Abbas's clear perceptions of this element, even his dependency on them and their empowerment through frequent interventions.

Safavid policy was inclusive but also exclusive. The Caucasian communities forcefully invited to Iranian soil were becoming a constituency of a social mosaic. Exclusive was their role as royal agents. The case of New Julfa is symbolic: for nearly a half century it was semi-closed suburb settlement in the imperial capital and Mohammad Beg, the only grand vizier of Armenian lineage in Safavid history, practically "opened" the district for other Armenians. Until then the main city of Isfahan and New Julfa were linked by a bridge constructed by Allah Verdi Khan. It boldly explains the forceful invitation and integration of peripheral elements in the making of early-modern empires[34]. This led to the preservation of collectiveness with their local background intact, and was one of the unique features of Iranian royal subjects. They were functioning both as the political elite and/or state slaves, being a trans-bordering middlemen who had complex identity assets.

The life of Parsadan Gorgijanidze, as we see, exemplified the role of intermediator between the central and peripheral societ(ies) which reflected his complex background. The imperial dependency on the human resources of cross-bordering zone paradoxically produced the central elite of the Middle Eastern polity. We will clearly observe the solid dynamism that Safavid Caucasian "subalterns" experienced and relied on, which offers more integrated view through the life of Parsadan Gorgijanize, a "Georgian" imperial officer serving the Safavid shahs in the second half of the seventeenth century.

Life of Parsadan Gorgijanidze

Parsadan Gorgijanidze was originally from Gori in Georgia and was probably born around 1626. He finished copying his Georgian translation of *Jamiʿ-i ʿAbbasi* (on which see further below) in October (*ghvinobis tve* or month of wine) 1691 at the age of 65, according to his own statement[35]. It is worth mentioning that he seemed to have no aristocratic lineage, and thus was not of the Georgian landed nobility which produced many powerful Safavid *gholam*s. M-F. Brossett suggested that he hailed from Armenians by citing a reference in Gorgijanidze's chronicle[36]. King Rostom, Safavid *vali* of Kartli (1633-58) and Kakheti (1648-56), a Bagratid (illegitimate) prince who was a Muslim and returned from the Safavid central court, picked him up when Gorgijanidze was ten years old and raised him at the Georgian court in a Perso-phile atmosphere[37].

In 1656 the reigning shah, ʿAbbas II, requested that King Rostom, who held the post of *darugha* (military mayor) of imperial capital Isfahan from around 1619 to his death in 1658, send a new *naib* (deputy) to the capital. Rostom chose Parsadan Gorgijanidze who converted to Islam for this occasion and was officially recognized as acting mayor of the city. After a short while, Gorgijanidze was forced to leave the post because of a quarrel with the *divanbegi* (supreme judge of the court), as will be discussed in the next section.

After his dismissal from the post, we cannot trace his career from the few Persian chronicles available on the central court during the long reign of Shah Solayman (r. 1666-94). However, as Parsadan Gorgijanidze was an enthusiastic writer, we can follow his career and some of personal life through his own statements. He was granted the post of *ishīk-aqasī* (royal chamberlain) and five villages near Gulpayigan as a fief by ʿAbbas II. A short while after his dismissal King Rostom died in 1658 and in consequence, Gorjijanidze chose to remain in Isfahan, spending the rest of his life in the shah's service[38].

At the Shah's court, Parsadan Gorgijanidze was an active and energetic state official. It is also worth noting that, according to his description, his brothers Aleksandre and Meliksadat were promoted to ranking positions as *zargarbashi* (head of the jewellers' department) and *yuzbashi* (centurion), respectively. Gorgijanidze's son Davit was given the post of *ishik-aqasi* when he was sixteen years old[39]. Certainly, Gorgijanidze was an example of the Caucasian servants who made a successful career in the Safavid political system as part of the royal *gholam* institution. At the same time, as Gorgijanidze describes in his *History of Georgia*, he sometimes suffered from the shah's wrath and fell from his grace. Despite serving at the imperial court, he was never cut off from his origins, but rather made use of his local connections. In his works, he repeatedly refers to his interventions in Georgian politics quite possibly with the power of Safavid imperial authority.

His cultural activity, no less energetic than his political one, represents a unique imprint of his identity as an imperial bureaucrat from a periphery. He edited a Georgian-Arabic-Persian dictionary and translated *Jami'-i 'Abbasi* into Georgian (discussed at the end of this article). Gorgijanidze also played an active role in producing a Georgian prose version of the *Shah-nama*. His *History of Georgia*, although no clear original title has yet been identified, written around the beginning of the 1690s in Isfahan, renewed Georgian historical writings which had been interrupted for centuries[40]. This work is important, as it completes Georgian history from the conversion of a Georgian king to Christianity up to Gorgijanidze's own time. It is worth noting that Gorgijanidze was engaged in this work a decade before the Georgian cultural revival of the eighteenth century. The most remarkable representative of this movement was a famous scholar-king Vakhtang IV (also called Hosaynqoli Khan), the last *Safavid vali* of Georgian Kartli[41]. Gorgijanidze used many Persian as well as Georgian and Armenian chronicles as source materials[42]. The original autograph manuscripts are now in the National Centre of Manuscripts (H-2140 and H-2492) in Tbilisi[43]. In this work he boasted of his service as well as the favours he received from King Rostom.

A "Georgian" Bureaucrat in the Safavid Political Society

Gorgijanidze would have been thirty years old when he arrived the imperial court and started his job. Gorgijanidze was sent to Isfahan as an acting mayor when his predecessor Mir Qasem had lost his job for having been accused of a soft attitude towards drinking. Parsadan Gorgijanidze converted to Islam since an "infidel never ruled the Muslims", which meant Gorgijanidze was still a Christian in Georgia. According to his statement, Gorgijanidze had visited Gilan and Qazvin before. As a close servant of Rostom, he must have been accustomed to Safavid court practices. However, the local resident turned their back on the acting mayor for he was harsh towards the city population, especially the craftsmen. Then, after a short while, Gorgijanidze was forced to leave the post because of a quarrel with the *divanbegī*[44].

Even if Gorgijanidze received a sufficient education and obtained administrative skills as an imperial official, the Caucasian elements, new participants to the Safavid political society, sometimes suffered and were opposed by older, established political blocs. The Safavid chronicler Valiquli Shamlu describes Gorgijanidze's name as *farsimadan beyg* (not Persian speaking) which clearly displays the Irano-Turkic perspectives towards those imperial subjects from the Caucasus[45]. This irony could be interpreted as an expression of resentment by a Turkic official from the Shamlu clan, a key member of the Qizilbash tribal confederation, towards an administrator from a periphery. The phrasing in fact is more complex as for Valiquli made his own career in the far-eastern provincial city of Qandahar, a rather exceptional 'man of the pen' from Qizilbash origin. He also occupied the post of *nazer* of Qandahar, an important civil post, while at the top of city's military-civil administration the governor-general was Zolfaqar Khan (Otar Khan), eldest brother of influential Georgian siblings of aristocratic origin (from Baratashvili-Orbelishvili or Orbeliani family). Things were getting more complicated because the family of Otar seems to have had poor political relations with Gorgijanidze, as we discuss later.

Gorgijanidze wrote about his son Davit's imprisonment, and refers to the antagonism between *qorchi*s and *gholam*s, thus attesting to visible tension between the two blocks of military-administrative elites). At the same time he was an outsider to Georgian aristocratic society which produced many powerful royal *gholam*s. When he describes that his patron Rostom enthroned Safi and Rostom became de fact ruler of the Safavid empire, he certainly recognizes himself an insider and a participant in Safavid imperial politics[46]. For all these contradictory standings in Safavid society Gorgijanidze seems to maintain his Georgian-ness or rather exposed his identity and experiences of a shah's servant hailing from a land of Georgia. But he was never fully synchronized with imperial "identity". Judging from his way of writing about Georgia's history in the Safavid period, Georgia was recognized as an historical entity contested by various Georgian groups. That is natural, for he would consult his writings from Queen Mariam's manuscript of "Life of Georgia", compiled during the zenith of Georgian united kingdom in twelveth-thirteenth centuries in the relevant part of his chronicle. Queen Mariam (from the Dadiani family, rulers of Samegrelo principality in western Georgia, strategic partner of Kartvelian king) behaved as a protector of Christianity in Georgia while her husband the Muslim king Rostom acted as the faithful servant and representative of Safavid authority in Georgia. The language of Gorgijanidze's writings was very simple and rather colloquial in style in contrast with previous and later Georgian chronicles (this phenomenon could reflect a kind of popularization or democratization of the culture in the late Safavid age). Thus Gogijanidze's "Georgian" identity was also not simply synchronized with its upper stratum. His political activity is worth considering from this perspective as well.

Considering the issues on his identification, a unique sentence described in the introduction of his translation of *Jami'-i 'Abbasi* is worth mentioning[47]. This work was originally written by Shaykh Baha' al-Din 'Ameli °n the commission of Shah 'Abbas I. As the first Shi'ite manual in Persian it explains the legal obligations to the average believers for their practical use[48]. At the beginning of his translation, Gorgijanidze states that 'Muslims are ruled by this knowledge, while it does not overwhelm Christians. Moreover, it is better for every man to know every religion to some extent, so that they can understand good and evil.[49]' This suggests an openness towards the value of both religions, possibly stemming from Gorgijanidze's mixed religious identity, that is a cosmopolitan viewpoint. It could also indicate strong resentment among Georgians against Safavid religious pressure if we understand his words as a justification to a certain degree. Parsadan Gorgijanidze made this translation during his six-year exile in Shushtar, in south-west Iran, in 1666-71[50].

Parsadan Gorgijanidze's Exile to Shushtar

How was Gorgijanidze involved in Georgian politics? As described in the introduction, the close involvement of *gholam-mamluk* elements in the politics of their homeland does not fit the generally accepted theory. Parsadan Gorgijanidze even boasts about his influence in Georgian politics in his chronicle. According to him, Kakhaberi's son, Gorjaspi, was appointed as acting governor of the Kakheti province of Georgia by Shah 'Abbas II as a result of Gorgijanidze's efforts[51]. This must have happened at the end of the 1650's or the beginning of the 1660's. It is worth noting that, according to his own statements, these interventions led to his downfall at least twice. First in 1666, when he went into a six-year internal exile in Shushtar, in south-western Iran[52]. Some twenty years later, in 1689, Gorgijanidze lost the confidence of Shah Solayman when his relationship with Qiasi, vizier of Erekle I/Shahnazar (king of Kartli 1688-1703), deteriorated and king Erekle I was also found to be hostile to him[53]. Thus he seemed to have repeated the same mistake, namely he failed to intervene in the political events in Georgia, thus causing his own downfall. Interestingly these downfalls gave him the time and the stimulus to probe his Georgian identity by composing Georgian prose and the chronicle; his withdrawal from the political scene may have provided him with the motivation and opportunity to take up cultural activities.

The short poetic phrases which Gorgijanidze inserted when he copied a Georgian version of the *Shah-nama* during his six-years exile in Shushtar are also worth consideration. These textual amendments give us interesting information on the life and activities of Parsadan Gorgijanidze, though they are yet to be investigated in a wider political context. By combining information garnered from Georgian and Persian sources we can shed light on the historical conditions in which Gorgijanidze lived. This also provides insight into the political relationship between Georgia and Iran at that time, which might have regulated and influenced the activities of Caucasians in Safavid service, a subject rarely investigated despite its specific significance. In this work interesting phrases can be found added by Gorgijanidze to the beginning and the end of the text.

> The Georgian king denounced me to the sovereign of Iran,
> Never hearing my case, they ordered to send me to the country of Arabs.
> I depart. I trust God, and Satan never deceives me.
> I never surrender if God's blessing is with me.
> k'art'velt'a mep'em mabezgha khemtsip'es eranelt'ana,
> ar gamikit'khes arabet's ubrdzanes ch'emi tsatana.
> tsamovel, ghmert'sa mivendev, ver mamatqueebs satana
> da aras vepoo, t'u ghmert'i tsqalobit' iqos ch'emt'ana[54].

> I, Parsadan, a poet, am kept in Shushtar as a common prisoner.
> I have no son to help me, neither a king nor a nation
> My younger brother, the handsome Meliksad(at) is here with me,
> God, give me hope and render me your assistance.[55]
> shushtars ubralod tqvet viqav p'arsadan leksis tseria,
> ara mqavs mshveli, momkhmare, artsmepe, artsa eria,
> dzma makhlavs ch'emi umtsrosi, meliksed shvenieria,
> da shvelad, imedad metsa mqavs mpqrobeli sakhieria[56]

As we see, the author laments his misfortune, his unjust exile to Shushtar, and prays to God for help. Parsadan Gorgijanidze blames the 'Georgian king' for his troubles. K. Kekelidze quoted the poem in his *History of Old Georgian Literature*[57]. One of the most knowledgeable researchers on Gorgijanidze's life and works, R. Kiknadze, assumed that by the 'Georgian king' Parsadan Gorgijanidze was referring to Vakhtang V/ Shahnavaz (*vali* of Georgian Kartli in 1658-76) in this passage, though he did not investigate this further[58].

Persian chronicles provide us with useful information concerning the Governor of Shushtar at the time of Gorgijanidze's exile. According to *Kholasat al-siyar* and *Khold-e barin*, Shah Safi I granted the title of sultan to certain Vakhushti beg, *yuzbashi* of the *gholam* corps, and appointed him the governor of Shushtar in 1632[59]. This date is attested by *Tazkera-ye Shushtar*, a work dedicated to the local history of Shushtar. The latter's author, 'Abd-Allah Husaynī Shushtari, wrote that Vakhushti ruled Shushtar until the year 1078/1667-68. After his death, Vakhushti's descendants continued to govern the territory and their activities are recorded even down to the time of Nader Shah Afshar (r. 1736-1747)[60]. This Vakhushti was the second brother of three (or four) siblings of the influential royal *gholam*s from Baratashvili-Orbelishvili clan in Georgia.

Vakhushti's elder brother Otar (Zolfaqar) later became the governor-general (*beglarbegi*) of Qandahar in the reign of Shah 'Abbas II (as already mentioned). Gorjaspi (Mansur), after working as the governor-general of Qandahar and Kerman, was appointed as commander-in-chief of Iranian army (*sepahsalar-e Iran*) and governor-general of Azarbaijan during the reign of Shah Solayman. He became commander of *gholam* corp (*qollar-aqasi*) too[61]. As a result, we can specify their original family name as Baratashvili-Orbelishvili, one of the most powerful landlords (*tavadi*) in Georgian Kartli, who ruled the southern province of its realm, Lower Kartli (*kvemo kartli*).

Vakhtang V Shahnavaz and Qaplan Baratashivli-Orbelishvili

The political situation of Georgia at the time of Gorgijanidze's exile should be taken into account. After the death of King Rostom in 1658, Vakhtang *Mukhranis batoni* (ruler of Mukhran) ascended the throne of Georgian Kartli (Vakhtang V, called Shahnavaz in Persian sources, king or *wali* of Kartli, 1658-76). Vakhtang's career was different from that of his foster-father King Rostom from the beginning. King Rostom spent almost all his life at the Safavid court, acting as *darugha* of Isfahan and *qullar-aqasi*. When he was appointed the *wali* of Georgian Kartli, he was already 67 years old[62]. In contrast Vakhtang had no career at the Safavid central court and spent almost all his life in Georgia. As a representative of Mukhran branch of Bagratid royal family, he was considered to be the greatest of the Georgian landlords for a long time before he came to the throne (Even his father Teimuraz was killed in 1625 in his fight with Safavid army).

Soon after his succession, Vakhtang started to intervene in Imereti, a kingdom in Western Georgia, putting his eldest son, Archil, who was then 14 years old, on its throne in 1661. This event strained relations between the Safavids and the Ottomans, as a peace treaty had given the Ottomans political suzerainty over Western Georgia. Two years later, Vakhtang abandoned his plan and brought Archil back to Kartli as a result of a strong demand made by Ottoman government to the Safavids. Shah 'Abbas II invited Archil to the central court and granted him the governorship of Georgian Kakheti on the condition of converting to Islam[63]. In spite of this initial failure, King Vakhtang continued to pursue a double-edged policy to be influential both in the Safavid court and in the whole of Georgia. For our interest, an essential fact is that Vakhtang's most powerful ally in Georgian Kartli was his father-in-law, the above-mentioned Qaplan Baratashvili-Orbelishvili, the cousin of Vakhushti, governor of Shushtar[64].

Parsadan Gorgijanidze must have been well aware of these family connections. In his work, he often refers to the activities of the Caucasians in the service of the Safavids. Included among those is a *qollar-aqasi* Mansur Khan Baratashvili, who stood by the side of Giorgi XI (also called Shahnavaz II, king or w*ali* of Kartli, 1677-88), heir successor of Vakhtang V Shahnavaz when the *eristavi* of Araghvi complained about him to the shah (this Giorgi later became the last Safavid governor of Qandahar under the name Gorgin Khan and was killed by Mir Wais, leader of the Afghans[65]). Through Mansur's mediation, Giorgi XI managed to gain the shah's confidence for a while. This Mansur Khan (originally Gorjasbi) was the younger brother of Vakhushti. Gorgijanidze must have known that the governor of Shushtar came from Baratashvili-Orbelishvili family and was related to Vakhtang V by marriage. Parsadan Gorgijanidze's poem, translated above, sheds light on his political biography and gains new historical significance by providing us insights into Persian-Georgian relations at that period. It suggests that Parsadan Gorgijanidze's exile to Shushtar occurred under certain political conditions; in other words, he was deported to that city at Vakhtang V Shahnavaz's request, since the governor of Shushtar at that time was Vakhushti Khan, a close relative of Vakhtang's first wife.

Parsadan Gorgijanidze and Georgian Politics

The above-mentioned episode definitely shows the complexity of the Persian-Georgian relationship in those days. Parsadan Gorgijanidze was never cut off from his homeland. The evidence gives the impression that the conflict at the Georgian court was "exported" to the Safavid court in the case of Gorgijanidze's exile. Gorgijanidze was in the service of Safavid central court and, as a result of antagonism with the Georgian king, was expelled from the imperial capital to the provincial city of Shushtar, which was governed by the latter's relative. This complexity was reflected in the political system of the Safavid dynasty as they constituted political elites of the dynasty and this event happened inside Safavid ruling institutions. Not only the Safavid dynasty influenced the politics in Georgia. By introducing the royal *gholams*, the Safavids embraced the local politics along with the Caucasians themselves, or the politics of the inner court and the Caucasian frontier was interrelated.

To understand his position on the Georgian political scene, Gorgijanidze's origin and career should be taken into account. Gorgijanidze was brought up by King Rostom and, despite his lowly origins, was singled out to be the acting mayor of Isfahan. According to his description, many Georgian nobles were opposed to the ascension of Vakhtang V, and the *eristavi* of Araghvi even declared that he never accepted Vakhtang as his patron, for his only patron after Rostom's death was the shah[66]. Vakhtang's initial power base was not strong enough; he was recognized as heir-successor only after Prince Luarsab, a close relative of King Rostom, was shot dead while out hunting (Gorgijanidze assumed the incident was not an accident but the act of an "evil" person) and his brother Vakhtang died shortly afterward in 1652[67]. According to Gorgijanidze, "those who were pleased with wept a great deal and beat their heads as to hide their visions when Luarsab was killed by the incident"[68]. We cannot be specific about the reason for Gorgijanidze's exile to Shushtar but his ability and influence over Georgian politics was never ignored by Vakhtang V. The presence of King Rostom's close servant at the Safavid central court looks disadvantageous to Vakhtang V.

We can also draw some inferences from another political conflict inside Georgia at that time. In 1662, Prince Erekle (I), who belonged to the dynastic branch of Georgian Kakheti and was the grandson of Teimuraz I, returned to Georgia from Russia, where he had been sent and grew up. He stayed in Tusheti, a province of Georgia in the mountains of the Great Caucasus, while trying to find an opportunity to regain the kingship of Kakheti. As mentioned above, Archil II, the eldest son of Vakhtang V, was made ruler of Kakheti in 1663. Prince Erekle was defeated by Vakhtang and failed to capture Kakheti at this time. Erekle finally left Georgia in 1666 and went back to Russia. Later he converted to Islam and was given the governorship of Georgian Kartli in 1688[69]. It is supposed that once the situation in Eastern Georgia was settled according to his interests, Vakhtang asked the shah to keep those opposed to him away from the Safavid central court.

Parsadan Gorgijanidze in-between

It is important to note that Gorgijanidze possessed a dual sense of his identity, as both a Georgian and a servant of the shah. His sense of belonging to the nation and religion should be discussed. He narrated a story from the twelfth century, according to which, the Georgian general Beka Jaqeli contributed much to the victory of the Il-Khanids over Qipchaks. The Il-Khan Hulagu wanted to reward him but this never happened because of the opposition of the Georgian king who envied his servant. Then Gorgijanidze added that a similar case happened to him twice. He contributed much to the profit of Georgian kings, but he not only received nothing in return, but, on the contrary, lost much. Thus, Gorgijanidze consciously had been putting into practice his multiple identities[70].

For his obvious self-identification with Georgian political society, still his "cultural" activity suggests further complicated aspects of its nature. In this regard, the revival of Georgian historical writing during the last quarter of seventeenth century and first quarter of eighteenth century also would be discussed with Parsadan

Gorgijanidze's activity from Safavid perspectives and from the view of changing climate of international surroundings as well. They were not subalterns who were treated badly, oppressed, a social class. They were representing the royal, that is to say "private (*khassa*)" but mostly political and publicized realms of the empire. They were influencing peripheral power politics. In Gorgijanidze's case we understand the Safavid central authority gave powers and means to subaltern element of the local society with its intriguing moments. The Safavid polity tried to increase its authority by inspiring, balancing and bargaining the rivalry among royal Bagratids, among Georgian servants at the court, among royal subjects connected with *khassa* or shah's private authority that was designed by 'Abbas I but they transformed it by their own activities.

In such circumstances, the Georgian political nation reemerged and even expanded though it should not be interpreted as a simple national awakening and exclusive of others. As is known, the Qajar governors of Kakheti issued documents in Georgian. They already became a local element and due to political events at the center and the place they were living, they shifted their allies and created new alliances. In fact, inter-Bagratid rivalry and inter-Qajar rivalry all happened in the framework of Safavid elite households. Each struggle was a result of reflections of their understanding of the self, and also a strategy for survival which thus had political connotations[71].

Conclusion

It is a misunderstanding to conceptualize those forcibly migrated and integrated peoples from the Caucasus (or "Caucasian elements" in a broad sense, a wording of V. Minorsky) as merely a subaltern or an oppressed minority for they were representing the "royal" in various social levels. Yet as Shah 'Abbas I tried to incorporate the "Caucasian society" with their social hierarchy in part, or to reorganize the two realms (geographical and structural) of the Safavid state, we should recognize the various tensions between the different social strata inside and outside the "Caucasus immigrant societies".

Parsadan Gorgijanidze, a "Safavid courtier" of "Georgian" origin, experienced the complex domains resulted from that forced "integration". For him Georgian politics was a major lever to strengthen his position at the Safavid imperial court and, in this regard, he primarily belonged to that political nation. The Safavid power was surely a suzerain authority, yet, paradoxically his account shows partly how Georgians were insiders insofar as imperial politics and that the inner dynamism of Georgian politics affected the sovereign center. At the same time Georgians struggled with each other to their own ends regardless of the imperial concern that had been a source of Gorgijanidze's lamentation but provided him a place in imperial politics.

We should exclude the simple interpretation of dichotomy including inner and outer dynamics, imperial and local tensions, "national" rivalries, directions from above and below. Parsadan Gorgijanidze is a good example to think of what we call "frontier phenomenon". We pay more attention to his "In-between-ness", rather than "subaltern" because Gorgijanidze is thought to have been a successful imperial courtier although, again we stress that, his chronicle contains lamentations and complaints about his political downfalls caused by his "national affiliations".

The Georgian case, or the Georgian angle, should be also discussed with regard to their multiple diplomatic orientations in the last quarter of the seventeenth century. Archil, eldest son of Vakhtang V, sought Russian aid late in his career for his Christian cause[72]. Ashotan Bagrationi, the ruler of Mukhran, also accelerated his activity as a donor to the monasteries in Mt. Athos[73]. The network spread far to the Aegean Sea. The subaltern moment of Safavid elite of the Caucasus origin should be investigated based on partly the geo-political dimension. Attention should be paid to the complexity of Gorgijanidze's various identities. Leaving aside his important Georgian historical works, however, Gorgijanidze was essentially a Georgian statesman of mixed background, pursuing a complicated career within the early modern Muslim world.

A man of complex identity, Gorgijanidze navigated the world between different religions and nations. The statement at the beginning of his translation represents his cosmopolitan world-view, and can thus be regarded as a unique expression and reflection of the social and political trends in late Safavid society by a member of the "Georgian" imperial elite. His lamentation could also reflect the conservative religious tendency in the late imperial society. The work requires more thorough study, but has clear value for comparative religious, cross-cultural and linguistic studies.

Bibliography

Anonymous, *Tadhkirat al-mulūk: A Manual of Safavid Administration*, ed. and tr. V. Minorsky, London: Messers, Luzac & Co., 1943.

Aksan, Virginia H., "What's Up in Ottoman Studies?", *Journal of the Ottoman and Turkish Studies Association*, 1:1-2 (2014), 3-21.

Babaie, Sussan, Kathryn Babayan, Ina Baghdiantz-McCabe, Massumeh Farhad, *Slaves of the Shah: New Elites of Safavid Iran*, London and New York: I.B.Tauris, 2004.

Bagrationi, Vakhushti, *Aghtsera sameposa sakartvelosa (Description of the Kingdom of Georgia)*, ed. S. Qaukhchishvili, *Kartlis tskhovreba (The Georgian chronicles)* IV, Tbilisi: Sabchota Sakartvelo, 1973.

Bakuradze, Lia, Marina Beridze and Zakharia Pourtskhvanidze, "A Georgian Language Island in Iran: Fereydani Georgian", *Iranian Studies*, 53-3/4 (2020), 489-550.

Baskins, Cristelle, "Lost in translation: Portraits of Sitti Maani Gioerida della Valle in Baroque Rome", *Early Modern Women: An Interdisciplinary Journal*, 7 (2012), 241–260.

Bosworth, C. E., "Ghulam ii. Persia", *Encyclopedia of Islam, The Encyclopaedia of Islam*, 2nd ed., vol. II, Leiden-London: E.J.Brill, 1991, 1081-1084.

Chagnon, Michael, "Cloath'd in Several Modes: Oil-on-Canvas Painting and the Iconography of Human Variety in Early Modern Iran", in *The Fascination of Persia: The Persian-European Dialogue in Seventeenth-Century Art & Contemporary Art of Teheran*, ed. Axel Langer, Zürich: Verlag Scheidegger & Spiess AG, 2013, 238-263.

Chardin, Jean, *Voyages de Chevalier Chardin, en Perse, et autres lieux de l'Orient*, ed. L. Langrès, 10 vols., Paris: Normant, 1811.

Chichinadze, Zurab, *Kartuli mtserloba mechvidmete saukuneshi* (Georgian writings in the seventeenth century), Tbilisi: Tipografiya Kheladze, 1888.

Chick, Herbert (ed. and tr.), *A Chronicle of the Carmelites in Persia: The Safavids and the Papal Mission of the 17th and 18th Centuries*, New York: I.B.Tauris, 2012.

Colley, Linda, *Captives: The Story of Britain's Pursuit of Empire and how its Soldiers and Civilians Were Held Captive by the Dream of Global Supremacy*, New York: Jonathan Cape Ltd, 2002.

Conermann, Stephan and Gül Şen, eds., *Slaves and Slave Agency in the Ottoman Empire*, Bonn: Bonn University Press, 2020.

Davitashvili, Sopio, "Ori Ashotan Mukhranbatonis moghvatseobis kvali Atonis tsm. mtaze (Two lords of Mukhrani with name Ashotan in the Iveron monastery of Holy Mountane)", *Kristianobis kvlevebi (Christian researches)*, V (2010), 9-17.

Davitashvili, Sopio, "Atonis Iveriis ghvtismshoblis khatis sachdilobelis khatis sachrdilobeli karavi (The shade tent of the Virgin's icon at the Iviron monastery on Mount Athos)", *Saistorio krebuli (Historical collections)*, II (2012), 313-347.

De Castelli, Don Kristoforo, *Tsnobebi da albomi Sakartvelos shesakheb (Information and Albam about Georgia)*, tr. and ed. B. Giorgadze, Tbilisi: Metsniereba, 1976.

De Silva Figueroa, Don Garcia, *Safarname-ye Don Garcia de Silva Figueroa*, tr. Gholamreza Sami'I, Tehran: Nashr-e nou, 1984/85 (1363).

Della Valle, Pietro, *Les Famevx voyages de Pietro della Valle, gentil-homme romain, svrnommé l'illvstre voyagevr; avec vn denombrement tres-exact des choses les plus curieuses, et les plus remarquables qu'il a veuës dans la Turquie, l'Egypte, la Palestine, la Perse, et les Indes orientales*, Paris: Chez Gervais Clovzier, 1663-64; *Safar-nama-ye Pietro Della Valle*, tr. Shoa-al-Din Shafa, Tehran: Entesharat-e benagah-e tarjome va nashr-e ketab, 1969 (1348).

Dikici, Ezgi, "The Making of Ottoman Court Eunuchs: Origins, Recruitment Paths, Family Ties, and 'Domestic Production'", *Archivum Ottomanicum*, 30 (2013), 105–136.

Dundua, Nugzar (ed.), *Kartul-sparsuli (orenovani) istoriuli sabutebi (XVI-XVII ss.) (Georgian-Persian (bilingual) historical documents XVI-XVII centuries)*, Tbilisi: Metsniereba, 1984.

Dumbadze, Mamia, V. Guchua, and B. Giorgadze, "Tsqaroebisa da literaturis mimokhilva-i Tsqaroebi da literature kartul da evropul enebze (Researches on the sources and literature i.: Sources and literature in Georgian and European languages)", in *Sakartvelos istoriis narkvevebi (Studies on the Georgian history)* IV, ed. Mamia Dumbadze, Tbilisi: Sabchota Sakartvelo, 1973, 21-61.

Dursteler, Eric R., *Renegade Women. Gender, Identity, and Boundaries in the Early Modern Mediterranean*, Baltimore: Johns Hopkins University Press, 2011.

Dursteler, Eric R., "Tobias P. Graf, *The Sultan's Renegades: Christian-European Converts to Islam and the Making of the Ottoman Elite, 1575–1610*", *International Journal of Middle East Studies*, 50 (2018), 804-806.

Encyclopedia Iranica (https://www.iranicaonline.org/ see the relevant web pages on the entries: "Della Valle, Pietro" by John Gurney; "Georgia iv. Literary contacts with Persia" by Aleksandre Gvakharia; "Jame'-e 'Abbasi" by Sajjad Rizvi; "Julfa i. Safavid period" by Vazken S. Ghougassian, "Gorgijanidze, Parsadan" by Jamshid Giunashvili; "Georgia vii. Georgian in the Safavid Administration" by Rudi Matthee)

Erdem, Y. Hakan, *Slavery in the Ottoman Empire and its Demise, 1800–1909*, New York: Palgrave Macmillan, 1996.

Esfahani, Mohammad-Ma'sum b. Khwajagi, *Kholasat al-siyar: tarikh-e ruzgar-e Shah Safi Safavi*, ed. Iraj Afshar, Tehran: Entesharat-e elmi, 1989.

Ferguson, Michael and Ehud R. Toledano, "Ottoman Slavery and Abolition in the Nineteenth Century", in *The Cambridge World History of Slavery*, vol.4, eds. David Eltis, Stanley L. Engerman, Seymour Drescher, David Richardson, Cambridge: Cambridge University Press, 2017, 197-225.

Gabashvili, Varelian, "Sep'iant'a sakhelmtsip'o (Safavid State)", *Narkvevebi Makhlobeli Aghmosavlet'is istoriidan (Studies on the history of Near East)*, Tbilisi: Tbilisis sakhelmtsipo universitetis gamomtsemloba, 1957, 234-245.

Gobejishvili, M. "Parsadan Gorgijaniżis saistorio tkhzulebis leningraduli H 41 nusxis minacerebi" (Scription of the H41 manuscript of Parsadan Gorgijanidze's historical writings in Leningrad), *Kartuli tsqarotmtsodneoba (Reserches on the Georgian sources)*, 5 (1978), 70-75.

Gorgijanidze, Parsadan, H-2140 and H-2492 (National Center of Manuscripts in Tbilisi) include his history of Georgia which was published as Gorgijanidze, Parsadan, "Parsadan Giorgijanidzis istoria" (Parsadan Gorgijanidze's history), *Saistorio moambe (The historical journal)*, 2 (1925), 198-316, also was published as a separate book in Tbilisi (Tpilisi) in 1926. French Translation: "Extraits de l'Histoire de Pharsadan Giorgidjanidzé" tr. M. Brosset, *Histoire de la Géorgie depuis l'Antiquité jusqu'au xixe siècle*, Partie 2, St. Petersburg: Académie impériale des sciences, 1856. 509-561; Russian Translation: *Istoriya Gruzii* tr. R. K. Kiknadze and V. S. Puturidze, Tbilisi: Metsniereba, 1990.

Gorgijanidze, Parsadan, S-174 (National Center of Manuscripts in Tbilisi) and M-27 (Institute of Oriental Manuscripts of the Russian Academy of Sciences in St. Petersburg) include *Jami'-i 'Abbasi ba lughat-i Gurji* or *Jamiabasi kartulad ('Jami'-i 'Abbasi in the Georgian language'* and other contents, a part is published as *Kartul-arabul-sparsuli leksikoni (Georgian-Arabic-Persian dictionary of P.Gorgijanidze)*, ed. Vladimer Puturidze, Tbilisi: Sakartvelos SSR metsnierebata akademiis gamomtsemloba, 1941.

Graf, Tobias P., *The Sultan's Renegades: Christian-European Converts to Islam and the Making of the Ottoman Elite, 1575–1610*, Oxford: Oxford University Press, 2017.

Güngörürle, Selim, "Diplomacy and Political Relations between the Ottoman Empire and Safavid Iran, 1649-1722", Ph. D. dissertation, Georgetown University, 2016.

Gürkan, Emrah Safa, "Mediating Boundaries: Mediterranean Go-Betweens and Cross-Confessional Diplomacy in Constantinople, 1560-1600", *Journal of Early Modern History*, 19 (2015), 107-128.

Inozemtseva, Elena, "On the History of Slave-Trade in Dagestan", *Iran and the Caucasus*, 10: 2 (2006), 181-189.

Jafariyan, Rasul, "Agahiha-ye taze darbare-ye gholaman va kanizegan dar doure-ye Safavi", *Payam-e baharestan*, 24 (2011-12/1390), 1833-1924.

Jamburia, Givi, "Sakartvelos politikuri vitareba XVII s. 30-90-ian tslebshi (Political condition of Goergia in the years of 30-90 of the seventeenth century)," in *Sakartvelos istoriis narkvevebi (Studies on the Georgian history)* IV, ed. Mamia Dumbadze, Tbilisi: Sabchota Sakartvelo, 1973, 312-356.

Janashvili, M., *Parsadan Gorgijanidze da misni shromani* (Parsadan Gorgijanidze and his works), Tbilisi: Stamba M. Sharadzisa da amkh., 1896.

Javakhishvili, Ivane, *Dzveli kartuli saistorio mtserloba* (Old Georgian historical writings), Tbilisi: Stalinis sakhelobis Tbilisis sakhelmtsipo universitetis gamomtsemloba, 1945.

Jikuri, Okropiri and Hirotake Maeda, "Georgian Antiquities from Karakallou Monastery (Mount Athos)", paper presented at *The 16th Annual International Kartvelological Conference in Memory of St. Grigol Peradze*, December 8, 2018, Warsaw: University of Warsaw.

Katsitadze, D., "Isev Parsadan Gorgijanidzis erti sparsulenovani tsqaros shesakheb" (Once again on a Persian source of Parsadan Gorgijanidze), *Aghmosavluri pilologia (Eastern Philology)*, 2 (1972), 153-159.

Kiknadze, Revaz, *Parsadan Gorgijanidze da "istoriani da azmani sharavandendtani" (Parsadan Gorgijanidze and 'A history and praise of the kings')*, Tbilisi: Metsniereba, 1975.

Kiknadze, Revaz, *Sakartvelos istoriis tsqarotmtsodneobis sakitkhebi (Studies on the source materials of history of Georgia)*, Tbilisi: Metsniereba, 1982.

Komaroff, Linda, *Gifts of the Sultan: The Arts of Giving at the Islamic Courts*, New Haven and London: Yale University Press, 2011.

Krstić, Tijana, "Contesting Subjecthood and Sovereignty in Ottoman Galata in the Age of Confessionalization: Moriscos and the Carazo Affair, 1613–1617", *Oriente Moderno*, 93-2 (2013), 422–453.

Kutsia, Karlo, "Kavkasiuri elementi Sep'ianta Iranis politikur sarbilze (Caucasian Elements in the Safavid Political Stage)", *Makhlobeli Aghmosavlet'is istoriis sakitkhebi (Questions on the Near Eastern History)*, vol.1, Tbilisi: Sakartvelos SSR metsnierebata akademiis gamomtsmloba, 1963, 65-79.

Maeda, Hirotake, "On the Ethno-Social Background of Four Gholam Families from Georgia in Safavid Iran," *Studia Iranica*, 32 (2003), 243-278.

Maeda, Hirotake, "The Forced Migrations and Reorganisation of the Regional Order in the Caucasus by Safavid Iran: Preconditions and Developments Described by Fazli Khuzani," in *Reconstruction and Interaction of Slavic Eurasia and its Neighbouring Worlds*, eds. Ieda, Osamu and Uyama, Tomohiko, Sapporo: Slavic Research Center, 2006, 237-271.

Maeda, Hirotake, "The Household of Allahverdi Khan: An Example of Patronage Network in Safavid Iran," in *Géorgie et sa capitale Tbilissi entre Perse et Europe*, eds. F. Hellot and I. Nathchebia, Paris-Tbilissi: l'Harmattan, 2007, 149-170.

Maeda, Hirotake, "Parsadan Gorgijanidze's Exile in Shushtar. A Biographical Episode of a Georgian Official in the Service of the Safavids", *Studies on Persianate Societies*, 1-2 (2008), 218-229.

Maeda, Hirotake, "Slave Elites Who Returned Home: Georgian *Vali*-king Rostom and the Safavid Household Empire," *Memoirs of the Research Department of the Toyo Bunko*, 69 (2011), 97-127.

Maeda, Hirotake, "Exploitation of the Frontier: The Caucasus Policy of Shah 'Abbas I," in Willem Floor and Edmund Herzig eds., *Iran and the World in the Safavid Age*, London: I. B. Tauris, 2012, 471-489.

Maeda, Hirotake, "Transcending Boundaries: When the Mamluk Legacy Meets a Family of Armeno-Georgian Interpreters", in *Constellations of the Caucasus: Empires, Peoples, and Faiths*, ed. Michael A. Reynolds, Princeton: Markus Wiener Publishers, 2016, 63-85.

Maeda, Hirotake, "Pasadan Gogijanidze" "Jami-i 'Abbasi bi lughat-i Gurji", in *Christian-Muslim relations. A bibliographical history volume 10 Ottoman and Safavid Empires (1600-1700)*, eds. David Thomas and John Chesworth, Leiden and Boston: Brill, 2017, 654-657, 658-659.

Maeda, Hirotake, "Against All Odds: the Safavids and the Georgians", in *The Safavid World*, ed. Rudi Matthee, London: Routledge, 2021, 125-43.

Marmon, Shaun, ed., *Slavery in Islamic Middle East*, Princeton: Markus Wiener Publishers, 1999.

Matthee, Rudi, "The Career of Mohammad Beg, Grand Vizier of Shah 'Abbas II (r. 1642-1666)", *Iranian Studies*, 24 (1991), 17-36.

Matthee, Rudi, *Persia in Crisis: Safavid Decline and the Fall of Isfahan*, London and New York: I.B.Tauris, 2012.

Metreveli, Elene, ed., *Kartul khelnatserta agtseriloba. Qopili kartvelta shoris tserakitkhvis gamavrtselebeli sazogadoebis (S) kolekts'ia* (Catalogue of Georgian manuscripts: Collections of the Former Society for the Spreading of Literacy among Georgians (S)), Tbilisi: Sakartvelos SSR metsnierebata akademiis gamomtsmloba, 1960.

Oberling, P. "Georgians and Circassians in Iran", *Studia Caucasica*, 1 (1963), 127-143.

Olearius, Adam, *Relation dv voyage de moscovie, tartarie, et de perse, fait a l'occasion d'vne ambassade, Enuoyée au Grand-Duc de Moscouie, et de Roy de Perse Par L.R.D.B.*, Paris: Chez Pierre Avbovin, 1656; *Safarnāme-ye Adam Olearius*, tr. Mohandes Hoseyn Kordbachche, 2 vols., Tehran: Sherkat-e ketab-e bara-ye hame, 1990/91 (1369).

Orbeli, R. R., *Gruzinskie rukopisi instituta vostokovedeniya, vypusk I, Istoriya, Geografiya, Puteshestviya, Arkheologiya, Zakonodatel'stvo, Filosofiya, Yazykoznanie, Bibliografiya*, Moskva-Leningrad: Izdatel'stvo Akademii Nauk SSSR, 1956.

Pirdousi, Abu-l-Qasim (Abu al-Qasim Firdawsi), *Shah-names anu mepeta tsignis kartuli versiebi (Georgian versions of Shahnama or the Book of the Kings)*, ed. Iustine Abuladze et al., 2 vols, Tbilisi, 1916, 1934.

Pollack, Sean, "'As One Russian to Another': Prince Petr Ivanovich Bagration's Assimilation of Russian Ways", *Ab Imperio*, no. 4 (2010), 113-142.

Połczyński, Michael, "The Relacyja of Sefer Muratowicz: 1601–1602 Private Royal Envoy of Sigismund III Vasa to Shah 'Abbas I", *Turkish Historical Review*, 5-1 (2014), 59–93.

Puturidze, Vladimir, ed., *Kartul-sparsuli istoriuli sabutebi (Georgian-Persian historical documents)*, Tbilisi: Sakartvelos SSR metsnierebata akademiis gamomtsemloba, 1955.

Puturidze, Vladimir, ed., *Sparsuli istoriuli sabutebi Sakartvelos tsigntsatsavebshi (Persian historical documents in the Georgian libraries)*, tsgni I, nakveti 1-3, Tbilisi: Sakartvelos SSR metsnierebata akademiis gamomtsemloba, Metsniereba, 1961, 1962, 1965.

Qazvini, Mirza Mohammad Taher Vahid, *Tarikh-e jahanara-ye 'Abbasi*, ed. Seyyed Said Mir Mohammad Sadeq, Tehran: Pazhuheshgah-e olum-e ensani va motalat-e farhangi, 2005 (1383); *'Abbas-name*, ed. Ebrahim Dehgan, Arak: Davudi, 1951 (1329).

Qazvini Esfahani, Mohammad Yusof Vale, *Iran dar zaman-e Shah Safi va Shah 'Abbas-e dovvom: Khold-e barin*, ed. Mohammad Reza Nasiri, Tehran: Anjoman-e athar va mofakher-e farhangi, 2001 (1380).

Rapp, Stephen H., *The Sasanian World through Georgian Eyes: Caucasia and the Iranian Commonwealth in Late Antique Georgian Literature*, Farnham: Ashgate, 2014.

Rota, Giorgio, ed. and trans., *La Vitae i Tempi di Rostam Khan. An Edition and Translation of the Manuscript British Library Add Ms 7655*, Wien: Österreichische Akademie der Wissenschaften, 2009.

Rothman, E. Natalie, *Brokering Empire: Trans-Imperial Subjects between Venice and Istanbul*, Itatha and London: Cornell University Press, 2012.

Qaukhchishvili, S., ed., *Kartlis Tskhovreba*, I, Tbilisi: Sakhelgami, 1955.

Qezelbashan, Amin, *Nasabname: Selsele-ye nasab-e gruhi az Gorji-ye tabarat-e Khuzestan va barkhi aqvam-e vayeste*, Tehran: Armaghan, 1395.

Savory, Roger M., *Iran under the Safavids*, Cambridge: Cambridge University Press, 1980.

Shamlu, Waliqoli, *Qesas al-khaqani*, Bibliothèque nationale de France, MS. Supplmént Persan 227.

Shurgaia, Tea, "The Proverbial Wisdom of a Georgian Language Island in Iran", *Iranian Studies*, 53-3/4 (2020), 551-571.

Shushtari, Sayyed 'Abd al-Allah b. Nur al-Din Hosayni, *Tazkera-ye Shuhtar*, eds. Khan Bahador Mawla Bakhsh and Mohammad Hedayat Hoseyn, Calcutta: Anjoman-e Asiyai-ye Bengal, 1924 (1343).

Sidiye, Simin, "Se sanad-e azadiname-ye bardegan az doure-ye Safavi", *Payam-e baharestan*, 1-2, 2008-09 (1387), 16-21.

Subrahmanyam, Sanjay, *Explorations in Connected History: From the Tagus to the Ganges*, New Delhi: Oxford University Press, 2005.

Tabatadze, K., "Isev Parsadan Gorgijanidzis tkhzulebis 15 saukunis tsqaroebis sakitkhisatvis (Once again on the question of the sources of Parsadan Gorgijanidze's writings on the fifteenth century)", *Kartuli tsqarotmtsodneoba (Studies on the Georgian sources)*, 4 (1973), 41-55.

Tarruell, Cecilia, "Prisoners of War, Captives or Slaves? The Christian Prisoners of Tunis and La Goleta in 1574", in *Micro-Spatial Histories of Global Labour*, eds. Christian G. De Vito and Anne Gerritsen, Cham: Palgrave Macmillan, 2018, 95-122.

Tiburcio, Alberto, *Muslim-Christian Polemics in Safavid Iran*, Edinburgh: Edinburgh University Press, 2020.

Todua, Magali, ed., *Tbilisskaya kollektsiya persidskikh firmanov*, I-II, Kutaisi and Tbilisi: Tsentralnyi gosudarstvennyi istoricheskii arkhiv CCCP and Gruzii, 1989-1995.

Toledano, Ehud, "Enslavement in the Ottoman Empire in the Early Modern Period", in *The Cambridge World History of Slavery*, vol.3, eds. David Eltis and Stanley L. Engerman, Cambridge: Cambridge University Press, 2011, 25-46.

Toledano, Ehud, "Ottoman and Islamic Societies: Were They "Slave Societie"?", in *What is a Slave Society? The Practice of Slavery in Global Perspective*, eds. Noel Lenski and Catherine M. Cameron, Cambridge: Cambridge University Press, 2018, 360-382.

Notes

1. This paper draws on Hirotake Maeda, "Parsadan Gorgijanidze's exile in Shushtar. A biographical episode of a Georgian official in the service of the Safavids", *Studies on Persianate Societies*, 1-2 (2008), 218-229, idem "Pasadan Gogijanidze" "Jami-i 'Abbasi bi lughat-i Gurji", in David Thomas and John Chesworth eds., *Christian-Muslim relations. A bibliographical history volume 10 Ottoman and Safavid Empires (1600-1700)* (Leiden and Boston, 2017), 654-657, 658-659. The author thanks the editors of above-mentioned volumes, Dr. Saïd Arjomand and Dr. John Chesworth for the permission to draw on both previous publications. The present article is also a product of the meeting in Edinburgh in June 2017. I thank Dr. Andrew Newman and colleagues who participated in the meeting for the intensive discussions.

2. S. Qaukhchishvili, (ed.), *Kartlis Tskhovreba*, I (Tbilisi, 1955), 20: "*ese parnavaz iqo mamulad kartleli...dedulad sparsi aspaneli da iqo igi dzmistsuli samarisi ...mtskhetel mamasakhlisi qopiliqo*" (Parnavaz was a Kartleli from his father... and Isfahan's Sparsi from his mother side. He was a nephew of Samari... who was a regent of Mtskheta). *Kartleli* means a people of Kartli, a part of Georgian provinces while Sparsi is of Persian.

3. Stephen H. Rapp, *The Sasanian World through Georgian Eyes: Caucasia and the Iranian Commonwealth in Late Antique Georgian Literature* (Farnham, 2014), 205-239.

4. See the relating entries in *Encyclopedia Iranica* on Persian literary influences in the Caucasus, Aleksandre Gvakharia provided a detailed introduction (Georgia iv. Literary contacts with Persia, https://www.iranicaonline.org/articles/georgia-iv--1. All the weblinks referred in this article was retrieved October 21, 2021). Persian epic tales always give literary impetus to the Georgian writers who have been translating and revising new Georgian versions for centuries, even the rendering Persian colloquial text inserted into one of the most important Georgian text which narrates the Georgian conversion to Christianity. King Mirian spoke a whole phrase in Persian in *Moktsevai Kartlisai* (*The conversion of Georgia*, ninth century): "*raïtmeboï khodzhat stabanug rasul psarzad*", or "*rast migui kojasta banu wa rasul-e pesar-e izad*" in modern Persian (You are speaking the truth, blessed lady and the messenger of the Son of God).

5. Hirotake Maeda, "Exploitation of the Frontier: The Caucasus Policy of Shah 'Abbas I," in Willem Floor and Edmund Herzig eds., *Iran and the World in the Safavid Age* (London, 2012), 471-489; idem, "Against All Odds: the Safavids and the Georgians", in Rudi Matthee (ed.), *The Safavid World* (London, 2021), 125-143. On the forced migration policy, also see idem, "The forced migrations and reorganisation of the regional order in the Caucasus by Safavid Iran: Preconditions and developments described by Fazli Khuzani," in Ieda, Osamu and Uyama, Tomohiko eds., *Reconstruction and interaction of Slavic Eurasia and its neighbouring worlds* (Sapporo, 2006), 237-271.

6. Anonymous, *Tadhkirat al-mulūk*, ed. and tr. V. Minorsky (London, 1943); Roger M. Savory, *Iran under the Safavids* (Cambridge, 1980); Sussan Babaie, Kathryn Babayan, Ina Baghdiantz-McCabe, and Massumeh Farhad, *Slaves of the Shah: New Elites of Safavid Iran* (London-New York, 2004).

7. The Georgian film "Mamluk" directed by Davit Rondeli in 1958 is a masterpiece taken from the Georgian perspective in the midst of the nation-state building period under the Soviet regime in the mid-twentieth century. Hirotake Maeda, "Transcending Boundaries: When the Mamluk Legacy Meets a Family of Armeno-Georgian Interpreters", in Michael A. Reynolds ed., *Constellations of the Caucasus: Empires, Peoples, and Faiths* (Princeton, 2016), 66-67.

8. On the classical framework developed in the influential works of B. Lewis, D. Ayalon, Patricia Crone and others, see the related entries of the second edition of *the Encyclopedia of Islam*, specifically C. E. Bosworth's summary in Ghulam ii. Persia (vol. II, 1083). Also see, Maeda "Transcending Boundaries", 64-66.

9. This closely connects with the broad reconceptualization of "diplomacy" and "captives" studies. See such examples as Sanjay Subrahmanyam, *Explorations in Connected History: From the Tagus*

to the Ganges (New Delhi, 2005) and Linda Colley, *Captives: The Story of Britain's Pursuit of Empire and how its Soldiers and Civilians Were Held Captive by the Dream of Global Supremacy* (New York, 2002).

10   Virginia H. Aksan, "What's Up in Ottoman Studies?", *Journal of the Ottoman and Turkish Studies Association*, 1:1-2 (2014): 8. Ehud Toledano gives major contribution towards "Ottoman society with slaves" including "Ottoman and Islamic Societies: Were They "Slave Societie"?," in Noel Lenski and Catherine M. Cameron, eds. *What is a Slave Society? The Practice of Slavery in Global Perspective* (Cambridge, 2018) 360-382, his publications in *The Cambridge World History of Slavery*, vol.3 and vol.4. Also see, Shaun Marmon (ed.), *Slavery in Islamic Middle East* (Princeton, 1999) and Stephan Conermann and Gül Şen (eds.), *Slaves and Slave Agency in the Ottoman Empire* (Bonn, 2020). On the Safavid case of polemical writings, see the important contribution by Alberto Tiburcio, *Muslim-Christian Polemics in Safavid Iran* (Edinburgh, 2020).

11   Ezgi Dikici "The Making of Ottoman Court Eunuchs: Origins, Recruitment Paths, Family Ties, and 'Domestic Production'," *Archivum Ottomanicum*, 30 (2013) 105–136. According to this article, castration inside Ottoman domains was officially censured for the first time at the beginning of eighteenth century. Also see, Y. Hakan Erdem, *Slavery in the Ottoman Empire and its Demise, 1800–1909* (New York, 1996). In the Safavid case, see the case of Yusof Aqa and his relatives: Mohammad-Ma'sum b. Khwajagi Esfahani, *Kholasat al-siyar: tarikh-e ruzgar-e Shah Safi Safavi*, ed. Iraj Afshar, (Tehran, 1989), 124, 140.

12   Eric R. Dursteler, *Renegade Women. Gender, Identity, and Boundaries in the Early Modern Mediterranean*, (Baltimore, 2011); Emrah Safa Gürkan, "Mediating Boundaries: Mediterranean Go-Betweens and Cross-Confessional Diplomacy in Constantinople, 1560-1600", *Journal of Early Modern History*, 19 (2015): 107-128; E. Natalie Rothman, *Brokering Empire: Trans-Imperial Subjects between Venice and Istanbul* (Itatha and London, 2012); Tijana Krstić, "Contesting Subjecthood and Sovereignty in Ottoman Galata in the Age of Confessionalization: Moriscos and the Carazo Affair, 1613–1617", *Oriente Moderno*, 93(2) (2013) 422–453; Tobias P. Graf, *The Sultan's Renegades: Christian-European Converts to Islam and the Making of the Ottoman Elite, 1575–1610* (Oxford, 2017). Also see, Eric R. Dursteler' review of Graf's monograph in *International Journal of Middle East Studies* 50 (2018) 804-806 and Cecilia Tarruell "Prisoners of War, Captives or Slaves? The Christian Prisoners of Tunis and La Goleta in 1574", in Christian G. De Vito and Anne Gerritsen eds., *Micro-Spatial Histories of Global Labour* (Cham, 2018) 95-122.

13   Varelian Gabashvili, "Sep'iant'a sakhelmtsip'o (Safavid State)," *Narkvevebi makhlobeli aghmosavlet'is istoriidan (Studies on the History of Near East)* (Tbilisi, 1957), 234-245; Karlo Kutsia, "Kavkasiuri elementi Sep'ianta Iranis politikur sarbilze (Caucasian Elements in the Safavid Political Stage)," *Makhlobeli Aghmosavlet'is istoriis sakitkhebi (Questions on the Near Eastern History)*, vol.1 (Tbilisi, 1963), 67, 78. On the details of Georgians' involvement in the Safavid policies, see Hirotake Maeda, "Against All Odds".

14   Hirotake Maeda, "On the Ethno-Social Background of Four Gholam Families from Georgia in Safavid Iran," *Studia Iranica*, 32 (2003), 243-278.

15   See the example of Papuna Tsitsishvili in Hirotake Maeda "Slave Elites Who Returned Home: Georgian *Vali*-king Rostom and the Safavid Household Empire," *Memoirs of the Research Department of the Toyo Bunko*, 69 (2011), 97-127.

16   Farmers were given lands in Mazandaran and other places, warriors were enrolled in the royal army and Jews in Georgia became royal merchants. See Maeda "Exploitation of the Frontier", 496.

17   Vladimir Puturidze edited Persian Documents and Persian-Georgian bilingual documents. Vladmir Puturidze (ed.), *Kartul-sparsuli istoriuli sabutebi (Georgian-Persian Historical Documents)* (Tbilisi, 1955). idem (ed.), *Sparsuli istoriuli sabutebi Sakartvelos tsigntsatsavebshi (Persian Historical Documents in the Georgian Libraries)*, tsgni I, nakveti 1-3, (Tbilisi, 1961, 1962, 1965). Also see, Magali Todua (ed.), *Tbilisskaya kollektsiya persidskikh firmanov*, I-II (Tbilisi, 1989-95); Nugzar Dundua (ed.), *Kartul-sparsuli (orenovani) istoriuli sabutebi (XVI-XVII ss.) (Georgian-Persian (bilingual) historical documents XVI-XVII centuries)* (Tbilisi, 1984).

18 There is still relatively little research on Safavid slave society including their lives and emancipations etc. Exceptional studies are Simin Sidiye, "Se sanad-e azadiname-ye bardegan az doure-ye Safavi", *Payam-e baharestan*, 1-2, 2008-09 (1387), 16-21 and Rasul Jafariyan, "Agahiha-ye taze darbare-ye gholaman va kanizegan dar doure-ye Safavi", *Payam-e baharestan*, 24, 2011-12 (1390), 1833-1924. Constituting an upper stratum of the Safavid society, Julfa merchants owned slaves. *Encyclopedia Iranica*, Julfa i. Safavid period, https://www.iranicaonline.org/articles/julfa-i-safavid-period.

19 Pietro Della Valle, *Les Famevx voyages de Pietro della Valle, gentil-homme romain, svrnommé l'illvstre voyagevr; avec vn denombrement tres-exact des choses les plus curieuses, et les plus remarquables qu'il a veuës dans la Turquie, l'Egypte, la Palestine, la Perse, et les Indes orientales, Chez Gervais Clovzier* (Paris, 1663-64), 413. *Safar-nama-ye Pietro Della Valle*, tr. Shoa-al-Din Shafa (Tehran, 1969) 303-04. The association of Safavid elite society with the artistic world would be a different and important theme to be investigated. Research on their appearances in the pictorial materials will lead us to the deep understanding of religious, ethnic, and political dynamism they experienced. See such examples of young courtier in a Georgian costume and other different nationalities discussed in Michael Chagnon, "Cloath'd in Several Modes: Oil-on-Canvas Painting and the Iconography of Human Variety in Early Modern Iran", in Axel Langer ed., *The Fascination of Persia: The Persian-European Dialogue in Seventeenth-Century Art & Contemporary Art of Teheran* (Zurich, 2013), 238-63. As far as the present author is concerned, the Qizlbash hat (taj haidariya) is not seen often in the visual arts during and after the reign of Shah 'Abbas I. An impressive painting on 'Abbas II's meeting with a Mughal ambassador includes hats highly deformative. See, Linda Komaroff, *Gifts of the Sultan: The Arts of Giving at the Islamic Courts* (New Haven and London, 2011), 142-143.

20 Davud cultivated his Georgian connections. He was the commander of Tbilisi Castle in 1625 and negotiated with Teimuraz I who at that time was in rebellion against Shah 'Abbas I. After the successful negotiation Davud was appointed to the governor-general of Qarabagh as a reward by the shah. Mohammad Qoli Khan Qajar, his predecessor, was given a daughter of Teimuraz I by 'Abbas once Teimuraz had revolted. Not only succeeding the post of general governorship Davud also put a daughter of Teimuraz I under his protection.sentence not clear. In early Safi's reign Davud rose in rebellion together with Teimuraz I which invited the total downfall of his brother Emamqoli Khan, governor-general of Fars and direct family members. The Italian missionary Teramo Cristoforo Castelli left a portrait of Davud Khan in exile. See the portrait published in Don Kristoforo De Castelli, B. Giorgadze tr. and ed., *Tsnobebi da albomi Sakartvelos shesakheb (Information and Albam about Georgia)*, (Tbilisi, 1976) plate 2b. On Allahverdi's military household in Fars, see Hirotake Maeda, "The Household of Allahverdi Khan: An Example of Patronage Network in Safavid Iran," in F. Hellot and I. Nathchebia, eds., *Géorgie et sa capitale Tbilissi entre Perse et Europe* (Paris and Tbilissi, 2007) 149-170.

21 Della Valle lamented the disharmony among Catholic subjects when the Spanish ambassador humiliated an Italian "private" traveller. His concern with Europeans in Iran in general is also worth mentioning, to think of their imagined "collectiveness" and concrete social behaviors. Della Valle, *Les Famevx voyages*, 117-119 etc.

22 Don Garcia de Silva Figueroa, *Safarname-ye Don Garcia de Silva Figueroa*, tr. Gholamreza Sami'i (Tehran, 1984/85) 92.

23 See Maeda, "Exploitation of the Frontier" and the above-mentioned note 20. An important chronicler on the reign of Shah 'Abbas I, Fazli Khuzani stressed these "ethnic bonds" and shah's manipulation of those in clear contrast with Eskandar Beg Torkoman Monshi.

24 Della Valle, *Les Famevx voyages*, 440.

25 On the life and activities of Della Valle, see John Gurney's article in Encyclopaedia Iranica, https://iranicaonline.org/articles/della-valle. Maani only arrived Rome in the casket while Mariuccia lived there with her 14 children. We also recall Anthony Sherly's Circassian wife Theressa who spent a latter life in Rome. Throughout the seventeenth century there were flows of people between Iran and the Caucasus beyond. Maani's nephew Ferdinand

was educated in Rome and shuttled between Italy and Iraq. His tragic death by a flood is described in the Camelites' record. Herbert Chick (ed. and tr.), *A Chronicle of the Carmelites in Persia : The Safavids and the Papal Mission of the1 7th and 18th Centuries* (New York, 2012), 387-88. On the image of Maani, see Cristelle Baskins, "Lost in translation: Portraits of Sitti Maani Gioerida della Valle in Baroque Rome," *Early Modern Women: An Interdisciplinary Journal*, 7 (2012), 241–260.

26 Adam Olearius, *Relation dv voyage de moscovie, tartarie, et de perse, fait a l'occasion d'vne ambassade, Enuoyée au Grand-Duc de Moscouie, et de Roy de Perse*; 392, *Safarnāme-ye Adam Olearius*, tr. Mohandes Hoseyn Kordbachche, 2 vols. (Tehran, 1990/91) 614.

27 Mohammad Yusof Vale Qazvini Esfahani, *Iran dar zaman-e Shah Safi va Shah 'Abbas-e dovvom: Khold-e barin*, ed. Mohammad Reza Nasiri (Tehran, 2001/02), 251-253, Mohammad-Ma'sum, *Kholasat al-siyar*, 247.

28 Shah 'Abbas I promoted Qarchaqay Sultan, a most influential courtier of Armenian origin, to the governor-general of Azarbaijan and ruler of Tabriz a day after he participated in the Armenian religious festival in 1619. Maeda, "Exploitation of the Frontier," 483.

29 Abedik was the donator of St. Maria Church in New Julfa and died in 1639. Della Valle was related to him through his half Armenian wife Maani. Della Valle, *Les Famevx voyages*, 592; *Safar-nama-ye Petro Dela Vala*, 445.

30 Della Valle, *Les Famevx voyages*, 430; *Safar-nama-ye Petro Dela Vala*, 320. Della Valle speculated on a Safavid-Catholic alliances through trans-Black Sea network when he met Cassak representative at the shah's court. Polish-Safavid connections through Armenian diaspora network are discussed in Michael Połczyński, "The Relacyja of Sefer Muratowicz: 1601–1602 Private Royal Envoy of Sigismund III Vasa to Shah 'Abbas I", *Turkish Historical Review* 5-1 (2014) 59–93. The early modern trans-Black Sea network should be further investigated from multiple perspectives, since the Ottoman sultans were entitled as the rulers of the two seas: Mediterranean and the Black Seas, and the investigations on the former trans-maritine network are rapidly advancing (see note 10 of this article).

31 On the slave trade in Daghestan", see Elena Inozemtseva, "On the History of Slave-Trade in Dagestan," *Iran and the Caucasus*, 10: 2 (2006), 181-189.

32 Activities of King Iese, half brother of Vakhtang VI, and his descendants show a complicated picture on the imperial subjecthood of trans-imperial military elites from the Caucasus. He ruled Kartli kingdom under his converted names twice: Aliquli Khan (Safavid regent king (vali-king) (1714-16) and Mustafa Pasha (Ottoman vassal 1723-1727).His grand son Pyotr Bagration became a Russian general and distinguished himself in the wars against Napoleon I. Sean Pollack, "As One Russian to Another': Prince Petr Ivanovich Bagration's Assimilation of Russian Ways," *Ab Imperio*, no. 4 (2010), 113-142.

33 Rudi Matthee's research on Muhammad Beg stressed the importance of family connections. Rudi Matthee, "The Career of Mohammad Beg, Grand Vizier of Shah 'Abbas II (r. 1642-1666)", *Iranian Studies*, 24 (1991), 17-36. See also Girogio Rota's intensive studies of the life of Rostom Khan Sipahsalar and Georgian *gholam*s: Giorgio Rota (ed. and trans.) *La Vitae i Tempi di Rostam Khan. An Edition and Translation of the Manuscript British Library Add Ms 7655* (Vienna, 2009).

34 To this day descendants who were forcefully migrated from the Caucasus remain relatively large communities on the Iranian plateau. P. Oberling, "Georgians and Circassians in Iran," *Studia Caucasica*, 1 (1963) 127-143. Also see Lia Bakuradze,Marina Beridze and Zakharia Pourtskhvanidze, "A Georgian Language Island in Iran: Fereydani Georgian" and Tea Shurgaia "The Proverbial Wisdom of a Georgian Language Island in Iran" *Iranian Studies*, 53, Issue 3-4 (2020), 489-550 and 551-571.

35 This manuscript starts saying that "I was from Gori, Kartili. I was given the post of the mayor (*mouravi* in Georgian and *darugha* in Persian) of Isfahan by King Rostom. The emperor granted me the post of chief chamberlain and there ordered me to translate the Muslim religious cannon into Georgia.(*kartlis Goreli viyav da ispahanis movraoba mepis rostomisagan mameca da shahabas*

khelmtsipem bokaultukhutsoba mibodza da manve mihmana musurmant rjulis kanoni kartulat atargmaneo)." St. Petersburg, Institute of Oriental Manuscripts of the Russian Academy of Sciences – M-27(1691. Oct.). fol. 1a. The author thanks Dr. Karen Hamada for the text of the Gorgijanidze's manuscript in St. Petersburg.

36 Parsadan Gorgijanidze "Extraits de l'Histoire de Pharsadan Giorgidjanidzé" tr. M. Brosset, *Histoire de la Géorgie depuis l'Antiquité jusqu'au xixe siècle*, Partie 2, St. Petersburg, 1856, 510. Kakabadze suggested he was from a merchant family. Sargis Kakabadze, "Parsadan Giorgijanidzis istoria" (Parsadan Gorgijanidze's history), *Saistorio moambe (The historical journal)*, 2 (Tbilisi, 1925), 198-316, published as a separate book in Tbilisi in 1926 (hereafter Kakabadze, *Parsadan Giorgijanidzis istoria*).

37 King Rostom played a crucial role for Safavid-Georgian relations as a military mayor of the imperial capital for about 40 years. On his political path, see Maeda "Slave Elites Who Returned Home".

38 On his life, see Jamshid Giunashvili, "Gorgijanidze, Parsadan", Encyclopaedia Iranica online edition, 2016, available at https://iranicaonline.org/articles/gorgijanidze-parsadan. Also see the following works in Georgian:. Zurab Chichinadze, *Kartuli mtserloba mechvidmete saukuneshi* (Georgian writings in the seventeenth Century), (Tbilisi, 1888), 17-18; M. Janashvili, *Parsadan Gorgijanidze da misni shromani* (Parsadan Gorgijanidze and his works), (Tbilisi, 1896), (includes an introduction about Gorgijanidze's biography and works) 20-27; 79-80, Ivane Javakhishvili, *Dzveli kartuli saistorio mtserloba* (Old Georgian historical writings), (Tbilisi, 1945), 283-297; Kakabadze, 204-206; Kiknadze; Puturidze, 5. K. Tabatadze, "Isev Parsadan Gorgijanidzis tkhzulebis 15 saukunis tsqaroebis sakitkhisatvis" (Once again on the question of the sources of Parsadan Gorgijanidze's writings on the fifteenth century), *Kartuli tsqarotmtsodneoba* 4 (1973) 41-55. D. Katsitadze, "Isev Parsadan Gorgijanidzis erti sparsulenovani tsqaros shesakheb", *Aghmosavluri pilologia* 2 (1972) 153-159 (Katsitadze has written several articles on Gorgijanidze's Persian sources). Gobejishvili, M. "Parsadan Gorgijaniżis saistorio tkhzulebis leningraduli H 41 nusxis minacerebi" (Scription of the H41 manuscript of Parsadan Gorgijanidze's historical writings in Leningrad), *Kartuli tsqarotmtsodneoba* 5 (1978) 70-75.

39 Gorgijanidze, 85, 90; Javakhishvili 286; Revaz Kiknadze, *Parsadan Gorgijanidze da "istoriani da azmani sharavandendtani" (Parsadan Gorgijanidze and 'A history and praise of the kings')*, Tbilisi, 1975, 12.

40 Vladimer Puturidze, P. Gorgijanidzis *kartul-arabul-sparsuli leksikoni (Georgian-Arabic-Persian dictionary of P. Gorgijanidze)* (Tbilisi, 1941) (includes an introduction about Gorgijanidze's biography and works) Kakabadze, 1925. 198-316, published as a separate book in Tbilisi in 1926; French Translation: "Extraits de l'Histoire de Pharsadan Giorgidjanidzé" 509-561; Russian Translation: *Istoriya Gruzii* tr. R. K. Kiknadze and V. S. Puturidze (Tbilisi, 1990). There are no published versions of Jami-i 'Abbasi ba lughat-i Gurji (fols 1-115 of Tbilisi manuscript), though the Georgian-Arabic-Persian vocabulary (fols 116r-126v) has been published twice. Elene Metreveli (ed.), *Kartul khelnatserta agtseriloba. Qopili kartvelta shoris tsera-kitkhvis gamavrtselebeli sazogadoebis (S) kolekts'ia* (Catalogue of Georgian Manuscripts: Collections of the Former Society for the Spreading of Literacy among Georgians (S)) (Tbilisi, 1960), 191-193. On the source materials Parsadan Gorgijanidze depended on, see Revaz Kiknadze, *Sakartvelos istoriis tsqarotmtsodneobis sakitkhebi* (includes a detailed study of Gorgijanidze's history).

41 Mamia Dumbadze, V. Guchua, and B. Giorgadze, "Tsqaroebisa da literaturis mimokhilva-i Tsqaroebi da literature kartul da evropul enebze (Researches on the sources and literature i.: Sources and literature in Georgian and European languages)," in M. Dumbadze, ed., *Sakartvelos istoriis narkvevebi (Studies on the Georgian hisotry)* IV (Tbilisi, 1973), 33.

42 Kiknadze, *Parsadan Gorgijanidze*, 25, 133-135.

43 It has never been published in its totality, though the part covering the Safavid era was edited and published by S. Kakabadze in Tbilisi in 1926. Also see, note 36.

44 Kakabadze, *Parsadan Giorgijanidzis istoria* 59. This incident was recorded in the following chronicles: Mirza Mohammad Taher Vahid Qazvini, *Tarikh-e Jahanara-ye 'Abbasi*, ed. Seyyed Said Mir Mohammad Sadeq (Tehran, 2004), 188, 219-221 (older edition: Mirza Mohammad-Taher Wahid Qazvini, 'Abbas-name, ed. E. Dehgan (Arak, 1960); Mohammad Yusof Vale Qazvini Esfahani, *Iran dar zaman-e Shah Safi va Shah 'Abbas-e dovvom*, ed. Mohammad Reza Nasiri, (Tehran, 2001). Waliqoli Shamlu, *Qesas al-khaqani*, Bibliothèque nationale de France, MS. Supplmént Persan 227. Because the riot happened at the heart of the empire, well-known European travellers including J. Chardin also describe the incident. Jean Chardin, *Voyages de Chevalier Chardin, en Perse, et autres lieux de l'Orient*, ed. L. Langrès, 10 vols. (Paris, 1811) vol. 9, 567-70. Also see, Matthee, "The Career of Mohammad Beg", 32.

45 Valiqoli Shamlu, *Qesas al-khaqani*, fol. 234r.

46 Maeda, "Slave Elites Who Returned Home" 123, note. 13.

47 It was written under the name of *Jami'-i 'Abbasi ba lughat-i Gurji* or *Jamiabasi kartulad ('Jami'-i 'Abbasi in the Georgian language'*

48 https://iranicaonline.org/articles/jame-e-abbasi.

49 Gorgijanidze, *Jami'-i 'Abbasi*, S-174 (Manuscript in Tbilisi), fol.1r: "*da amaebis ts'odna musurmant' mart'ebs da arts'a ras k'ristians daumarts'khebs da kidev ujobs qovels kats'sa, rom qovlis rjulisa rame its'odes da kargisa da avis garkueva sheedzlos*".

50 Gorgijanidze maintained that he was commissioned to translate this work by Shah 'Abbas II. See note 35. Also see, Brossett, *Histoire de la Géorgie*, Partie 2, 513. There are two known manuscripts in Tbilisi and St. Petersburg. The manuscript in the Georgian National Centre of Manuscripts (S-174) covers 140 folios. As for the manuscript in St. Petersburg, see R. R. Orbeli, *Gruzinskie rukopisi instituta vostokovedeniya, vypusk I, Istoriya, Geografiya, Puteshestviya, Arkheologiya, Zakonodatel'stvo, Filosofiya, Yazykoznanie, Bibliografiya,* (Moskva-Leningrad, 1956), 20-22, 113-114. This manuscript (M27) was copied in 1691 (1103 Hijri or 379 Georgian chalender). Also see Puturidze, *Gorgijanidzis kartul-arabul-sparsuli leksikoni*, vii. The manuscript, which still awaits full study, also contains the following short works: a notebook or dictionary of Georgian-Arabic-Persian vocabulary, based on Abu Nasr Farrahi's *Nisab al-sibyan*, with a description of the Muslim calendar (fols 116r-126v); secret code of Georgian writings (*anjanis anbana*) and explanation of dreams (fols 126v-127v); translation of *Ikhtilajat-i a'za* (fols 128r-133v); and, a genealogy of Ottoman sultans (*Osman jugi*) (fols 134r-140). Writing down a "secret code of Georgian writings" could have regarded to an act of false to show the secret. We know, however, that Shah 'Abbas I already made his causes for his notorious Georgian campaign when he confiscated a letter of Teimura I, the king of Kakheti who revolted, written in secret code. Because Georgian politics was played inside at the shah's court for a long time, the secret code could no longer have been secret at Gorgijanidze's time. Still the manuscript clearly reflects the imperial objection and Gorgijanidze should have been one of the bearers and conductors of the policy, it also exposes his Georgianness and some in-between characters which should be thought a typical of (part of) Georgian political thinking of that time.

51 Kakabadze, *Parsadan Giorgijanidzis istoria*, 69. "A post of acting governor of Kakheti was given to Gorjaspi, son of Kakhaberi, by fortunate *qaen* (Shah 'Abbas II) through the effort of Parsadan Gorgijanidze (*kakhetis janishnoba bednierman qaenman kakhabris shvils gorjaspis ubodza parsadan gorgijanidzis sakmita)*".

52 Kiknadze, *Parsadan Gorgijanidze*,15.

53 Kakabadze, *Parsadan Giorgijanidzis istoria* 80; Kiknadze, *Parsadan Gorgijanidze*, 16.

54 Abu-l-Qasim P'irdousi (Abu al-Qasim Firdawsi), *Shah-names anu mepeta tsignis kartuli versiebi (Georgian versions of Shahnama or the Book of the Kings)*, ed. Iustine Abuladze et al., 2 vols, Tbilisi, 1916, 1934 (Georgian trans. of Firdawsi's *Shahname*, called *Rostomiani* in Georgian), 317.

55 Kiknadze, *Parsadan Gorgijanidze*,15; see also Gorgijanidze, Russ. tr. 15.

56 Ferdowsi ed. by Iustine Abuladze et al., 366.

57 Kekelidze, II, 336.

58 Kiknadze, *Parsadan Gorgijanidze*, 16.
59 Mohammad-Ma'sum, *Kholasat al-siyar*, 142; Mohammad Yusof Vale Qazvini Esfahani, *Iran dar zaman-e Shah Safi va Shah 'Abbas-e dovvom*, 121.
60 Rudi Matthee, "Georgia vii. Georgian in the Safavid Administration," in *Encyclopaedia Iranica* X, 493-96; Sayyed 'Abd al-Allah b. Nur al-Din Hosayni Shushtari, *Tazkera-ye Shuhtar*, ed. Khan Bahador Mawla Bakhsh (Calcutta, 1924). Recently Amin Qezelbashan, himself a descendant of Vakhushti Khan, published several important works on the history of this family living in Khuzestan for four centuries. Amin Qezelbashan, *Nasabname: Selsele-ye nasab-e gruhi az Gorji-ye tabarat-e Khuzestan va barkhi aqvam-e vayeste* (Tehran, 1395).
61 On this family, see Maeda, "On the Ethno-Social Background", 247-253.
62 Bagrationi, Vakhushti, "Aghtsera sameposa sakartvelosa (Description of the Kingdom of Georgia)," in S. Qaukhchishvili, ed., *Kartlis tskhovreba (The Georgian chronicles)*, IV (Tbilisi, 1973), 70.
63 Givi Jamburia, "Sakartvelos politikuri vitareba XVII s. 30-90-ian tslebshi (Political condition of Goergia in the years of 30-90 of the seventeenth century)," in Dumbadze, ed., *Sakartvelos istoriis narkvevebi*, 342-349. Also see, Mohammad Yusof Vale Qazvini Esfahani, *Iran dar zaman-e Shah Safi va Shah 'Abbas-e dovvom*, 652; Mohammad Taher, *Tarikh-e Jahan-ara-ye 'Abbasi*, 750-751, 755.
64 Maeda, "Against All Odds", 138-139.
65 Rudi Matthee, *Persia in Crisis: Safavid Decline and the Fall of Isfahan* (London and New York, 2012), 233-34; Maeda, "Kaykhosrow Khan," in *Encyclopaedia Iranica*.
66 Kakabadze, *Parsadan Giorgijanidzis istoria*, 59-60.
67 On Prince Luarsab, see Maeda "Slave Elites Who Returned Home", 107.
68 Kakabadze, *Parsadan Giorgijanidzis istoria*, 54-56. "*visats ukharoda, is upro stiroda da tavs itsemda azris ar mikhvdomisatvis.*"
69 Jamburia, "Sakartvelos politikuri vitareba," 347. Maeda, "Against All Odds", 139.
70 Judging from his anti-Vakhtang V Shahnavaz standings and his career at the Safavid central court, Gorgijanidze could have been close to Shaykh 'Ali Khan Zangane, longtime grand vezir of Shah Soleyman. Shaykh 'Ali's relationship with Vakhtang was known to be deteriorated. Matthee, *Persia in Crisis*, 68.
71 For example, a compilation of Georgian-Persian bilingual documents edited by V. Puturidze includes three orders issued by 'Abbas Qoli Khan Qajar and six orders by Kalb 'Ali Khan Qajar from 1689-1701. Puturidze, *Kartul-sparsuli istoriuli sabutebi*, Document no. 142, 152, 154, 157, 159, 160, 162, 165, 167.
72 Archil's political activities continued to fuel tensions in the Caucasian frontier regions which was of concern to the Ottoman, Safavid, Russian goverments. On this topic specifically, and also in general to the Ottoman-Safavid diplomatic relations in the second half of the seventeenth century, see Selim Güngörürle, "Diplomacy and Political Relations between the Ottoman Empire and Safavid Iran, 1649-1722" Ph. D. dissertation subjected to Georgetown University, 2016.
73 This episode represents the geo-political dimension Georgians possessed. Ashton II's activity remains less known. Sopio Davitashvili, however, recently discussed his political life in detail. See Sopio Davitashvili, "Ori Ashotan Mukhranbatonis moghvatseobis kvali Atonis tsm. mtaze" and "Atonis Iveriis ghvtismshoblis khatis sachdilobelis khatis sachrdilobeli karavi" *Saistorio krebuli (Journal of History)* II. Together with a Georgian scholar Okuropiri Jikuri, I eventually discovered a book of Gospel in Karkalo monastery in Athos, Greece in the spring of 2018. We also saw the precious green umbrella beautifully embroidered in Iviron monastery. "Georgian-Greek Colophons, Added to the Greek Four Gospels, as well as Bilingual Inscriptions of the Plated Covers and Miniatures' Georgian Inscriptions, preserved in Athos Karakalou Monastery Library. Hirotake Maeda and Okropiri Jikuri, "Georgian Antiquities from Karakallou Monastery (Mount Athos)", *The 16th Annual International Kartvelological Conference in Memory of St. Grigol Peradze*, December 8, 2018, University of Warsaw.

About the Contributors

Ines Asceric-Todd is Lecturer in Arabic and Middle Eastern Cultures at the University of Edinburgh. Her research interests are in cultural and religious history of the Middle East and the Ottoman Empire, and she is particularly interested in Sufism and dervish orders, and interfaith relations in the Ottoman Empire and wider Middle East during the Ottoman period. She is the author of *Dervishes and Islam in Bosnia: Sufi Dimensions to the Formation of Bosnian Muslim Society* (Leiden, 2015), and a co-editor of *Travellers in Ottoman Lands: The Botanical Legacy* (Oxford, 2018).

Jaimee K. Comstock-Skipp will receive her PhD from Leiden University and is writing a dissertation on Firdausi's *Shahnama* epic and illustrated manuscript production in Abulkhairid-administered Transoxiana in the sixteenth century. She holds MA degrees from The Courtauld Institute of Art in London and the Williams College Graduate Program in the History of Art. Her BA in Near Eastern Studies was obtained from the University of California, Berkeley.

Valérie Gonzalez, Research Associate, SOAS, University of London. Specialisms: Islamic art history and aesthetics. Gonzalez obtained her Ph.D. in Islamic Studies at the University of Provence Aix-Marseille, and a Master of Fine Arts, School of Fine Arts, Marseille-Luminy. She got scholarships from Kunsthistorisches Institut-Max-Planck-Institut, Florence, Trinity College, Dublin, The Getty Research Institute, the Aga Khan Program for Islamic Architecture (MIT), the Institute for Advanced Study, Princeton. Books: *Aesthetic Hybridity in Mughal Painting, 1526-1658*, Ashgate 2015; *Le piège de Salomon, La pensée de l'art dans le Coran*, Albin Michel, 2002, and *Beauty and Islam, Aesthetics of Islamic Art and Architecture* IB Tauris, 2001.

Selim Güngörürler is researcher at the Austrian Academy of Sciences in Vienna since 2020. He formerly worked as a post-doctoral fellow at Istanbul's Boğaziçi University and holds a PhD from Georgetown University (2017). He studies the early modern diplomacy of the Middle East, particularly that of the Ottoman State with its neghboring polities. His research has also been supported by grants from the German Academic Exchange Service (DAAD), Koç University's Research Center for Anatolian Civilizations, and the Austrian Academic Exchange Service.

Hirotake Maeda is a professor in the Faculty of Humanities and Social Sciences at Tokyo Metropolitan University. He investigates the history of the Caucasus peoples in the Middle East and the Central Eurasia. His main publications are "On the Ethno-Social Background of the Four Gholam Families from Georgia in Safavid Iran", *Studia Iranica* Tome 32, 2003 (Translated into Georgian ქართველები სეფიანთა ირანში"(Tbilisi, 2008) and into Persian "چهار دودمان گرجی در عصر صفوی" (Tehran, 2018); "Exploitation of the Frontier," Willem Floor and Edmund Herzig (eds.), *Iran and the World in the Safavid Age*, (London, 2012); "Lives of Enikolopians", Abbas Amanat and Assef Ashraf (eds.), *The Persianate World* (Leiden and Boston, 2019).

Andrew J. Newman Professor of Islamic Studies and Persian at the University of Edinburgh. He holds a BA in History from Dartmouth College and an MA and PhD in Islamic Studies from UCLA. He came to Edinburgh in 1996 from the Wellcome Unit for the History of Medicine and Green College, Oxford, where he was researching topics in the history of Islamic medicine. Newman has published on early Twelver Shi'ism and Shi'i history and thought and on Shi'ism in Safavid Iran. His most recent monograph is *Twelver Shiism, Unity and Diversity in the Life of Islam, 632 to 1722* (Edinburgh, 2013). He is the founder/moderator of *Shī'ī News and Resources*.

Babak Rahimi is the Director of the Program for the Study of Religion at the Department of Literature, University of California San Diego. His monograph, *Theater-State and Formation of the Early Modern Public Sphere in Iran: Studies on Safavid Muharram Rituals, 1590-1641 C.E.* (Brill 2011), traces the origins of the Iranian public sphere in the early-seventeenth century Safavid Empire with a focus on the relationship between state-building, urban space and ritual culture. Rahimi is also the co-editor (David Faris) of *Social Media in Iran* (SUNY Press 2015), coeditor (Armando Salvatore and Roberto Tottoli) of *The Wiley Blackwell History of Islam* (Wiley Blackwell 2018), co-editor (Peyman Eshaghi) of *Muslim Pilgrimage in the Modern World* (University of North Carolina Press 2019), Theatre in the Middle East (Anthem Press, 2020) and *Performing Iran: Culture, Performance, Theatre* (Bloomsbury 2021). His articles have appeared in *Thesis Eleven: Critical Theory and Historical Sociology, International Political Science Review, International Communication Gazette, International Journal of Middle East Studies, The Middle East Journal, The Communication Review*, and *Journal of the International Society for Iranian Studies*. Rahimi's research interests concern the relationship between culture, religion, and technology. The historical and social contexts that inspire his research range from the early modern Islamicate societies to the Global South.

Alberto Tiburcio (PhD McGill, 2015) is Guest Professor of Iranian Studies at the Ludwig Maximilian University of Munich. He previously held postdoctoral appointments at the Philipps University of Marburg and at the Max Planck Institute for the History of Science.

Barry Wood (Ph.D., Harvard University, 2002) is an art historian and philologist with a special interest in the preservation and transmission of cultural memory. His work on Persian art, manuscripts, and cultural memory has appeared in *Ars Orientalis, Iranian Studies,* and the *Metropolitan Museum Journal*; his translation of one of the "Anonymous Histories of Shah Isma'il" was published by Brill in 2019 as *The Adventures of Shah Esma'il: A Seventeenth-Century Persian Popular Romance.*

Studies in Late Antiquity and Early Islam

Averil Cameron, Lawrence I. Conrad,
John Haldon, Geoffrey King (eds.)
The Byzantine and Early Islamic Near East
– 4 Volumes Set –
SLAEI 1 – ISBN 9783959941365

Averil Cameron and Lawrence I. Conrad (eds.)
The Byzantine and Early Islamic Near East
Volume 1: Problems in the Literary Source Material
SLAEI 1.1 – ISBN 9783959940849

Geoffrey King and Averil Cameron (eds.)
The Byzantine and Early Islamic Near East
Volume 2: Land Use and Settlement Patterns
SLAEI 1.2 – ISBN 9783959940863

Averil Cameron (ed.)
The Byzantine and Early Islamic Near East
Volume 3: States, Resources and Armies
SLAEI 1.3 – ISBN 9783959940887

John Haldon and Lawrence I. Conrad (eds.)
The Byzantine and Early Islamic Near East
Volume 4: Elites Old and New
SLAEI 1.4 – ISBN 9783959940900

Robert Schick
The Christian Communities of Palestine
from Byzantine to Islamic Rule.
An Historical and Archaeological Study
SLAEI 2 – ISBN 9783959940924

Albrecht Noth with Lawrence I. Conrad
The Early Arabic Historical Tradition.
A Source-Critical Study
Translated from the German by Michael Bonner
SLAEI 3 – ISBN 9783959940948

Martin Hinds; ed. by Jere Bacharach,
Lawrence I. Conrad, and Patricia Crone
Studies in Early Islamic History
With an Introduction by G. R. Hawting
SLAEI 4 – ISBN 9783959940962

Uri Rubin
The Eye of the Beholder: The Life of Muhammad
as Viewed by the Early Muslims. A Textual Analysis
SLAEI 5 – ISBN 9783959940986

Jean Maurice Fiey; edited by Lawrence I. Conrad
Saints Syriaques
SLAEI 6 – ISBN 9783959941006

Elizabeth Savage
A Gateway To Hell, A Gateway To Paradise.
The North African Response to the Arab Conquest
SLAEI 7 – ISBN 9783959941082

Suliman Bashear
Arabs and Others in Early Islam
SLAEI 8 – ISBN 9783959941020

Milka Levy-Rubin (ed.)
The Continuatio of the Samaritan Chronicle of
Abū l-Fatḥ al-Sāmirī al-Danafī
Annotated Translation
SLAEI 10 – ISBN 9783959941044

Josef Horovitz, edited by Lawrence I. Conrad
The Earliest Biographies of the Prophet and
Their Authors
SLAEI 11 – ISBN 9783959941068

Fred M. Donner
Narratives of Islamic Origins.
The Beginnings of Islamic Historical Writing
SLAEI 14 – ISBN 9783959941105

Hugh N. Kennedy (ed.)
Al-Ṭabarī. A Medieval Muslim Historian and His Work
SLAEI 15 – ISBN 9783959941129

Uri Rubin
Between Bible and Qur'an.
The Children of Israel and the Islamic Self-Image
SLAEI 17 – ISBN 9783959941143

Josef W. Meri (ed.)
A Lonely Wayfarer's Guide to Pilgrimage. ʿAlī ibn Abī Bakr
al-Harawī's Kitāb al-ishārāt ilā maʿrifat al-ziyārāt
Translated and Introduced by the Editor
SLAEI 19 – ISBN 9783959941167

James E. Lindsay (ed.)
Ibn ʿAsākir and Early Islamic History
SLAEI 20 – ISBN 9783959941181

David Cook
Studies in Muslim Apocalyptic
SLAEI 21 – ISBN 9783959941204

Andreas Goerke
Das Kitab Al-Amwal des Abu ʿUbaid Al-Qasim b. Sallam.
Entstehung und Überlieferung eines frühislamischen
Rechtswerkes
SLAEI 22 – ISBN 9783959941228

Michael Lecker
The „Constitution of Medina".
Muhammad's First Legal Document
SLAEI 23 – ISBN 9783959941242

Andreas Goerke and Gregor Schoeler
Die ältesten Berichte über das Leben Muhammads.
Das Korpus ʿUrwa ibn az-Zubair
SLAEI 24 – ISBN 9783959941266

Robert G. Hoyland (ed.)
The Late Antique World of Early Islam.
Muslims among Christians and Jews
in the East Mediterranean
SLAEI 25 – ISBN 9783959941280

Jens Scheiner and Damien Janos (eds.)
The Place to Go:
Contexts of Learning in Baghdad, 750-1000 C.E.
SLAEI 26 – ISBN 9783959941303

Note:
Volume nos 9, 12, 16 and 18 were never published.
Vol 13 was reissued by Gorgias Press.

www.gerlachpress.com